Computer Science with *Mathematica*

Computer algebra systems have revolutionized the use of computers within mathematics research, and are currently extending that revolution to the undergraduate curriculum. But the power of such systems goes beyond simple algebraic or numerical manipulation. This book shows how computer-aided mathematics has reached a level where it can support effectively many of the computations in science and engineering. In addition to treating traditional computer science topics, an introductory course should show scientists and engineers how these computer-based tools can be used to do scientific computations.

This introduction to computer science studies algorithms through use of *Mathematica*. This powerful interactive tool encourages experimentation and allows each algorithm to be tested separately and its behavior studied. Examples from number theory, differential geometry, numerical mathematics, symbolic computation, computer algebra, linear algebra, electronic circuits, semiconductors, mechanical engineering, celestial mechanics, and chaotic systems are included. Computer science topics include abstract data types, complexity of algorithms, searching and sorting, optimization problems, functional and object-oriented programming, term rewriting, computability, and databases.

A valuable text for introductory courses in computer science for mathematicians, scientists, and engineers, this book should also prove useful to *Mathematica* users at all levels. Covering Version 4, the latest release of *Mathematica*, the book includes useful tips and techniques that will help even seasoned users.

Roman E. Maeder was a co-founder of Wolfram Research and was responsible for developing central parts of the *Mathematica* software system, such as polynomial factorization and language design. Maeder received his Ph.D. from the Swiss Federal Institute of Technology (ETH) in Zurich. Formerly a professor of computer science at ETH, he is now an independent computing consultant.

Computer Science with *Mathematica*

Theory and Practice for Science, Mathematics, and Engineering

Roman E. Maeder

CAMBRIDGE UNIVERSITY PRESS
Cambridge, New York, Melbourne, Madrid, Cape Town, Singapore, São Paulo

Cambridge University Press
The Edinburgh Building, Cambridge CB2 2RU, UK

Published in the United States of America by Cambridge University Press, New York

www.cambridge.org
Information on this title: www.cambridge.org/9780521631723

First published 2000
Reprinted with corrections 2006

A catalogue record for this publication is available from the British Library

Library of Congress Cataloguing in Publication data
Maeder, Roman.
    Computer science with Mathematica : theory and practice for
science, mathematics, and engineering / Roman E. Maeder.
        p.   cm.
    Includes index.
    ISBN 0-521-63172-6. – ISBN 0-521-66395-4 (pbk.)
    1. Mathematica (Computer file) 2. Mathematics – Data processing.
3. Mathematica (Computer programming language) I. Title.
QA76.95.M34   1999
510′.285′5369–dc21   99-38932
                                                         CIP

ISBN-13 978-0-521-63172-3 hardback
ISBN-10 0-521-63172-6 hardback

ISBN-13 978-0-521-66395-3 paperback
ISBN-10 0-521-66395-4 paperback

Transferred to digital printing 2006

Contents

Preface

This book provides an introduction to computer science, and shows how modern computer-based tools can be used in science, mathematics, and engineering. Computer-aided mathematics has reached a level where it can support effectively many computations in science and engineering. In addition to treating traditional computer-science topics, an introductory book should show scientists and engineers how these computer-based tools can be used to do scientific computations. Students must get to know these possibilities, and they must gain practical experience. Learning a traditional programming language becomes less important, just as learning arithmetic is not a main topic of mathematics education. In an introductory book, it is clearly necessary to limit ourselves to a small part of the huge field of computer science. We emphasize topics that are related to possible applications in mathematics and the sciences. Technical and practical computer science have therefore been neglected.

It is certainly worthwhile to combine an introductory computer-science course with exercises. In the same way as we learn a foreign language by speaking the language and by studying literature in that language, we should apply algorithmic knowledge by studying programs and writing our own. If we can solve an interesting problem from mathematics or the sciences at the same time, all the better! Traditionally, such introductory courses use languages such as Pascal, C, or FORTRAN. These languages have in common that the effort to develop even a small program (one that adds two numbers, for example) is considerable. One has to write a main program that deals with input and output, and to compile the program. Furthermore, these languages cannot be used easily to solve nonnumerical problems. Leaving aside these practical difficulties gives us room to look at other topics in computer science, an extension that is not offered in traditional programming courses. In this way, we gain insight into computer *science*, which consists of much more than writing small programs.

Another disadvantage of traditional languages is that they support only *procedural* programming. This style is an important one, but it is not the only option and it is not always the best approach. I prefer a language that does not force this programming style on programmers. The programming style should be chosen to fit the problem to be solved, rather than vice versa. The language should be interactive, to encourage experimentation and to allow us to call individual functions without having to write a whole program.

Mathematica was first released in 1988, and it is being used with increasing frequency in teaching, research, and industry. A by-product of the symbolic computation system, it is a programming language that differs from traditional languages in many important ways.

Conventional languages are not well suited to expressing mathematical formulae and algorithms. LISP and other functional languages showed alternatives. An important aspect of scientific computation is an easy way to express mathematical rules. Application of rules by machine requires good pattern-matching capabilities of the kind found in Prolog. Another prerequisite is that it be simple to manipulate structured data. Such structural operations have been pioneered by APL. Object-oriented elements and modularization are important tools for developing larger projects. Ideas were taken from Simula, Smalltalk, and C++. We also want to support traditional procedural programming in the style of Pascal and C. All these objectives lead to a large language with many built-in functions. It nevertheless has a consistent and uniform style, made possible through the use of *rewrite rules,* which underly all other programming constructs. Such a language is also interactive and therefore easy to use. It is not necessary to compile functions or to embed them into a main program to use them. The additional step of compilation increases the difficulty of program development and requires special tools (debuggers) to study the behavior of programs.

Because *Mathematica* also contains most operations needed in mathematics and physics, it is especially well suited for an introductory course in computer science for readers interested primarily in the sciences and engineering. It allows us to treat interesting examples easily. There is no good reason, for example, to restrict the range of integers to $2, 147, 483, 647$, as is done in most programming languages. This restriction makes no sense in mathematics. Programming with recursively defined functions is often treated as extraordinary and difficult. We can express naturally many mathematical algorithms, however, by using recursion, and it should be possible to formulate recursion easily in a language. For example, the properties of the greatest common divisor of two integers leading directly to Euclid's algorithm,

$$
\begin{aligned}
\gcd(a, b) &= \gcd(b, a \bmod b) \\
\gcd(a, 0) &= a \,,
\end{aligned}
$$

can be expressed verbatim in *Mathematica* and tried out immediately. As in LISP, the technique of tail-recursion elimination in *Mathematica* ensures that the corresponding program runs as fast as the loop that is normally used (which is not the case in most procedural languages). Deriving the loop invariant and programming the same function as a loop leads naturally to systematic programming and considerations of program correctness.

Mathematica is helpful in all areas of computer use in mathematics, in the sciences, and in engineering:

- Its numerical part, which allows arithmetic to arbitrary precision, can be used to treat numerical mathematics, including traditional floating-point arithmetic.

- Its symbolic part does computations with formulae, solves equations, performs series expansions and transformations, and knows calculus to the level required for an undergraduate degree.

- The programming language supports all traditional programming styles, including procedural programming. The language can therefore be used for traditional computer-science classes (algorithms and data structures) as well.

- The rule-based programming system allows a natural expression of scientific facts.

- Graphics allows the meaningful presentation of results and experimental data. It is also useful for showing how algorithms work.

- We can call external programs and exchange results, so we can use external software libraries and even control laboratory experiments.

This book grew out of class notes for a course given at the Department of Mathematics and Physics at the Swiss Federal Institute of Technology, Zurich. It was originally published in my native German language [48], and I am glad to present now my own English translation and adaptation.

I am thankful to Erwin Engeler, John Gray, and Stephen Wolfram for their inspiration and many interesting discussions. Helpful suggestions on particular topics came from R. Marti and H. Mössenböck. Lyn Dupré proofread an early version of the manuscript, and Karen Tongish copyedited the final version. The publishers of the German and English editions, Ekkehard Hundt and Alan Harvey, helped me to keep going. Many thanks to the anonymous reviewer whose favorable comments and useful suggestions motivated me to finish this project.

R. E. M.
Wollerau, March 1999

About This Book

The emphasis of this introduction to computer science is *algorithmics* – that is, the study of algorithms. We do not want this activity to become a dry exercise, so we shall try out all algorithms as soon as possible. Our programs will often consist of only a few lines of code. Such simplicity allows us to concentrate on the essentials and to ignore peripheral matters such as input, output, and driver programs. Often, however, we shall develop whole packages, collections of various procedures grouped around a topic. The methods for writing such packages will be explained in Chapter 4. After all, computer science is not about writing small, throwaway programs but rather developing larger applications. In addition to finding suitable algorithms, this entails techniques of documentation and maintenance of software. We shall present some of these techniques.

Mathematica does have a major advantage over traditional programming languages: It is *interactive*. Interactivity encourages experimentation and allows us to test each function separately and to study its behavior. In the first section we shall study recursively defined functions, a topic often considered difficult and therefore treated with caution. We also have at our disposal a symbolic, numerical, and graphic computation system – an added benefit that we shall use in many ways.

Overview of Contents

Each chapter after the first two introductory ones presents a topic from computer science together with its applications and examples in mathematics, the sciences, and engineering. You can choose from the many applications presented those that correspond to your background. Because only one system (*Mathematica*) is used for all programs and all calculations, the extra work of learning about practical matters such as editing or working with the application is minimized. My experiences have shown that *Mathematica* is rather easy to learn; you will be able to work with it quite soon, after overcoming any initial difficulties you might encounter.

Chapter 1 is not a prerequisite for the rest of the text, if you already know something about computers. It shows how computers can be used in the sciences, explains the history and current state of computers, and discusses what computer science is all about.

The quick introduction to *Mathematica*'s syntax in Chapter 2 should be studied with a computer at hand, so you can try out the calculations for yourself and get a feeling for what it is like to work with *Mathematica*. The elements of programming presented in Sections 2.1–2.3 are the foundation of our programs.

In Chapter 3, we use two simple examples to show how mathematical questions can be turned into computer programs. The most important concepts are iteration and recursion. The section on loop invariants gives a method for proving programs correct.

Chapter 4 explains how programs in *Mathematica* are structured. We start with simple commands, which we turn into a program by defining a few functions. We will give guidelines for turning a program into a package. Packages allow for easier use of programs and prevent unwanted side effects on other programs, which might have similar function names. The tools we use are modularization and separation of the interface (for the user of our program) and the implementation (for the program developer). You can use these techniques as recipes, even if you do not know how they work in detail. You can use our template package as a starting point.

Abstract data types, presented in Chapter 5, constitute one of the most important tools for the design of programs. These methods allow a clean separation of design and implementation. We shall use them in most of our programs in this book.

Algorithms for searching and sorting are the basic building blocks of many programs. The algorithms presented in Chapter 6 are part of basic computer-science knowledge.

Problems can be solved in many ways. One aspect to consider when choosing a method is the complexity of the resulting algorithm. Chapter 7 provides an introduction to algorithmic complexity. As an example, we look at the computation of large Fibonacci numbers, optimization problems, and arbitrary-precision arithmetic.

Vectors and matrices are important data structures for mathematical applications. We present several important operations on them and look at a few algorithms from linear algebra in Chapter 8.

In Chapter 9, we program in LISP, a language that we can interpret in *Mathematica* easily. Recursion is the most important tool for solving problems in LISP, where it replaces iteration.

For many scientific problems, *rule-based programming* is the simplest method of solution. It is also the foundation of *Mathematica*'s programming language. In Chapter 10, we shall look at the important concepts of simplification and normal forms, as well as at some applications.

Functions are of central importance in mathematics. They play a lesser role in computer science, because many programming languages have only rudimentary means of dealing with them. An important exception are the functional languages, including *Mathematica*. Functions are the topic of Chapter 11. That chapter highlights the differences between the symbolic computation system *Mathematica* and ordinary languages.

In Chapter 12, we give a short introduction to theoretical computer science. There we see that this topic is not necessarily as "theoretical" as is often feared. We answer the question of what the fundamental limits of computers are and show that some problems cannot be solved by machine, even disregarding the practical matters of limited memory and computing time.

Databases are the most important commercial application of computers. Managing large volumes of data demands reliable and powerful programs. A precise mathematical model of collections of data provides the tools for their easy manipulation. We treat these concepts in Chapter 13.

Chapter 14 introduces an important programming style: object-oriented programming. It is especially useful for larger applications and for the design of reusable software.

Appendix A is an annotated bibliography on the topics programming methods, teaching with *Mathematica*, and literature about *Mathematica*; it includes a section with references for the topics treated in this book, followed by the bibliographical data.

The more detailed explanations about the structure of *Mathematica* given in Appendix B are useful for self-study and are also meant as a reference. For a complete reference to *Mathematica*, you should consult *The Mathematica Book* [74]. The appendix of that manual contains an alphabetical listing of all built-in functions, commands, and other objects. This listing, as well as the complete manual, is available on-line in *Mathematica* (in the *Help Browser*). Looking up an item there is much easier than is looking it up in a heavy book. Studying the *Mathematica* manual is not a prerequisite for reading this book.

Appendix B also contains a section that demonstrates *Mathematica*'s more advanced capabilities. Finally, we give the programs used to generate the chapter-opener pictures.

Certain sections are labeled "Advanced Topic." They presume that the reader has a more complete mathematical background than is required for the rest of the book; they are optional.

Sections marked "Special Topic" are independent from the rest of the book. Sections marked "Example" or "Application" develop a topic using a larger example that is of interest in its own right.

At the end of most sections, there is a review list, entitled "Key Concepts," of new concepts that have been introduced. At the end of the chapters, you will find numerous exercises.

The verso page following a chapter title contains a brief overview of the sections in the chapter, and an explanation of the graphic illustration on the title page. The programs for generating these pictures are in the package Pictures.m; see Section B.2.

Comments on Exercises

We assume that you already know how to work with your computer. The installation of *Mathematica* on your machine is explained in the documentation that comes with the software. This documentation includes a manual that explains the machine-specific features of *Mathematica*. The best way to learn *Mathematica* is to do practical exercises at the machine. In the beginning, you may want to look at one of the included demonstration documents before moving on to your own small examples. You can also find simple examples in the section titled "A Tour of *Mathematica*" in *The Mathematica Book*. We recommend that you work through such examples.

There are two ways to use *Mathematica* on a computer: the Notebook frontend and a simple dialog with the kernel of *Mathematica* (the kernel is the part that does the actual computations; the frontend serves as a user interface to the kernel). The Notebook frontend is more comfortable to use, but is not required for the examples in this book, which have all been computed by direct interaction with the kernel. All examples have been tested with Version 4.0 of *Mathematica*.

If you use the Notebook frontend, your interaction with *Mathematica* will look a bit different from the way it is presented in the book, but the results will be the same. Numbering of your inputs happens only after they have been sent to kernel for evaluation (with SHIFT-RETURN or ENTER), because the number is given out by the kernel, rather than by the frontend. An example Notebook is reproduced on page 95.

Please note that each example has been computed in a fresh *Mathematica* session. We recommend that you begin new sessions to avoid any influences from previous computations whenever the numbering of the input lines restarts at 1. Under the Notebook frontend, you can choose the menu command Quit Kernel to start a fresh kernel.

The frontend allows you to store your programs and your sample computations in the same document (the Notebook) and to open them again in the future. We recommend, however, that you store *packages* in separate files, and read them into *Mathematica* using <<*file*`. This command to read in a package is often not shown in the dialogs in this book. If you want to reproduce the examples, you must read the appropriate programs into *Mathematica* first.

Electronic Resources

All programs mentioned in this book are available in machine-readable form from the book's Web site, located at http://www.mathconsult.ch/CSM/. There, you will find compressed archives of all files ready to download. Packages have the extension .m; Notebooks have the extension .nb. Both kinds of files can be opened with the frontend. Packages can be read into the kernel directly (using <<CSM`*file*`) and can also be opened with any text editor (in ASCII mode).

The archive should be extracted into the AddOns/Applications subdirectory of your *Mathematica* installation directory. Extraction will create a subdirectory CSM inside the Applications directory.

Mathematica can display its own installation directory. The value of $TopDirectory will reflect the actual place where you installed *Mathematica* on your computer.

```
In[1]:= $TopDirectory
Out[1]= /usr/local/Mathematica
```

If you installed the files correctly, this simple test should give the result shown here. Note the use of the backquote ` as a machine-independent way to specify directories and files.

```
In[2]:= << CSM`Test`
The CSM packages are correctly installed in
/usr/local/Mathematica/AddOns/Applications/CSM
```

All packages mentioned in this book can be loaded by prefixing their name with the directory, CSM.

```
In[3]:= << CSM`ComplexParametricPlot`
```

Please refer to the book's Web site for up-to-date information on available archive formats and detailed installation instructions.

In addition to the programs, the book's Web site contains other information, such as notebooks, updates, a list of errata, and the archive of the mailing list intended for readers of this book. I encourage you to join the mailing list. Please see the Web site for details.

Notation and Terminology

Mathematica input and output is typeset in a typewriterlike style (in the Courier font): Expand[(x+y)^9]. Parts of *Mathematica* expressions not to be entered verbatim, but denoting (meta) variables, are set in italic: f[*var_*] := *body*.

Functions or *commands* are denoted by their name, followed by an empty argument list in square brackets: Expand[]. Program listings are delimited by horizontal lines:

```
a[1] = a[2] = 1
a[n_Integer?Positive] := a[n] = a[a[n-1]] + a[n-1-a[n-1]]
```

A sequence by John H. Conway.

A program package is identified by name (the context name, as we shall see) – for example, Complex. The files used for storing successive versions of this package will be named Complex1.m, Complex2.m, and so on. The final version will be called Complex.m.

Mathematica dialog is set in two columns. The left column contains explanations; the right column contains input and output, including graphics. This form of presentation is derived from *The Mathematica Book*.

As usual, we will clarify program structure by indentation. *Mathematica* allows writing deeply nested expressions. It is, therefore, often necessary to break such expressions into multiple lines.

Here is an example of such a dialog. You would enter only the input set in boldface. The prompt `In[1]:=` is printed by *Mathematica*. If you work with the Notebook frontend, this prompt will appear *after* you evaluate your input with ENTER.

```
In[1]:= Factor[ x^34 - 1 ]
Out[1]= (-1 + x) (1 + x)
                 2    3    4    5    6    7    8    9
       (1 - x + x  - x  + x  - x  + x  - x  + x  - x  +
          10    11    12    13    14    15    16
         x   - x   + x   - x   + x   - x   + x   )
                 2    3    4    5    6    7    8    9
       (1 + x + x  + x  + x  + x  + x  + x  + x  + x  +
          10    11    12    13    14    15    16
         x   + x   + x   + x   + x   + x   + x   )
```

In most programming languages, you can define procedures, functions, or subroutines. *Mathematica* uses only one mechanism, called *definitions*, which look like $f[x\_] := def$. Chapter 2 provides a short explanation of the elements of *Mathematica*'s programming language. A more in-depth presentation is given in Appendix B.

The table on page xx lists the mathematical notations that we use. Equations, figures, program listings, and tables are numbered by section. For example, Equation 3.1–1 is the first equation in Section 3.1.

Colophon

Mathematica dialogs were computed on a Sun ULTRAsparc II with Version 4.0 of *Mathematica* using the initialization file init.m reproduced here.

```
Format[Continuation[_]] := ""

SeedRandom[10000]

Off[ General::spell, General::spell1 ]

Unprotect[Short]
Short[e_] := Short[e, 2]        (* lines are very short *)
Protect[Short]

SetOptions[ Plot3D, AspectRatio -> Automatic, PlotPoints -> 35 ]
SetOptions[ Graphics3D, AspectRatio -> Automatic ]
SetOptions[ ParametricPlot, AspectRatio -> Automatic ]
SetOptions[ ParametricPlot3D, Axes -> None ]

Needs["ProgrammingInMathematica`Options`"]
SetAllOptions[ ColorOutput -> GrayLevel ]

$DefaultFont = {"Times-Roman", 9.0} (* font in graphics *)

SetOptions["stdout", PageWidth->56] (* line width *)
```

init.m: *Mathematica* initialization for this book.

The manuscript is written in LaTeX [40] (with many custom macros). It contains only the input of the sample computations. The results were computed by *Mathematica* and were inserted automatically into the file. The bibliography was produced with BIBTEX [59], and the index was sorted with makeindex [41]. Those figures not produced with *Mathematica* were designed with FrameMaker and included in PostScript form. The reproductions of Notebooks and help screens were taken from the computer's screen. Finally, the output of LATEX was converted into PostScript and phototypeset.

$\lg x$	logarithm to base 2, $\log_2 x$
$\log x$	natural logarithm (base e)
$\gcd(a, b)$	greatest common divisor
$a \mid b$	a divides b
$a \bmod b$	remainder when a is divided by b
$a \operatorname{div} b$	integer part of the quotient a/b
$\operatorname{sign} x$	sign of x
$n!$	n factorial, $n! = n(n-1)(n-2)\cdots 1; 0! = 1$
$\mathbf{N}$	set of nonnegative integers $\{0, 1, 2, \ldots\}$
$\mathbf{Z}$	ring of integers $\{0, \pm 1, \pm 2, \ldots\}$
$\mathbf{Z}_p$	residue classes modulo p
$\mathbf{R}$	field of real numbers
$\mathbf{C}$	field of complex numbers
i	imaginary unit, $i = \sqrt{-1}$
$\lfloor r \rfloor$	largest integer $\leq r$
$\lceil r \rceil$	smallest integer $\geq r$
$x \approx y$	approximate equality of x and y
$\pi(x)$	number of primes $\leq x$
a^t	transpose of matrix a
$v.w$	dot product of vectors v and w
$a \otimes b$	outer product of tensors a and b
$\operatorname{div} v$	divergence of vector field v
$\operatorname{grad} s$	gradient of scalar field s
$\nabla^2 s$	Laplace operator, $\nabla^2 s = \operatorname{div} \operatorname{grad} s$
$\dfrac{d}{dx}$	total derivative w.r.t. x
$\dfrac{\partial}{\partial x}$	partial derivative w.r.t. x
$x \mapsto y$	mapping of x to y
$\lambda x.t(x)$	lambda expression (pure function)
$[x \rightarrow a]e$	substitution of x by a in e
$p \wedge q$	p AND q
$p \vee q$	p OR q
$p \rightarrow q$	p implies q
$r \cup s$	union of sets r and s
$r \cap s$	intersection of sets r and s
$r - s$	difference of sets r and s
$r \bowtie s$	join of relations r and s

Mathematical Notation Used in This Book.

Chapter 1
Computers and Science

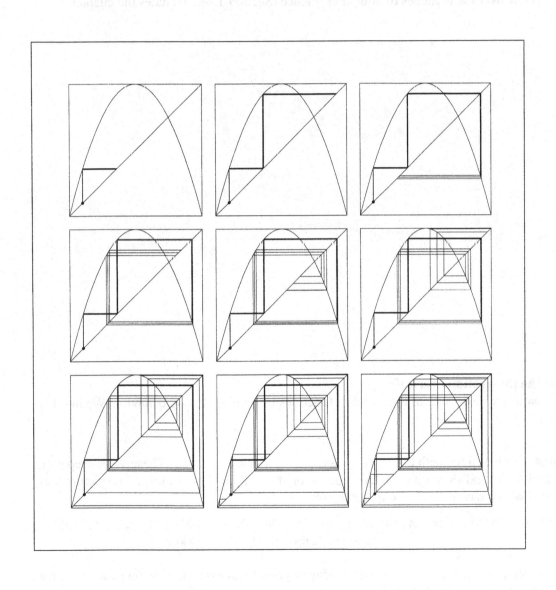

In the first section of this chapter we show how typical scientific problems can be solved with the help of a computer. We also discuss methods to develop programs to solve these problems. Section 1.2 covers computers and operating systems. We describe the historic development and operating principles of a modern workstation.

Programming languages have developed along with hardware. In Section 1.3, we look at a program in several forms – from machine language to a higher-level programming language. An overview over the branches of computer science (Section 1.4) concludes the chapter.

About the illustration overleaf:

The illustration shows one of the simplest functions leading to chaotic behavior. We iterated the map

$$f: x \mapsto 4x(1-x).$$

The first nine iterations with three nearby starting values are displayed. These values separate more and more, and show quite different behavior after only eight iterations. The picture was produced with the command (see Pictures.m):

```
Animate[ FunctionIteration[4#(1-#)&, {0.099,0.1,0.101}, 0, n, {0, 1},
                    Frame->True, FrameTicks->None],
      {n, 1, 9, 1} ];.
```

With the *Mathematica* frontend you can produce a genuine animation; here, on paper, we have to put the frames next to each other.

1.1   From Problems to Programs

For computer users, the possibility of solving problems by machine is the most interesting aspect of computer science. Many textbooks and introductory classes deal exclusively with (procedural) programming, however. Programming constructs are explained with the help of simple programming exercises. Because traditional languages are not well suited to solving mathematical and scientific problems, the courses usually fail to show how such problems – which are, after all, our main interest – can be solved. The overhead stemming from the low mathematical level of even so-called higher-level programming languages shadows the underlying scientific problem and requires knowledge of memory organization, operating systems, and so on. Many of these languages were developed by computer scientists for their own use (e.g., to write compilers). In this book, we want to show that there is another way of studying both computer science and its application to the sciences and engineering.

The following subsections describe some typical uses of computers in the sciences. The examples are simpler than what you would encounter in practice, however.

We have not yet talked about how to program in *Mathematica*, so do not dwell on the syntactic details; instead, observe how easy it is to solve a problem by computer. Most of the time, the syntax will be similar to traditional mathematical notation. In the rest of this book, you will learn how to express your computations in *Mathematica*.

1.1.1   Newton's Formula

A *zero* of a function f is a value x, such that $f(x) = 0$. Newton's method for approximate determination of zeroes of functions f proceeds as follows. From a rough estimate x_0 of the zero, we can find a better estimate x_1 according to the formula

$$x_1 = x_0 - \frac{f(x_0)}{f'(x_0)}, \qquad (1.1-1)$$

where f' denotes the derivative of f. This formula is of the form

$$x_1 = g(x_0), \qquad (1.1-2)$$

with

$$g(x) = x - \frac{f(x)}{f'(x)}. \qquad (1.1-3)$$

We apply the same method to x_1 to get an even better approximation $x_2 = g(x_1)$, then repeat the process. This method leads to the following iteration:

$$x_{i+1} = g(x_i), \qquad i = 0, 1, 2, \ldots. \qquad (1.1-4)$$

If this sequence converges, we have found a zero of f. For an example, let us compute square roots.

The function `RootOf2` has $\sqrt{2}$ as its zero.

```
In[1]:= RootOf2[x_] := x^2 - 2
```

Here is the right-hand side of the iteration.

```
In[2]:= x - RootOf2[x]/RootOf2'[x]
```

$$Out[2]= x - \frac{-2 + x^2}{2\,x}$$

This equivalent form is often given in the literature.

```
In[3]:= (2/x + x)/2
```

$$Out[3]= \frac{\frac{2}{x} + x}{2}$$

Let us define the iteration function g.

```
In[4]:= g[x_] = (2/x + x)/2;
```

The start value $x_0 = 1$ gives this value of x_1.

```
In[5]:= g[1.0]
Out[5]= 1.5
```

Here is x_2. The shorthand notation % refers to the previous result in `Out[5]` above.

```
In[6]:= g[%]
Out[6]= 1.41667
```

After seven iterations, successive values of x are already equal; that is, we have found the solution. This computation was done to 30-digit accuracy.

```
In[7]:= NestList[ g, N[1, 30], 7 ] // TableForm
Out[7]//TableForm= 1.00000000000000000000000000000
                   1.50000000000000000000000000000
                   1.41666666666666666666666666667
                   1.41421568627450980392156862745
                   1.41421356237468991062629557889
                   1.41421356237309504880168962350
                   1.41421356237309504880168872421
                   1.41421356237309504880168872421
```

For verification of the result, we square the final value. It is correct to 29 decimal places.

```
In[8]:= Last[%]^2
Out[8]= 2.00000000000000000000000000000
```

Here is another example that shows that Newton's method does not always perform this well.

The zero of this function is 0, of course.

```
In[9]:= slow[x_] := x^3

In[10]:= slow[0]
Out[10]= 0
```

Again, we define the iteration function h.

```
In[11]:= h[x_] = x - slow[x]/slow'[x]
```

$$Out[11]= \frac{2\,x}{3}$$

With the function h we get slow convergence, as you can see here.

```
In[12]:= NestList[ h, N[1, 30], 22 ] // TableForm
Out[12]//TableForm= 1.0000000000000000000000000000000
                    0.66666666666666666666666666666667
                    0.44444444444444444444444444444444
                    0.29629629629629629629629629629296
                    0.19753086419753086419753086419198
                    0.13168724279835390946502057632
                    0.087791495198902606310013717421
                    0.058527663465935070873342478280
                    0.039018442310623380582228318853
                    0.026012294873748920388152212569
                    0.017341529915832613592101475046
                    0.011561019943888840906140098336
                    0.0077073466292589393742673222427
                    0.0051382310861726262495115481618
                    0.0034254873907817508330076987745
                    0.0022836582605211672220051325163
                    0.0015224388403474448146700883442
                    0.0010149592268982965431133922295
                    0.00067663948459886436207559481966
                    0.00045109298973257624138372987977
                    0.00030072865982171749425581991985
                    0.00020048577321447832950387994656
                    0.00013365718214298555300258663104
```

Even after 100 iterations, we have only 18 digits of the zero.

```
In[13]:= Nest[h, N[1, 30], 100]

Out[13]= 2.45965442657982926924379399594 10
                                             -18
```

We can visualize easily the progress of Newton's method. We draw a line from the point $(x_0, 0)$ up to $(x_0, f(x_0))$, then along the tangent to the intersection with the x axis, which is the point $(x_1, 0)$, then back to $(x_1, f(x_1))$, and so on.

These steps have been collected in an extension of *Mathematica*, which we can read into our session. Doing so will define the command `NewtonIteration`.

```
In[14]:= << CSM`Iterate`
```

The start value is 2, and we perform four steps. Because of the fast convergence of the square-root iteration, we can see only the first two steps; the remaining lines are too close to the graph of the function.

```
In[15]:= NewtonIteration[ RootOf2, 2, 4, {1, 2} ];
```

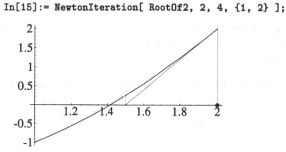

The second example shows slow convergence so we can see several more steps.

```
In[16]:= NewtonIteration[ slow, 0.6, 6, {0, 0.65},
                          PlotRange->All ];
```

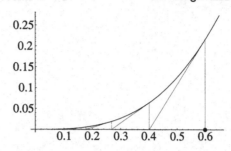

The zero of the cosine at $x = \pi/2$ can also be found with this method. The values x_i alternate between being too small and too large, giving this picture.

```
In[17]:= NewtonIteration[ Cos, 0.5, 4, {0, 3} ];
```

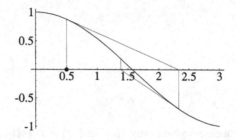

Numerical approximation techniques were among the first algorithms developed for computers. One of the most important methods for numerical approximation is iteration. It is also used to solve systems of equations and differential equations.

1.1.2 Formulae: Uniformly Accelerated Motion

A standard topic in an introductory physics course is uniformly accelerated motion. The formulae for its special cases, such as free fall and braking distance, are easily derived from the general formula by symbolic manipulation.

The velocity at time t is $v(t) = v_0 + at$. The constant acceleration is denoted by a, and v_0 is the initial velocity.

```
In[1]:= v[t_] = v0 + a t
Out[1]= a t + v0
```

The distance traveled is the integral of the velocity

$$s(t) = \int_0^t v(\tau)d\tau$$

```
In[2]:= s[t_] = Integrate[v[tt], {tt, 0, t}]

                 2
                a t
Out[2]=  ------ + t v0
                 2
```

If we set v_0 to 0 and a to g, we get the formula for the distance traveled in free fall.

```
In[3]:= s[t] /. {v0 -> 0, a -> g}

           2
        g t
Out[3]= ----
          2
```

The time it takes to bring a vehicle to a complete stop is obtained as the solution of this equation for final velocity 0.

```
In[4]:= Solve[v[tb] == 0, tb][[1]]

                 v0
Out[4]= {tb -> -(--)}
                 a
```

This time gets us the braking distance. The value grows quadratically with initial velocity v_0. When the brakes are applied, the acceleration a is negative. The value is therefore positive, despite the minus sign.

```
In[5]:= s[tb] /. %

              2
          -v0
Out[5]= ----
          2 a
```

This kind of formula manipulation is typical of many scientific problems. A symbolic computation system can work with formulae and equations just as easily as an ordinary programming language can work with numbers.

How such a symbolic computation system works is quite a different matter. The first symbolic computation systems were written in LISP, which allows us to work with symbolic expressions directly. We need "only" implement the underlying mathematical algorithms. We shall take a look at LISP in Section 9.2.

1.1.3   Simulation: The Value of π

A simple physical experiment allows us to measure the area of a quarter of a disk and thus to determine the value of π. We choose repeatedly a uniformly distributed random point in the unit square and count how often it lies in the unit circle as well. The ratio of the number of points in the unit circle to the total number of points is equal to the ratio of the areas of the quarter disk and the unit square. Instead of performing the experiment in reality, we can simulate it on the computer.

Each invocation of `Random[]` returns a real number distributed uniformly in the interval from 0 to 1.

```
In[1]:= Random[]
Out[1]= 0.753989
```

This function (which has no arguments) gives a randomly chosen point in the unit square.

```
In[2]:= randomPoint := { Random[], Random[] }
```

Here is a list of 200 simulations in abbreviated form.

```
In[3]:= (data = Table[ randomPoint, {200} ]) // Short
Out[3]//Short=
   {{0.524444, 0.759749}, {0.989753, 0.518709},
    {0.46092, <<7>>31}, <<196>>, {0.51534, 0.801726}}
```

We can take a better look at the simulation results by drawing the points in the unit square.

```
In[4]:= ListPlot[ data, AspectRatio->Automatic ];
```

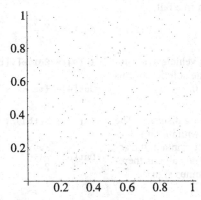

We are interested in the number of points in the circle. This picture highlights the circle inside the unit square.

```
In[5]:= Show[
          Graphics[{
          {GrayLevel[0.89], Disk[{0,0}, 1, {0,Pi/2}]},
          Line[{{0,0},{1,0},{1,1},{0,1},{0,0}}] }],
          %, AspectRatio->Automatic ];
```

This predicate tests whether a point lies in the circle, that is, whether the point's distance from the origin is ≤ 1.

```
In[6]:= inCircle[pt_] := Apply[Plus, pt^2] <= 1
```

Here is the fraction of points lying in the circle.

```
In[7]:= Count[ data, _?inCircle ] / Length[data] // N
Out[7]= 0.845
```

We repeat the experiment with 100,000 points. The result is an approximation of $\pi/4$.

```
In[8]:= data = Table[ randomPoint, {100000} ]; \
        Count[ data, _?inCircle ] / Length[data] // N
Out[8]= 0.78338
```

Here are six exact decimals of $\pi/4$.

```
In[9]:= N[ Pi/4 ]
Out[9]= 0.785398
```

This example uses the computer to simulate a physical experiment. One requirement for such a simulation is a *random-number generator*. It is used in *Monte Carlo* simulation methods to simulate a large number of trials. The results are then evaluated statistically. (Here, we simply calculated an average.)

1.1.4   Solution of Equations: Operational Amplifiers

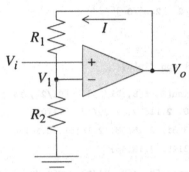

The circuit shown on the left is a noninverting amplifier, realized using an *operational amplifier* (*op amp*). Because of the almost ideal properties of op amps, this circuit can be computed with a linear system of equations. We can assume that the difference of the two input voltages is zero, that is, $V_i = V_1$. Furthermore, the input resistance is infinite, which implies that the current through the two resistors R_1 and R_2 is the same. From Ohm's law, we arrive at equations $V_1 = IR_2$ and $V_o - V_1 = IR_1$. We are interested in the *voltage gain* $A_v = V_o/V_i$.

Here are the equations.

```
In[1]:= g1 = { vi == v1,
               v1 == i r2,
               vo - v1 == i r1,
               av == vo/v1    };
```

Solving for A_v, we immediately get the standard formula for the voltage gain.

```
In[2]:= Solve[ g1, av, {vi, vo, v1, i} ]

                        r1 + r2
Out[2]= {{av -> ---------}}
                          r2
```

1.1.5   Numerical Computation: Kepler's Equation

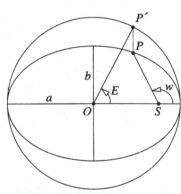

A planet P moves on an elliptic orbit with one focal point S being the sun. To determine its location on the orbit, according to the illustration, we need to determine the angle w, the *true anomaly*. The time M, called the *mean anomaly*, is measured starting from the point closest to the sun, such that one revolution is equal to 2π.

First, we determine the angle E, called the *eccentric anomaly*, according to Kepler's equation:

$$M = E - \varepsilon \sin E, \qquad (1.1\text{–}5)$$

where $\varepsilon = (a^2 - b^2)/a$ denotes the eccentricity of the ellipse with semimajor axes a and b. Equation 1.1–5 cannot be solved for E in closed form, but we can use an iterative method.

We write the equation in the form

$$E = M + \varepsilon \sin E . \qquad (1.1-6)$$

The equation is now of the form $E = f(E)$, with $f(E) = M + \varepsilon \sin E$, and it can be solved by iteration. We let $e_0 = M$ and iterate $e_i = f(e_{i-1})$, for $i = 1, 2, 3, \ldots$.

In our example, the ratio of the axes is $a/b = 3/2$. Here is the corresponding value of the eccentricity.

```
In[1]:= eps = N[ Sqrt[3^2 - 2^2]/3 ]
Out[1]= 0.745356
```

Here is the iteration function.

```
In[2]:= f[E_, M_] := M + eps Sin[E]
```

We perform 14 iterations for $M = \pi/2$, that is, after one-quarter of a revolution. We can see that values converge quickly toward a solution.

```
In[3]:= NestList[ Function[E, f[E, Pi/2]], N[Pi/2], 14 ]
Out[3]= {1.5708, 2.31615, 2.11852, 2.20712, 2.17028,
    2.18618, 2.17942, 2.18231, 2.18108, 2.18161, 2.18138,
    2.18148, 2.18144, 2.18145, 2.18145}
```

The command FixedPoint[] performs the iteration as many times as is necessary to find the solution.

```
In[4]:= FixedPoint[ Function[E, f[E, Pi/2]], N[Pi/2] ]
Out[4]= 2.18145
```

The function Kepler[M] allows us to compute E for any given value of M.

```
In[5]:= Kepler[M_] :=
            FixedPoint[ Function[E, f[E, M]], N[M],
                SameTest -> Equal ]
```

Again, here is the solution for $M = \pi/2$.

```
In[6]:= Kepler[ Pi/2 ]
Out[6]= 2.18145
```

This curve shows the difference between mean and eccentric anomalies during one revolution of the planet.

```
In[7]:= Plot[ Kepler[M] - M, {M, 0, 2Pi} ];
```

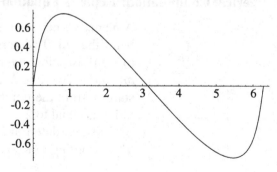

This example uses one of the simplest approximation methods for solving equations that do not have a solution in closed form. Because most equations occurring in practice are of this kind, such methods are important.

1.1.6 Everything Together: The Diode Equation

This example shows the interplay of symbolic computation, numerics, and graphics for solving a problem from electronics.

The relationship between voltage V and current I of a diode is

$$I = I_0(e^{qV/kT} - 1), \tag{1.1-7}$$

where I_0 is the leakage current, q is the elementary charge, k is the Boltzmann constant, and T is (absolute) temperature. *Mathematica* contains a table of such physical quantities. We read it in and verify first that the dimensions in the equation are correct.

This package contains conversion functions for all units imaginable (and then some).	`In[1]:= Needs["Miscellaneous`Units`"]`
We read in a table of physical constants.	`In[2]:= Needs["Miscellaneous`PhysicalConstants`"]`

This symbol is the elementary charge.	`In[3]:= q = ElectronCharge`
	
	`Out[3]= 1.60218 10^-19 Coulomb`

Finally, we introduce Boltzmann's constant. SI units are used.	`In[4]:= k = BoltzmannConstant` $Out[4]= \dfrac{1.38066\ 10^{-23}\ Joule}{Kelvin}$
Here is the dimension of the exponent qv/kT. The units should cancel.	`In[5]:= q Volt/(k Kelvin)` $Out[5]= \dfrac{11604.4\ Coulomb\ Volt}{Joule}$

This command converts the units to fundamental SI units and shows that the result is correct.	`In[6]:= Convert[%, 1]`
	
	`Out[6]= 11604.4`

Let us now replace q and k by dimensionless numbers to simplify the following computations.	`In[7]:= q = q/Coulomb; k = k Kelvin/Joule;`

Next, we define the diode equation and investigate the relationship between current and voltage.

This definition gives the current in terms of voltage and temperature.	`In[8]:= Diode[v_, t_] := i0(Exp[q v/(k t)] - 1)`
The leakage current is typically of this magnitude.	`In[9]:= i0 = 10.0^-9;`

This diagram shows the current for a voltage from 0 to 0.5 V at room temperature (70°F = 294 K). In the forward direction, the current increases rapidly above 0.5 V because the diode becomes a conductor.

```
In[10]:= Plot[ Diode[v, 294], {v, 0, 0.5},
            PlotRange->All, AxesLabel->{v, i} ];
```

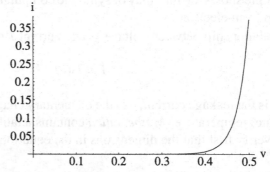

For an exponential relationship, a *log-linear* plot shows more detail. The `LogPlot[]` command is from the standard package `Graphics`Graphics``.

```
In[11]:= LogPlot[ Diode[v, 294], {v, 0.001, 0.6} ];
```

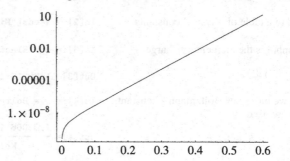

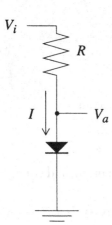

So that the diode is not destroyed, it is usually put in series with a resistor R, as shown here. This resistor limits current. The current becomes equal to $(V_i - V_a)/R$, according to Ohm's law. The current through the resistor and that through the diode are equal. By combining Ohm's law with the diode equation, we get

$$(V_i - V_a)/R = I_0(e^{qV_a/kT} - 1). \qquad (1.1\text{--}8)$$

We are mainly interested in the output voltage V_a in relation to the input voltage V_i. Because of the transcendent dependency, this equation cannot be solved exactly for V_a so we use a numerical approximation technique.

The function `FindRoot[`*equation*`, {`*var*`, `*start*`}]` solves the given equation for the unknown *var*. The search for a solution starts with the value *start*. We know that the voltage across the diode is about 0.5 V, and so we use this value as our start value. This simple equation does not need a good initial value.

We can solve the equation with FindRoot. Here, we set $V_i = 12$ V and $R = 100$ Ω.

```
In[12]:= FindRoot[ (12-va)/100 == Diode[va, 294],
                    {va, 0.5} ]

Out[12]= {va -> 0.470296}
```

This definition solves the equation for V_a, and returns the solution.

```
In[13]:= Va[vi_, r_, t_] :=
            va /. FindRoot[ (vi-va)/r == Diode[va, t],
                            {va, 0.5} ][[1]]
```

Here, we can see how the diode works as rectifier. It cuts off voltages above ≈ 0.5 V.

```
In[14]:= Plot[ Va[vi, 100, 294], {vi, -2, 5},
            AxesLabel -> {Subscript[V,i], Subscript[V,a]}
         ];
```

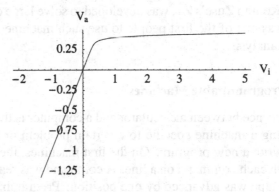

Our circuit dampens variations of input voltage by this factor.

```
In[15]:= (11 - 10)/(Va[11, 100, 294] - Va[10, 100, 294])
Out[15]= 396.695
```

Here is the *temperature coefficient*. A temperature change of 1 K changes the voltage by only this much.

```
In[16]:= (Va[10, 100, 294] - Va[10, 100, 293])
Out[16]= 0.00157909
```

1.2 Computers

Although they are called *computers,* these machines can do much more than compute. The term hints at their first use. Before the age of computers, a computer was a human, equipped with a mechanical calculator, who performed numerical computations. The first machines in the United States (Howard Aiken's Mark I and the first machine with electron tubes, the ENIAC) were used to solve numerical problems. The first machine using the binary number system, Konrad Zuse's Z1, was developed to solve large computations in fluid dynamics. Alan Turing was one of the first people to use such machines for nonnumerical purposes, namely, for cryptanalysis.

1.2.1 Programmable Machines

The difference between a calculator and a computer is that the latter is *programmable.* Instead of building a machine specific to a certain problem or rewiring one for a new problem, we simply write a new program. On the first machines, these programs were written onto paper tape, with each command on a line. A command was read and was executed immediately, and then the tape was advanced by one position. Programmers implemented loops by gluing the ends of the tape together.

The next major advance was storing programs inside the machine itself, as was first done on the EDSAC, the successor of the ENIAC. This new idea allowed the implementation of *jumps,* that is, commands that continue the program at a different place. Moreover, the place where the program would continue could depend on the data being processed. Such conditional statements were a major breakthrough. Konrad Zuse said:

> This idea often scared me in the beginning, because until then with the computers Z1–Z4 one could understand what was going on. You could even follow the calculations. In the moment that I allowed the computed data to influence the program – for that only a small wire connecting the arithmetic unit and the stored program is required – I could no longer monitor the calculations. [75, p. 25]

The programs for such computers were also often stored on tape or punched cards, but the *whole* program was read into the machine before it was executed. Today, programs are stored like data, and they are loaded into main memory as needed.

1.2.2 Computer Architecture

Computer architecture is the study of the various functional units and their connections. Figure 1.2–1 shows the main parts of a modern workstation computer. The way such a

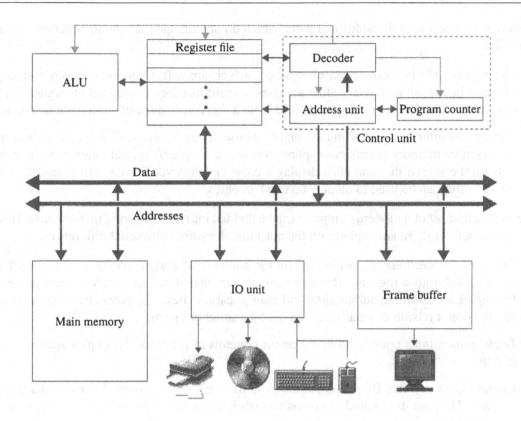

Figure 1.2–1   Building blocks of a computer.

machine works has not changed much since John von Neumann formulated the *von Neumann architecture* in 1945. Accordingly, a computer consists of the following building blocks:

1. The *control unit* loads instructions from memory and decodes them. Depending on the kind of instruction, it configures the other parts of the machine to execute the instruction.

2. The *arithmetic and logic unit (ALU)* performs arithmetic and logic computations.

3. The *main memory* is divided into sequentially numbered cells each of which contains a word of memory of a certain size. The *address* tells the memory unit which word to read or write. Words are represented in binary. The main memory contains both instructions and data.

4. The *input–output (IO) unit* is used to exchange data with external devices, such as secondary memory, printer, keyboard, mouse, terminal, or the network.

Modern computers contain additional parts, which do not change the overall structure fundamentally:

5. The *register file* is a collection of *registers,* which are a fast version of main memory. The number of comparatively slow accesses to main memory is reduced by organizing a computation so that operands can be read from a register, instead of from main memory.

6. The *frame buffer* is a part of main memory whose contents can be displayed on a screen. Consecutive memory words correspond to consecutive *pixels* (picture elements), that is, dots on the screen that can each display a color or graylevel from a certain range. The frame buffer can be used to display text and graphics.

The *instruction set* of a modern computer can be divided into the following main groups. How many instructions there are depends on the machine; there are substantial differences.

1. *Arithmetic operations* are performed on the contents of certain registers. The result is written back into a register. Register contents are interpreted as binary coded numbers. Examples are addition, subtraction, and multiplication. Few computers have instructions for division; division is usually carried out by a small program.

2. *Logical operations* operate bit by bit on the contents of registers. Examples are AND, OR, and NOT.

3. *Comparisons* perform Boolean operations on the registers and store the result in a status register. They are used mainly to prepare conditional jumps. Examples are $r_1 = 0$, $r_1 \neq 0$, $r_1 > 0$, and $r_1 = r_2$.

4. *Memory operations* transfer data between registers and memory.

5. *Jumps* change the ordinary sequential instruction sequence by writing a new value into the program counter. Jumps can be conditional. A conditional jump is executed only if the status register contains a certain value. If the condition is not satisfied, the next instruction in sequence is executed. The value of the status register is set by a preceding comparison instruction.

6. *Subroutine calls* are unconditional jumps that write the old value of the program counter into another register. The `return` instruction restores the program counter from this saved value, which causes the previous program to be continued.

The control unit can also react to external influences. A key being pressed, for example, creates an impulse that causes the control unit to interrupt the current instruction sequence, and to jump to another one. This interrupt sequence can use the IO unit to find out which key was pressed. As soon as the key has been identified, a return instruction is used to continue the interrupted program. Most external devices can generate such interrupts.

1.2.3 Operating Systems

Running a modern computer itself requires a large program: the *operating system*. The operating system coordinates the different parts of the computer and guides the correct running of user programs. Most of today's computers work in time-sharing mode, meaning that several programs can run concurrently. Chunks of the available processor time and the peripheral devices are made available to the programs in turn.

The *kernel* is the program that starts running when a computer is powered on. It maintains the interface between programs and the hardware. In addition to this kernel, an operating system consists of several *utilities*, or auxiliary programs that are needed to operate a computer. The *linker*, or *loader*, takes programs from secondary memory, connects them with the kernel, and puts them into main memory for execution. The *back-up program* writes copies of files from secondary memory onto off-line storage devices, such as magnetic tape, to protect the files in case of human or technical error. The *command interpreter* reads the commands entered on the keyboard and runs the corresponding programs. Many of these interpreters are small interpreted languages in their own right. An example is the Unix shell.

More and more frequently, *graphical user interfaces* (GUIs) that use a mouse or another pointing device are taking over the task of the command interpreter. A GUI performs two main functions:

- It manages the *windows*, that is, the rectangular areas on the screen that are used to interact with programs.

- It organizes your "desktop." It shows *icons* – graphical representations of your files – and allows you to perform such tasks as copying or deleting files or to start programs by a few clicks with the buttons of the mouse.

The first GUI was developed by Xerox. The first commercially successful GUI was part of the Macintosh operating system. The Macintosh interface's ease of use is legendary, whereas the two competing systems initially developed for the IBM PC – *Windows 3* and the *Presentation Manager* of OS/2 – failed on this measure. True progress was made only with NextStep. Most high-end Unix-based scientific workstations use graphical interfaces derived from the X Window System.

1.3 Programming Languages

With the increasing performance levels and growing commercial use of computers, people
came to realize that writing programs is a difficult task. What was more natural than to use
computers to write programs?

1.3.1 Machine Language and Assembler Programming

The first step toward easier programming was the simplification of producing machine-
language programs. People built *assemblers* – programs that allow you to write machine
instructions in symbolic form and that can compute jump addresses. Listing 1.3–1 shows an
example of an assembly-language program. It was written for Sun Microsystems' SPARC
processor.

```
        .proc   16                              cmp     %i1,%i2
        .global _vecMultLoop                    inc     2,%i0
_vecMultLoop:                                   bne     L77016
        save    %sp,-96,%sp                     srl     %i5,16,%i5
        sll     %i2,16,%i2              L77018:
        srl     %i2,16,%i4                       tst     %i5
        sll     %i3,1,%i3                        be      L77023
        add     %i1,%i3,%i2                      nop
        cmp     %i1,%i2                 L77020:
        be      L77018                          lduh    [%i0],%o7
        mov     0,%i5                           add     %i5,%o7,%i5
L77016:                                         sth     %i5,[%i0]
        lduh    [%i1],%o1                        srl     %i5,16,%i5
        call    .umul,2                          tst     %i5
        mov     %i4,%o0                          bne     L77020
        lduh    [%i0],%o3                        inc     2,%i0
        inc     2,%i1                   L77023:
        add     %o3,%o0,%o3                      ret
        add     %i5,%o3,%i5                      restore
        sth     %i5,[%i0]
```

Listing 1.3–1 An assembly program (written in two columns).

Typically, assembly-language programs contain *labels*: symbolic names of program lines (in
our example, they begin in column 1 and are terminated by a colon – e.g., L77016:). The
names of machine instructions are indented: for example, add is used to add the contents
of two registers. Instructions are followed by their arguments, that is, by the names of the
registers or the memory addresses to use. The instruction bne L77016 is a conditional jump.
If the result of the preceding test is not equal to zero, the program will jump back to label
L77016. This test is the preceding instruction cmp %i1,%i2, which compares registers i1
and i2.

The assembler transforms the assembly-language program into machine language by generating the bit patterns that correspond to the individual instructions and by replacing the labels in the jump instructions by the *length* of the jump, that is, by the number of instructions between the jump instruction and its target. The machine program generated from the program in Listing 1.3–1 is shown in Listing 1.3–2. Nowadays, it is almost never necessary to work with a program at this low level. *Disassemblers* and *debuggers* can transform such programs back into higher-level languages.

```
0000000   0103 0107 0000 0080 0000 0000 0000 0000
0000020   0000 0018 0000 0000 0000 000c 0000 0000
0000040   9de3 bfa0 b52e a010 b936 a010 b72e e001
0000060   b406 401b 80a6 401a 0280 000e ba10 2000
0000100   d216 4000 4000 0000 9010 001c d616 0000
0000120   b206 6002 9602 c008 ba07 400b fa36 0000
0000140   80a6 401a b006 2002 12bf fff6 bb37 6010
0000160   8090 001d 0280 0009 0100 0000 de16 0000
0000200   ba07 400f fa36 0000 bb37 6010 8090 001d
0000220   12bf fffb b006 2002 81c7 e008 81e8 0000
0000240   0000 0024 0000 0186 ffff ffdc 0000 0004
0000260   0500 0000 0000 0000 0000 0011 0100 0000
0000300   0000 0000 0000 0018 5f76 6563 4d75 6c74
0000320   4c6f 6f70 002e 756d 756c 00a3
```

Listing 1.3–2   A machine program in hexadecimal notation.

1.3.2   Higher-Level Languages

The next step in the development of programming languages was the advent of *higher-level languages*. In a higher-level language, we use symbolic names, or *variables*, instead of memory addresses to denote values. Another important aspect is that we can write loops and branches in a more human-readable form than is possible with assembler. One of the first higher-level languages was FORTRAN. Over time, many other languages have been developed. Depending on their intended usage and the personal preferences of their developers, they show a (sometimes too) rich variety of features. A few of the better-known examples are LISP, BASIC, COBOL, ALGOL 60, Prolog, C, Pascal, and Java. Listing 1.3–3 shows a small program in C.

Eventually, a program written in a higher-level language, like one in assembler, must also be converted into machine language so that it can be run on a computer. The translation from higher-level language to assembler is done by a *compiler*. Because of the power of expression that such languages offer, compilers are usually very complicated programs. Incidentally, the assembly-language program in Listing 1.3–1 is the result of compilation of the C program from Listing 1.3–3. It is the inner loop of the multiplication of two long integers, carried out as in *Mathematica*.

```
typedef unsigned short bigit;
typedef unsigned int accu;
const BigBits = 16;
#define BigRem(a) ((bigit) (a))
#define Carry(a)  ((a) >> BigBits)

void vecMultLoop(bigit a, bigit b, unsigned int si, unsigned int lb)
{ /* inner multiplication loop: a[0 .. lb-1] += s*b[0 .. lb-1] */
    accu        ac = 0;
    bigit       s = si, *bil;

    for (bil = b + lb; b != bil; b++, a++) {
        ac += *a + s * *b;
        *a = BigRem(ac);
        ac = Carry(ac);
    }
    while (ac != 0) {
        ac += *a;
        *a++ = BigRem(ac);
        ac = Carry(ac);
    }
}
```

Listing 1.3–3   A C program.

1.3.3 Application-Specific Environments

After the development of higher-level languages, the emphasis in research and in commercial software production shifted toward *application-specific problem-solving environments*. These programs "know" the language of the application and have built in the most important methods used in a certain area. Examples are database systems, spreadsheets, expert systems, desktop-publishing systems, and symbolic computation systems – among them *Mathematica*. *Mathematica*, in turn, offers a programming language – the one we are using in this book.

Scientific Astronomer is an application package written in *Mathematica*.

```
In[0]:= Needs["Astronomer`"];
Astronomer is Copyright (c) 1997 Stellar Software
```

We can specify our location on Earth; the Bürgenstock mountain in Switzerland, in this case.

```
In[1]:= SetLocation[ {8+23/60., 47.0},
            GeoAltitude -> 0.8 KiloMeter, TimeZone -> 2]
Out[1]= {GeoLongitude -> 8.38333 Degree,
    GeoLatitude -> 47. Degree,
    GeoAltitude -> 0.8 KiloMeter, TimeZone -> 2}
```

Figure 1.3–1 shows a view of the northern night sky over Bürgenstock at the given date and time.

```
In[2]:= CompassStarChart[ North, {1997,8,17,21,30,0},
            Mesh -> True, MagnitudeRange -> 4.0,
            ConstellationLabels -> True, MilkyWay -> True
        ];
```

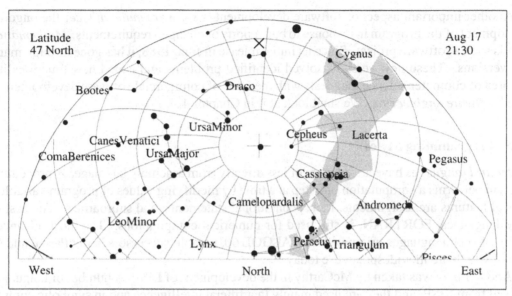

Figure 1.3–1   The northern night sky on August 17, 1997.

1.3.4 Problem Solving by Computer

We do not do programming for its own sake. It is only one part of problem solving. Solving a problem begins with *analyzing* that problem. If you ask a stupid machine to perform a task, you have to spell out all the steps accurately. As the saying goes,

> *The computer does not do what you want it to do; it does only what you tell it to do.*

There is usually a broad choice of methods for solving any given problem, and the next step is *selecting* one. Experience will teach you which ones to use in which situations. Once you choose a method, you begin *programming*. Programming is an interactive process in *Mathematica*: you can try out each small program piece immediately and see whether it does what it should do. Thus you can do *testing* both as you write your program as well as once you finish it. Part of testing is the simple but often-neglected step of thinking about whether the output *could* be right. An important part of programming is writing the *program documentation*. Then, if you are convinced that the program is correct, you can solve the original problem. Finally, you need to format the output. There are few cases where the output of a program is already the final answer to a scientific problem. Using graphics is often a good way to present a result, as demonstrated by the examples given in Section 1.1.

If software is developed commercially, these steps are formalized in a software project. The project documentation becomes an important part of software development and the work is often split among many people.

Another important aspect of software development is *software maintenance*: the ongoing development of the program in response to bug reports or changed requirements. *Mathematica* itself is such a software project. Since its initial release in June 1988, it has gone through many new versions. These new versions solved identified problems and added new functionality. The area of computer science that deals with methods of commercial software development is called *software engineering*. We shall look at it in Chapter 4.

1.3.5 Programming Styles

Procedural languages have arisen more or less directly from assembly language. A procedural program performs a computation one step at a time by modifying values of program variables. Typical features are assignments, loops, conditional statements, and subroutines. The first of these languages, FORTRAN, is still used for numerical computations. The most advanced family of such languages originated with ALGOL 60, notable successors being Pascal and C, both of which are in widespread use today.

Another path was taken by McCarthy in the development of LISP. A number of languages evolved from LISP, and they are used mainly in artificial intelligence and in symbolic computation. A modern member of this family of *functional languages* is Standard ML. A functional program performs a computation by applying functions to values. This style of programming is often neglected when traditional procedural languages are taught. We shall treat functional programming in Section 9.2.

Declarative programming, or *logic programming*, is exemplified by the language Prolog. A logic program states logic properties of predicates. A computation is a proof of the validity of a predicate. We shall discuss *rule-based programming* – another variant of declarative programming – in Section 10.1.

Object-oriented programming is rapidly gaining in popularity. It began with Simula. Nowadays, Smalltalk and C++ are widely used, with Java rapidly gaining in popularity. *Objects* are collections of data and procedures. Computations are performed by sending *messages* to objects. We shall treat object-oriented programming in Chapter 14.

Apart from these major languages, many other languages have been developed for specific problems and cannot be put into one of the main categories. COBOL is the most widely used programming language because it is used for commercial data processing. PostScript has become the standard for the description of printed material, especially for laser printers. APL and BASIC are other members of this heterogeneous group.

Mathematica incorporates features from all major programming styles, which allows us to use the one best suited for a given problem.

1.4 Computer Science

Computers have become so important in science and engineering – and in everyday life – that a new science has been established to deal with all aspects of computers. Its origins include both electronics and mathematics. The earliest research institutes for computer science belonged to one of these two fields. At most universities, independent departments of computer science have been established during the last 20 years. Here is a somewhat biased overview of the branches of computer science.

1.4.1 Theoretical Computer Science

Theoretical computer science studies the mathematical foundations of computer science. One area is *theory of computation*, which investigates the relation between programs and mathematical functions. Are there functions that cannot be computed by a program, even if we have unlimited memory and time? We shall answer this question in Chapter 12.

Complexity theory is the second main topic of theoretical computer science. It focuses on the difficulty of computing functions. How many operations does it take to solve a certain problem? Are there lower bounds and, if so, can we write an optimal program? We shall look at aspects of algorithmic complexity in Chapter 7.

Semantics is an important aspect of theoretical computer science. The semantics of a program is its meaning. On the lowest level, the meaning of a program is the sequence of states of the computer that executes the program. The final state after the completion of the program is the result of the program. The state of a computer is the complete information about the contents of each register and each word of memory. Usually, we are interested in only a small subset of this state – for example, the contents of the frame buffer. This semantics is called *operational semantics*. It is not satisfactory because it depends too much on the details of the machine on which the program is run. A better approach to semantics is to find a well-defined mathematical function that describes the program's output in terms of its input. Because of the self-referential nature of programs (programs can have other programs as their input or can produce programs as output), and because of recursion, the domains and ranges of these mathematical functions are complicated. They are called *universal domains*. This kind of semantics is termed *denotational semantics*. The *denotation* of a program is the function it computes. *Axiomatic semantics* proves statements about the values of program variables before and after a program is executed. We shall look at axiomatic semantics in Section 3.3.

1.4.2 Practical Computer Science

Practical computer science examines the tools needed to use computers efficiently. These tools are the compilers and interpreters for our languages and the operating systems (described

in Section 1.2.3). Gaining in importance are computer-aided tools for software development
– CASE tools – as well as the other problem-solving tools mentioned in Section 1.3.

1.4.3 Technical Computer Science

Technical computer science studies the computers themselves, from how to design integrated
circuits (chips) to how best to connect the parts of a computer (see Section 1.2.2). The main
area of research is to find alternatives to the traditional von Neumann architecture, such as
parallel and vector computers, often termed *supercomputers*. Development of peripherals,
secondary storage devices such as hard disks, and fast data-transmission channels also is part
of technical computer science.

1.4.4 Applied Computer Science

As a universal machine, computers can be found in almost all areas of science and engineering.
Applications in these areas cannot all be taken to be part of computer science, of course. Certain
types of applications, however, have been recognized as important areas of computer science
and have become part of *applied computer science*. Examples are numerical analysis, scientific
computation, computer graphics, databases, and real-time computation.

1.4.5 Computer Algebra

A significant part of *Mathematica* owes its existence to *computer algebra*, the study of algorithms for symbolic (nonnumeric) computation. This field started soon after LISP was
developed. Early progress showed that it was feasible to perform many of the seemingly hard
computations from high-school mathematics efficiently by computer, and computer algebra
benefitted in turn from the increasing demand for tools for computer-aided mathematics in
research and industry.

Chapter 2
Mathematica's Programming Language

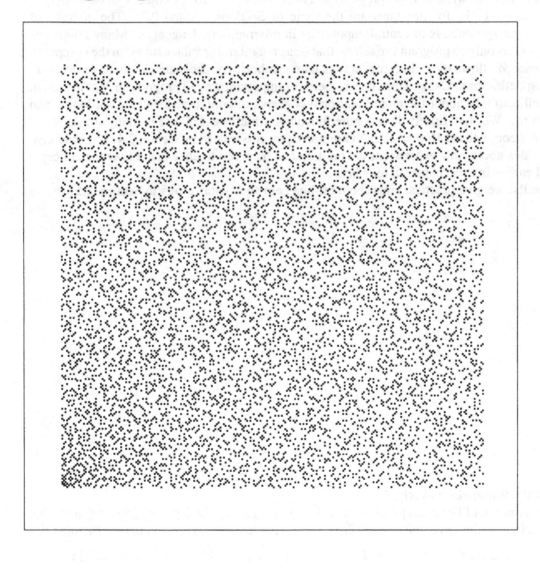

In this chapter, we examine *Mathematica*'s programming language. Every language has a unique syntax that we must understand before we can write even a simple program. Learning an interactive language is easier than learning a language that has to be compiled. We recommend strongly that you try out the examples on your own machine; only by working them through will you get practical experience with *Mathematica*.

Section 2.1 covers arithmetic and logic expressions. Such expressions appear in most programs. In *Mathematica*, we can do computations with arithmetic expressions immediately; we do not have to write a whole program just to compute 2^{100}, for example.

Building blocks for programs are the topic of Sections 2.2 and 2.3. The concept of variables, or symbols, is of central importance in programming languages. Many languages treat symbols only as program variables – that is, as notations for values stored in the computer. *Mathematica* allows us to do computations with symbols. Symbols are also used to organize function definitions. Using definitions is the most important way to program in *Mathematica*. We shall also talk about the more traditional concepts of conditional statements, loops, and procedures. We shall briefly discuss pure functions, which we shall use in many situations.

The theory behind *Mathematica*'s expressive power is treated in Section 2.4. It should give you an idea about how expressions are built up and help you to understand how the concepts treated earlier in this chapter fit together.

Finally, we give practical hints about on-line help and syntax errors in Section 2.5.

About the illustration overleaf:

The distribution of Gaussian primes (black dots) among $x + iy$ for $0 \leq x \leq 255, 0 \leq y \leq 255$. The origin is in the lower left corner. The plot was made with this command (see Pictures.m):

```
grid = Table[If[PrimeQ[x + I y], 0, 1], {x, 0, 255}, {y, 0, 255}];
Show[Graphics[Raster[grid]], AspectRatio -> Automatic].
```

2.1   Arithmetic and Logic

Arithmetic expressions can be found in nearly every program. Most languages – including *Mathematica* – allow you to write arithmetic expressions with traditional mathematical notation. Logic expressions are used to test properties of numbers.

2.1.1   Arithmetic Expressions

Mathematica can be used like a calculator. Using the four arithmetic operations and parentheses, you can enter arbitrarily complex expressions, the results of which will then be displayed.

The arithmetic operations have their usual precedence; therefore, the sum $3 + 4$ must be in parentheses.

```
In[1]:= (3 + 4)*5
Out[1]= 35
```

Without parentheses, we get this result, corresponding to $3 + (4 \cdot 5)$.

```
In[2]:= 3 + 4*5
Out[2]= 23
```

The multiplication sign can be left out.

```
In[3]:= (3 + 4)5
Out[3]= 35
```

Mathematica always computes an exact result, if all inputs are exact numbers.

```
In[4]:= 1 + 1/3
         4
Out[4]= -
         3
```

You have to ask explicitly for a floating-point approximation.

```
In[5]:= N[%]
Out[5]= 1.33333
```

Exponentiation a^b is written as a∧b.

```
In[6]:= 2∧10
Out[6]= 1024
```

Observe that exponentiation is *right associative*. This input is read as a∧(b∧c).

```
In[7]:= a∧b∧c
             c
           b
Out[7]= a
```

Parentheses are necessary for $(a^b)^c$.

```
In[8]:= (a∧b)∧c
          b c
Out[8]= (a )
```

There is no built-in limit for the size of the numbers you can use. (Only available memory will set practical limits.) The number 100! has 158 digits.

```
In[9]:= 100!
Out[9]= 933262154439441526816992388562667004907159682640\
        38162146859296389521759999322991560894146397615651828\
        62536979208272237582511852109168640000000000000000000\
        00000
```

Here is a sum of three fourth powers.

```
In[10]:= 95800^4 + 217519^4 + 414560^4
Out[10]= 31858749840007945920321
```

The result is again a fourth power, as this calculation shows. The fourth root is computed
only if doing so is possible exactly.

```
In[11]:= % ^ (1/4)
Out[11]= 422481
```

2.1.2 Logical (Boolean) Expressions

Logical, or Boolean, expressions are tests whose results can be *true* or *false*. *Mathematica* uses
the symbols `True` and `False` to denote the two truth values. Ordering relations are expressed
with the usual symbols: $n_1 < n_2$, $n_1 >= n_2$, and so on. Equality of numbers is written with
two equal signs:

$$n_1 \text{ == } n_2 .$$

Inequality is expressed as follows:

$$n_1 \text{ != } n_2 .$$

Negation of a logical expression r is written as $!r$. The AND connection of two expressions r_1
and r_2 is written

$$r_1 \text{ \&\& } r_2 ,$$

and the OR connection as

$$r_1 \text{ || } r_2 .$$

Mathematica can figure out this inequality
immediately.

```
In[12]:= 2 < 5
Out[12]= True
```

Different comparison operators can be
mixed. The result is `True`, because both
$0 \le 2$ and $2 < 5$ are true.

```
In[13]:= 0 <= 2 < 5
Out[13]= True
```

The same test can be expressed like this.

```
In[14]:= 0 <= 2 && 2 < 5
Out[14]= True
```

Negation changes a truth value to the opposite value.

```
In[15]:= (!False)
Out[15]= True
```

Because variables can have symbolic values, not every logical expression can be figured out
immediately. If *Mathematica* finds a logical expression whose value cannot be determined,
that expression is left as is.

Because the variables a and b have no values, the value of this equation cannot yet be
found; the expression is left as is.

```
In[16]:= a == b
Out[16]= a == b
```

The first expression 2<5 returns True; the second one does not matter anymore.

```
In[17]:= 2 < 5 || a == b
Out[17]= True
```

For the AND connection, all parts must return True. The first expression is already True; therefore, only the second one matters.

```
In[18]:= 2 < 5 && a == b
Out[18]= a == b
```

Mathematica looks ahead and sees the second expression, which returns True.

```
In[19]:= a == b || 2 < 5
Out[19]= True
```

2.1.3 Lists

Lists are linearly ordered collections of data. In *Mathematica*, lists are written with curly braces, as $\{e_1, e_2, \ldots, e_n\}$. The e_i are the *elements* of the list, n is the *length* of the list.

Lists can hold together arbitrary elements. The last element of this list is again a list (with two elements).

```
In[1]:= {a, 2, Pi, {1, 0}}
Out[1]= {a, 2, Pi, {1, 0}}
```

Mathematica provides many operations on lists; here we reverse the order of the elements of the preceding list.

```
In[2]:= Reverse[ % ]
Out[2]= {{1, 0}, Pi, 2, a}
```

Here is the list's length.

```
In[3]:= Length[ % ]
Out[3]= 4
```

The function Part[*list*, *i*] returns a list's *i*th element. It is most often written with double square brackets, as *list*[[*i*]]. This notation was chosen in analogy to the notation for array elements in many traditional programming languages.

Here is the second element of the list {a, b, c}.

```
In[4]:= Part[{a, b, c}, 2]
Out[4]= b
```

This alternate syntax gives the same result.

```
In[5]:= {a, b, c}[[2]]
Out[5]= b
```

Negative indices count from the end of the list. Here is the list's *last* element.

```
In[6]:= Part[{a, b, c}, -1]
Out[6]= c
```

Mathematica uses lists to represent arrays or vectors; nested lists are used for matrices, see Chapter 8.

2.2 Definitions

Simple mathematical functions can be defined almost in the usual notation. The function that
squares its argument is normally written as follows:

$$f(x) = x^2 \,. \tag{2.2-1}$$

Mathematica uses square brackets for function arguments. The operator for definition is `:=`.
The formal parameter x corresponds to a pattern that is denoted by `x_`. We have already seen
how powers are written. Therefore, in *Mathematica* Equation 2.2–1 looks like this:

$$\texttt{f[x\_] := x\^2} \,. \tag{2.2-2}$$

The function f is defined like this.

```
In[1]:= f[x_] := x^2
```

We use the new function f immediately. For
numerical arguments, the result can be calculated.

```
In[2]:= f[2]
Out[2]= 4
```

For symbolic arguments, no further simplification takes place.

```
In[3]:= f[1 + y]
               2
Out[3]= (1 + y)
```

A question mark at the beginning of a line
can be used to show all definitions made for
a symbol.

```
In[4]:= ?f
Global`f
f[x_] := x^2
```

2.2.1 Several Definitions

A new definition for a symbol overwrites an existing one only if the left side is the same.

This definition overwrites the old one given
for f.

```
In[5]:= f[x_] := x^3
```

We can see that only the new one remains.

```
In[6]:= ?f
Global`f
f[x_] := x^3
```

If the left side of a new definition is different from those already stored, the new definition is
added to the list of definitions. Definitions that are more specialized than existing ones are put
before more general ones.

Here is the general rule for the factorial function.

```
In[1]:= factorial[n_] := n factorial[n-1]
```

This definition establishes the initial condition.

```
In[2]:= factorial[0] = 1
Out[2]= 1
```

Even though the initial condition is given second, it is put before the general rule.

```
In[3]:= ?factorial
Global`factorial

factorial[0] = 1

factorial[n_] := n*factorial[n - 1]
```

Only in this way can the function work at all.

```
In[4]:= factorial[30]
Out[4]= 265252859812191058636308480000000
```

`Clear[f]` clears all definitions made for a symbol f.

```
In[5]:= Clear[factorial]
```

Mathematica no longer knows any definitions for the symbol `factorial`.

```
In[6]:= ?factorial
Global`factorial
```

> If you set up definitions interactively and want to modify existing ones, you should make sure that the new ones do in fact overwrite the old ones. Often, it is better to use `Clear[symbol]` to clear all definitions and then to start over. With `?symbol`, you can always check which definitions are in effect.

2.2.2 Piecewise-Defined Functions

Piecewise-defined functions can be implemented with several definitions with the appropriate conditions on their validity. Definitions valid under only certain conditions are given as follows:

$$ls \ /; \ cond := rs \ .$$

The condition *cond* is a logical expression.

The absolute value of a real number is defined thus:

$$\text{abs}(x) = \begin{cases} x & \text{for } x \geq 0; \\ -x & \text{for } x < 0. \end{cases} \tag{2.2--3}$$

These two conditional definitions can be entered into *Mathematica* similarly as two separate definitions.

The absolute value of x is equal to x, if $x \geq 0$.

```
In[7]:= abs[x_] /; x >= 0 := x
```

The absolute value of x is equal to $-x$, if $x < 0$.

```
In[8]:= abs[x_] /; x < 0 := -x
```

The first rule that matches is used.

```
In[9]:= {abs[-1], abs[0], abs[1]}
Out[9]= {1, 0, 1}
```

Of course, our own functions can also be plotted.

```
In[10]:= Plot[ abs[x], {x, -1, 1} ];
```

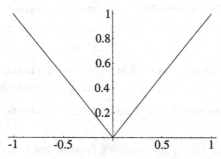

For symbolic arguments, nothing is known about their sign. The function `abs[]` therefore remains unevaluated.

```
In[11]:= abs[a]
Out[11]= abs[a]
```

2.2.3 Immediate and Delayed Definitions

You will encounter two kinds of definitions; those with *ls* = *rs*, and those with *ls* := *rs*. The difference lies in *when* the right side (*rs*) is evaluated. The first kind, *immediate definitions*, evaluates the right side when the definition is given; the second kind evaluates it only when the definition is used later on. The second kind, *delayed definition*, should be used if the left side (*ls*) contains pattern variables – for example, in `f[x_] := x^2`. As we have seen in the preceding sections, these definitions are usually used to define functions. The right side of function definitions, called the *body* of the function, should be evaluated only when the function is used, not when it is defined.

Immediate definitions can be used if the left side is constant – for example, in `fib[0] = 1`, or when a value for a symbol is defined, as in `a = 5`.

To make the difference visible, we give a value to the variable `x`.

```
In[1]:= x = 77
Out[1]= 77
```

This delayed definition is not influenced by the global value of `x`.

```
In[2]:= f[x_] := x^2
```

First, the value of the pattern variable `x` is inserted; then, the right side is evaluated.

```
In[3]:= f[2]
Out[3]= 4
```

As you can see, the definition for `f` still contains `x`, not its value.

```
In[4]:= ?f
Global`f

f[x_] := x^2
```

The right side of this definition is evaluated immediately.

```
In[5]:= g[x_] = x^2
Out[5]= 5929
```

The value of the pattern variable **x** is not used at all because it does not appear in the evaluated right side. Normally, this is not what we want.

```
In[6]:= g[2]
Out[6]= 5929
```

Here, you can see that the definition for **g** does not contain **x** at all. It was replaced by its value when the definition was made.

```
In[7]:= ?g
Global`g
g[x_] = 5929
```

> Functions should normally be set up with delayed definitions (with :=).
> For constants and for symbols, immediate definitions (with =) can be given.

2.3 Simple Program Structures

In this section, we shall look at building blocks of programs. Every program in the rest of this book is composed of the language elements described here.

2.3.1 Variables and Symbols

You can use variables for symbolic computation (without giving them a value).

The variable x is treated as an *indeterminate*, as is customary in mathematics.

```
In[1]:= Expand[(1+x)^6]
                        2         3          4          5     6
Out[1]= 1 + 6 x + 15 x  + 20 x  + 15 x  + 6 x  + x
```

Even without a value for x, we know that it is equal to itself.

```
In[2]:= x == x
Out[2]= True
```

Here is a symbolic sum of the powers 0 through 5 of x.

```
In[3]:= Sum[ x^i, {i, 0, 5} ]
                    2    3    4    5
Out[3]= 1 + x + x  + x  + x  + x
```

You can assign values to variables. The values can be numbers or formulae. Every time a variable is used, its value is inserted.

We set the value of the variable n to 4.

```
In[4]:= n = 4
Out[4]= 4
```

This value of n is now used in this formula.

```
In[5]:= 1 + n + n^2
Out[5]= 21
```

The value of x is another formula.

```
In[6]:= x = a+b
Out[6]= a + b
```

This value, too, is used.

```
In[7]:= x^2
                  2
Out[7]= (a + b)
```

By expanding products and powers with the command Expand[], we get the well-known formula $(a + b)^2 = a^2 + 2ab + b^2$.

```
In[8]:= Expand[%]
             2            2
Out[8]= a  + 2 a b + b
```

You can do assignments in parallel by enclosing the left and right sides in lists (curly braces).

```
In[9]:= {x, y} = {2, 3}
Out[9]= {2, 3}
```

The assignments are done in parallel. Therefore, this command interchanges the values of x and y.

```
In[10]:= {x, y} = {y, x}
Out[10]= {3, 2}
```

2.3.2   Sequences of Assignments

Expressions or statements can be separated by a semicolon (;). They are then evaluated one after the other.

The commands are executed in the order given. The value of the last one is returned.

```
In[1]:= n = 5; a = (1 + n)^5; Expand[(a + x)^2]
                                          2
Out[1]= 60466176 + 15552 x + x
```

If the last command (after the semicolon) is empty, no value is returned.

```
In[2]:= Expand[(1+x)^100];
```

The percent sign (%) can still be used to access the value of the last expression before the semicolon. This possibility is useful if a command would produce a large output.

```
In[3]:= Length[ % ]

Out[3]= 101
```

2.3.3   Conditional Expressions

Conditional expressions are programmed with If[]. The syntax is

$$If[predicate,\ true,\ false].$$

First, the predicate (a logical expression) is tested. If it evaluates to True, the value returned is equal to the value of the expression *true*. If it evaluates to False, the value returned is the value of *false*.

This is a second way of defining the absolute value: If $x \geq 0$, then x; else, $-x$.

```
In[1]:= abs[x_] := If[ x >= 0, x, -x ]
```

This definition works exactly like the ones in Section 2.2.2.

```
In[2]:= abs[-2]

Out[2]= 2
```

The If[] expression also remains unevaluated, if the truth value of the predicate cannot be determined.

```
In[3]:= abs[a]

Out[3]= If[a >= 0, a, -a]
```

There are three truth values in *Mathematica*: *true, false,* and *don't know.*

2.3.4   Loops

Loops are programmed with While[]. The syntax is

$$While[predicate,\ statements].$$

First, the predicate (a logical expression) is tested. If it evaluates to True, the expression *statements* is evaluated once. Then, *predicate* is evaluated again, and so on, until the value of *predicate* is no longer True.

Here is a parallel assignment for the variables a and b.	`In[4]:= {a, b} = {1999, 2999}` `Out[4]= {1999, 2999}`
This loop computes the greatest common divisor of the integers a and b. (See also Section 3.1.)	`In[5]:= While[ b != 0, {a, b} = {b, Mod[a, b]} ]`
The greatest common divisor of 1999 and 2999 is now in the variable a.	`In[6]:= a` `Out[6]= 1`

There are two ways to change the flow of control in a loop: Break[] and Continue[], which can be used in exceptional circumstances.

The Break[] command exits the loop immediately. The following loop searches for an element e in a list l and exits the loop as soon as e has been found:

```
i = 1;
n = Length[l];
While[ i <= n,
    If[ l[[i]] === e, Break[] ];
    i = i + 1
]
```

You can often avoid such a special exit by changing the loop predicate accordingly. The preceding example would be expressed more clearly as follows:

```
i = 1;
n = Length[l];
While[ i <= n && l[[i]] =!= e,
    i = i + 1
]
```

Sometimes we use Break[] because it makes certain programs more readable (see Sections 6.1.1 and 8.4.3). Before using it, however, you should try to find a more elegant way to express your loop because jumping around in a program usually makes it more difficult to understand.

The Continue[] command causes the rest of the current loop iteration to be skipped. The program continues testing the loop predicate. An example using Continue[] can be seen in the function walk[] in Listing 8.5–1.

2.3.5 Iterators

An iterator evaluates an expression several times, while changing the value of an *iterator variable*. The general form is

$$command[expression, iterator] ,$$

where *command* is Do, Table, Sum, or Product. The iterations are specified by *iterator*, which gives the values over which the iterator variable ranges. There four forms; in the following box, *var* is the iterator variable taking on certain values in turn:

{*var*, *from*, *to*}	*var* takes successive values *from*, *from* + 1, ..., *to*
{*var*, *to*}	initial value *from* defaults to 1
{*var*, *from*, *to*, *step*}	step size is *step* (instead of 1)
{*n*}	evaluates *expression* n times, without an iterator variable

Forms of iterators in *Mathematica*.

The iterator Do[*statements*, *iterator*] simply evaluates *statements* without returning a value. To see what happens, we can use a Print[] command, for example.

The iterator is evaluated five times, with i taking on the values 1, 2, ..., 5.

```
In[1]:= Do[ Print[i], {i, 1, 5} ]
1
2
3
4
5
```

Here, the value of i is incremented by 2 and ends at 9.

```
In[2]:= Do[ Print[i], {i, 1, 9, 2} ]
1
3
5
7
9
```

Let's set x to 1.0.

```
In[3]:= x = 1.0
Out[3]= 1.
```

Now, we replace x by $1 + 1/x$, a total of 10 times.

```
In[4]:= Do[ x = 1 + 1/x, {10} ]
```

This value is the final value of x – an approximation to the Golden Ratio.

```
In[5]:= x
Out[5]= 1.61798
```

We can see all intermediate values with a
`Print[]` statement.

```
In[6]:= x = 1.0; Do[ x = 1 + 1/x; Print[x], {10} ]

2.
1.5
1.66667
1.6
1.625
1.61538
1.61905
1.61765
1.61818
1.61798
```

Normally, we see only a few digits of a
floating-point number. With this command,
we can see all digits.

```
In[7]:= InputForm[x]

Out[7]//InputForm= 1.6179775280898876
```

The iterator `Table[]` returns the results of the iterations in a list.

`Table[]` collects the results of all iterations
in a list.

```
In[8]:= Table[ i^2, {i, 1, 10} ]

Out[8]= {1, 4, 9, 16, 25, 36, 49, 64, 81, 100}
```

This list contains the first 10 primes.

```
In[9]:= Table[ Prime[j], {j, 10} ]

Out[9]= {2, 3, 5, 7, 11, 13, 17, 19, 23, 29}
```

`Sum[]` and `Product[]` give sums and products, respectively, according to the mathematical
notation $\sum$ and $\prod$.

$$\sum_{i=1}^{100} i^2$$

```
In[1]:= Sum[ i^2, {i, 1, 100} ]
Out[1]= 338350
```

$$\prod_{k=1}^{5}(x-k)$$

```
In[2]:= Product[ x-k, {k, 1, 5} ]
Out[2]= (-5 + x) (-4 + x) (-3 + x) (-2 + x) (-1 + x)
```

2.3.6   Local Variables

In Section 2.3.4, we saw how we can compute easily the greatest common divisor (gcd) of
two numbers. Now we want to define a *function* to perform these calculations, taking the two
numbers as arguments. Inside this function, we need two *local variables* a and b, to which
we assign the values of the arguments in the same way as we did it on page 36. Local variables
are declared with `Module[{`*variables*`}, `*body*`]`. The function is shown in Listing 2.3–1.

The two local variables a and b get the arguments of the function as initial values.
The body of the module consists of the two expressions `While[...]` and a, separated by a
semicolon. The value of last expression (simply a in our case) is returned.

```
gcd[a0_, b0_] :=
    Module[{a = a0, b = b0},
        While[ b != 0, {a, b} = {b, Mod[a, b]} ];
        a
    ]
```

Listing 2.3–1   A function for the gcd.

Now we can compute the gcd of two numbers without having to enter all the calculation steps every time.

```
In[1]:= gcd[ 1999, 2999 ]

Out[1]= 1
```

The declaration of local variables with initial values is necessary here. The reason is that the
pattern variables a0 and b0 are not program variables! Their values are *inserted* into the body
of the definition. Let's see what the consequences are. Without local variables, our program
would look like the one shown in Listing 2.3–2.

```
gcd[a_, b_] :=
        While[ b != 0, {a, b} = {b, Mod[a, b]} ];
        a
```

Listing 2.3–2   An erroneous function for the gcd.

If we call the function as gcd[1999, 2999], all occurrences of a and b are replaced by
the arguments 1999 and 2999. The resulting expression is

```
While[ 2999 != 0, {1999, 2999} = {2999, Mod[1999, 2999]} ];
1999
```

There are many errors in this expression (can you find them?). Therefore, we must assign the
parameter values to local variables, and then do all computations with these local variables.
That is the purpose of

$$\text{Module}[\{var_1 = val_1, \ var_2 = val_2, \ \ldots\}, \ body] \ .$$

Local variables are not used only for parameters of functions. *Auxiliary variables* also
should be declared in a Module. These are variables used inside the body of a definition. If
there was no parallel assignment of the form $\{var_1, \ var_2\} = \{e_1, \ e_2\}$ in *Mathematica*, we
would need an additional variable to exchange the values of the variables a and b, as shown
in Listing 2.3–3.

Hint: the program in Listing 2.3–3 would run even if we did not declare the local variables.
Mathematica would simply use global symbols with names a, b, and c. Using a function
that changes the values of global variables is bad programming style and can introduce errors
that are hard to find.

```
gcd[a0_, b0_] :=
    Module[{a = a0, b = b0, c},
        While[ b != 0,
                c = b;
                b = Mod[a, b];
                a = c
        ];
        a
    ]
```

Listing 2.3–3   Exchanging values using an auxiliary variable.

Here is the last version of the gcd function without declarations for the local variables. Observe the parentheses: They make
all statements be part of the definition.

```
In[1]:= gcd[a0_, b0_] := (
            a = a0; b = b0;
            While[ b != 0,
                c = b;
                b = Mod[a, b];
                a = c
            ];
            a
        )
```

Perhaps we performed other computations
before using our gcd function. If so, the
symbol c may already have a value.

```
In[2]:= c = SpeedOfLight
```

$$Out[2]= \frac{299792458 \; Meter}{Second}$$

Now, we compute a gcd.

```
In[3]:= gcd[1999, 2999]

Out[3]= 1
```

As a side effect, the value of c has changed.

```
In[4]:= c

Out[4]= 1
```

2.3.7 Constants

Closely related to Module[] is

$$With[\{var_1 = val_1, \; var_2 = val_2, \; \ldots\}, \; body]$$

that introduces local *constants*. A local constant is similar to a local variable (as declared with
Module[]), but it cannot be changed after its initialization. The use of constants can make a
program easier to read and can also make it more efficient.

This function definition is a bit inefficient
because x^2 is computed twice.

```
In[1]:= f[x_] := (x^2-1)(x^2+1)
```

In this equivalent definition, x^2 is computed only once.

```
In[2]:= f[x_] := With[ {x2 = x^2}, (x2-1)(x2+1) ]
```

With this definition we intend to measure the time it takes to multiply two n-digit numbers, but we also measure the time it takes to compute the two numbers in the first place.

```
In[3]:= time1[n_] := Timing[ (10^n-1)*(10^n-3); ]
```

Here we compute the two numbers outside `Timing[]`, and then insert their values in the timing command (see Section 7.4.3).

```
In[4]:= time2[n_] :=
            With[ {a = 10^n-1, b = 10^n-3}, Timing[a*b;] ]
```

2.3.8 Pure Functions

Pure functions are treated in detail in Chapter 11. Because we use them in many places, we present the basic idea here.

Before we can use a function, we have to define it.

```
In[1]:= f[x_] := x^2
```

We apply a function `f` to an argument by putting the argument inside square brackets.

```
In[2]:= f[5]
Out[2]= 25
```

Here is another way to specify a function. A preceding definition is not necessary. The function that squares its argument can be applied immediately.

```
In[3]:= Function[x, x^2][5]
Out[3]= 25
```

This expression is the function itself. It can be read as "the function whose value at x is x^2."

```
In[4]:= Function[x, x^2]
                          2
Out[4]= Function[x, x ]
```

This function (on the preceding line) can be applied to an argument.

```
In[5]:= %[5]
Out[5]= 25
```

We can differentiate a function. The result is the function that multiplies its argument by 2, according to the formula $\frac{d}{dx} x^2 = 2x$.

```
In[6]:= Function[x, x^2]'
Out[6]= Function[x, 2 x]
```

The value on the preceding line is a *function* that we can apply to an argument in the usual way.

```
In[7]:= %[5]
Out[7]= 10
```

The special symbol `#` can be used as the variable in a function. In need not be declared, so this form of the pure function has only one element.

```
In[8]:= Function[#^2]
                   2
Out[8]= #1  &
```

This short form, given in the previous output, can be input as well. We say more about the operator `&` in Section 11.1.3.

```
In[9]:= #^2&
                2
Out[9]= #1  &
```

2.3.9 Functional Operations

With a simple way to specify a function we can take a look at *Mathematica*'s many functional operations, that is, commands that take a function as argument. Here is a short introduction to four of these functional operations: `Map`, `Apply`, `Nest`, and `Fold`.

We can show how a functional operation works by giving it an undefined, symbolic function, such as `f`, as argument. The result will still contain the symbol `f` so we can see what is going on.

`Map` applies a function to each element of a list in turn. It returns the list of the results of these applications.

```
In[1]:= Map[ f, {a, b, c, d} ]
Out[1]= {f[a], f[b], f[c], f[d]}
```

Here we apply the function that squares its argument to a list of integers. The result is the list of the squares of these numbers.

```
In[2]:= Map[ #^2&, {1, 2, 3, 4} ]
Out[2]= {1, 4, 9, 16}
```

`Apply` applies a function to all elements of a list.

```
In[3]:= Apply[ f, {e1, e2, e3, e4} ]
Out[3]= f[e1, e2, e3, e4]
```

Applying the function `Plus` gives the sum of the elements of a list.

```
In[4]:= Apply[ Plus, {e1, e2, e3, e4} ]
Out[4]= e1 + e2 + e3 + e4
```

`Nest` applies a function repeatedly to the result of the previous application, starting with the value `x`.

```
In[5]:= Nest[ f, x, 5 ]
Out[5]= f[f[f[f[f[x]]]]]
```

The repeated application of the function $f(x) = 1 + 1/x$ to a symbol `x` gives a continued fraction.

```
In[6]:= Nest[ Function[x, 1+1/x], x, 7 ]
```

$$Out[6]= 1 + \cfrac{1}{1 + \cfrac{1}{1 + \cfrac{1}{1 + \cfrac{1}{1 + \cfrac{1}{1 + \cfrac{1}{1 + \cfrac{1}{x}}}}}}}$$

The same function applied to an integer gives a rational number. Here we nested the function 200 times.

```
In[7]:= Nest[ Function[x, 1+1/x], 1, 200 ]
```

$$Out[7]= \frac{734544867157818093234908902110449296423351}{453973694165307953197296969697410619233826}$$

`Fold` applies a function `g` of two arguments repeatedly to the result of the previous application (as first argument) and another element from the given list (as second argument).

```
In[8]:= Fold[ g, x0, {x1, x2, x3} ]
Out[8]= g[g[g[x0, x1], x2], x3]
```

This function multiplies the previous result by z and adds the next element from the list. The result is the Horner form of a polynomial.

```
In[9]:= Fold[ Function[{x,y}, x z + y], 0,
              {a5, a4, a3, a2, a1, a0}]

Out[9]= a0 + z (a1 + z (a2 + z (a3 + z (a4 + a5 z))))
```

The expanded form shows that the a_i are the coefficients of an ordinary polynomial. The Horner from is often used for numerical computations because it is more efficient than the expanded form.

```
In[10]:= Expand[ % ]

                         2        3        4        5
Out[10]= a0 + a1 z + a2 z  + a3 z  + a4 z  + a5 z
```

Functional operations are treated in more detail in Section 11.2.3.

2.4 Structure of Expressions

Programming languages usually have a rigid structure with precise rules about the form of valid expressions. A program is understood by the interpreter or compiler only if it satisfies these syntactic requirements. In Sections 2.4–2.4.4, we examine fundamental aspects of the structure of the expressions that are understood by *Mathematica*.

In the preceding sections, we saw some of the possible forms of expressions in *Mathematica*. Even though it contains a large collection of operators, the language has a simple fundamental structure. It is the same as the structure of the language LISP, one of the oldest languages still in use today. All expressions are built from fundamental building blocks with a single method. The building blocks are termed *atoms*. Formally, an expression is either an atom or a *normal expression*.

2.4.1 Normal Expressions

A normal expression has the form

$$h \: [\: e_1, \: e_2, \: \ldots, \: e_n \:] \: , \qquad\qquad (2.4\text{--}1)$$

where h and the e_i are themselves expressions. Such an *inductive* definition of expressions is typical for formal languages. The h is called the *head* of the expression; the e_i are the *elements*. The number of elements may be zero. In this case, the expression looks as follows:

$$h \: [\:] \: . \qquad\qquad (2.4\text{--}2)$$

Here, for example, is an expression according to the preceding definition:

$$\texttt{f[a,b][][g[1], h[x, y]]} \: . \qquad\qquad (2.4\text{--}3)$$

It has two elements: `g[1]` and `h[x, y]`. Its head is `f[a,b][]`, which is again a normal expression (without elements), whose head is `f[a, b]`, and so on.

The head of an expression *expr* can be extracted with `Head[`*expr*`]`. The ith element is obtained by `Part[`*expr*`, `*i*`]`. Instead of `Part[`*expr*`, `*i*`]`, you can also write *expr*`[[`*i*`]]`. `Length[`*expr*`]` gives the *length* of a normal expression, that is, the number of elements.

Here again is an example of a normal expression.	`In[1]:= expr = f[a,b][][ g[1], h[x, y] ];`
It has two elements.	`In[2]:= Length[ expr ]`
	`Out[2]= 2`
Here is the first element.	`In[3]:= Part[ expr, 1 ]`
	`Out[3]= g[1]`

Here is the second element. `Part[expr, i]` can alternatively be written as *expr[[i]]* (with double square brackets).

```
In[4]:= expr[[2]]
Out[4]= h[x, y]
```

The head of `expr` is again a normal expression.

```
In[5]:= Head[ expr ]
Out[5]= f[a, b][]
```

Its head is a normal expression, too.

```
In[6]:= Head[ % ]
Out[6]= f[a, b]
```

At some point, we always reach an atom; here, it is a symbol.

```
In[7]:= Head[ % ]
Out[7]= f
```

2.4.2   Atoms

There are three kinds of atoms:

1. *Symbols* are the identifiers; they are words beginning with a letter and containing only letters or digits. The dollar sign, $, is treated as a letter.

2. *Strings* are sequences of arbitrary characters, enclosed in quotation marks. They are used mainly to denote external objects, such as file names.

3. *Numbers* include integers, rational numbers, floating-point numbers, and complex numbers.

Even though they are not normal expressions, atoms also have heads. This head describes the type of the atom according to the preceding list.

The head of a symbol is the symbol `Symbol`.

```
In[8]:= Head[ aSymbol ]
Out[8]= Symbol
```

Its head is again the same symbol, of course.

```
In[9]:= Head[%]
Out[9]= Symbol
```

The head of an integer is the symbol `Integer`.

```
In[10]:= Head[ 1024 ]
Out[10]= Integer
```

The head of a rational number is the symbol `Rational`.

```
In[11]:= Head[ 1/3 ]
Out[11]= Rational
```

The head of a floating-point number is the symbol `Real`.

```
In[12]:= Head[ 3.14159 ]
Out[12]= Real
```

The head of a complex number is the symbol `Complex`.

```
In[13]:= Head[ 1 + I ]
Out[13]= Complex
```

The head of a string is the symbol `String`.

```
In[14]:= Head[ "a string" ]
Out[14]= String
```

2.4.3   Operators

Having a large number of operators simplifies input and makes output more readable. Inputs in operator notation are transformed into internal form by the *parser*. We could refrain from using operators, and instead write a + b as Plus[a, b], for example. This notation, however, would be cumbersome and nonstandard.   Any expression using operators is transformed into an internal form (as a normal expression).   You can look at this internal form with FullForm[*expr*].

The head belonging to addition is the symbol Plus.	In[15]:= FullForm[a + b + c] Out[15]//FullForm= Plus[a, b, c]
Even a list is an ordinary normal expression with head List.	In[16]:= FullForm[{x, y, z}] Out[16]//FullForm= List[x, y, z]
A subtraction is turned into an addition and multiplication by −1.	In[17]:= FullForm[x - y] Out[17]//FullForm= Plus[x, Times[-1, y]]
A division is turned into a multiplication and exponentiation by −1.	In[18]:= FullForm[2/x] Out[18]//FullForm= Times[2, Power[x, -1]]

Because FullForm[] evaluates its argument in the usual way, what we just saw was the internal form of the *result,* rather than of the input, as claimed. In the preceding examples, no evaluation took place, so there was no difference. If you want to see the internal form of an expression *before* evaluation, enclose the expression in HoldForm[*expr*].

Even typical assignments are ordinary expressions.	In[19]:= FullForm[HoldForm[x = 2]] Out[19]//FullForm= HoldForm[Set[x, 2]]
Without the wrapper HoldForm[], this assignment is evaluated, and we see only the internal form of the *result*.	In[20]:= FullForm[x = 2] Out[20]//FullForm= 2

The operator // allows us to write function application with a trailing function symbol (instead of f[x], as usual).	In[21]:= a // f
	 Out[21]= f[a]

Sometimes we use this notation to apply commands such as Short[] and N[] to an input line.	In[22]:= Expand[(1 + a + b)∧10] // Short Out[22]//Short=

$$1 + 10\ a + 45\ a^2 + 120\ a^3 + 210\ a^4 + <<59>> +$$
$$10\ a\ b^9 + b^{10}$$

Section B.4 contains a list of operators and their internal forms.

2.4.4   The Meaning of Expressions

All inputs are nothing but ordinary expressions. Depending on usage, we nevertheless talk about different kinds of expressions.

This expression is understood as a *function call* sin x. Observe the square brackets.

```
In[1]:= Sin[x]

Out[1]= Sin[x]
```

Ordinary parentheses are used for grouping only. They are necessary here because multiplication has a higher precedence than does addition.

```
In[2]:= a(b + c)

Out[2]= a (b + c)
```

A *list* serves to hold together expressions.

```
In[3]:= {x, y, z}

Out[3]= {x, y, z}
```

This expression serves as a *definition* of a function.

```
In[4]:= f[x_] := x^2
```

This *command* calls an internal algorithm for solving equations.

```
In[5]:= Solve[ x^2 + x + 1 == 0, x ]

Out[5]= {{x -> -(-1)^{1/3}}, {x -> (-1)^{2/3}}}
```

Here is a *sequence* of statements.

```
In[6]:= alpha = Sqrt[2]; beta = 1-alpha; gamma = beta^2

Out[6]= (1 - Sqrt[2])^2
```

2.4.5   Structural Operations

Structural operations change the structure of an expression. Many of the operations available in *Mathematica* are inspired by the language APL, which is particularly rich in such operations. Here we look at `Apply`, `Flatten`, `Transpose`, and `Thread`.

`Apply` changes the head of an expression to the given new head `h`.

```
In[1]:= Apply[ h, f[a, b, c, d] ]

Out[1]= h[a, b, c, d]
```

In this way we can easily compute the product of the elements of a list. See also Section 2.3.9.

```
In[2]:= Apply[ Times, {a, b, c, d} ]

Out[2]= a b c d
```

`Flatten` removes nested occurrences of the head of an expression; here this head is `List`.

```
In[3]:= Flatten[{a, {b, {c, d}, {}}, {e, f}}]

Out[3]= {a, b, c, d, e, f}
```

`Transpose` exchanges the levels of nested lists. The result corresponds to the transpose of a matrix written as a nested list.

```
In[4]:= Transpose[ {{a, b, c}, {x, y, z}} ]

Out[4]= {{a, x}, {b, y}, {c, z}}
```

Thread exchanges the head of the whole expression f with the head List of the elements of the expression. It is a generalization of Transpose.

```
In[5]:= Thread[ f[{a, b, c}, {x, y, z}] ]
Out[5]= {f[a, x], f[b, y], f[c, z]}
```

We can use it to turn an equation involving lists into a list of equations, see Section 8.1.2.

```
In[6]:= Thread[ {x, y} == {1, 2} ]
Out[6]= {x == 1, y == 2}
```

2.5 Help with Problems

Mathematica is documented in *The Mathematica Book*. Simply to find out what a certain command does, you need not consult this manual, however; the information is available on-line. Section 2.5.1 describes two ways to obtain on-line help.

When you read a program into *Mathematica* from a file or when you enter a definition directly, *Mathematica* signals any syntax errors it encounters. Section 2.5.2 shows what error messages look like and points out a few common sources of errrors.

2.5.1 Information about Commands

One possibility to obtain information about a command is the on-line help that you can look at by using ?*symbol* at the beginning of a line. Figure 2.5–1 shows an example in which we ask for information about NestList. The message always begins with the *template*, here NestList[*f*, *expr*, *n*]. The template shows a typical call of the command with symbolic arguments. This form of description is also used in this book. Using the Notebook frontend, you can extract the template from the message with the menu command Make Template and then fill in your values for the symbolic arguments, as shown.

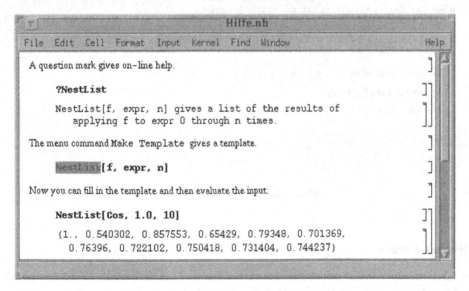

Figure 2.5–1 On-line help and templates.

The second information source is the *Help Browser*. It gives you access to the on-line help, including information about all commands. In Figure 2.5–2, you can see the topic

"Programming," again with `NestList`. The reference to *The Mathematica Book* is a hyperlink that you can click to obtain immediate access to the section mentioned.

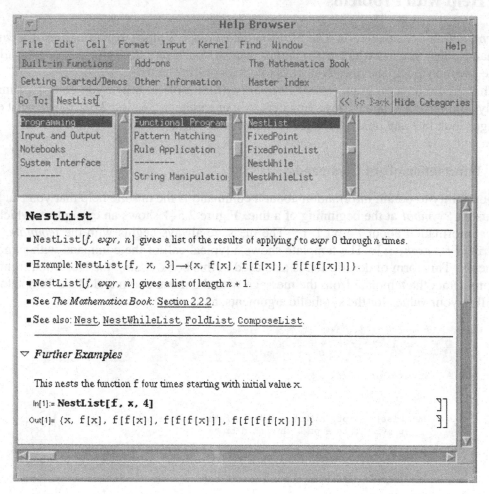

Figure 2.5–2   The Help Browser.

2.5.2   Syntax Errors

Because of its many built-in operators, *Mathematica* has a rich syntax. A list of operators and special characters is given in Section B.4. If an input is syntactically incorrect, *Mathematica* displays an error message. In the following dialog with the kernel, a curly brace has been used instead of a square bracket. Because the same error could also be caused by a forgotten opening brace, such error messages are not always accurate.

```
In[1]:= NestList[ 1 + 1/#&, N[1, 20}, 5]

Syntax::bktmch: "N[1, 20" must be followed by "]", not "}".

In[1]:= NestList[ 1 + 1/#&, N[1, 20], 5]

Out[1]= {1.0000000000000000000, 2.0000000000000000000,

    1.5000000000000000000, 1.6666666666666666667,

    1.6000000000000000000, 1.6250000000000000000}
```

If input comes from a Notebook, the cursor is put at the place where the error occurred, and a beep is sounded. It is then easy to correct the input and to evaluate it again. The frontend can even help you to balance parentheses.

One particular kind of error is worth pointing out. Because *Mathematica* does not require a multiplication sign, expressions with missing operators, such as the comma or semicolon, can nevertheless be syntactically correct. Of course, they are wrong semantically; that is, they do not have the intended meaning. In many such cases, a warning message is printed. Here is an example.

In our first attempt, the semicolon (;) between the two statements in the loop is missing. As a consequence, the body of the loop is read as

    x = (x + 2/x)/2*Print[x] .

The value of the Print statement is Null. Therefore, x is set to 1.5 Null.

```
In[1]:= x = 1.0;\
        While[ x != (x + 2/x)/2,
               x = (x + 2/x)/2
               Print[x]
             ]; x
Syntax::newl:
    The newline character after "         x = (x + 2/x)/2"
        is understood as a multiplication operator.

1.

Out[1]= 1.5 Null
```

Here is the correct piece of code. It computes an approximation to $\sqrt{2}$ (see page 3).

```
In[2]:= x = 1.0;\
        While[ x != (x + 2/x)/2,
               x = (x + 2/x)/2;
               Print[x]
             ]; x
1.5
1.41667
1.41422
1.41421
1.41421

Out[2]= 1.41421
```

There is always one more bug!

2.6 Exercises

2.1 Operators

1. Go through the examples given in Sections 2.1–2.3, and determine the internal forms of the expressions that occur in these examples. *Mathematica* can help you; see Section 2.4.3.

2. What is the internal form of these expressions *before* evaluation?

   a. `f @ {a, b, c}`

   b. `f /@ {a, b, c}`

   c. `f @@ {a, b, c}`

2.2 Structure of Expressions

Investigate this expression:

$$f'[x+1]/5!$$

1. Write the expression in internal form, without using any operators.

2. Denote the building blocks of the expression, that is, head and elements. Continue in this way with any parts that are still composite. Give the type of atomic parts.

3. To what does this expression evaluate?

Hint: Use the tables in Appendix B.4.

2.3 Simple Evaluations[1]

Give the result of evaluating the following expressions. If there are any nested functions, also give the most important intermediate steps. Assume that each example is evaluated in a fresh *Mathematica* session. Consecutive expressions in one example are evaluated one after another in the same session.

1. `Sum[ z^i/i!, {i, 0, 4} ]`

2. `Sum[ Product[(x - i)^j, {i, 0, 2}], {j, 2} ]`

3. `Expand[ Product[x - i, {i, -2, 2}] ]`

4. `{1, 2, 3}^2 + 1`

---

[1]Written examination, ETH Zürich, Department of Mathematics and Physics.

5. a = 5; b := 6;
    c = a; d = b;
    e := a; f:= b;
    a = 7; b := 8;
    {a, b, c, d, e, f}

2.4 The Arithmetic-Geometric Mean (AGM)

For positive reals a and g, the two sequences a_i and b_i, with

$$
\begin{aligned}
a_0 &= a \\
g_0 &= g \\
a_{i+1} &= \frac{a_i + g_i}{2} \\
g_{i+1} &= \sqrt{a_i g_i}
\end{aligned}
$$

(2.6–1)

converge to a common limit. Observe that a_{i+1} is the arithmetic mean of a_i and g_i, and that g_{i+1} is the geometric mean.

1. Compute the common limit numerically for a few values of a and g with a simple `While` loop.

2. Define a function `AGM[a, g]` that computes this limit.

Chapter 3
Iteration and Recursion

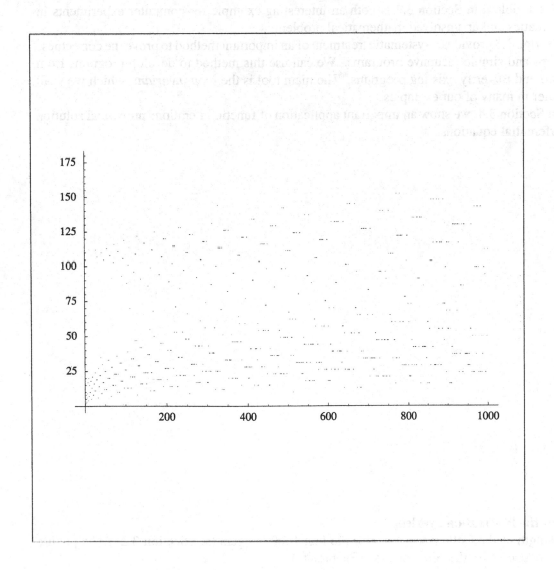

In this chapter, we introduce algorithmics. We develop systematically a few small example programs. Often, we have a choice among different methods to solve a problem. Two of the most important methods are loops and recursion. We can program recursion easily in *Mathematica* by giving a few definitions.

In Section 3.1, we look at the oldest known algorithm, Euclid's algorithm for the computation of the greatest common divisor (gcd) of two numbers. Starting with the definition of the gcd, we derive several programs for its computation.

The problem in Section 3.2 is both an interesting example for computer experiments in mathematics and an unsolved mathematical problem.

Section 3.3 provides a systematic treatment of an important method to prove the correctness of loops and simple recursive programs. We can use this method to develop programs from scratch and to verify existing programs. The main tool is the *loop invariant,* which we shall use later in many of our examples.

In Section 3.4, we show an important application of function iteration: numerical solution of differential equations.

About the illustration overleaf:
The length of the Collatz sequence for the first 1000 integers (see Section 3.2). The picture was produced with the command (see Pictures.m):

```
ListPlot[Table[CollatzLength[i],{i,1,1000}]]
```

3.1 The Greatest Common Divisor

The *greatest common divisor* (*gcd*) of two integers a and b (not both zero) is the largest integer c that divides both a and b:

$$\gcd(a, b) = \max(c : c \mid a \wedge c \mid b). \qquad (3.1\text{--}1)$$

(The notation $x \mid y$ means "x divides y.") We shall look only at nonnegative integers a and b.

To find the gcd, we need to turn this definition into an algorithm. This translation is possible only if the definition is *constructive* – that is, if it gives a method to compute the result *in principle*. We note that there are infinitely many integers; it is therefore not immediately obvious that we can find the gcd in finite time. By deriving further properties of the gcd, we can see that we can indeed do so.

3.1.1 Finite Search

An immediate consequence of the properties of divisibility (a divisor cannot be greater than the number it divides) is $\gcd(a, b) \leq \min(a, b)$ (for $a \neq 0$, $b \neq 0$). Because the integer 1 is always a divisor of a and b, we have restricted the search for the gcd to a *finite set* of numbers. (If $a = 0$, the gcd is equal to b; if $b = 0$, the gcd is equal to a.) In our program, shown in Listing 3.1–1, we first define an auxiliary function Divides[], give the definitions for the two special cases $a = 0$ or $b = 0$, and then define the general case with the loop that searches for the gcd.

```
Divides[x_, y_] := Mod[y, x] == 0      (* x divides y *)

gcd[0, b_] := b  (* special cases *)
gcd[a_, 0] := a

gcd[a_, b_] :=
    Module[{c},
        c = Min[a, b];
        While[ !(Divides[c, a] && Divides[c, b]), c-- ];
        c
    ]
```

Listing 3.1–1   GCD1.m: First version of the gcd algorithm.

The auxiliary function Divides[x, y] checks whether $x \mid y$. It returns True if the remainder of the division of y by x is zero. In the loop, we start with the largest possible value – the minimum of a and b – and search *downward*. The local variable c is initialized with the minimum of a and b. As long as the value of c does not divide both a and b, it is decremented by 1. The first number found to divide both a and b is the gcd. Because there is at least one divisor (1), we know that the search terminates after a finite number of steps. The maximum number of loop traversals is equal to $\min(a, b)$. (When is this maximum attained?)

3.1.2 The Division Method

We are not satisfied with the first algorithm found in Section 3.1.1, so we try to find a better one. Such an algorithm could be especially simple, or it could find the result with fewer operations.

To improve the gcd algorithm, we continue to find additional properties of the gcd. Looking at division properties leads to success. If c is a divisor of a and b, $b \neq 0$, then it also divides the remainder of the division of a by b. Thus,

$$c \mid a \wedge c \mid b \rightarrow c \mid (a \bmod b). \tag{3.1--2}$$

Therefore,

$$\gcd(a, b) = \gcd(b, a \bmod b). \tag{3.1--3}$$

If $b = 0$, we have

$$\gcd(a, 0) = a. \tag{3.1--4}$$

Equations 3.1–3 and 3.1–4 lead to a much faster and simpler algorithm, which is shown in Listing 3.1–2. The two equations can be programmed into *Mathematica* directly!

```
gcd[a_, 0] := a
gcd[a_, b_] := gcd[b, Mod[a, b]]
```

Listing 3.1–2 GCDR.m: A rule-based algorithm for the gcd.

We read in the file with the two rules.

```
In[1]:= << CSM`GCDR`
```

The gcd of 1999 and 2999 is 1.

```
In[2]:= gcd[1999, 2999]
Out[2]= 1
```

If one of the two numbers is zero, the gcd is equal to the other one.

```
In[3]:= gcd[0, 5]
Out[3]= 5
```

This command makes the application of rules visible. We see how the rules first interchange the arguments, and then make them smaller step by step, until one of them becomes zero.

```
In[4]:= Trace[ gcd[5, 8], gcd[__Integer] ] // TableForm
Out[4]//TableForm= gcd[5, 8]
                   gcd[8, 5]
                   gcd[5, 3]
                   gcd[3, 2]
                   gcd[2, 1]
                   gcd[1, 0]
```

3.1.3 The Division Method in a Loop

The two rules derived in Section 3.1.2 are probably the best way to program the gcd in *Mathematica*. Many conventional languages do not allow this kind of programming. There are also cases (see Section 3.2.1) where such rules are inefficient – even in *Mathematica*.

Therefore, we shall show how we can derive a program working with a loop from these two rules. The rule

$$gcd[a\_, \ b\_] := gcd[b, \ Mod[a, \ b]]$$

says basically that the two arguments a and b should be replaced by b and $(a \bmod b)$, after which we continue in the same way. This formulation leads to a *loop*. The termination condition for the loop is obtained from the other rule $gcd[a\_, \ 0] := a$. Because we must test this rule first (if b happens to be zero in the beginning), we shall use a While-loop (see Section 2.3.4): As long as b is not yet zero, we replace a and b by b and $(a \bmod b)$. The two assignments to a and b must happen simultaneously (see Section 2.3.1). We declare a and b as local variables in the way shown in Section 2.3.6. The program is given in Listing 3.1–3.

```
gcd[a0_, b0_] :=
    Module[{a = a0, b = b0},
        While[ b != 0, {a, b} = {b, Mod[a, b]} ];
        a
    ]
```

Listing 3.1–3   GCDS.m: The division method in a loop.

The correctness of this program can be shown in the following way. Let a and b be the values of the variables a and b on entering the loop, and let a' and b' be their values at the end of one iteration of the loop. At the end of the iteration the following three conditions hold:

$$\begin{aligned} a' &> b', \\ gcd(a', b') &= gcd(a, b), \\ b' &< b. \end{aligned} \tag{3.1–5}$$

Then we set $a = a'$ and $b = b'$, and run through the loop once more. Because the numbers get smaller and smaller, we eventually reach $b = 0$. (If $a < b$ holds at the beginning, the first iteration will simply interchange the two values.)

3.1.4   Key Concepts

1. The properties of the gcd lead directly to an algorithm for the computation of the gcd.

2. We can derive more efficient algorithms by taking into account further properties of the gcd. This allows us to narrow the range of the search or to proceed in larger step sizes.

3. Rule-based or recursive programs can often be converted to loops, and vice versa.

3.2   The $3x + 1$ Problem

The $3x + 1$ problem is also known as the *Collatz problem*. The structure of the iterations of the function c is an unsolved mathematical problem:

$$c(n) = \begin{cases} 3n + 1, & n \text{ odd}; \\ n/2, & n \text{ even}. \end{cases} \qquad (3.2\text{--}1)$$

Starting with an integer, we get a sequence of integers by repeatedly applying c to the previous term. If the number is even, it is halved; if it is odd, it is multiplied by 3 and 1 is added to the result. For example, for $n = 1$, we get this sequence by iterating c: 1, 4, 2, 1, 4, ...

Formally, we define the sequence $n_1, n_2, \ldots$ as follows:

$$\begin{aligned} n_1 &= n, \\ n_{i+1} &= c(n_i), \qquad i = 1, 2, \ldots. \end{aligned} \qquad (3.2\text{--}2)$$

A few experiments show that the sequence $\{n_i\}$ falls into the cycle 1, 4, 2, 1, ... for each choice of $n_1 = n$.

These two rules define the function c. Note that you can put the predicates directly into the left side of the rules with the notation `f[x_?pred]`.

```
In[1]:= c[n_?OddQ]  := 3n + 1; \
        c[n_?EvenQ] := n/2
```

This loop applies the function c repeatedly to 5 until the result is 1 for the first time.

```
In[2]:= n = 5; While[ n != 1, n = c[n]; Print[n] ]
16
8
4
2
1
```

The same computation, starting with 11.

```
In[3]:= n = 11; While[ n != 1, n = c[n]; Print[n] ]
34
17
52
26
13
40
20
10
5
16
8
4
2
1
```

So far, nobody has been able to prove that this property does indeed hold for all positive integers or to find any counterexample. We shall study *experimentally* some properties of this sequence. We are especially interested in *how long* it takes to reach 1, starting from a number n.

3.2.1 The Length of the Collatz Sequence

The *length* $L(n)$ of the Collatz sequence is defined as the smallest index i such that $n_i = 1$. We simply count how long it takes to reach 1 for the first time. By *induction*,

$$L(1) = 1,$$
$$L(n) = 1 + L(c(n)), \qquad n > 1, \tag{3.2–3}$$

we immediately get this definition for computing the length in the function `CollatzLength`.

```
CollatzLength[1]  =  1
CollatzLength[n_] := 1 + CollatzLength[c[n]]
```

Listing 3.2–1   Part of Collatz1.m: Recursive computation of the length.

With this computation method, the intermediate results accumulate and the program needs more space for larger results. (The gcd program in Section 3.1.2 did not suffer from this drawback.) An iterative version that does not have this problem can be obtained easily. The number of evaluations of the second rule is obviously equal to the value of `CollatzLength` because we add 1 to the previous result. So, we simply count this number in a `While`-loop. The termination condition is obtained from the first rule. If the input is 1, the loop is never executed.

```
CollatzLength[n0_] :=
    Module[{n = n0, l = 1},
        While[ n != 1, n = c[n]; l = l + 1 ];
        l
    ]
```

Listing 3.2–2   Part of Collatz2.m: Iterative computation of the length.

You can see a graph of the length of the Collatz sequence for the integers up to 1,000 on page 55. Here we look at the length for much larger inputs.

We read in the improved package.	`In[1]:= << CSM'Collatz2'`
Here is the length of the Collatz sequence for $n = 2^{100} - 1$.	`In[2]:= CollatzLength[ 2^100-1 ]` `Out[2]= 1466`
With this command, we generate the 1,466 elements of the sequence.	`In[3]:= seq = NestList[ c, 2^100-1, %-1 ];`

We want to measure the size of these numbers. The size of a number is equal to the latter's *logarithm* to base 10.

```
In[4]:= logs = Log[ 10.0, seq ];
```

Here is a diagram of the sizes of the elements. First, the size increases rapidly; finally, it drops to zero.

```
In[5]:= ListPlot[ logs ];
```

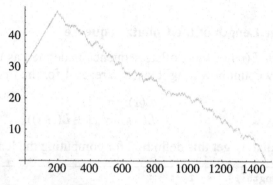

```
Display::pserr:
    PostScript language error:
    Warning: substituting font Utopia-Regular for
    Times-Roman
```

3.2.2 Computation of the Collatz Sequence

Like the length, the sequence itself can be computed inductively (as a list). Instead of adding 1 at each iteration, we prepend the current value in front of the list. We call this function CollatzSequence. Program Collatz1.m is shown in Listing 3.2–3.

```
c[n_?OddQ]   := 3n + 1      (* for n odd *)
c[n_?EvenQ] := n/2          (* for n even   *)

CollatzLength[1]  = 1
CollatzLength[n_] := 1 + CollatzLength[c[n]]

CollatzSequence[1]  = {1}
CollatzSequence[n_] := Prepend[ CollatzSequence[c[n]], n ]
```

Listing 3.2–3   Collatz1.m: Recursive computation of the Collatz sequence.

The function Prepend[*list, elem*] adds the element *elem* to the front of the list *list*. (If you reach the default recursion limit of *Mathematica* during a longer computation you can turn it off with $RecursionLimit = Infinity.)

The function Prepend[] adds a new element to the front of a list.

```
In[6]:= Prepend[ {a, b, c}, x ]
Out[6]= {x, a, b, c}

In[7]:= << CSM`Collatz1`
```

The is the Collatz sequence for the integer 23 until it reaches 1 for the first time.

```
In[8]:= CollatzSequence[23]
Out[8]= {23, 70, 35, 106, 53, 160, 80, 40, 20, 10, 5,
     16, 8, 4, 2, 1}
```

Here, too, we can avoid recursion. The operation $l = l + 1$, which increases the value of l by 1, corresponds to *var*=Append[*var*, *elem*], which adds an element to the value of *var at the end*. The computation now takes place in the opposite order (the order did not matter for computing the length because addition of numbers is commutative). Program Collatz2.m is reproduced in Listing 3.2–4.

```
c[n_?OddQ]  := 3n + 1      (* for n odd *)
c[n_?EvenQ] := n/2         (* for n even  *)
CollatzLength[n0_] :=
    Module[{n = n0, l = 1},
        While[ n != 1, n = c[n]; l = l + 1 ];
        l
    ]
CollatzSequence[n0_] :=
    Module[{n = n0, l = {n0}},
        While[ n != 1, n = c[n]; l = Append[l, n] ];
        l
    ]
```

Listing 3.2–4   Collatz2.m: Iterative computation of the Collatz sequence.

Operations such as Prepend[] and Append[] are inefficient when used in a loop. For this example, there is no simpler, more efficient solution because the length of the result is not known at the beginning. If we knew the length of the result beforehand, it would be better to generate the whole result with Table[], NestList[], or FoldList[].

3.2.3   Key Concepts

1. Iterations with an unknown number of repetitions lead to While loops.

2. An inductive proof generates a recursive program.

3. Recursive function calls inside another function can lead to inefficient programs. If possible, such a program should be turned into a loop.

3.3 Advanced Topic: Loop Invariants

There is one important question that we must ask ourselves each time we write a program: Does it do what we want it to do? We have seen a few algorithmic problems that lead to simple programs with a loop or recursive rules. For such programs, there is a method to prove them correct. The most important tool is the loop invariant.

3.3.1 Deriving the Loop Invariant

A *loop invariant* is a statement about the values of the variables occurring in a loop that is valid at each iteration of the loop. Such an invariant gives us a tool for proving a loop correct. Let us look at a simple example:

```
i = 0;
k = 1;
                        (* 1: before the loop *)
While[i != n,
                        (* 2: before an iteration *)
    k = k*(i+1);
    i = i+1;
                        (* 3: after an iteration *)
];
                        (* 4: after the loop *)
k
```

We analyze the program in four places:

1. Before entering the loop

2. Before an iteration of the loop body

3. After an iteration of the loop body

4. After leaving the loop

After the two assignments, immediately before the loop, we have

$$k = i! \tag{3.3--1}$$

($i!$ is i factorial) because $0! = 1$. Before an iteration, we still have $k = i!$. Because of $(i+1)! = i! \cdot (i+1)$, we get $k = (i+1)!$ after the first statement in the loop; then i is incremented by 1, and we have, at the end of an iteration, $k = i!$. This equation is our loop invariant. After leaving the loop, we also have $i = n$, the *negation* of the termination condition for the loop, because the loop is left as soon as the condition is no longer satisfied. After the loop, we therefore have

$$i = n,$$
$$k = i!,$$

(3.3–2)

and we have shown that, at the end, we have $k = n!$; that is, we have computed $n!$ with the result in k.

We still have to think about whether the loop terminates at all. Assume that n is a nonnegative integer. Therefore, we have $i \leq n$ before the loop. In the loop, we increment i by 1 in each iteration, and we must reach $i = n$ sometime (after n steps), which means that the loop terminates. The *precondition* $n \in \mathbf{Z}$, $n \geq 0$ implies the *postcondition* $k = n!$.

This kind of concluding a desired postcondition from a necessary precondition and the termination of the loop is typical for analysis of loop programs. We already used it when we looked at the loop for the gcd in Section 3.1.3. The invariant was $\gcd(a', b') = \gcd(a, b)$.

Because we regard our small program as a function of n, we should write it as such. We can use the precondition to test the input n of the function. We restrict the argument of factorial[n] to be a nonnegative integer. Listing 3.3–1 shows the program.

```
factorial[n_Integer?NonNegative] :=
    Module[{i = 0, k = 1},
        While[i != n,
            k = k*(i+1);
            i = i+1;
        ];
        k
    ]
```

Listing 3.3–1 Factorial.m: A definition of the factorial function.

3.3.2 Correctness Proofs

We can derive the following steps for finding a correctness proof:

1. Formulate the loop invariant. It can be derived from the desired result and the loop body. (This step requires some clever thinking or intuition.)

2. Make sure that the loop invariant is satisfied before entering the loop. We can make this assurance by correctly initializing the local variables.

3. Show that the invariant is satisfied at the end of an iteration if it was satisfied before that iteration.

4. Derive the postcondition from the loop invariant and the negation of the termination test.

5. Find the necessary precondition under which the loop terminates.

Another example will explain these steps in more detail. The program given in Listing 3.3–2 computes the sum of the integers x_0 and y_0 exclusively by adding 1 to numbers. We want to prove that it behaves correctly.

```
x = x0;
y = 0;
While[y != y0,
    x = x + 1;
    y = y + 1;
];
x
```

Listing 3.3–2   Computing the sum of two numbers by elementary operations.

Here are the five steps in the proof for this program:

1. The invariant is $x - y = x_0$.

2. The invariant is satisfied with the assignments $x = x_0$ and $y = 0$ before the loop because in this case $x - y = x_0 - 0 = x_0$.

3. If $x - y = x_0$ holds before an iteration, it also holds afterward because $x - y$ is not changed if we increment x and y both by 1: $(x + 1) - (y + 1) = x + 1 - y - 1 = x - y$.

4. After the loop, we have the invariant $x - y = x_0$ as well as the negation $y = y_0$ of the termination test $y \neq y_0$. Therefore, $x = x_0 + y = x_0 + y_0$, and we did, in fact, compute the sum of x_0 and y_0 in the variable x.

5. The precondition for termination is that y_0 must be nonnegative. Because y is incremented by 1, starting with 0, it must eventually reach y_0 (after $y_0 + 1$ steps).

To summarize, we just proved:

$$\text{For } x_0, y_0 \in \mathbf{Z}, y_0 \geq 0 \text{ our program computes } x = x_0 + y_0.$$

Note that the elementary operation "add 1" plays an important role in theory of computation; see Section 12.1.

3.3.3   Recursions and Loops

We would like to show how simple recursion can be transformed into a loop systematically, and vice versa.

For the conversion of a loop into a recursion, let us look once more at the factorial function in the package Factorial.m (see Listing 3.3–1). The input is in the variable n, and the output is in the variable k. Which function $f(n) = k$ does our program compute?

If $n = 0$, the loop is never traversed. Therefore, we get

$$f(0) = 1 \qquad (3.3\text{–}3)$$

from the initialization $k = 1$.

Let $f(n-1)$ be the value obtained after we traverse the loop $n-1$ times. If we traverse the loop one more time, we get

$$f(n) = (i+1) \cdot f(n-1) = n \cdot f(n-1), \qquad (3.3\text{–}4)$$

because $i+1$ is equal to n in the last traversal. Thus we have derived the well-known recursive form of the definition of the factorial function

$$
\begin{aligned}
f(0) &= 1, \\
f(n) &= n \cdot f(n-1).
\end{aligned}
\qquad (3.3\text{–}5)
$$

We can also transform a simple recursive definition into a loop. Here is the recursive definition of addition from Section 12.1:

$$
\begin{aligned}
x + 0 &= x, \\
x + (y+1) &= (x+y) + 1.
\end{aligned}
\qquad (3.3\text{–}6)
$$

The recursion is by y. From the termination condition $x + 0 = x$, we derive the necessary initialization and the following skeleton for the loop, using y as the loop variable.

```
y = 0;
While[y != ?,
    ⋮
    y = y + 1;
];
x
```

To go from y to $y+1$, we simply add 1 to the old result in x, according to the recursive equation $x + (y+1) = (x+y) + 1$, so we get:

```
y = 0;
While[y != ?,
    x = x + 1;
    y = y + 1;
];
x
```

The loop should terminate when we reach the desired value y_0 of y, and we may want to initialize x with the desired value x_0. The loop is the one we just studied in Section 3.3.2 (Listing 3.3–2).

3.3.4   Key Concepts

1. Loop invariants are statements about values of program variables that are valid before and after a loop.

2. The loop invariant and the negation of the termination condition give the postcondition of the loop.

3. Loop invariants can be used in correctness proofs for programs.

4. Recursive and iterative programs can be transformed into each other with the help of a loop invariant.

3.4 Application: Differential Equations

Iterative methods for the numerical solution of ordinary differential equations are of great practical importance because most equations cannot be solved in closed form.

3.4.1 Systems of First-Order Equations

A system of n autonomous differential equations of first order has the form

$$
\begin{aligned}
\dot{x}_1 &= f_1(x_1, \ldots, x_n), \\
\dot{x}_2 &= f_2(x_1, \ldots, x_n), \\
&\ \ \vdots \\
\dot{x}_n &= f_n(x_1, \ldots, x_n).
\end{aligned}
\tag{3.4-1}
$$

The quantities x_i are functions of the independent variable t, and $\dot{x}$ is the differentiation with respect to t. In addition, we have an initial condition

$$
\begin{aligned}
x_1(0) &= a_1, \\
x_2(0) &= a_2, \\
&\ \ \vdots \\
x_n(0) &= a_n.
\end{aligned}
\tag{3.4-2}
$$

This is called an *autonomous system*, because the functions f_i do not depend explicitly on t. It is easier to write such systems in vector notation. With the definitions $\mathbf{x} = (x_1, x_2, \ldots, x_n)$ and $\mathbf{f}(\mathbf{x}) = (f_1(\mathbf{x}), \ldots, f_n(\mathbf{x}))$, we get

$$
\begin{aligned}
\dot{\mathbf{x}} &= \mathbf{f}(\mathbf{x}), \\
\dot{\mathbf{x}}(0) &= \mathbf{a}.
\end{aligned}
\tag{3.4-3}
$$

3.4.2 Example: The Harmonic Oscillator

The equation of an harmonic oscillator is

$$
\ddot{x} = -x - \alpha \dot{x}.
\tag{3.4-4}
$$

Equation 3.4–4 is a second-order equation. We can write it as a system of two first-order equations by setting $x_1 = x$ and $x_2 = \dot{x}$:

$$
\begin{aligned}
\dot{x}_1 &= x_2, \\
\dot{x}_2 &= -x_1 - \alpha x_2.
\end{aligned}
\tag{3.4-5}
$$

We can get an overview over the system by looking at the *direction field*.

This standard package draws vector fields.

```
In[1]:= << Graphics`PlotField`
```

Now we can plot the direction field of an harmonic oscillator. We set $\alpha = 0.1$. The first argument of `PlotVectorField` is the list of the right sides of Equation 3.4–5.

```
In[2]:= ho = PlotVectorField[{x2, -x1 - 0.1 x2},
            {x1, -2, 2}, {x2, -2, 2}, Frame->True];
```

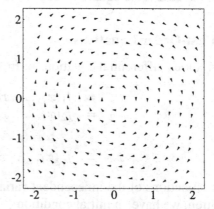

3.4.3   The Euler–Cauchy Method for Numerical Solution

The simplest solution method for ordinary differential equations is that of Euler–Cauchy. We start with a vector $\mathbf{x}^{(0)}$ set equal to $\mathbf{x}$ at time 0:

$$\mathbf{x}^{(0)} = \mathbf{x}(0) = \mathbf{a}, \tag{3.4–6}$$

and we go a small step δ in the direction given by the direction field. Thus, we arrive at the point

$$\mathbf{x}^{(1)} = \mathbf{x}^{(0)} + \delta\mathbf{f}(\mathbf{x}^{(0)}). \tag{3.4–7}$$

We can iterate this procedure, which leads to

$$\begin{aligned}
\mathbf{x}^{(0)} &= \mathbf{a}, \\
\mathbf{x}^{(i+1)} &= \mathbf{x}^{(i)} + \delta\mathbf{f}(\mathbf{x}^{(i)}) \quad i = 0, 1, 2, \dots
\end{aligned} \tag{3.4–8}$$

It is not difficult to write a small function to compute the list of the $\mathbf{x}^{(i)}$. It is given in Listing 3.4–1.

We read in the function `ODE1[]`.

```
In[3]:= << CSM`ODE1`
```

Here, we define f for the harmonic oscillator.

```
In[4]:= f[{x1_, x2_}] := {x2, -x1 - 0.1x2}
```

```
ODE1[f_, x0_List, delta_, n_Integer] :=
    Module[{xi = x0, res = {x0}},
        Do[ xi = xi + delta f[xi]; AppendTo[res, xi],
            {n} ];
        res
    ]
```

Listing 3.4–1   ODE1.m: A simple loop.

We set the step size δ = 0.05, and perform 250 steps, starting at the point {1.5, 0}. The result is a list with 251 coordinates.

```
In[5]:= ODE1[f, {1.5, 0}, 0.05, 250] // Short
Out[5]//Short=
  {{1.5, 0}, {1.5, -0.075}, {1.49625, -0.149625},

   <<247>>, {1.09159, 0.0671304}}
```

We can plot the result. Such plots are called *phase portraits*, because they show the solution in *phase space* with position and velocity coordinates $(x, \dot{x})$.

```
In[6]:= ListPlot[%, PlotJoined->True, AspectRatio->1];
```

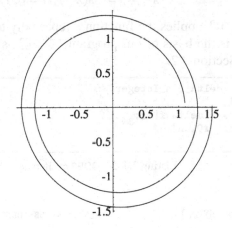

It is also interesting to superimpose the solution and the direction field.

```
In[7]:= Show[ho, %];
```

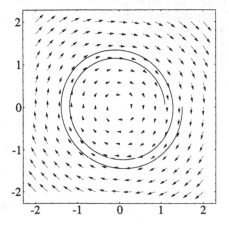

3.4.4 Iteration of Function Application

Our program becomes even simpler if we adopt a functional viewpoint. Equation 3.4–8 describes how $\mathbf{x}^{(i+1)}$ is obtained from $\mathbf{x}^{(i)}$. This formula does not depend on i (i.e., it is the same for every step). Therefore, we can write

$$\mathbf{x}^{(i+1)} = s(\mathbf{x}^{(i)}), \tag{3.4–9}$$

where the *step function s* is given by

$$s(\mathbf{x}) = \mathbf{x} + \delta \mathbf{f}(\mathbf{x}). \tag{3.4–10}$$

Now the iteration looks like this:

$$\begin{aligned} \mathbf{x}^{(0)} &= \mathbf{a}, \\ \mathbf{x}^{(i+1)} &= s(\mathbf{x}^{(i)}) \quad i = 0, 1, 2, \ldots \end{aligned} \tag{3.4–11}$$

NestList[s, x, n] applies the function s repeatedly to x, and returns the list of all intermediate steps. It is the basis of our program ODE2[], shown in Listing 3.4–2. We already used this idea in Section 3.2.

```
ODE2[f_, x0_List, delta_, n_Integer] :=
    Module[{s, x},
        s[x_] := x + delta f[x];
        NestList[s, x0, n]
    ]
```

Listing 3.4–2   ODE2.m: Iteration of functions.

We read in the function ODE2[].

ODE2 works the same way that ODE1 does. Here, we doubled the step size (and halved the number of steps) compared to the previous example. It is easy to see that this step size is too large, the solution differs substantially from the previous one.

```
In[8]:= << CSM`ODE2`
```

```
In[9]:= ListPlot[ODE2[f, {1.5, 0}, 0.1, 125],
            PlotJoined->True, AspectRatio->1];
```

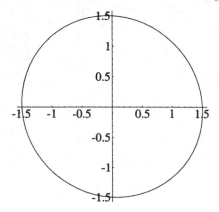

With half the step size (0.025) and twice the number of steps, we get a more accurate result.

```
In[10]:= ListPlot[ODE2[f, {1.5, 0}, 0.025, 500],
              PlotJoined->True, AspectRatio->1];
```

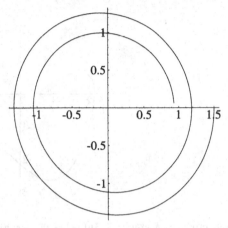

3.4.5   Example: van der Pol's Equation

Van der Pol's equation describes a simple electron-tube oscillator with a resonator consisting of a capacitor and a coil. Its equation is

$$x + \ddot{x} = \varepsilon(1 - x^2)\dot{x}. \tag{3.4--12}$$

The variable x represents the charge in the capacitor, which is also the voltage across the latter. The first derivative $\dot{x}$ is the change in voltage, that is, the current. The change in current $\ddot{x}$ is the induced voltage in the coil. A feedback provided by the tube serves to excite the resonator. The value of ε describes the coupling constant and the amplification of the tube.

Again, we can write Equation 3.4–12 as a system of two first-order equations:

$$\begin{aligned}
\dot{x}_1 &= x_2, \\
\dot{x}_2 &= \varepsilon(1 - x_1^2)x_2 - x_1.
\end{aligned} \tag{3.4--13}$$

We want to show that the system approaches a limit cycle for any initial condition. We shall generate the solutions for various starting points and combine them in one picture.

Here is the right side of the equation with $\varepsilon = 0.9$.

```
In[11]:= vdP[{x1_, x2_}] := {x2, 0.9 (1-x1^2) x2 - x1}
```

We compute the solution starting at $(3, -3)$.

```
In[12]:= l1 = ODE2[vdP, {3, -3}, 0.05, 500];
```

Here is the picture.

```
In[13]:= gl1 = ListPlot[l1, PlotJoined->True,
                        AspectRatio->1];
```

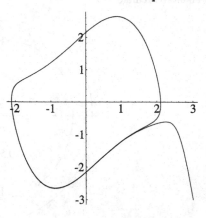

This auxiliary function produces a graphic like the one here for a given initial point.   We can suppress generation of the picture itself with the option setting `DisplayFunction->Identity`.

```
In[14]:= ODEGraphics[ f_, x0_, delta_, n_ ] :=
         ListPlot[ ODE2[f, x0, delta, n],
             PlotJoined->True,
             DisplayFunction->Identity
         ]
```

Here, we generate several solutions whose initial points lie on the top margin of the picture (with $y = 4$).

```
In[15]:= top =
         Table[ ODEGraphics[vdP, {i,  4}, 0.05, 100],
                {i, -4, 0} ];
```

These initial points lie at the lower margin.

```
In[16]:= bot =
         Table[ ODEGraphics[vdP, {i, -4}, 0.05, 100],
                {i, 0, 4} ];
```

Now, we can combine the graphics and render the image. We need to reset the option `DisplayFunction` to its normal value.

```
In[17]:= Show[ {top, bot}, AspectRatio->1, Frame->True,
              PlotRange->{{-4.5, 4.5}, {-5, 5}},
              DisplayFunction->$DisplayFunction ];
```

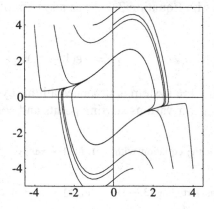

3.4.6 Advanced Topic: Higher-Order Methods

The simple numerical methods presented so far are not efficient. We have to choose small step sizes to obtain a reasonable accuracy for the result, and – more important – we do not know how accurate our results are. For practical applications, there are more efficient methods. One of them, the Runge–Kutta Method, is described in our book [54]. Even more advanced methods can predict the numerical error and choose the step size accordingly. The built-in function `NDSolve[]` uses such methods.

Here is again van der Pol's equation with a starting point of $(0.1, 0)$. The result is returned in terms of an interpolating function object.

```
In[1]:= NDSolve[ {x1'[t] == x2[t],
                  x2'[t] == 0.9(1-x1[t]^2)x2[t] - x1[t],
                  x1[0] == 0.1, x2[0] == 0},
                 {x1, x2}, {t, 0, 6Pi} ]
Out[1]= {{x1 ->
    InterpolatingFunction[{{0., 18.8496}}, <>],
  x2 -> InterpolatingFunction[{{0., 18.8496}}, <>]}}
```

In this way, we get the values of $x_1(t)$ and $x_2(t)$ for the first (and only) solution.

```
In[2]:= {x1[t], x2[t]} /. %[[1]];
```

Because the result is returned as a function, instead of as a simple list of values, we can produce a parametric plot of it. This picture shows how the solution approaches the limit cycle from a point in the latter's interior, rather than from the exterior, as we showed on page 74.

```
In[3]:= ParametricPlot[ Evaluate[%], {t, 0, 6Pi},
                       AspectRatio->1 ];
```

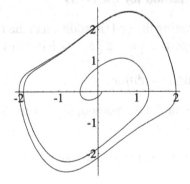

3.4.7 Key Concepts

1. Differential equations can be solved numerically by proceeding along the direction field in small time steps.

2. An equation of higher order can be transformed into a system of first-order equations.

3. Mechanical systems can be visualized in phase space.

3.5   Exercises

3.1   Reduction Rules for the GCD

With the following rules, we can find the gcd of two nonnegative integers.

```
Gcd[a_, 0] := a

Gcd[a_, b_] := Gcd[b, Mod[a, b]]
```

---

1. Find the evaluation steps for the example `Gcd[8, 13]`.

2. For which numbers a and b, with $a \geq b > 0$, are these rules applied exactly twice to find their gcd?

3. For which numbers less than 100 do we need the largest number of rule applications to find their gcd?

3.2   The Subtraction Method for the GCD

A third method for computing the gcd (in addition to the two methods presented in Section 3.1) is obtained from the property $c \mid a \wedge c \mid b, a > b$ implies $c \mid a - b$.

1. What is the termination condition?

2. Find rules that implement this method, similar to the rules for the division method from Section 3.1.2.

3. Write a function with a `While[]` loop that uses this idea.

4. Find the loop invariant and prove correctness and termination using the methods outlined in Section 3.3.2.

Test your programs for a set of inputs that includes all special cases.

Hints: The result $a - b$ is generally not smaller than b. If necessary, the variables a and b should be exchanged. Rules that are applicable under only certain conditions can be given as follows (our condition is $a > b$):

$$\text{Gcd[a\_, b\_] /; a > b := ...}$$

3.3 Local Maxima of the Collatz Sequence

In this exercise, we want to find numbers whose Collatz sequence is longer than the sequence of all other numbers in a certain range. See Section 3.2 for an explanation of Collatz sequences.

1. Write a function FindMax[a_, b_] that finds the maximal length of the Collatz sequence for all numbers between a and b. The value of the function should be the number whose Collatz sequence is the longest.

2. Which number $n < 1,000$ has the longest Collatz sequence?

3.4 Invariants for the Fibonacci Numbers

Prove the correctness of the program fibc[n] from Section 7.2.2 (Listing 7.2–2) by following the methods given in Section 3.3.2.

```
fibc[n_] := Module[{fi = 1, fi1 = 0},
            Do[ {fi, fi1} = {fi + fi1, fi}, {n - 1} ];
            fi
         ]
```

Listing 7.2–2 A loop for the nth Fibonacci number.

Hint: First transform the Do loop into a While loop.

3.5 Continued Fractions[1]

The continued fraction expansion of an irrational number r is the sequence $a_0, a_1, a_2, \ldots, a_i \in$ **N**, such that (in the limit)

$$r = a_0 + \cfrac{1}{a_1 + \cfrac{1}{a_2 + \ldots}}$$

The a_i can be found as follows. Let $r_0 = r$. The first term, a_0, is equal to the integer part of r_0:

$$a_0 = \lfloor r_0 \rfloor .$$

The fractional part of r_0 is $r_0 - a_0$. Its reciprocal, $r_1 = 1/(r_0 - a_0)$, is therefore

$$r_1 = a_1 + \cfrac{1}{a_2 + \cfrac{1}{a_3 + \ldots}} .$$

Thus, we get

$$a_1 = \lfloor r_1 \rfloor ,$$

and so on.

---

[1] Written examination, ETH Zürich, Department of Mathematics and Physics.

1. Write a function `continuedFraction[r_, n_Integer]` that computes the first n elements of the continued fraction expansion of r as the list $\{a_0, a_1, \ldots, a_{n-1}\}$. You can use a loop or program recursively.

2. Write a function `continuedValue[l_List]` that returns the number belonging to the initial segment $l = \{a_0, a_1, \ldots, a_{n-1}\}$ of a continued fraction.

3. Write a simple definition for `continuedError[r, n]`, which finds the absolute error of the continued fraction approximation of length n. This error is the absolute value of the difference of r and the approximation with n terms.

Here are the first 10 elements of π's continued fraction expansion.

```
In[1]:= continuedFraction[Pi, 10]
Out[1]= {3, 7, 15, 1, 292, 1, 1, 1, 2, 1}
```

The numerical value of the previous continued fraction is this rational number.

```
In[2]:= continuedValue[%]
           1146408
Out[2]= ───────────
           364913
```

Here is the error of the 10-term approximation of π.

```
In[3]:= N[continuedError[Pi, 10]]
                   -12
Out[3]= 1.61071 10
```

Note that coth 1 has an interesting expansion.

```
In[4]:= continuedFraction[Coth[1], 12]
Out[4]= {1, 3, 5, 7, 9, 11, 13, 15, 17, 19, 21, 23}
```

Hint: The function `Floor[r]` gives the integer part of r.

Chapter 4

Structure of Programs

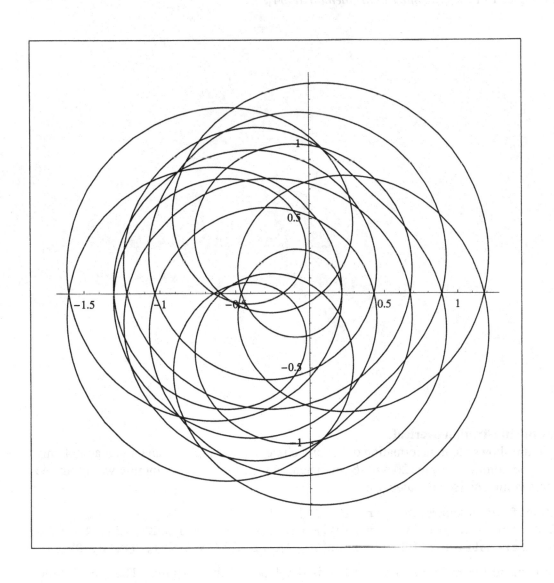

In this chapter, we use the example of plotting complex-valued parametric lines to discuss the development of programs. The methods used for structuring programs can be used like recipies in a cookbook, but it is nevertheless a good idea to understand something about how they work.

The method presented in this chapter is the framework for building packages in *Mathematica*. It is used for all nontrivial programs in the rest of this book. The material is adapted from Chapter 1 of *Programming in Mathematica* [54].

About the illustration overleaf:

The picture shows the transformation of the unit circle in the complex plane under a randomly chosen polynomial of degree 20 whose coefficients are all 1 or -1. The picture was produced with this command (see Pictures.m):

```
randCoeff := 2Random[Integer, {0, 1}] - 1
RandHorner[n_Integer, x_] := Nest[Function[p, p x + randCoeff], 1, n]
ComplexParametricPlot[ RandHorner[20, Exp[I t]]/Sqrt[21], {t, 0, 2Pi}].
```

The command `ComplexParametricPlot` is developed in this chapter. The idea for this picture is from A. Odlyzko.

4.1 Complex Parametric Lines

This chapter explains step by step how a package is built in *Mathematica*. A *package* consists of the definitions that constitute the program itself, as well as documentation and declarations for interfacing the programs with *Mathematica*. To show you how to build packages, we use a realistic example, complete with all necessary details. The package should plot parametric lines in the complex plane.

A complex number consists of two components: the *real* and *imaginary* parts. They can be viewed as the coordinates of a point in the plane. The complex number describing the point with coordinates (a, b) is written as $a + ib$, where i is the *imaginary unit* and stands for $\sqrt{-1}$. In *Mathematica*, we have to write it as I or $\dot{\imath}$ instead of i, because by convention, all built-in symbols begin with a capital letter.

4.1.1 Plotting Lines

A complex-valued function $z(t)$, depending on a real parameter t describes a line in the complex plane. *Mathematica*'s ParametricPlot command requires a list with two explicit coordinates for plotting parametric lines. We can simply calculate the real and imaginary parts of $z(t)$ to draw the line.

Here is the formula for the unit circle in the complex plane.

```
In[1]:= z1 = Exp[I t]
              I t
Out[1]= E
```

By calculating its real and imaginary part, we can easily plot it. The parameter t ranges from 0 to 2π for one revolution around the circle.

```
In[2]:= ParametricPlot[{Re[z1], Im[z1]}, {t, 0, 2Pi}];
```

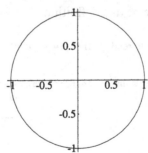

To see how a complex-valued function transforms these lines, we can simply apply the function to the parametric representation of the desired line, then plot it as before.

Here is the unit circle transformed by the complex-valued sine function.

```
In[3]:= z2 = Sin[ Exp[I t] ]
                  I t
Out[3]= Sin[E    ]
```

We can plot it as before. By comparing the previous graphic with this one, you can see how the sine function transforms the unit circle.

In[4]:= ParametricPlot[{Re[z2], Im[z2]}, {t, 0, 2Pi}];

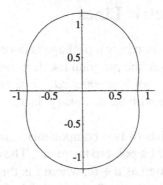

4.1.2   A Simple Procedure to Draw the Lines

If we want to draw pictures of several different lines, it is worthwhile to collect the necessary commands in a procedure, so that we do not have to enter them every time. The variable parts of the computation – that is, the expression that describes the line and the range of the parameter – are defined as arguments of the procedure. This first version of ComplexParametricPlot[z, {t, t_0, t_1}] in the file ComplexParametricPlot1.m is shown in Listing 4.1–1.

```
ComplexParametricPlot[z_, range_List]:=
    ParametricPlot[{Re[z],Im[z]}, range]
```

Listing 4.1–1   ComplexParametricPlot1.m: The first version of ComplexParametricPlot[].

Here is an example for the use of this definition.

Before using the commands we have to read in the file containing them.

In[5]:= << CSM`ComplexParametricPlot1`

Here is a picture of the unit circle transformed by the tangent function.

In[6]:= ComplexParametricPlot[
        Tan[Exp[I t]], {t, 0, 2Pi}];

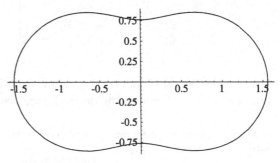

4.1.3   Drawing Several Lines

We can greatly enhance the visual presentation of a complex function by drawing several parametric lines in one picture. `ParametricPlot[]` allows us to give a list of coordinate pairs to draw several lines at once.

Here is an expression for the transformation of circles with radius r under the tangent function.

```
In[1]:= z = Tan[r Exp[I t]]
                I t
Out[1]= Tan[E   r]
```

We generate a list of pairs of real and imaginary parts, using `Table[]`, for $r = 0.1, 0.2, \ldots, 1.0$.

```
In[2]:= Table[{Re[z], Im[z]}, {r, 0.1, 1, 0.1}] // Short
Out[2]//Short=
                     I t                I t
   {{Re[Tan[0.1 E   ]], Im[Tan[0.1 E   ]]}, <<8>>,
                  I t              I t
     {Re[Tan[1. E   ]], Im[Tan[1. E   ]]}}}
```

Here we plot the resulting lines for $0 \le t \le 2\pi$.

```
In[3]:= ParametricPlot[ Evaluate[%], {t, 0, 2Pi} ];
```

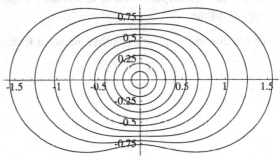

There is no need to define a new function for drawing several lines. This capability is a natural *extension* of our command `ComplexParametricPlot[]`. We can simply give a second definition with an additional parameter to be used as the range in the table. The result is the second version of our package, in ComplexParametricPlot2.m, see Listing 4.1–2.

```
ComplexParametricPlot[z_, range_List]:=
    ParametricPlot[{Re[z],Im[z]}, range]

ComplexParametricPlot[z_, range_List, table_List]:=
    ParametricPlot[Evaluate[Table[{Re[z],Im[z]}, table]], range]
```

Listing 4.1–2   ComplexParametricPlot2.m: An extension for several lines.

We read the new version of our package.

```
In[4]:= << CSM`ComplexParametricPlot2`
```

The exponential function converts vertical lines into circles around the origin. This follows from $e^{x+iy} = e^x e^{iy}$, which is a circle e^{iy} with radius e^x.

```
In[5]:= ComplexParametricPlot[ Exp[x + I y],
            {y, -Pi, Pi}, {x, -1, 1, 0.2} ];
```

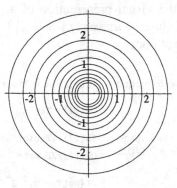

4.1.4 Key Concepts

1. We can visualize complex-valued functions by showing the images of parametric lines in the complex plane.

2. Procedures combine statements that we want to execute for different parameter values.

4.2   The First Package

In Section 4.1, we developed the first version of `ComplexParametricPlot[]`. Although already useful, it is not yet in a state to be published or made available to other users. The goal of writing a *package* is to make the defined commands behave as much as possible like built-in commands. They should have documentation, accessible with `?ComplexParametricPlot`, and their working should not depend on any other calculations we may have performed before reading the package.

The commands `BeginPackage[]`, `Begin[]`, `End[]`, and `EndPackage[]` are used to make definitions in a package independent from other calculations. For this purpose, every symbol belongs to a *context*. Searching for symbols and creating new ones (if a symbol entered at the keyboard is not found) are governed by two global variables:

`$Context`	the context in which new symbols are created
`$ContextPath`	a list of contexts to be searched

These two variables govern the lookup of contexts.

Context names are strings, ending in a backquote (` ) – for example, `"Global`"`. Note that you must enclose strings in quotation marks to enter them into *Mathematica*; the normal output form does not show these quotation marks, however. `Context[symbol]` returns the context of *symbol*.

If a symbol is entered, *Mathematica* searches the *current context* (the value of `$Context`) and all contexts on the list `$ContextPath` for the symbol. If none is found, a new one is created in the current context. More information about the details of this process can be found in *Programming in Mathematica* [54].

Normally, the value of `$Context` is `"Global`"`.

```
In[1]:= $Context
Out[1]= Global`
```

Input form shows the quotation marks.

```
In[2]:= InputForm[ % ]
Out[2]//InputForm= "Global`"
```

These contexts are searched before new symbols are created.

```
In[3]:= $ContextPath
Out[3]= {Global`, System`}
```

This symbol does not exist yet, and a new one is created.

```
In[4]:= newSymbol
Out[4]= newSymbol
```

A new symbol is put into the context `$Context`.

```
In[5]:= Context[ newSymbol ]
Out[5]= Global`
```

Symbols already existing in one of the contexts in $ContextPath are not created anew.

```
In[6]:= Context[ Integrate ]
Out[6]= System`
```

ComplexParametricPlot3.m (Listing 4.2–1) contains our program as a complete package. The part of the package between BeginPackage["CSM`ComplexParametricPlot`"] and Begin["`Private`"] is the *interface part*. It declares the functions *exported* by this package – that is, the functions that the package provides. The best way to declare a function is to give it a usage message – that is, a documentation for the function. The argument of BeginPackage[] is the context for the functions in the package.

```
BeginPackage["CSM`ComplexParametricPlot`"]

ComplexParametricPlot::usage =
    "ComplexParametricPlot[z, {t, t0, t1}] plots a complex parametric line.
    ComplexParametricPlot[z, {t, t0, t1}, {r, r0, r1, dr}] plot several lines."

Begin["`Private`"]

ComplexParametricPlot[z_, range_List]:=
    ParametricPlot[{Re[z],Im[z]}, range]

ComplexParametricPlot[z_, range_List, table_List]:=
    ParametricPlot[Evaluate[Table[{Re[z],Im[z]}, table]], range]

End[]

EndPackage[]
```

Listing 4.2–1   ComplexParametricPlot3.m: Our functions in a package.

The part of the package between Begin["`Private`"] and End[] is the *implementation part*. Here, the already-declared functions are implemented. The implementation part uses its own private context. The use of a separate context prevents details of the implementation from being exported: The implementation is *encapsulated*. This implementation part is identical to the code in ComplexParametricPlot2.m from Listing 4.1–2.

Users of our package should have to look at only the interface to use the package. This separation of interface and implementation is an important principle of software engineering. *Software engineering* studies the methods and principles of good programming. One of these principles is that declaration and implementation should be separated. Separation establishes a clear *interface* between user and programmer. The declaration contains all aspects important for the user. The implementation realizes these aspects. *How* we do the implementation is unimportant for users. Users must not depend on the properties of the program that are mentioned only in the implementation part. Programmers are then free to change the implementation at any time provided the declaration is not affected by the change.

Contexts are a means for realizing this separation of declaration and implementation. We just saw how it works. This knowledge is, however, not important for us. Our package is rather small, and it may seem that the use of all of this overhead is not justified. Because the package is only the first in a series, however, we are providing a good foundation for future developments.

The command << for reading in the package does not return a value, because the command `EndPackage[]`, which is the last one in the package, does not return one.

```
In[1]:= << CSM`ComplexParametricPlot3`
```

ComplexParametricPlot has been defined in this context.

```
In[2]:= Context[ ComplexParametricPlot ]
Out[2]= CSM`ComplexParametricPlot`
```

The context of our package has been put on the search path. That is why we found the symbol `CartesianMap`.

```
In[3]:= $ContextPath
Out[3]= {CSM`ComplexParametricPlot`, Global`, System`}
```

The function works as before. Here is the image of several circles with radii $r = 0$, $0.2, \ldots, 2$ under the sine function, rotated by $90°$.

```
In[4]:= ComplexParametricPlot[ I Sin[r Exp[I t]],
            {t, 0, 2Pi}, {r, 0, 2, 0.2} ];
```

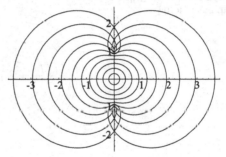

4.2.1   A Second Function in the Package

To help visualize the effect of a complex-valued function on a set of parametric lines, it is convenient to draw the lines and their images side by side.

Here are several circles around the origin.

```
In[5]:= ComplexParametricPlot[ r Exp[I t],
            {t, -3.1, 3.1}, {r, 0.01, 2.01, 0.2} ];
```

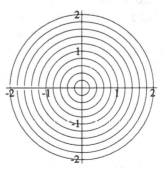

Here are their images under the logarithm function.

```
In[6]:= ComplexParametricPlot[ Log[r Exp[I t]],
              {t, -3.1, 3.1}, {r, 0.01, 2.01, 0.2} ];
```

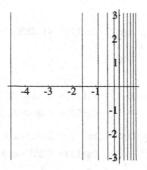

Here the two pictures are shown side by side. `GraphicsArray[{gr_1, ..., gr_n}]` assembles several graphics in a row.

```
In[7]:= Show[ GraphicsArray[{%%, %}] ];
```

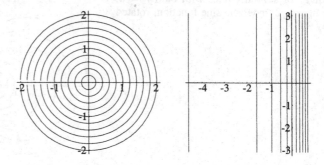

It is easy to see that the logarithm maps circles into vertical straight lines.

```
In[8]:= PowerExpand[ Log[r Exp[I t]] ]
Out[8]= I t + Log[r]
```

Listing 4.2–2 shows the code for the command `ComplexParametricMap[]` that takes the function to map, the expression for the lines, and the ranges as arguments. It generates the two pictures without showing them (by setting the option `DisplayFunction` to `Identity`), then combines them in the way just shown. The display function is reset to its default value `$DisplayFunction`. The argument `ranges__` is declared with two underscore characters, because it should match one or two parameters, depending on whether we want to draw a single line or several lines. The parameter is simply passed unchanged to `ComplexParametricPlot[]`.

4.2.2 Key Concepts

1. Each symbol belongs to a context.

2. New symbols are created in the *current context*.

3. A package consists of an interface and an implementation part.

4. A package uses its own context for the exported functions.

5. The implementation is hidden in its own private context.

```
BeginPackage["CSM`ComplexParametricPlot`"]

ComplexParametricPlot::usage =
    "ComplexParametricPlot[z, {t, t0, t1}] plots a complex parametric line.
    ComplexParametricPlot[z, {t, t0, t1}, {r, r0, r1, dr}] plot several lines."

ComplexParametricMap::usage = "ComplexParametricMap[f, z, ranges..] shows
    the image of the parametric lines defined by z and their images
    under f side by side."

Begin["`Private`"]

ComplexParametricPlot[z_, range_List]:=
    ParametricPlot[{Re[z],Im[z]}, range]

ComplexParametricPlot[z_, range_List, table_List]:=
    ParametricPlot[Evaluate[Table[{Re[z],Im[z]}, table]], range]

ComplexParametricMap[f_, z_, ranges__]:=
Module[{pre,post},
    pre = ComplexParametricPlot[z,    ranges, DisplayFunction->Identity];
    post = ComplexParametricPlot[f[z], ranges, DisplayFunction->Identity];
    Show[ GraphicsArray[{pre,post}], DisplayFunction:>$DisplayFunction ]
]

End[]

EndPackage[]
```

Listing 4.2–2   ComplexParametricPlot4.m: A second function in the package.

4.3   Optional Arguments

Optional arguments of a procedure are arguments that you can leave out when calling the procedure. In this case, a *default value* is used.

A (constant) default for an argument can be declared with *var_:default*. If an argument in a definition is declared in this way (i.e., with a default), the definition is also applied if the argument is missing. The pattern variable *var* takes on the value *default* in this case.

This rule says that the default for the second argument of f should be 17.

```
In[1]:= f[ x_, y_:17 ] := {x, y}
```

If the second argument is given, the default is ignored.

```
In[2]:= f[ 4, 6 ]
Out[2]= {4, 6}
```

If the second argument is missing, the default value is used, and the rule matches even though only one argument was given.

```
In[3]:= f[ 4 ]
Out[3]= {4, 17}
```

4.3.1   Options

If a command takes many optional arguments, this solution will become confusing; there is a better way to specify optional arguments out of a large number of such arguments. The arguments are given in the form *name -> value*. These are *named optional arguments*, in *Mathematica* referred to simply as *options*.

In this parametric plot we change the settings of the AspectRatio and Frame options.

```
In[4]:= ParametricPlot[
            {Sin[t], Sin[2t]/2}, {t, 0, 2Pi},
            AspectRatio -> 0.5,
            Frame -> True
        ];
```

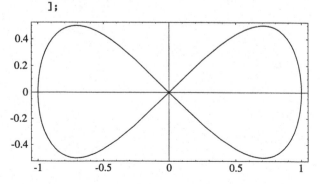

Graphics commands have many such optional arguments. Normally, you need to specify only a small number of them when you use the command. All other options assume the default values shown here.

```
In[5]:= Options[ParametricPlot]
Out[5]= {AspectRatio -> Automatic, Axes -> Automatic,
   AxesLabel -> None, AxesOrigin -> Automatic,
   AxesStyle -> Automatic, Background -> Automatic,
   ColorOutput -> GrayLevel, Compiled -> True,
   DefaultColor -> Automatic, Epilog -> {},
   Frame -> False, FrameLabel -> None,
   FrameStyle -> Automatic, FrameTicks -> Automatic,
   GridLines -> None, ImageSize -> Automatic,
   MaxBend -> 10., PlotDivision -> 30.,
   PlotLabel -> None, PlotPoints -> 25,
   PlotRange -> Automatic, PlotRegion -> Automatic,
   PlotStyle -> Automatic, Prolog -> {},
   RotateLabel -> True, Ticks -> Automatic,
   DefaultFont :> $DefaultFont,
   DisplayFunction :> $DisplayFunction,
   FormatType :> $FormatType, TextStyle :> $TextStyle}
```

You can also change the default value. We did so for all images in this chapter to preserve the true aspect ratio.

```
In[6]:= SetOptions[ ParametricPlot,
                    AspectRatio -> Automatic ];
```

4.3.2 Handling Options

In our commands `ComplexParametricPlot[]` and `ComplexParametricMap[]` we call the graphic functions `ParametricPlot[]` and `GraphicsArray[]`. These graphic functions have many options that we may want to change. To make such changes possible, we should allow options to be given for our commands and pass these options along to the graphic commands.

We declare an additional parameter `opts___?OptionQ`, which accepts any options given after the required arguments. The built-in predicate `OptionQ` gives true if the extra arguments are valid options, that is, rules of the form *name -> value* or *name :> value*. The triple blank `___` matches any number of such options, including none at all. Inside `ComplexParametricPlot[]`, we can simply pass the parameter `opts` to the command `ParametricPlot[]`.

In `ComplexParametricMap[]` we invoke two commands whose options we may want to change, our own `ComplexParametricPlot` and the standard `GraphicsArray[]`. We have to be careful to pass on only those options that are valid for the respective graphic function. The auxiliary function `FilterOptions[]` selects from a sequence of options those that are valid for a certain function. It is defined in the standard package `Utilities`FilterOptions`.

To use the function `FilterOptions[]`, we have to *import* this package into our own package. We do so by mentioning the imported package as a second argument of `BeginPackage[]`. The imported package is then read in, and its functions can be used in the implementation part of our own package. This final version of our package, ComplexParametricPlot.m, is given in Listing 4.3–1.

Now that our package is final and its file-name corresponds to the name of the context given in `BeginPackage["Context`"]`, we should read it in with the command `Needs["Context`"]`.

```
In[1]:= Needs["CSM`ComplexParametricPlot`"]
```

The function $f(z) = z + 1/z$ maps the unit circle to the real line segment between -2 and 2 and the outside of the unit circle to the whole complex plane.

```
In[2]:= ComplexParametricMap[Function[z, z + 1/z],
            r Exp[I t], {t, 0, 2Pi}, {r, 1, 2, 0.1},
            AspectRatio -> Automatic, GraphicsSpacing ->
            0.2];
```

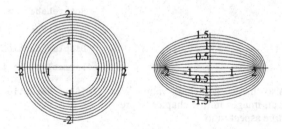

Similarly, the inside of the unit circle is also mapped to the whole complex plane.

```
In[3]:= ComplexParametricMap[Function[z, z + 1/z],
            r Exp[I t], {t, 0, 2Pi}, {r, 0.2, 1, 0.1},
            AspectRatio -> Automatic, PlotRange -> All];
```

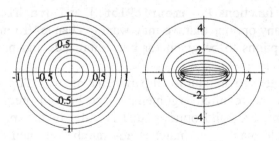

4.3.3   Key Concepts

1. Optional arguments of a functions have a default that is used if the argument is left out.

2. Options are named arguments that can be given in any order.

3. Options look like rules.

```
BeginPackage["CSM`ComplexParametricPlot`", "Utilities`FilterOptions`"]

ComplexParametricPlot::usage =
    "ComplexParametricPlot[z, {t, t0, t1}] plots a complex parametric line.
    ComplexParametricPlot[z, {t, t0, t1}, {r, r0, r1, dr}] plot several lines."

ComplexParametricMap::usage = "ComplexParametricMap[f, z, ranges..] shows
    the image of the parametric lines defined by z and their images
    under f side by side."

Begin["`Private`"]

ComplexParametricPlot[z_, range_List, opts___?OptionQ]:=
    ParametricPlot[{Re[z],Im[z]}, range, opts]

ComplexParametricPlot[z_, range_List, table_List, opts___?OptionQ]:=
    ParametricPlot[Evaluate[Table[{Re[z],Im[z]}, table]], range, opts]

ComplexParametricMap[f_, z_, ranges__, opts___?OptionQ]:=
Module[{pre,post},
    pre = ComplexParametricPlot[z, ranges,
            DisplayFunction->Identity, FilterOptions[ParametricPlot,opts]];
    post = ComplexParametricPlot[f[z], ranges,
            DisplayFunction->Identity, FilterOptions[ParametricPlot,opts]];
    Show[GraphicsArray[{pre,post}], FilterOptions[GraphicsArray,opts],
        DisplayFunction:>$DisplayFunction]
]

End[]

EndPackage[]
```

Listing 4.3–1 ComplexParametricPlot.m: The final version of complex lines.

4.4   A Template Package

You can use Template.m (Listing 4.4–1) as the starting point for your own packages. Copy it to a new file and change the context name in the command `BeginPackage["`*Context*`‘"]`. Normally, the file name is chosen as *Context*.m. The template contains the package framework, as discussed in Section 4.2.

```
BeginPackage["Template`"]

Function1::usage = "Function1[n] does nothing."

Function2::usage = "Function2[n, (m:17)] does even less."

Begin["`Private`"]

Aux[f_] := Do[something]      (* an auxiliary function *)

Function1[n_] := n

Function2[n_, m_:17] /; n < 5 := n m

End[]

EndPackage[]
```

Listing 4.4–1   Template.m: A template package.

In addition to the direct interaction with the kernel of *Mathematica* as it is used in the examples in this book, there is the Notebook frontend, with which you will most likely work. A *Notebook* is a structured document that contains text and graphics, as well as *Mathematica* input and output. It allows calculations to be annotated.

A package can also be developed as a Notebook. A Notebook version of Template.m with name Template.nb is shown in Figure 4.4–1. In this example, you can see a few of the features of Notebooks. A Notebook is divided into cells. The cells are marked at the right margin by cell brackets. Groups of cells are kept together by the outer brackets. The squares mark sections and subsections. In the section "Examples," the function just defined is immediately tried out. The visual presentation of a Notebook depends on what kind of operating system is used. The files themselves, however, are portable between different operating systems.

The cells marked by a short vertical line are initialization cells. These are the cells that contain the package proper. The menu command Kernel>Evaluate Initialization allows you to have your package evaluated by the kernel just as if you had read in the corresponding Template.m package. When you save this Notebook, the initialization cells are optionally written into a package (Template.m) file, so you can read it in later with the usual command `<<Template`` or `Needs["Template`"]`.

Template.nb

Roman E. Maeder

You can use this package as a template for your own packages. When you save it, the corresponding package (with the .m extension) is created automatically; it will contain all cells marked as initialization cells (vertical mark in cell bracket).

■ Implementation

■ Definition of the package context

```
BeginPackage["Template'"]
```

■ Declaration of exported functions

```
Function1::usage = "Function1[n] does nothing."

Function2::usage = "Function2[n, (m:17)] does even less."
```

■ Begin the implementation part

```
Begin["'Private'"]
```

■ Definition of auxiliary functions

```
Aux[f_] := Do[something]
```

■ Definition of exported functions

```
Function1[n_] := n

Function2[n_, m_:17] := n m /; n < 5
```

■ Epilogue

```
End[]        (* end of the implementation part *)

EndPackage[] (* end of package *)
```

■ Examples

```
Function1[5]

5
```

Figure 4.4–1   The template package as a Notebook Template.nb.

4.5   Exercises

4.1   A Package for the Collatz Problem

Collect the functions that we developed for the Collatz sequence (Section 3.2) in a package Collatz.m. They are:

> CollatzLength[n]
> CollatzSequence[n]
> CollatzMaximum[a, b]   (FindMax in Exercise 3.3)

Auxiliary functions should be defined in the implementation part. Add documentation and the necessary context declarations.

4.2   Möbius Transforms

A Möbius transform is a complex-valued function of the form

$$f(z) = \frac{az + b}{cz + d} \tag{4.5--1}$$

(a, b, c, and d are complex numbers).

1. Find a, b, c, and d, such that

$$\begin{aligned} f(0) &= 1, \\ f(1) &= 1 + i, \\ f(1 + i) &= \infty. \end{aligned} \tag{4.5--2}$$

2. Illustrate f using ComplexParametricMap[] by choosing suitable sets of lines that show the essential features of f. Identify the values $f(0)$ and $f(\infty)$ in the diagrams.

Chapter 5
Abstract Data Types

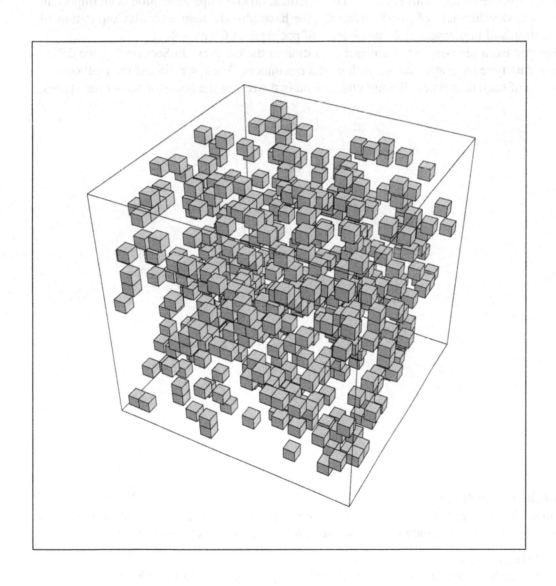

In this chapter, we look at one of the most important concepts in programming languages: data types. A data type is a set of elements together with the operations defined on them. This simple definition implies an important assertion: Data and operations belong together. Modern programming languages allow us to make this connection visible by special means of defining new data types.

A data type is abstract if it is defined only in terms of its properties, without concern for its possible implementation. This separation of specification and implementation is an important tool for the development of good software. We have already seen a similar separation of specification and implementation on the level of packages in Chapter 4.

Our first example will be the abstract definition of the integers. In Section 5.2, we define our own data type for computations with modular numbers. Then, we discuss the methods for the design of such data types. We use this method in the rest of the book for all our data types.

About the illustration overleaf:
This image comprises 500 unit cubes whose coordinates have been chosen as random integers in the range $0 \ldots 19$. The picture was produced with this command (see Pictures.m):

```
Cuboids[n_, m_] :=
   Graphics3D[Cuboid /@ Table[Random[Integer, {0, m-1}], {n}, {3}]]
Show[ Cuboids[500, 20] ].
```

5.1   Definition of Abstract Data Types

A *data type* is a set of *elements* (the data of this type) and the *operations* defined on them, together with their *relationships* (equations between the operations).

An example is the data type `Integer`. The data elements are the integers, the operations are addition `+`, multiplication `*`, and so on. `Integer` is a built-in type that we can use as is.

In *Mathematica* and in many other programming languages, we can define new data types ourselves. The data elements of type `Integer` are *atomic*, that is, they cannot be subdivided further. In general, data elements are composite meaning that they consist of several parts. A data type for addresses, for example, contains at least these parts: name, street, ZIP code, and city. All these parts have their own type.

A data type is *abstract* if it is defined solely in terms of its properties, without regard to possible implementation. This separation of definition or *specification* and implementation is an important tool for the design of good software. It serves the user of the software who can rely on a specification without having to know the implementation, and it also serves the programmer who can choose a suitable implementation as long as the specification is satisfied. The choice of implementation has then no consequences for the user.

These aspects of software development are often neglected in teaching because we usually work with small programs consisting of a few lines of code (in contrast to *Mathematica* itself, for example, which consists of more than 500,000 lines of code). But we always define abstract data types in the rest of this book, even for small programs. Because abstract data types are wholly defined by their specification, these ideas are independent of the programming language chosen. If you ever have to program in C or Java, you can still use these concepts – only the implementation will look different.

5.1.1   Example: Abstract Definition of the Natural Numbers

The well-known natural numbers $\mathbf{N} = \{0, 1, 2, \ldots\}$ can also be defined in an abstract way. This has always been done in mathematics, long before the introduction of abstract data types. It is the description of natural numbers by *Peano*. The natural numbers can be defined from a constant 0 and the successor function $\mathbf{s}$ as the smallest set $\mathbf{N}$ with these properties:

$$0 \in \mathbf{N} \tag{5.1–1}$$

$$n \in \mathbf{N} \Rightarrow \mathbf{s}(n) \in \mathbf{N} \tag{5.1–2}$$

Intuitively, $\mathbf{s}$ is the function that adds 1 to a number. This construction obviously gives us all natural numbers if we start with zero.

Let us now look at a set T_N of *Mathematica* expressions with these properties:

- The expression z (a symbol) is an element of T_N:

$$z \in T_N.$$ (5.1–3)

- All expressions of the form s[s[...s[z]...]] are elements of T_N:

$$\underbrace{s[s[...s[z]...]]}_{n \text{ times } s} \in T_N, \qquad n = 1, 2, \ldots.$$ (5.1–4)

That is, the expressions s[z], s[s[z]], ...

A function s operating on these expressions can be defined as follows:

$$s: t \mapsto s[t].$$ (5.1–5)

For example, $s(z) = $ s[z], $s(s[z]) = $ s[s[z]]. Please observe the distinction between the *function s* and the *symbol* s. We use these similar notations on purpose.

It is easy to see that T_N and the function s satisfy the conditions of Equations 5.1–1 and 5.1–2 because we constructed the set T_N such that the result of applying s to an element gives another element of the set. The expression z serves as our zero. The set T_N is therefore a *model* of the natural numbers – the *term model*.

Addition **add** and multiplication **mult** can be defined inductively:

$$\begin{aligned}
\mathbf{add}(n, 0) &= n, \\
\mathbf{add}(n, \mathbf{s}(m)) &= \mathbf{s}(\mathbf{add}(n, m)), \\
\mathbf{mult}(n, 0) &= 0, \\
\mathbf{mult}(n, \mathbf{s}(m)) &= \mathbf{add}(\mathbf{mult}(n, m), n).
\end{aligned}$$ (5.1–6)

You can easily verify that ordinary addition and multiplication of natural numbers satisfy these equations.

These equations can be realized in *Mathematica* as *rules*. We can enter them almost verbatim. We have only to mark the variables n and m on the left side as pattern variables by appending an underscore character. Note that the symbol z is not a variable, but rather a constant.

```
add[n_, z] := n
add[n_, s[m_]] := s[add[n, m]]

mult[n_, z] := z
mult[n_, s[m_]] := add[mult[n, m], n]
```

This example computes $2 + 1$ in the term model.	`In[1]:= add[ s[s[z]], s[z] ]` `Out[1]= s[s[s[z]]]`
Here is $2 \times 2 = 4$.	`In[2]:= mult[ s[s[z]], s[s[z]] ]` `Out[2]= s[s[s[s[z]]]]`

It is easy to prove that T_N is isomorphic to $\mathbf{N}$. The term $\mathbf{z}$ corresponds to the natural number 0. The term $\mathbf{s[s[\ldots s[z]\ldots]]}$ corresponds to the number n, where there are exactly n occurrences of $\mathbf{s[\ldots]}$. The built-in nonnegative integers are also a model of $\mathbf{N}$. The function s becomes

$$\mathbf{s[n\_] := n + 1}.$$

Note that the data type $\mathtt{int}$ (or $\mathtt{integer}$) in most programming languages is not a model of $\mathbf{N}$, because there is a limit on the size of these numbers (often this limit is $2^{31} - 1$). In this number system, we have

$$(2^{31} - 1) + 1 = -2^{31},$$

which is rather strange.

5.1.2   Composite Data Types in *Mathematica*

For composite data types, there is a simple representation as *normal expressions* in *Mathematica* (see Section 2.4). The name *type* of the data type is used as head for the data elements. All information that describes a data element is stored as elements e_i of the normal expression. A data element therefore looks as follows:

$$type[e_1, \, e_2, \, \ldots, \, e_n].$$

These ideas are best made clear with an example. We introduce a data type for modular numbers in Section 5.2.

5.1.3   Key Concepts

1. A data type consists of elements and operations.

2. The natural numbers are defined by the number zero and the successor function.

3. The term model is a set of formal expressions that satisfy certain equations.

5.2 Example: Modular Numbers

Let us look at modular numbers for an example of the design and implementation of a new data type. The ring of modular numbers is normally designated by $\mathbf{Z}_p$, for $p > 0$ (often chosen to be a prime number). We use the name mod for this data type. A modular number can be described by a *representative* (an integer) and the modulus p. This observation suggests the implementation mod[n, p]. The component n is a representative of the residue class $n + kp$, for $k \in \mathbf{Z}$. The choice is not unique: Each number congruent to n (modulo p) is also a representative.

5.2.1 Unique Representation of Data Elements

If possible, data elements should be represented in a unique way. In our example, we can always find a representative n with $0 \le n < p$. A simple rule reduces representations outside this interval to standard form:

```
mod[ n_, p_ ]/; n < 0 || n >= p := mod[ Mod[n, p], p]
```

(Mod[n, p] is the built-in integer remainder function whose result for positive p is always in the range $0 \le n < p$.) One advantage of a unique representation is that equality of two data elements is easy to check.

5.2.2 Arithmetic with Modular Numbers

The sum of two modular numbers is found by adding the representatives, and then reducing to normal form; in a similar way we can find the product of two modular numbers. Here are these simple definitions for modPlus and modTimes, respectively:

```
modPlus[ mod[a_,p_], mod[b_,p_] ]  := mod[ a + b, p ]
modTimes[ mod[a_,p_], mod[b_,p_] ] := mod[ a * b, p ]
```

Observe that we use the same pattern variable p_ for the modulus in the two arguments on the left side of the definitions. This restriction ensures that both operands have the same modulus. Note that we do not need to program the reduction to normal form; this task is already performed by the code of mod.

This solution is rather cumbersome. We would better express the sum of two modular numbers m_1 and m_2 in the form $m_1 + m_2$ instead of modPlus[m_1, m_2]. That is, we want to use the existing operator + also for our new data type. Not many programming languages

allow us to *overload* existing operators to work with new data types in the way we can in
Mathematica.

Overloading an operator means adding definitions for an existing operator in such a way
that it can handle new data types. Here are the new definitions in terms of + and *, instead of
modPlus and modTimes, respectively:

```
mod/: mod[a_,p_] + mod[b_,p_] := mod[ a + b, p ]
mod/: mod[a_,p_] * mod[b_,p_] := mod[ a * b, p ]
```

The declaration mod/: binds the definitions to the data type mod, instead of to the operations
Plus and Times. This binding emphasizes the close connection of data and operations, and
leads to more efficient evaluation.

The additive inverse −a mod p can be found as follows, by overloading the unary minus
operator:

```
mod/: -mod[a_, p_] := mod[-a, p]
```

We can use the built-in function PowerMod[a, n, p] for positive integer powers of modular numbers. This function computes a^n mod p faster than does the integer operation
Mod[$a \wedge n$, p]. With $n = -1$, we get the *modular inverse* in the same way.

```
mod/: mod[a_,p_] ^ n_Integer := mod[ PowerMod[a, n, p], p ]
```

This modular number is immediately reduced to normal form. Obviously, we have
$13 \equiv 6$ (mod 7).

```
In[1]:= mod[13, 7]
Out[1]= mod[6, 7]
```

The sum of 5 and 3 is 1.

```
In[2]:= mod[5, 7] + mod[3, 7]
Out[2]= mod[1, 7]
```

The product 5 × 4 is 6.

```
In[3]:= mod[5, 7] mod[4, 7]
Out[3]= mod[6, 7]
```

The negative of 5 is 2.

```
In[4]:= -mod[5, 7]
Out[4]= mod[2, 7]
```

Subtraction is turned into addition with the
negative automatically. Therefore, we do
not need to give any additional rules for subtraction.

```
In[5]:= mod[5, 7] - mod[4, 7]
Out[5]= mod[1, 7]
```

The inverse of 5 is 3.

```
In[6]:= mod[5, 7]^-1
Out[6]= mod[3, 7]
```

By multiplying the inverse with the original number, we can verify the preceding result. The inverse of 5 multiplied by 5 must give 1.

```
In[7]:= % mod[5, 7]
Out[7]= mod[1, 7]
```

Very big powers (here, $2^{10^{100}}$ mod 7) can be found in a fraction of a second.

```
In[8]:= mod[2, 7]^10^100
Out[8]= mod[2, 7]
```

5.2.3 Output Formatting

The (external) representation is also a part of a data type. The usual notation in mathematics is n mod p, which we can program as follows:

```
Format[m_mod] := Infix[m," mod "]
```

The formatting rule is applied to each result.

```
In[1]:= mod[13, 7]
Out[1]= 6 mod 7
```

Formatting does not influence our computations. Internally, modular numbers are still stored in the same way.

```
In[2]:= % ^ 2
Out[2]= 1 mod 7
```

`InputForm[]` allows us to look at this internal form.

```
In[3]:= InputForm[ % ]
Out[3]//InputForm= mod[1, 7]
```

5.2.4 Type Conversion

It is convenient to extend arithmetic to combinations of modular numbers and integers (which is justified mathematically by the canonical homomorphism $\mathbf{Z} \rightarrow \mathbf{Z}_p$). We can do this extension by defining additional rules for mixed argument types.

```
mod/: mod[a_,p_] + b_Integer := mod[ a + b, p ]
mod/: mod[a_,p_] * b_Integer := mod[ a * b, p ]
```

Integers are transformed into modular numbers whenever they come in contact with the latter.

```
In[4]:= 2 mod[5, 7]
Out[4]= 3 mod 7
```

The order of the operands does not matter; *Mathematica* knows that addition and multiplication are commutative.

```
In[5]:= mod[5, 7] 2
Out[5]= 3 mod 7
```

The complete package for computing with modular numbers is in Modular.m; it is reproduced in Listing 5.2–1.

```
BeginPackage["CSM`Modular`"]
mod::usage = "mod[n, p] is a representation of the number (n mod p)."
Begin["`Private`"]
(* Constructor and Normal Form *)
mod[n_, p_]/; n < 0 || n >= p := mod[ Mod[n, p], p ]
(* Arithmetic *)
mod/: mod[a_,p_] + mod[b_,p_] := mod[ a + b, p ]
mod/: mod[a_,p_] * mod[b_,p_] := mod[ a * b, p ]
mod/: mod[a_,p_] ^ q_Integer  := mod[ PowerMod[a, q, p], p ]
(* Output Formatting *)
Format[m_mod] := Infix[m," mod "]
(* Type Conversion of Integers *)
mod/: mod[a_,p_] + b_Integer := mod[ a + b, p ]
mod/: mod[a_,p_] * b_Integer := mod[ a * b, p ]
End[]
EndPackage[]
```

Listing 5.2–1 Modular.m.

5.2.5 Key Concepts

1. Modular numbers are described by a representative and the modulus.

2. A unique representation of data elements simplifies equality tests.

3. The standard arithmetic operators can be overloaded for new data types.

5.3 Design of Abstract Data Types

For most programming projects, designing the data types should be the first activity of the
programmer. A good data type design helps the implementation of the algorithms in the
program.

5.3.1 Constructors and Selectors

We are not yet satisfied with the data type of modular numbers. We violated one important
principle: We should not access the internal representation of data elements directly. If we
define the operations on modular numbers as we did in Section 5.2, we have to change all
our definitions if the representation of our data type needs to be changed for some reason.
To avoid this undesirable dependency, we try to formulate our algorithms independently of
the implementation. Access to data elements happens then exclusively through certain access
functions: the constructors and selectors. A *constructor* is a function that creates new data
elements; a *selector* is a function that returns a component of a data element.

In our example of modular numbers, we need one constructor to create modular numbers
and two selectors, one each for the two components, the representative and the modulus. We
can define the constructor Modular[n, p] and the selectors Representative[*mod*] and
Modulus[*mod*] as follows:

```
Modular[n_Integer, p_Integer?Positive] := mod[Mod[n, p], p]

Representative[mod[n_, p_]] := n
Modulus[mod[n_, p_]] := p
```

The constructor Modular[n, p] assembles n and p to a modular number mod[n, p]. At the
same time, we make the representation unique as we did at the beginning of Section 5.2. The
selectors simply return the components n and p. Using these access functions, we can write
the rule for addition in the following implementation-independent way:

```
mod/: a_mod + b_mod /; Modulus[a] == Modulus[b] :=
    Modular[ Representative[a] + Representative[b], Modulus[a] ]
```

We no longer use patterns in the form mod[n_, p_] that access the representation of a modular
number directly. Instead, we declare only variables of type mod using a_mod, and so on. We
access the components of the modular number using the selectors Representative[a] and
Modulus[a]. We build the result of addition using the constructor. We implement the test for
equality of the two moduli with a condition.

Constructors and selectors must fit together. The conditions can be expressed as equations. Here, we have the usual laws about modular numbers.

$$
\begin{aligned}
\text{Modular[Representative}[n]\text{, Modulus}[n]\text{]} &== n, \\
\text{Representative[Modular}[n, p]\text{]} &== n \quad (\mathrm{mod}\ p), \qquad (5.3\text{--}1) \\
\text{Modulus[Modular}[n, p]\text{]} &== p.
\end{aligned}
$$

The first equation says that we must get the same modular number m if we take it apart (using the selectors) and then put it back together (using the constructor). The second equation says that the chosen representative must be congruent to n.

The correctness of the definition for the addition can now be proved using these identities alone. We no longer have to know how modular numbers are implemented. This fact ensures the desired independence of representation. Assume that a and b have the same modulus. Let us look at `Representative`$[a + b]$. According to our definition of addition, we get

$$
\text{Representative[Modular[Representative}[a]\text{ + Representative}[b]\text{,} \\
\text{Modulus}[a]]\text{] ,}
$$

which, according to Equation 5.3–1, is congruent to

$$
\text{Representative}[a]\text{ + Representative}[b]\text{ .}
$$

This last form is exactly the definition of modular addition, which is defined in terms of representatives.

5.3.2   Design Principles for Abstract Data Types

The task of finding a useful data type for a problem can be divided into two parts: *specification* and *implementation*. These two steps are independent. In larger programming projects, they might even be done by different programmers. Specification declares which operations are needed and which properties they should have. A specification consists of the following elements:

- *Constants* are the fundamental building blocks of data structures. Often, they are termed *atoms*.

- *Constructors*, *selectors*, and *predicates* are the functions used to build and to access data elements. If used exclusively, such access functions make algorithms using the data type independent of implementation.

- *Equations* describe the properties of constructors, selectors, and predicates.

5.3.3 Implementation of Data Types

Implementation takes the specification and tries to satisfy it as well as possible. The measure of satisfaction may be *efficiency* (in terms of run time or memory usage), or our goal may be to produce a working *prototype* as quickly as possible. This prototype allows us to test the design. Later, we can change the implementation to be more efficient without making any changes to existing code, as we have seen. Implementation consists of these elements:

- A *representation* of data elements; often, we can use normal expressions with the name of the data type as head

- *Definitions* for the constructors, selectors, and predicates

- *Rules for reduction to normal form*; these rules are derived from the equations and can often be built into the constructors

- A useful *output representation*; a good output format makes data more readable and hides the implementation

- *Overloading* of standard operators, where useful

- Automatic *type conversion*

We present only one more example at this point because these design principles are used in the rest of the book in many places.

5.3.4 Example: *Mathematica* Expressions

The expressions used by *Mathematica* can also be defined as elements of an abstract data type, of course. We have already defined them as such in Section 2.4. The constants are the atoms (numbers, symbols, and strings). For every integer $n \geq 0$, there is one constructor

$$h \, [\, e_1, \, e_2, \, \ldots, \, e_n \,] \, ,$$

which produces a normal expression with a head and n elements. The selectors are `Head[e]` and `Part[e, i]`, for $1 \leq i \leq n$. The equations are of the form

$$\begin{aligned}
\texttt{Head[} h[e_1, e_2, \ldots, e_n] \texttt{]} &== h \, , \\
\texttt{Part[} h[e_1, e_2, \ldots, e_n], \, i \texttt{]} &== e_i \, , \\
\texttt{Head[e] [Part[e, 1]}, \ldots, \texttt{Part[e, n]]} &== e \, .
\end{aligned} \qquad (5.3\text{--}2)$$

See also Section 9.1.2, where a similar data type for LISP is presented.

This example is special insofar as we do not have to implement anything. Expressions are already built into *Mathematica*. But we can see that, to use these expressions, we do not have to know how they have been implemented. All we need is the specification.

5.3.5 Key Concepts

1. Constructors build elements of data types.

2. Selectors return components of data elements.

3. Equations between constructors and selectors lead to simplification of data elements and to unique representations.

5.4 Exercises

5.1 Rational Numbers[1]

A data type for rational numbers can be defined with the constructor makeRational[n, d] and the selectors numerator[r] and denominator[r]. The representation of a data element is simply rational[n, d]. It should represent the rational number n/d. In this exercise, you should not use the built-in rational numbers; use only integers.

1. Give the definitions of makeRational, numerator, and denominator. Complete the right side:

$$\begin{aligned}
\text{makeRational[n\_, d\_]} &:= \quad \ldots \\
\text{numerator[rational[n\_, d\_]]} &:= \quad \ldots \\
\text{denominator[rational[n\_, d\_]]} &:= \quad \ldots
\end{aligned}$$

2. The representation rational[n, d] for rational numbers is not yet unique. For example, the expressions rational[-1, 2], rational[1, -2], and rational[-2, 4] describe the same number. The representation becomes unique if we demand that the denominator is always positive and the numerator and denominator are relatively prime; that is, they have no factors in common. Find two rules for rational[n_, d_] that ensure that data elements are transformed into a unique form.

   Hint: the function GCD[] computes the greatest common divisor (gcd) of two integers.

3. Give definitions for addition and multiplication of rational numbers that work exclusively with constructors and selectors. Complete the right side:

$$\begin{aligned}
\text{rational/: a\_rational + b\_rational} &:= \quad \ldots \\
\text{rational/: a\_rational * b\_rational} &:= \quad \ldots
\end{aligned}$$

5.2 Complex Numbers[1]

A data type for complex numbers can be defined with a constructor complexCartesian[x, y] and the selectors re[c] and im[c]. The representation is by a data element of the form cartesian[x, y]. It describes the number $x + iy$. These definitions implement the constructor and the selectors (The built-in complex numbers must not be used for this exercise).

```
complexCartesian[x_, y_] := cartesian[x, y]
re[cartesian[x_, y_]] := x
im[cartesian[x_, y_]] := y
```

---

[1]Written examination, ETH Zürich, Department of Mathematics and Physics.

1. Give definitions for addition, multiplication, and inverse of complex numbers that work exclusively with constructors and selectors. Complete the right side:

$$\begin{aligned}
\texttt{cartesian/: a\_cartesian + b\_cartesian :=} &\quad \texttt{...}\\
\texttt{cartesian/: a\_cartesian * b\_cartesian :=} &\quad \texttt{...}\\
\texttt{cartesian/: a\_cartesian \^\ -1 :=} &\quad \texttt{...}
\end{aligned}$$

Give similar definitions for the sum of a complex number and an integer or a rational number, as well as the product of a complex number with an integer or a rational number.

2. Are the rules from part 1 sufficient for all four arithmetic operations (addition, subtraction, multiplication, and division)?

   - If yes, show how `cartesian[1, 2] - cartesian[0, 1]` and `cartesian[1, 2] / cartesian[0, 1]` are computed.

   - If no, give more definitions sufficient for all four arithmetic operations. Show how the above two examples are now computed.

3. Complex numbers can also be given in polar coordinates as $re^{i\varphi} = r\cos\varphi + ir\sin\varphi$. Here is the definition of a constructor `complexPolar[r, φ]` that creates a data element `polar[r, φ]` describing the complex number $re^{i\varphi}$:

$$\texttt{complexPolar[r\_, p\_] := polar[r, p].}$$

Give definitions for the selectors `re[]` and `im[]` for data of type `polar`. With these definitions, `re[polar[1, Pi/4]]` evaluates to `Sqrt[2]/2`, because $e^{i\pi/4} = \sqrt{2}/2 + i\sqrt{2}/2$.

Chapter 6

Algorithms for Searching and Sorting

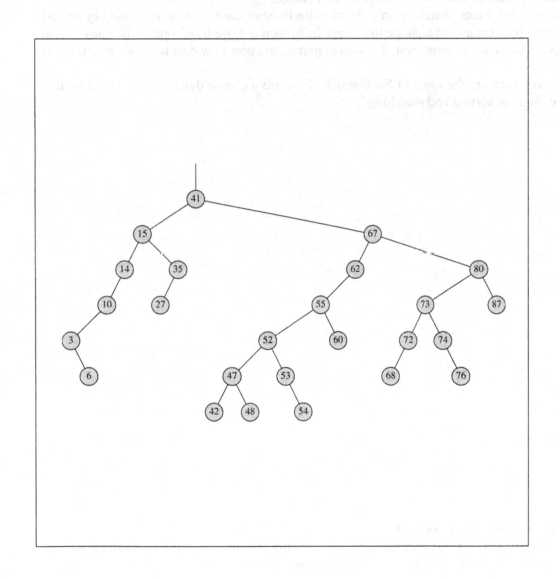

In this chapter, we present algorithms for sorting collections of data and for searching in ordered collections. The algorithms treated here are fundamental to computer science. Algorithms for sorting and searching are part of many programs. In a broad sense, they serve to collect and process data.

In this chapter we use *Mathematica*'s graphics capabilities to visualize the behavior of algorithms. One of the features of an interactive symbolic computation systems is that program runs are themselves data and can be processed accordingly.

Section 6.1 treats searching in ordered collections of data. Ordering is the key to fast searching, for example in a phone directory. In Section 6.2, we treat sorting. Because sorted data collections are so important, it is also important to know how data becomes sorted in the first place.

Binary trees are the topic of Section 6.3. They are a classic dynamic data structure that can be used for sorting and searching.

About the illustration overleaf:
A picture of a binary tree. It was obtained by inserting 30 random numbers into an empty tree. The picture was produced with this command (see also Pictures.m):

```
TreePlot[RandomTree[30]];
```

6.1 Searching Ordered Data

It is easy to find the phone number of a person in the phone directory, but difficult to find the name, given the number. The reason is that the directory is *sorted* by name. Let us see how we can take advantage of the order present in a collection of data. The most important searching technique is binary search, or bisection, which we treat in this section.

6.1.1 Bisection (Binary Search)

How can we find an entry in a sorted directory? If we search by hand, we use our experience to find the approximate location of the entry, and then search sequentially through the page that contains the entry. This is a *heuristic* method, which is not well suited for computers. We need a purely algorithmic procedure, one that can be explained to a machine.

We want to solve this task with the minimum number of accesses to the directory. First, we look at the entry in the middle of the directory and compare it with the entry we are looking for. This step tells us in which half of the directory the entry must lie. The other half does not have to be looked at again. The part of the directory that contains the entry can again be divided into two halves, and so on. Each step halves the number of entries in which we have to search. After $\log_2 n$ steps, where n is the number of entries in the original directory, the directory has been reduced to a single entry. If it is the one we are looking for, we have located it; otherwise, it is not in the directory at all. Of course, if at any step the entry in the middle happens to be the right one, we can stop the search immediately. The function `BinarySearch[]` shown in Listing 6.1–1 finds the position of a number in a sorted list using bisection.

```
BinarySearch::usage = "BinarySearch[list, elem] finds the position of elem
    in the sorted list. If elem does not occur in list, 0 is returned."
BinarySearch[list_, elem_] :=
    Module[{n0 = 1, n1 = Length[list], m},
        While[n0 <= n1,
            m = Floor[(n0 + n1)/2];
            If[ list[[m]] == elem, Return[m] ];        (* found *)
            If[ list[[m]] < elem, n0 = m+1, n1 = m-1 ] (* continue *)
        ];
        0  (* not found *)
    ]
```

Listing 6.1–1 BinarySearch1.m: The bisection method for searching.

A directory with 1 million entries can be searched with at most 20 accesses.

```
In[1]:= Log[2.0, 10^6]
Out[1]= 19.9316
```

The number 5 occurs in the third position in
the list.

```
In[2]:= BinarySearch[
            {1, 3, 5, 7, 9, 11, 13, 15, 17},
            5 ]

Out[2]= 3
```

The number 6 does not occur. Zero is returned to indicate this fact.

```
In[3]:= BinarySearch[
            {1, 3, 5, 7, 9, 11, 13, 15, 17},
            6 ]

Out[3]= 0
```

To prove correctness of this algorithm, we look at the loop invariant:

If *elem* occurs in *list*, then it is in the range $n_0, \ldots, n_1$.

This invariant is satisfied trivially if *elem* does not occur at all or if the list is empty. In the beginning, it is always satisfied if we set $n_0 = 1$ and $n_1 = n$. Then, we look at the middle element with index $m = \left\lfloor \frac{n_0 + n_1}{2} \right\rfloor$. If the mth element happens to be the one we are looking for, we can terminate the loop and return m. Otherwise, we continue the search in that half that must contain the element, if it occurs at all. Therefore, we can either set n_0 to $m + 1$ to search in the upper half, or we can set n_1 to $m - 1$ to search in the lower half. In each case, the loop invariant remains true and the range $n_0 \ldots n_1$ is made smaller. After a few steps of the algorithm, we must reach $n_0 > n_1$. Because the range to be searched is then empty, it is clear that the element did not occur in the list. In this case, we return 0 to indicate an unsuccessful search.

Such considerations have to be performed with care. A special case exists for $n_1 = n_0 + 1$. We cannot find an m in between the only two elements present. Please convince yourself that the algorithm also works in this case. How does the program work if the list contains just one element?

6.1.2 Observation of the Algorithm

Mathematica makes it easy to observe how an algorithm works. In the simplest case, we can insert a `Print[]` command in the loop. This statement allows us to see the progress of the computation. The information of interest in binary search is the value of the pair $\{n_0, n_1\}$. We print it out at the beginning and after each iteration of the loop. The modified program is shown in Listing 6.1–2.

We see the values of n_0 and n_1 at the beginning and after each iteration.

```
In[1]:= BinarySearch[
            {1, 3, 5, 7, 9, 11, 13, 15, 17},
            5 ]

{1, 9}
{1, 4}
{3, 4}

Out[1]= 3
```

```
BinarySearch[list_, elem_] :=
    Module[{n0 = 1, n1 = Length[list], m},
        Print[{n0, n1}];
        While[n0 <= n1,
            m = Floor[(n0 + n1)/2];
            If[ list[[m]] == elem, Return[m] ];           (* found *)
            If[ list[[m]] < elem, n0 = m+1, n1 = m-1 ];   (* continue *)
            Print[{n0, n1}]
        ];
        0   (* not found *)
    ]
```

Listing 6.1–2   BinarySearchA.m: Print commands in the loop.

The algorithm needs the largest number of
iterations if the element does not occur.

```
In[2]:= BinarySearch[
            {1, 3, 5, 7, 9, 11, 13, 15, 17},
            6 ]

{1, 9}
{1, 4}
{3, 4}
{4, 4}
{4, 3}

Out[2]= 0
```

A better idea is to generate the information about the algorithm as a *Mathematica* object itself.
We can then process it further. The version of `BinarySearch[]` shown in Listing 6.1–3
returns the list of all n_0, n_1 pairs.

```
BinarySearch[list_, elem_] :=
    Module[{n0 = 1, n1 = Length[list], m, res = {}},
        AppendTo[res, {n0, n1}];
        While[n0 <= n1,
            m = Floor[(n0 + n1)/2];
            If[ list[[m]] == elem, Break[] ];
            If[ list[[m]] < elem, n0 = m+1, n1 = m-1 ];
            AppendTo[res, {n0, n1}];
        ];
        res
    ]
```

Listing 6.1–3   BinarySearchB.m: Returning trace information.

We generate a list of the first 10,000 integers.

```
In[1]:= Short[ l = Range[10000] ]
Out[1]//Short=
{1, 2, 3, 4, 5, 6, 7, 8, 9, 10, 11, 12, 13, <<9981>>,
 9995, 9996, 9997, 9998, 9999, 10000}
```

We search for a number that does not occur in 1. The result is the list of all n_0, n_1 pairs generated during the search.

```
In[2]:= pairs = BinarySearch[ 1, 7200.5 ]
Out[2]= {{1, 10000}, {5001, 10000}, {5001, 7499},
         {6251, 7499}, {6876, 7499}, {7188, 7499},
         {7188, 7342}, {7188, 7264}, {7188, 7225},
         {7188, 7205}, {7197, 7205}, {7197, 7200},
         {7199, 7200}, {7200, 7200}, {7201, 7200}}
```

In this way, we generate rectangles that correspond to the intervals in our search. The lower left corner is $(n_0, -(i - 1/2))$; the upper right corner is $(n_1, -i)$.

```
In[3]:= Table[
            Rectangle[ {pairs[[i, 1]], -i+1/2},
                       {pairs[[i, 2]], -i} ],
         {i, Length[pairs]} ];
```

This command shows the rectangles. We can see how the intervals are halved at each step (from top to bottom).

```
In[4]:= Show[ Graphics[%], Axes->None, Frame->True,
              FrameTicks->{Automatic,None,None,None},
              AspectRatio->1/3, PlotRange->All ];
```

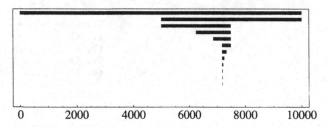

6.1.3   Abstract Formulation of Binary Search

Searching and sorting benefits much from an abstract formulation. The details of the algorithm do not depend on the kind of data searched or sorted. All we need is that the data elements contain a *key field* that can be compared with key fields of other data elements. Therefore, we need to know only the selector for the key field. The data elements are usually called *records*. One component of these records is the key. The possible values of the key can be ordered linearly. (Such an order is called a *total order*.) *Mathematica* provides a general comparison function Order[e_1, e_2] that returns 1, 0, or -1, depending on whether $e_1 < e_2$, $e_1 = e_2$, or $e_1 > e_2$ holds.

The selector GetKey[*record*], which returns the key, is made an additional argument of the binary search procedure. The procedure can, therefore, be used to sort arbitrary types of records. The program BinarySearch.m is reproduced in Listing 6.1–4.

The package Telephone.m (Listing 6.1–5) contains the definition of an abstract data type for a simple phone directory. We use the name as key.

We need these two packages.

```
In[5]:= << CSM`Telephone`; \
        << CSM`BinarySearch`;
```

Here, we enter a few records into the directory. These records are the phone numbers of branches and offices of Cambridge University Press in various countries. Note that we must enter the records in alphabetical order.

```
In[6]:= directory = {
          entry["Argentina", "+541 322-5040"],
          entry["Australia", "+61 3 9568 0322 9"],
          entry["Brazil",    "+55 11 259 2122"],
          entry["Egypt",     "+202 3935157"],
          entry["France",    "+331 39 14 46 91"],
          entry["Greece",    "+30 1 9213020"],
          entry["India",     "+91 11 3274196"],
          entry["Japan",     "+81 813 32914541"],
          entry["Poland",    "+48 2 654 18 09"],
          entry["Spain",     "+34 1 360 45 65"],
          entry["Thailand",  "+66 2 255 4620"],
          entry["Turkey",    "+216 346 3046"],
          entry["USA",       "+1 212 924 3900"]
        };
```

We can extract a record with the name as key.

```
In[7]:= BinarySearch[ directory, "Brazil", name ]
Out[7]= phonerecord[Brazil, +55 11 259 2122]
```

The procedure `BinarySearch` is a *polymorphic* operation. It can be used to search collections of data of different types.

```
BinarySearch::usage = "BinarySearch[list, key, getkey] finds the position
    in list of a record whose key value is equal to key. The function getkey
    is applied to records to retrieve the key for comparisons."

BinarySearch[list_, key_, getkey_] :=
    Module[{n0 = 1, n1 = Length[list], m},
        While[n0 <= n1,
            m = Floor[(n0 + n1)/2];
            Switch[ Order[ getkey[list[[m]]], key ],
                1,  n0 = m + 1,            (* record is above m *)
                0,  Return[ list[[m]] ],   (* found! *)
                -1, n1 = m - 1             (* record is below m *)
            ]
        ];
        Null    (* record is not in list *)
    ]
```

Listing 6.1–4   BinarySearch.m.

```
entry[name_String, number_String] :=
    phonerecord[name, number]                    (* constructor *)

number[phonerecord[name_, number_]] := number    (* selector *)

name[phonerecord[name_, number_]] := name         (* selector *)
```

Listing 6.1–5   Telephone.m.

6.1.4   Key Concepts

1.   An ordered list of data can be searched in logarithmic time.

2.   The key of a record is the field used for sorting and searching.

6.2 Sorting Data

For simplicity, we shall sort only lists of numbers. We saw in Section 6.1.3 how methods for searching can be extended to arbitrary data types. The same extension is possible for sorting algorithms. The algorithms we discuss are *internal* sorting algorithms. They are used to sort a list of numbers residing in the main memory of our computer. The sorting of external data (residing on the hard disk) requires different methods. All our algorithms work *in place*, that is, they sort the data without requiring any auxiliary memory. The elementary operation for internal, in-place sorting is the *exchange*, or swap, of two elements. A list can be sorted by a sequence of such exchanges.

Here is a list of numbers.	`In[1]:= l = {3, 1, 2, 4}`
	`Out[1]= {3, 1, 2, 4}`
This command exchanges the first and second element. It is an example of parallel assignment (see Section 2.3.1).	`In[2]:= {l[[1]], l[[2]]} = {l[[2]], l[[1]]}; l`
	`Out[2]= {1, 3, 2, 4}`
After exchanging the second and third element, the list is sorted.	`In[3]:= {l[[2]], l[[3]]} = {l[[3]], l[[2]]}; l`
	`Out[3]= {1, 2, 3, 4}`

The auxiliary command swap[*l*, *i*, *j*] performs such an exchange on the value of *l*. The attribute HoldFirst prevents the evaluation of *l* as argument of swap[]. We shall use program SortAux.m (Listing 6.2–1) in all sorting programs to follow.

```
BeginPackage["CSM`SortAux`"]

swap::usage = "swap[l, i, j] exchanges elements i and j of the value of l."

Begin["`Private`"]

SetAttributes[swap, {HoldFirst}]

swap[l_Symbol, i_, j_] := ({l[[i]], l[[j]]} = {l[[j]], l[[i]]}; l)

End[]

EndPackage[]
```

Listing 6.2–1   SortAux.m: Exchanging elements of a list.

The use of swap[] instead of the explicit assignment will make our sorting programs more readable.	`In[4]:= swap[l, 1, 3]`
	`Out[4]= {3, 2, 1, 4}`

We shall compare the algorithms by the number of comparisons $C(n)$ and the number of exchanges $E(n)$ necessary to sort a list of length n. In most algorithms, these numbers depend on the input and are lower for input lists that are almost sorted. This dependency makes it necessary to look at the best and worst cases. Most important, however, is the expected *average* performance. In the formulae we assume that our input is the list $l = \{e_1, e_2, \ldots, e_n\}$ with n elements.

6.2.1   Selection Sort

The idea of selection sort is to gradually build up the sorted list. The first element of the sorted list is the smallest of all elements of l. It is brought at position 1 of the result by exchanging it with the element that happens to be in position 1 of l. Then, the smallest among elements 2 through n is found. It comes in second place in the sorted list. Before the ith step, the first $i - 1$ elements are the initial part of the final result; the remaining elements are still unsorted. This partition of l into two parts is shown here:

$$\underbrace{e_1 \ldots e_{i-1}}_{\text{final}} \underbrace{e_i \ldots e_n}_{\text{unsorted}} \tag{6.2--1}$$

These considerations lead to the following loop invariant:

Elements $e_1 \ldots e_{i-1}$ are the initial segment of the sorted version of l.

In the beginning, we set $i = 1$ to satisfy the loop invariant trivially. If elements $e_1 \ldots e_{i-1}$ are the initial segment of the sorted version of l, they must be smaller than the remaining elements $e_i \ldots e_n$. We locate the smallest among these elements. It belongs in position i in the sorted list because it is larger than elements $e_1 \ldots e_{i-1}$ but smaller than the remaining elements. An exchange puts it into position i. This operation establishes the loop invariant for $i + 1$. Finally, we reach $i = n$, and the whole list is sorted. (Strictly speaking, only elements $e_1 \ldots e_{n-1}$ are sorted, but this is sufficient!)

The smallest element among $e_i \ldots e_n$ is found in an inner loop by *sequential search*. Sequential search is performed by looking at the elements in turn and recording the smallest one found so far, as well as its index. Program Selection.m is shown in Listing 6.2--2.

The number of comparisons $C_s(n)$ is approximately equal to $n^2/2$, because we perform one comparison in the body of the inner loop. The number of iterations of the inner loop is $n - (i + 1) + 1 = n - i$. In the outer loop, i varies from 1 to $n - 1$. Together, we get

$$C_s(n) = \sum_{i=1}^{n-1}(n - i) = \sum_{i=1}^{n-1} i = \frac{1}{2}n(n - 1) \approx \frac{n^2}{2}. \tag{6.2--2}$$

The number of exchanges $E_s(n)$ is $n - 1 \approx n$, because we perform one exchange in the outer loop. Note that these numbers do not depend on the input.

```
Needs["CSM`SortAux`"]

SelectionSort::usage = "SelectionSort[l] sorts the list l."

SelectionSort[list_List] :=
    Module[{l = list, i, n = Length[list]}, min, minj, j},
        Do[
            min = l[[i]]; minj = i;
            Do[ If[l[[j]] < min, min = l[[j]]; minj = j], {j, i+1, n} ];
            swap[l, i, minj],
            {i, 1, n-1}];
        l
    ]
```

Listing 6.2–2 Selection.m: Selection sort.

6.2.2 Insertion Sort

Insertion sort works by maintaining a sorted list of elements of l. Elements of l are taken one by one and inserted into this list in their proper place. This sorted list is kept at the beginning of l. Before the ith step, the first i elements are sorted; the remaining elements are still unsorted. This arrangement is similar to selection sort (see Section 6.2.1), but here we do not require this sorted part to be the beginning of the final result; we require only that it be sorted. The partition of l into two parts is shown here:

$$\underbrace{e_1 \ldots e_i}_{\text{sorted}} \underbrace{e_{i+1} \ldots e_n}_{\text{unsorted}} \tag{6.2–3}$$

The loop invariant is the following:

Elements $e_1 \ldots e_i$ are sorted.

In the beginning, we set $i = 1$ to satisfy the loop invariant trivially. We look at element e_{i+1} and put it at its proper place among $e_1 \ldots e_{i+1}$. We do this by first comparing e_{i+1} with e_i. If $e_{i+1} \geq e_i$, element e_{i+1} is already in the right place (e_i is the largest element among $e_1 \ldots e_i$ because these elements are sorted). If $e_{i+1} < e_i$, we exchange elements e_i and e_{i+1} and continue comparing e_{i-1} and e_i. Eventually, the two elements compared are in their proper order, or we reach $i = 1$. When this happens, the elements $e_1 \ldots e_{i+1}$ are sorted, and we have established the loop invariant for $i + 1$. As soon as we reach $i = n$, the whole list is sorted. Listing 6.2–3 shows the program.

The number of comparisons and exchanges are of the same order because each comparison is immediately followed by an exchange, except possibly the last one in the inner loop. How often the inner loop is traversed depends on the input list l. On average, we can expect the

```
Needs["CSM`SortAux`"]

InsertionSort::usage = "InsertionSort[l] sorts the list l."

InsertionSort[list_List] :=
    Module[{l = list, i, n = Length[list], j},
        Do[
            j = i-1;
            While[ j >= 1 && l[[j]] > l[[j+1]], swap[l, j, j+1]; j-- ],
            {i, 2, n}];
        l
    ]
```

Listing 6.2–3   Insertion.m: Insertion sort.

inner loop to be traversed about $(i - 1)/2$ times. This consideration leads to

$$V_i(n) \approx A_i(n) = \sum_{i=2}^{n} \frac{i - 1}{2} = \frac{1}{2} \sum_{j=1}^{n-1} j = \frac{1}{4}n(n - 1) \approx \frac{n^2}{4}. \tag{6.2–4}$$

In the worst case (for which inputs does it happen?), the algorithm takes twice this number of steps. If the input is already sorted, there will be only n comparisons and no exchanges. This number is optimal because we have to perform at least that many comparisons just to find out whether the input is sorted.

6.2.3 Quicksort

Quicksort (Listing 6.2–4) is the most often used algorithm because it performs better on average than the algorithms we have looked at so far. Its implementation is more complicated than that of insertion sort or selection sort. The idea is to partition the input list into two parts (using exchanges), so that all elements in the first part are smaller than the elements in the second part. We do not require the two parts to be sorted. The key observation is that the two parts can now be sorted *independently.* We do this sorting by two recursive calls to quicksort. In these recursive calls, we have to specify which part of the original list is to be sorted. Therefore, we define an auxiliary function QSort[l, n_0, n_1] that sorts only the range $e_{n_0} \ldots e_{n_1}$ of l. To sort the whole list, we simply call this auxiliary function with bounds $n_0 = 1$ and $n_1 = n$: QSort[l, 1, n].

The recursion ends as soon as $n_0 \geq n_1$. This case is treated with a separate definition for QSort[]. For the following analysis of the algorithm, we can assume $1 \leq n_0 < n_1 \leq n$. The partition is obtained by maintaining two indices, i and j. Here is our loop invariant:

> Elements $e_{n_0} \ldots e_{i-1}$ are smaller or equal to e,
> Elements $e_{j+1} \ldots e_{n_1}$ are larger or equal to e,

where e is an arbitrary element among $e_{n_0} \ldots e_{n_1}$. The invariant is satisfied trivially with $i = n_0, j = n_1$. We try to increase i and decrease j, and maintain the invariant. In general, our list is divided into three parts:

$$\underbrace{e_{n_0} \dots e_{i-1}}_{\leq e} \underbrace{e_i \dots e_j}_{?} \underbrace{e_{j+1} \dots e_{n_1}}_{\geq e} . \tag{6.2-5}$$

Our goal is to reach either $i = j + 1$, or $i = j$ and $e_i = e$. If one of these two cases is satisfied, we have obtained the partitioning of the list into two parts that can be sorted independently.

$$
\begin{aligned}
i = j : \quad & \underbrace{e_{n_0} \dots e_{i-1}}_{\leq e} e \underbrace{e_{j+1} \dots e_{n_1}}_{\geq e}, \\
i = j + 1 : \quad & \underbrace{e_{n_0} \dots e_{i-1}}_{\leq e} \underbrace{e_{j+1} \dots e_{n_1}}_{\geq e} .
\end{aligned}
\tag{6.2-6}
$$

Increasing i and decreasing j is done as follows: While $e_i < e$ holds, we can increment i; while $e_j > e$ holds, we can decrement j. This operation is done in the two inner `While` loops. Because e occurs among $e_{n_0} \dots e_{n_1}$, there is an $i \leq n_1$ with $e_i \geq e$, and there is a $j \geq n_0$ with $e_j \leq e$. The loops will therefore terminate with valid values of i and j. After the two loops, one of the following three cases is true:

- If $i < j$, we can exchange e_i and e_j, and then increment i and decrement j. This operation keeps the invariant valid and we can continue with the outer loop.

- If $i = j$, we have $e_i = e = e_j$, and all elements $e_{n_0} \dots e_{i-1}$ are $\leq e$, and all elements $e_{j+1} \dots e_{n_0}$ are $\geq e$. We can terminate the loop because the partitioning has been obtained.

```
Needs["CSM`SortAux`"]

QuickSort::usage = "QuickSort[list] sorts the list."

QuickSort[list_] := Module[ {l = list}, QSort[l, 1, Length[l]]; l ]

SetAttributes[QSort, HoldFirst]

QSort[l_, n0_, n1_]/; n0 >= n1 := l   (* nothing to do *)

QSort[l_, n0_, n1_] :=
    Module[{lm = l[[ Floor[(n0 + n1)/2] ]], i = n0, j = n1},
        While[ True,
            While[ l[[i]] < lm, i++ ];
            While[ l[[j]] > lm, j-- ];
            If[ i >= j, Break[] ];     (* l is partitioned *)
            swap[l, i, j];
            i++; j--
        ];
        QSort[ l, n0, i-1 ]; (* recursion *)
        QSort[ l, j+1, n1 ]  (* recursion *)
    ]
```

Listing 6.2–4 QSort.m: Quicksort.

▪ If $i > j$, the partitioning has been obtained as well. This case can happen only after at least one exchange has taken place. Therefore, we are sure that $i \leq n_1$ and that $j \geq n_0$ (furthermore, $i = j + 1$).

After termination of the loop, the list has been partitioned into the parts $e_{n_0} \ldots e_{i-1}$ and $e_{j+1} \ldots e_{n_1}$. Both of them are shorter than the input list $e_{n_0} \ldots e_{n_1}$ and can now be sorted by a recursive call of QSort[]. The whole list is sorted with a call of QSort[] with $n_0 = 1, n_1 = n$.

We still must determine the element e used for partitioning. The algorithm runs best if e is chosen from the middle of the *sorted* list. Both partitions are then of half the original length. Because we do not yet know which element will lie in the middle of the sorted list, we have to use some other means of selecting e. In our program, we simply choose an element from the middle of the unsorted input.

The number of comparisons in the main loop is equal to n because we compare each element of the list once with e. This comparison happens in the two inner loops. In the best case, i and j will meet in the middle, and we obtain the following equation for the number of comparisons $C_q(n)$:

$$C_q(n) = n + 2C_q\left(\frac{n}{2}\right). \tag{6.2-7}$$

The second term on the right is the contribution of the two recursive calls of half the original length. This recursive equation can be solved exactly (see Section 7.1.2). The solution is

$$C_q(n) \approx n \lg n. \tag{6.2-8}$$

($\lg n$ is the logarithm to base 2.) A deeper analysis for the *average* case shows that we need approximately

$$C_q(n) \approx 2n \log n \approx 1.38 n \lg n \tag{6.2-9}$$

comparisons. The function $n \lg n$ grows slower than n^2. This property is the reason that quicksort is preferred to insertion or selection sort for most applications.

In the worst case, quicksort is much slower than in the average case. If we happen to choose the element e that is always equal to the smallest of the remaining elements, we always get $i = n_0, j = n_0$. The first of the two recursive calls is then trivial, but the second one is shorter by only one element. The depth of the recursion is equal to n, and we need $n^2/2$ comparisons (and a lot of computer memory).

6.2.4   Observation of Quicksort

The following pictures show the state of the list to be sorted after the two inner loops (see Listing 6.2–4), that is, at the place where the invariant is violated. Elements e_i and e_j are shown by gray squares. These are the elements that are then exchanged. After reaching $i > j$, the place of partitioning is shown by a vertical bar. The special case where the partitioning happens with $i = j$ is shown by a frame around the square i. The pictures for the two recursive calls follow.

This version of the package draws the pictures.

```
In[1]:= << CSM`QSortG`
```

After one exchange, we get a left part of length four and a right part of length two. In the left part, the element $e_2 = 1$ is selected, which leads to a bad partitioning; only one element is removed. The right part is sorted with a single exchange.

```
In[2]:= QuickSort[{2, 1, 5, 3, 6, 4}];
```

2	1	5	3	6	4
2	1	4	3	6	5
2	1	4	3
1	2	4	3
	2	4	3
	2	3	4
	2	3
			6	5
			5	6

This picture shows how quicksort behaves if the input is sorted in reverse.

```
In[3]:= QuickSort[{8, 7, 6, 5, 4, 3, 2, 1}];
```

8	7	6	5	4	3	2	1
1	7	6	5	4	3	2	8
1	2	6	5	4	3	7	8
1	2	3	5	4	6	7	8
1	2	3	4	5	6	7	8
1	2	3	4
	3	4
			5	6	7	8
				7	8

Here is an example for the worst case. Only a single element is removed in every partitioning.

Try to find an example of this behavior for each length n.

```
In[4]:= QuickSort[{2, 4, 6, 7, 1, 5, 3}];
```

2	4	6	7	1	5	3
2	4	6	3	1	5	7
2	4	6	3	1	5
2	4	5	3	1	6
2	4	5	3	1
2	4	1	3	5
2	4	1	3
2	3	1	4
2	3	1
2	1	3
2	1
1	2

6.2.5 Key Concepts

1. A list of records can be sorted by a sequence of exchanges.

2. The simplest sorting methods are selection sort and insertion sort.

3. Quicksort works recursively and has a better average running time than other sorting methods.

6.3 Binary Trees

A *dynamic data structure* is a means to maintain a collection of data elements (records). It allows insertion and deletion of records and provides a function for locating records by a key field (retrieval if records). The phone directory from Section 6.1.3 was an example. There are many implementations of dynamic data structures. The choice of an implementation depends on many aspects. Some data structures allow fast insertion or retrieval of data, but are slow for deletion of records. Often, data structures maintain their contents at least partially ordered. This ordering speeds up retrieval operations, as we have seen in Section 6.1. The study of dynamic data structures is one of the most important fields of computer science. Here are some of the aspects to consider when choosing a data structure for an application:

- The expected relative frequency of the various operations such as insertion, retrieval, and deletion

- The maximal number of records needed (if known)

- Whether several records with identical keys should be allowed

A simple dynamic data structure is the *binary tree*. Binary trees are easy to implement. Insertion of records is fast, and retrieval is also fast (it is similar to binary search). The total number of records in a binary tree is not limited. Deletion of records is a bit more complicated, however.

In computer science, trees are drawn with the root pointing upward. There are at most two branches at each node. The numbers are stored in the nodes. A binary tree is ordered: The numbers in the left subtree are smaller than the number in the node itself; the numbers in the right subtree are larger. This condition holds for every node.

```
In[1]:= plotTree[ Tree[{3, 7, 5, 4, 8, 6, 2}] ];
```

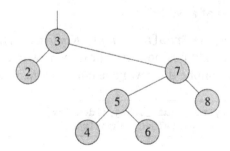

A node of a binary tree consists of a *data*, or *information*, field, and a left and right *subtree*. The information field is used to store the records contained in the tree. Binary trees are ordered. The keys of the information fields in the left subtree are smaller than the key in the node; the keys in the right subtree are larger. If a tree is balanced, it can be searched in logarithmic time because each subtree has only half the size of the whole tree. We assume that key values are unique. An abstract data type for trees is the following:

Constants	`emptyTree`	an empty tree
Constructors	`node[`*info*`,` *left*`,` *right*`]`	a tree with this root
Selectors	`information[`*tree*`]`	the information at the root
	`leftTree[`*tree*`]`	the left subtree
	`rightTree[`*tree*`]`	the right subtree

Here is an implementation. A node is represented by `tree[`*info*`,` *left*`,` *right*`]`. This representation makes constructors and selectors quite simple. All code shown in this section is part of the package BinaryTree.m.

```
node[info_, left_, right_] := tree[info, left, right]

leftTree[tree[_, left_, _]] := left
rightTree[tree[_, _, right_]] := right
information[tree[info_, _, _]] := info
```

Key fields are compared with the built-in function `Order[`e_1`,` e_2`]`. We assume that we can extract the key from the information with the selector *Key*. A default value of `Identity` for this selector (see Section 4.3) causes the whole record to be treated as key. For simplicity, we will use numbers as our data. Such a default is therefore convenient.

A binary tree is either empty or consists of a left and right subtree. Most functions on binary trees can therefore be implemented with two definitions: one for the empty tree and a recursive one for the general case.

6.3.1 Insertion of a Node

The function `insertTree[`*tree*`,` *info*`,` *Key*`]` inserts the record *info* into the tree by creating a new node in the right position. It returns the new tree.

If the tree is empty, the new node comes at the root and its two subtrees are empty:

```
insertTree[emptyTree, info_, Key_:Identity] :=
      node[info, emptyTree, emptyTree]
```

If the key of the root is equal to the key of the new record, we do not insert it because keys are supposed to be unique. (We could perhaps generate an error message in this case.)

```
insertTree[tree_, info_, Key_:Identity] /;
   Order[Key[info], Key[information[tree]]] == 0 := tree
```

If the new key is smaller than the key at the root, the new node must go into the left subtree. It is inserted there recursively. Because the left subtree might change as a consequence of this insertion, we have to assemble it together with the old right subtree and the information at the root into a new tree.

```
insertTree[tree_, info_, Key_:Identity] /;
    Order[Key[info], Key[information[tree]]] > 0 :=
        node[ information[tree],
            insertTree[leftTree[tree], info, Key],
            rightTree[tree]
        ]
```

Otherwise, the new key is larger than the key at the root, and the new node must go into the right subtree. The roles of left and right are simply interchanged.

```
insertTree[tree_, info_, Key_:Identity] :=
        node[ information[tree],
            leftTree[tree],
            insertTree[rightTree[tree], info, Key]
        ]
```

Observe that the algorithm for insertion has been derived directly from the defining properties of a binary tree. A binary tree is ordered. By inserting a new node at the right place, this order is preserved. The rest is done by recursion. Nothing could be simpler!

This command inserts the number 5 into an empty tree. The whole record (a simple number in our case) is the key.

```
In[1]:= b = insertTree[emptyTree, 5]
Out[1]= tree[5, emptyTree, emptyTree]
```

The number 3 is inserted into the previous tree.

```
In[2]:= b = insertTree[b, 3]
Out[2]= tree[5, tree[3, emptyTree, emptyTree],
    emptyTree]
```

Now, we insert the number 7.

```
In[3]:= b = insertTree[b, 7]
Out[3]= tree[5, tree[3, emptyTree, emptyTree],
    tree[7, emptyTree, emptyTree]]
```

A diagram provides us with a better look at the tree than the nested expression does.

```
In[4]:= plotTree[b];
```

Note that we assigned the result of an insertion back to the variable holding the previous tree. This technique allows us to build a tree step by step. Here we insert the number 4 into the previous tree.

`In[5]:= plotTree[ b = insertTree[b, 4] ];`

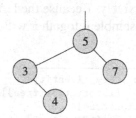

The following constructor is useful for inserting a list of records one by one into a tree:

```
Tree[l_List, Key_:Identity] :=
    Fold[ Function[{t, i}, insertTree[t, i, Key]], emptyTree, l ]
```

The function `insertTree[]` is applied to the result of the previous application and the next element from the list. This iteration is performed by `Fold[]`, see Section 2.3.9.

The tree obtained from a list depends on the order of the elements in the list. In the next two examples, we build two trees with the same elements, but inserted in different order.

This picture shows the tree obtained from inserting the numbers 5, 3, 7, 4, 2, 8, and 6 in this order.

`In[6]:= plotTree[ Tree[{5, 4, 7, 3, 2, 8, 6}] ];`

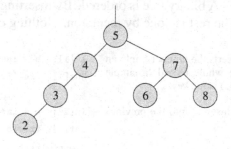

If we insert the same numbers in a different order, we get a different tree.

`In[7]:= plotTree[ Tree[{3, 7, 5, 4, 8, 6, 2}] ];`

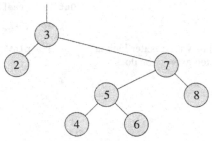

6.3.2 Retrieval of a Node

The function searchTree[*tree*, *key*, *Key*] returns the information of a node whose key is equal to *key* and where *Key* is the name of the selector for the key field. Its default is again the identity. We can proceed in the same way we did with insertion.

The method is similar to binary search. The key is compared with the key at the root of the tree. If it is identical, we have found the record. Otherwise, we search in the left or right half, depending on whether the key is smaller or larger than the key in the root. If we reach the empty tree, we know that the record is not in the tree, and we return Null to signal this fact.

```
searchTree[ emptyTree, key_, Key_:Identity ] := Null

searchTree[ tree_, key_, Key_:Identity ] /;
    Order[ Key[information[tree]], key ] == 0 :=
        information[ tree ]

searchTree[ tree_, key_, Key_:Identity ] /;
    Order[ Key[information[tree]], key ] < 0 :=
        searchTree[ leftTree[tree], key, Key ]

searchTree[ tree_, key_, Key_:Identity ] :=
        searchTree[ rightTree[tree], key, Key ]
```

6.3.3 Balanced Trees

The *depth* of a tree is the maximum number of nodes between the root and a leaf. A *leaf* is a node without any subtrees. The depth can be computed recursively:

```
depth[emptyTree] := 0
depth[tree_] := 1 + Max[ depth[leftTree[tree]], depth[rightTree[tree]] ]
```

Let us investigate trees obtained by inserting the numbers 1 to 7 in different orders.

This tree is perfectly balanced. All leaves are at the same level (the tree does not have any holes).

In[8]:= plotTree[b1 = Tree[{4, 2, 1, 3, 6, 5, 7}]];

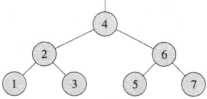

This tree degenerates into a linear list because each node has at most one nonempty
subtree.

`In[9]:= plotTree[ b2 = Tree[{1, 2, 3, 4, 5, 6, 7}] ];`

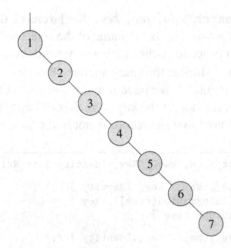

The second tree is far deeper than is the first
one.

`In[10]:= {depth[b1], depth[b2]}`

`Out[10]= {3, 7}`

The depth of a tree with n nodes is at least $\lg n$. This fact follows from the observation that a
tree with depth k can have at most $2^k - 1$ nodes because

$$\sum_{i=0}^{k-1} 2^i = 2^k - 1. \tag{6.3--1}$$

6.3.4 Advanced Topic: Deletion of Nodes

We said that deletions are not as simple as insertions. If the node to be deleted has at most one
subtree, deleting it is easy, however. The root of its single subtree can be put at its place.

This is again the tree from Section 6.3.1.

`In[1]:= plotTree[ b1 = Tree[{5, 4, 7, 3, 2, 8, 6}] ];`

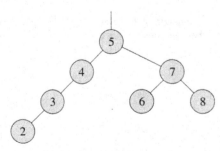

The node with information 4 can be deleted easily. Its successor 3 is put at its place.

`In[2]:= plotTree[ b2 = deleteTree[b1, 4] ];`

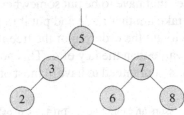

The node 6 has no successors and can simply be removed.

`In[3]:= plotTree[ b3 = deleteTree[b2, 6] ];`

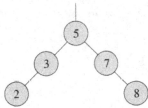

The following rules implement recursion. The place of deletion is found with a variant of the search from Section 6.3.2.

```
deleteTree[emptyTree, key_, Key_:Identity ] := emptyTree

deleteTree[ tree_, key_, Key_:Identity ] /;
    Order[ Key[information[tree]], key ] < 0 :=
        node[ information[tree],
              deleteTree[leftTree[tree], key, Key],
              rightTree[tree]
        ]

deleteTree[ tree_, key_, Key_:Identity ] /;
    Order[ Key[information[tree]], key ] > 0 :=
        node[ information[tree],
              leftTree[tree],
              deleteTree[rightTree[tree], key, Key]
        ]
```

Here are the rules for the cases where the deleted node has at most one subtree.

```
deleteTree[ tree_, key_, Key_:Identity ] /;
    leftTree[tree] == emptyTree := rightTree[tree]

deleteTree[ tree_, key_, Key_:Identity ] /;
    rightTree[tree] == emptyTree := leftTree[tree]
```

Now we treat the difficult case where the deleted node d has two subtrees. If d is removed, there are two subtrees that have to be put somewhere but only one place to put them – the place of d. The idea is to take another node and put it in place of d. We must be careful to choose a node that does not violate the ordering of the tree if it is moved. A candidate is the node with the next higher key value than the key of d. This node can be found as the smallest node in the right subtree of d. It is guaranteed to have at most one subtree itself, so we can easily remove it.

The node 5 has two successors an cannot be removed easily.

`In[4]:= plotTree[b1];`

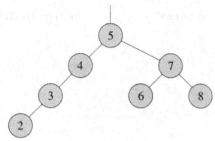

The next higher node 6 is put at its place. The left and right subtrees of 5 are made subtrees of 6. In the right subtree we have to remove the node 6, because it is now in another place in the tree.

`In[5]:= plotTree[ deleteTree[b1, 5] ];`

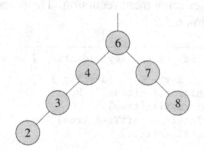

The auxiliary function `smallestNode[`*tree*`]` finds the node with the smallest key in *tree*. We simply descend along the left subtree. If the left subtree is empty the current node is the smallest one.

```
smallestNode[emptyTree] = Null
smallestNode[tree_] /; leftTree[tree] === emptyTree := information[tree]
smallestNode[tree_] := smallestNode[ leftTree[tree] ]
```

The new tree without d consists, therefore, of the information in the smallest node in the right subtree at the root, and of the former left and right subtrees – with the smallest node removed from the right subtree.

```
deleteTree[ tree_, key_, Key_:Identity ] :=
      With[{nextinfo = smallestNode[ rightTree[tree] ]},
          node[ nextinfo,
                leftTree[tree],
                deleteTree[rightTree[tree], Key[nextinfo], Key]
            ]
        ]
```

6.3.5 Key Concepts

1. Binary trees are the most important dynamic data structure.

2. Binary trees are ordered.

3. Different orders of insertion of the same set of nodes leads to different binary trees.

4. Binary trees can be searched in logarithmic time.

6.4   Exercises

6.1   Counting Prime Numbers

Write a function `primePi[x]` that finds the number $\pi(x)$ of primes $\leq x$ using binary search (see Section 6.1.1). (This function already exists in *Mathematica* under the name `PrimePi[]`.)
Hints:

- The function `Prime[n]` computes the nth prime number.

- x can be an arbitrary real number.

- An upper bound for `primePi[x]` for $x > 2$ is obtained by the logarithmic integral `LogIntegral[x]`.

- You can use bisection without first generating the list to be searched. Generate only the primes that are actually needed.

Examples:

Because `Prime` is quite fast, large arguments of `PrimePi[]` are no problem.

```
In[1]:= {PrimePi[-2], PrimePi[1.5], PrimePi[2],
          PrimePi[10], PrimePi[10^8]}
Out[1]= {0, 0, 1, 4, 5761455}
```

The function is defined for all real numbers and can, therefore, be plotted.

```
In[2]:= Plot[ PrimePi[x], {x, 1, 20} ];
```

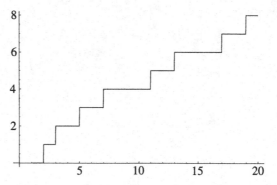

6.2   Binary Trees

Binary trees can be used to implement a sorting method.

1. Extend the package BinaryTree.m from Section 6.3 by a function `InOrder[tree]`. The function should return all records of the tree in a list in the following order: first, the

elements of the left subtree (recursively); then, the element at the root; finally, the elements of the right subtree. Because of the ordering of the binary tree, the resulting list will be sorted.

2. Use `InOrder[`*tree*`]` to implement a sorting function `TreeSort[`*list*`]` that sorts the list by first inserting all its elements into a binary tree and then converting the tree back into a list.

6.3 Merging Lists[1]

Write a function `Merge[`l_1`, `l_2`]` that merges the elements of the two lists l_1 and l_2 into a single list. The elements of l_1 and l_2 are assumed to be numbers sorted in ascending order (you do not have to check this property). The result should also be sorted in ascending order. The result should be obtained without sorting the list anew.

Write a single procedural definition that works on the input lists in a loop. You can use any list operations, such as `First[`*l*`]`, `Rest[`*l*`]`, `Prepend[`*l*`, `*elem*`]`, `Append[`*l*`, `*elem*`]`, or `Join[`l_1`, `l_2`]`. Use `Module[]` to declare local variables.

The result contains all elements of the two input lists in ascending order.

```
In[1]:= Merge[{1, 5, 7}, {2, 3, 8}]
Out[1]= {1, 2, 3, 5, 7, 8}
```

Your function should also treat such special inputs correctly.

```
In[2]:= Merge[{}, {2, 3}]
Out[2]= {2, 3}
```

If an element appears more than once, it must appear in the result the same number of times.

```
In[3]:= Merge[{1, 1, 2, 3}, {2, 3}]
Out[3]= {1, 1, 2, 2, 3, 3}
```

6.4 Observation of a Sorting Algorithm

We restrict the inputs of our sorting functions to permutations of the numbers $1 \ldots n$. A simple way to visualize the amount of "sortedness" in such a list of numbers is a picture obtained with `ListPlot`.

This definition is used to plot permutations of the numbers $1 \ldots n$ with suitable settings of graphics options.

```
In[1]:= PermutationPlot[l_List, opts___] :=
            ListPlot[ l,
                PlotRange -> { {0.5, Length[l]+0.5},
                               {0.5, Length[l]+0.5} },
                PlotStyle->PointSize[0.75/Length[l]],
                opts, Axes->None, FrameTicks->None,
                Frame->True, AspectRatio->1 ]
```

Here is a random permutation.

```
In[2]:= p1 = PermutationPlot[
            {9, 10, 6, 8, 2, 4, 12, 1, 7, 5, 3, 11},
            DisplayFunction->Identity ];
```

---

[1]Written examination, ETH Zürich, Department of Mathematics and Physics.

Here is the list after the first phase of QuickSort (Section 6.2.3).

```
In[3]:= p2 = PermutationPlot[
           {3, 1, 4, 2, 8, 6, 12, 10, 7, 5, 9, 11},
           DisplayFunction->Identity ];
```

Now, the list is sorted.

```
In[4]:= p3 = PermutationPlot[
           {1, 2, 3, 4, 5, 6, 7, 8, 9, 10, 11, 12},
           DisplayFunction->Identity ];
```

Here, finally, are the three pictures.

```
In[5]:= Show[GraphicsArray[{p1, p2, p3}]];
```

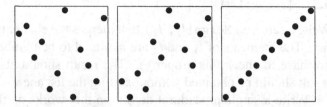

Write a program that allows you to draw such pictures after each exchange step in the sorting procedures (insertion sort, selection sort, and quicksort). If you wish, you can animate these sequences of pictures to see how the algorithm runs.

Hint: You do not have to change anything in the sorting procedures themselves. A special version of SortAux.m (see Listing 6.2–1) is all you need.

6.5 Abstract Sorting Algorithm

Develop an abstract version of quicksort (see Section 6.2.3). As in the abstract searching procedure from Section 6.1.3, you should assume that arbitrary records are to be sorted. The records have a key field that is used for comparisons.

Chapter 7

Complexity of Algorithms

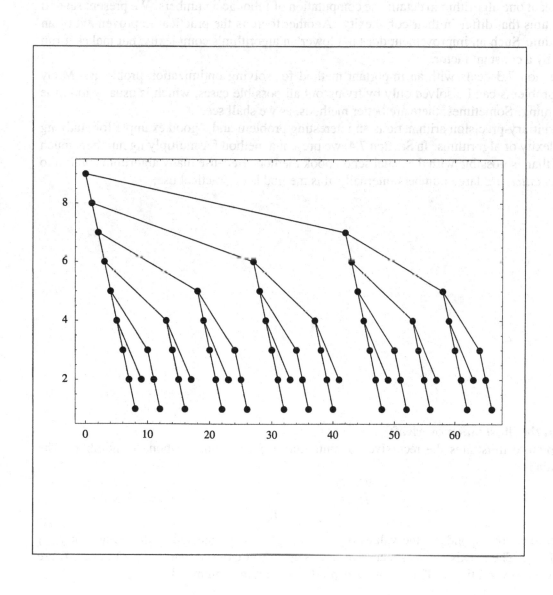

In this chapter we study complexity of algorithms. Complexity theory studies the amount of computations necessary for solving a certain problem. One important question in complexity is how the number of computation steps grows with the size of the input, disregarding machine-specific details. The main results concern the asymptotic behavior of an algorithm – that is, the number of steps for arbitrarily large inputs.

Section 7.1 discusses the main complexity classes for algorithms. Then, in Section 7.2, we look at one algorithm in detail: the computation of Fibonacci numbers. We present several algorithms that differ in their complexity. Another topic is the practical improvement of an algorithm. Such an improvement does not lower an algorithm's complexity, but makes it run faster by a constant factor.

Section 7.3 deals with an important method for solving optimization problems. Many such problems can be solved only by trying out all possible cases, which is usually too time consuming. Sometimes, there are better methods, as we shall see.

Arbitrary-precision arithmetic is an interesting problem and a good example for studying complexity of algorithms. In Section 7.4, we present a method for multiplying numbers much faster than is possible with the usual schoolbook method. Because many algorithms built into *Mathematica* use large numbers internally, this method is of practical use.

About the illustration overleaf:
The picture illustrates the recursive computation of f_9, the ninth Fibonacci number. The formula is

$$
\begin{aligned}
f_1 &= 1, \\
f_2 &= 1, \\
f_n &= f_{n-1} + f_{n-2}.
\end{aligned}
$$

The y-axis corresponds to the values of n. Each point is connected to the points for f_{n-1} and f_{n-2}. The x-axis shows successive time steps. You can see that many values of f_i are computed several times. The picture was produced with the command

```
FibonacciPlot[9] .
```

7.1   Complexity of Computations

The *complexity* $R(n)$ of an algorithm is the number of computation steps necessary to solve a problem of input size n. An algorithm is of *order* not larger than $g(n)$, if there is a constant c such that

$$R(n) < cg(n), \qquad \forall n . \tag{7.1-1}$$

We write $R(n) = O(g(n))$. This definition means that $R(n)$ does not grow essentially faster than $g(n)$. Of course, we are interested in small functions g.

The binary searching method in Section 6.1 needs at most $\log_2(n)$ steps to search n records. It is of complexity $O(\log n)$. (Logarithms of different bases differ only by a constant; therefore, we can use the natural logarithm.) Observe that we treat several elementary computation steps as a single *step,* for example, the whole body of the `While` loop in program `BinarySearch`. This simplification is possible if the computations inside the loop take a constant number of more elementary steps, independent of input size. Also, we assume that we can access an element in a list of records in constant time. This kind of idealizations is typical for complexity considerations. All these simplifications affect only the constant c in Equation 7.1–1.

7.1.1   Input Size

The definition of *input size* depends on the kind of problem we are analyzing. For the sorting and searching algorithms presented in Chapter 6, the input size is the number of data elements to sort or to search through.

If we perform calculations with big numbers, the measure of input size is the *length* of the number. The *length* of a number m is the number of digits we need to write down the number; it is equal to $\log_b(m)$, where b is the base of the positional number system used to represent m (our ordinary decimal system uses base 10, the base of the binary system is 2). The base does not matter for complexity; it is customary to use the natural logarithm $\log m$.

7.1.2   Complexity Classes

The functions g used to measure the complexity of computations can be divided into different *complexity classes.* An algorithm of order $O(\log n)$ has *logarithmic complexity.* Searching algorithms are often in this class. Logarithmic algorithms are very efficient: If the input size doubles, we need only *one* additional computation step.

An algorithm of order $O(n)$ is *linear.* For many problems, this complexity is the best possible because we have to look at the whole input at least once, which takes already $O(n)$ steps. Searching in an unordered collection of data is an example of a linear algorithm. Addition of two numbers of length n is another example.

The phone directory of New York City has
about 685, 750 entries for residents.

```
In[1]:= entries = 685750;
```

Searching for an entry by name has logarithmic complexity; it takes only this many
steps (see Section 6.1.1).

```
In[2]:= Ceiling[ Log[2, entries] ]
Out[2]= 20
```

A sequential search for a phone number, for
example, is a linear algorithm; it would take
on average this many steps.

```
In[3]:= entries/2
Out[3]= 342875
```

Another important complexity class are algorithms of order $O(n \log n)$. Many sorting problems
are of this kind. Let us consider quicksort from Section 6.2.3. In the first phase, we look at
each element once, which takes n steps. Then, the problem is subdivided into two problems of
half size. From these considerations we can establish the following equation for the number
of steps $R(n)$:

$$R(n) = n + 2R(n/2), \tag{7.1–2}$$

as well as the boundary condition $R(1) = 0$. This recursive equation has the following solution:

$$R(n) = n \lg n \tag{7.1–3}$$

($\lg n$ is the logarithm with base 2, $\log_2 n$). This result can easily be proved by induction. The
equation is exact only for input sizes of the form $n = 2^k$ (that is, powers of two). For such
input sizes, the induction proof is sketched here:

$$
\begin{aligned}
R(n) &= n + 2R(n/2) \\
     &= n + 2(\tfrac{n}{2} \lg(\tfrac{n}{2})) \\
     &= n + n \lg(\tfrac{n}{2})) \\
     &= n + n(\lg n - \lg 2) \\
     &= n + n(\lg n - 1) \\
     &= n \lg n.
\end{aligned}
\tag{7.1–4}
$$

If $g(n)$ is a polynomial in n, the algorithm has *polynomial complexity*. Many important
algorithms are in the range $O(n^2)$ to $O(n^3)$. For larger exponents, polynomial algorithms
usually become impractical.

If $g(n)$ is an exponential function of n, we say that the algorithm has *exponential complexity*.
Most of these algorithms are not practical. We can reverse the statement about logarithmic
problems for exponential ones: If the speed of our computer is doubled, we can solve only a
problem that is larger by one. Even a base b of the exponential function that is near 1 leads to
an asymptotic growth far larger than that of any polynomial. If we compare $p(n) = n^{100}$ with
$e(n) = 1.01^n$, for example, the polynomial $p(n)$ grows much faster at first, but at $n \approx 117, 308$,
the exponential takes over.

Here is a diagram of the ratio of the *logarithm* of the two functions for $n = 10 \ldots 10^{5.5}$, that is, of

$$\frac{\log(1.01^{10^m})}{\log(10^{m^{100}})} = \frac{10^m \log 1.01}{100m \log 10},$$

for $m = 1 \ldots 5.5$. The exponential grows faster than the polynomial. The point where the ratio becomes 1 is where the two functions are equal.

```
In[4]:= Plot[ 10^m Log[1.01] / (100 m Log[10.]),
             {m, 1, 5.5}, PlotRange->All,
             Frame->True, GridLines->Automatic ];
```

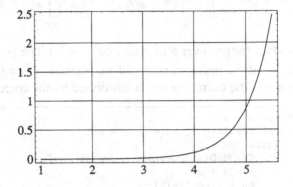

The solution of this numerical equation is the point where numerator and denominator are equal, that is, where $p(10^m) = e(10^m)$.

```
In[5]:= FindRoot[ 10^m Log[1.01] == 100m Log[10.0],
             {m, 5.1} ]

Out[5]= {m -> 5.06933}
```

Here is the corresponding value of $n = 10^m$.

```
In[6]:= 10^m /. %

Out[6]= 117308.
```

The point $n = 10^m$, where the two functions $p(n)$ and $e(n)$ are equal, corresponds to a number of computation steps equal to $p(n) = e(n) = 10^{507}$. This number of steps is far beyond the practical range. The conclusion is that in this example the exponential function is smaller in the whole range where we could actually perform such a computation, even though it grows much faster asymptotically. We can see that asymptotic complexity considerations are not the only important aspect of an algorithm.

7.1.3   Example: Fast Integer Powers

Often, computations can be rearranged for an impressive run-time improvement. Let us look at the computation of integer powers.

The straightforward method to compute m^n, where n is a nonnegative integer, starts with an intermediate result of 1, and multiplies it successively by m, a total of n times. This method takes n steps. There is a much faster method that takes only $\lg n$ steps. To see how it works, we write the exponent n in the binary number system as

$$n = \sum_{i=0}^{k-1} n_i 2^i, \qquad (7.1\text{--}5)$$

where the n_i are the binary digits, or *bits* (all either 0 or 1), and k is the number of binary digits of n. Now, we can express m^n as

$$m^n = m^{\sum_{i=0}^{k-1} n_i 2^i} = \prod_{i=0}^{k-1} m^{n_i 2^i} = \prod_{i:n_i=1} m^{2^i}. \qquad (7.1\text{–}6)$$

(The product ranges over all i such that $n_i = 1$.) The powers m^{2^i} can be found by successive squaring of of the previous power of m, because $m^{2^i} = (m^{2^{i-1}})^2$, and $m^{2^0} = m$. For each 1 in the exponent, the current result is multiplied by the corresponding power of m.

```
BinaryPower[m_, n_] :=
    Module[{result = 1, nn = n, s = m},
        While[ nn > 1,
            If[OddQ[nn], result = result * s];
            s = s * s;
            nn = Floor[nn/2];
        ];
        result * s
    ]
```

Listing 7.1–1   Fast computation of powers.

The binary digits of n can be found iteratively. First we determine n_0, the last bit of the number n. It is equal to 1 for *odd* numbers and equal to 0 for *even* numbers. Afterward, we divide n by 2, discarding any remainder. This operation brings the second-to-last bit n_1 into last position. In this way, the method can be continued. If $n = \sum_{i=0}^{k-1} n_i 2^i$, we get $\lfloor n/2 \rfloor = \sum_{i=1}^{k-1} n_i 2^{i-1} = \sum_{i=0}^{k-2} n_{i+1} 2^i$. ($\lfloor n/2 \rfloor$ is the result of the division without remainder of n by 2.) Observe that we run the loop only to $nn = 1$, and that we perform the last multiplication `result * s` outside the loop. This method avoids squaring s once more. The new value of s would not be used anymore. This last squaring would take about half of the *total* run time of the algorithm.

7.1.4 Key Concepts

1. Algorithmic complexity describes the relation between input size and the number of computation steps.

2. A complexity class is a set of problems with the same asymptotic behavior.

3. Logarithmic complexity is typical for searching in ordered data.

4. Linear complexity is the best possible if the whole input needs to be examined.

5. Exponential complexity is almost always impractical.

6. An nth power can be computed in $\log n$ steps.

7.2   Example: Computing the nth Fibonacci Number

We use the computation of the nth Fibonacci number as an example to compare the complexity of different algorithms. We shall see algorithms of different asymptotic complexity, as well as algorithms of different run time (but equal complexity). We shall see that Fibonacci numbers grow exponentially. As a consequence, the computing time for ordinary arithmetic influences the complexity. We can no longer treat an arithmetic calculation as a single step in the computation.

Fibonacci numbers f_n are defined by this second-order recurrence:

$$
\begin{aligned}
f_1 &= 1, \\
f_2 &= 1, \\
f_n &= f_{n-1} + f_{n-2}.
\end{aligned}
\tag{7.2--1}
$$

All methods for the computation of Fibonacci numbers in this section are in the package Fib.m.

7.2.1   A Recursive Algorithm

As usual, Equation 7.2–1 can be programmed directly. This translation leads to a recursive computation, shown in Listing 7.2–1.

```
fiba[1] = fiba[2] = 1;
fiba[n_] := fiba[n-1] + fiba[n-2]
```

Listing 7.2–1   Recursive computation of Fibonacci numbers.

Here are the first 10 Fibonacci numbers.
```
In[1]:= Table[ fiba[i], {i, 1, 10} ]
Out[1]= {1, 1, 2, 3, 5, 8, 13, 21, 34, 55}
```

A measure of the complexity of this method is the number $t(n)$ of recursive calls of fiba necessary for the computation of fiba[n]. fiba[1] and fiba[2] need one call each. For larger n, the number of calls is equal to the number of calls for $n - 1$ and $n - 2$. This observation leads to the following equation for $t(n)$:

$$
\begin{aligned}
t(1) &= 1, \\
t(2) &= 1, \\
t(n) &= t(n - 1) + t(n - 2).
\end{aligned}
\tag{7.2--2}
$$

This equation is the same as Equation 7.2–1 for $f(n)$ itself. Therefore, $t(n) = f_n$. We shall see that f_n grows exponentially in n. This algorithm is therefore inefficient: it has exponential complexity. An improvement by *dynamic programming* is treated in Section 7.3.1.

Here is a table of the computation times for f_i, for $i = 10, \ldots, 25$. The times grow rapidly. Observe that each time is approximately equal to the sum of the preceding two times.

```
In[2]:= Table[ First[Timing[ fiba[i] ]],
             {i, 10, 25} ] /. Second->1

Out[2]= {0., 0.01, 0.01, 0.02, 0.03, 0.05, 0.08, 0.12,
         0.21, 0.33, 0.54, 0.87, 1.41, 2.29, 3.71, 6.}
```

7.2.2 A Loop

The Fibonacci recursion can be turned into iteration (see Section 3.3.3). The computation of each Fibonacci number requires only the two previous values. Therefore, we need two local variables for these two values, as shown in Listing 7.2–2.

```
fibc[n_] :=
    Module[{fi = 1, fi1 = 0},
        Do[ {fi, fi1} = {fi + fi1, fi}, {n - 1} ];
        fi
    ]
```

Listing 7.2–2   A loop for the nth Fibonacci number.

Starting with $i = 1$, the value of `fi` is f_i, and the value of `fi1` is f_{i-1}. This fact is the loop invariant. The sum of f_i and f_{i-1} is f_{i+1}. Therefore, we must set `fi` to `fi + fi1`, and `fi1` to `fi` (simultaneously), to fulfill the invariant for $i + 1$. After $n - 1$ iterations, the value of `fi` is f_n, as desired.

What is the complexity of this loop? The length of the ith Fibonacci number is proportional to i, as we shall see. In the ith iteration, we therefore add two numbers of length i. This addition takes i steps. The total number of steps is the sum over all iterations:

$$\sum_{i=1}^{n-1} i = \frac{n(n-1)}{2} \approx n^2. \tag{7.2-3}$$

This algorithm has quadratic complexity. It is quite fast for small n, but there are better algorithms for larger n, as we shall see soon.

Here is a table of computation times for f_i, $i = 10,000, 20,000, \ldots, 100,000$. This method allows much larger values than the recursive one does.

```
In[3]:= Table[ First[Timing[ fibc[10000 i] ]],
             {i, 1, 10} ] /. Second->1

Out[3]= {0.64, 1.55, 2.67, 4.15, 6.08, 7.96, 10.32,
         12.93, 15.64, 18.35}
```

A least-squares fit of the measured times to a quadratic functions shows the linear and quadratic terms.

```
In[4]:= Fit[ %, {1, i, i^2}, i ]

Out[4]= -0.198833 + 0.616992 i + 0.125568 i
                                            2
```

7.2.3 A Formula for f_n

To be faster than the simple loop in Section 7.2.2, we must find a method to compute f_n without computing all previous f_i. Indeed, there is a closed formula for Fibonacci numbers. The equation $f_n = f_{n-1} + f_{n-2}$, or $f_n - f_{n-1} - f_{n-2} = 0$, is an example of a *second-order recurrence*. The general form of such an iteration is $f_n + bf_{n-1} + cf_{n-2} = 0$. Its solutions are of the form

$$f_n = a_1 e_1^n + a_2 e_2^n, \tag{7.2-4}$$

where e_1 and e_2 are the two solutions of the *characteristic equation*

$$x^2 + bx + c = 0. \tag{7.2-5}$$

For Fibonacci numbers, we have $b = -1$ and $c = -1$. We can use *Mathematica* to help us solve the characteristic equation for e_1 and e_2 and find the coefficients a_1 and a_2.

Here are the two solutions of the characteristic equation for Fibonacci numbers.

```
In[1]:= Solve[ x^2 - x - 1 == 0, x ]
Out[1]= {{x -> (1 - Sqrt[5])/2}, {x -> (1 + Sqrt[5])/2}}
```

We assign them to the two variables e1 and e2.

```
In[2]:= {e1, e2} = x /. %
Out[2]= {(1 - Sqrt[5])/2, (1 + Sqrt[5])/2}
```

The two constants a_1 and a_2 can be determined from the initial conditions $f_1 = 1$ and $f_2 = 1$:

$$\begin{aligned} f_1 &= a_1 e_1 + a_2 e_2 = 1, \\ f_2 &= a_1 e_1^2 + a_2 e_2^2 = 1. \end{aligned} \tag{7.2-6}$$

Here is Equation 7.2–6 in *Mathematica*. There is a unique solution.

```
In[3]:= Solve[ {a1 e1 + a2 e2 == 1,
                a1 e1^2 + a2 e2^2 == 1},
               {a1, a2} ] // FullSimplify
Out[3]= {{a1 -> -(1/Sqrt[5]), a2 -> 1/Sqrt[5]}}
```

We assign the solution to the two variables a1 and a2.

```
In[4]:= {a1, a2} = {a1, a2} /. %[[1]]
Out[4]= {-(1/Sqrt[5]), 1/Sqrt[5]}
```

By expansion and simplification of the powers of the square roots, we can compute f_n according to Equation 7.2–4.

```
In[5]:= fibd[n_] := Expand[ a1 e1^n + a2 e2^n ]
```

The complicated symbolic computations make this method rather slow. Observe that all square roots cancel, and we do get an integer answer.

```
In[6]:= Timing[fibd[1000]]
Out[6]= {1.36 Second, 43466557686937456435688527675040 6\
         25802564660517371780402481729089536555417949051890 40\
         38798400792551692959225930803226347752096896232398 73\
         32247116164299644090653318793829896964992851600370 44\
         76137795166849228875}
```

The asymptotic complexity of this method depends on the internal algorithms used for simplifying symbolic powers and can, therefore, not be analyzed exactly.

7.2.4   Numerical Computation

Equation 7.2–4 allows us to find the length of f_n. The number of digits is the logarithm $\log f_n$. Because $|e_1|$ is smaller than 1, higher powers e_1^n do not contribute anything to the length. Therefore, we get

$$\log f_n = \log(a_1 e_1^n + a_2 e_2^n) \approx \log(a_2 e_2^n) = \log(a_2) + n \log(e_2) \approx n \log(e_2). \qquad (7.2\text{--}7)$$

The length of f_n is proportional to n. The Fibonacci numbers themselves grow exponentially!

In Section 7.2.3, we evaluated Equation 7.2–4 exactly. A approximate numerical evaluation is sufficient, however. Because $a_1 e_1^n$ is smaller than 0.5 for large n, we can simply compute $a_2 e_2^n$ numerically with sufficient precision, and then round it to the nearest integer (we know that the result must be an integer). The necessary precision is at least the number of digits of the result. We can find it as $\log_{10}(a_2 e_2^n) = \log_{10}(a_2) + n \log_{10}(e_2)$. Machine precision is sufficient for this calculation of the length of the result. Now, we can compute $a_2 e_2^n$ again, but this time using the extended precision just determined. To perform a calculation with precision *prec*, we can use N[*expr*, *prec*]. The resulting program is fibe[], shown in Listing 7.2–3.

```
fibe[n_] :=
   Module[{digits, approx},
       digits = N[Log[10, a2] + n Log[10, e2]];
       digits = Ceiling[digits] + 10; (* some digits extra *)
       approx = N[a2, digits] N[e2, digits]^n;
       Round[approx]
   ]
```

Listing 7.2–3   Numerical computation of Fibonacci numbers.

The numerical method is quite fast, due to *Mathematica*'s efficient numerical computations. Note that it is much faster than the loop-based computation with fibc.

```
In[7]:= Timing[fibe[10^5];]
Out[7]= {1.54 Second, Null}
```

Note that *Mathematica* can figure out the required precision for the rounding all by itself, which allows us to express this method in a natural way. Some overhead is involved in the exact computation of the power of `e1`, however.

```
In[8]:= Timing[Round[a2 e2^10^5];]
Out[8]= {2.93 Second, Null}
```

An nth power can be computed in $\log n$ steps (see Section 7.1.3). Each step requires the multiplication of two numbers with n digits. Let $M(n)$ be the complexity of multiplying two n-digit numbers. The complexity of the numerical computation is therefore $M(n) \log n$. For ordinary (schoolbook) multiplication, we have $M(n) \approx n^2$. Therefore, this method is asymptotically worse than the simple loop, even though it is faster for small n.

There are faster methods for multiplying numbers, for example the *Karatsuba algorithm* (see Section 7.4.3) with $M(n) \approx n^{1.58}$, used in *Mathematica* Version 3, and the *fast Fourier transform* (FFT) with $M(n) \approx n log(n)$, used in *Mathematica* Version 4 for very large numbers. With one of these algorithms, our numerical computation becomes asymptotically faster than the loop.

7.2.5   Matrix Methods

We can use the method of iterated squaring from Section 7.1.3 to compute Fibonacci numbers, if we apply it to matrices m. The Fibonacci numbers appear in the powers of the matrix

$$m = \begin{pmatrix} 1 & 1 \\ 1 & 0 \end{pmatrix}. \tag{7.2–8}$$

The number f_n is at the top left corner of m^{n-1} because

$$m^{n-1} = \begin{pmatrix} f_n & f_{n-1} \\ f_{n-1} & f_{n-2} \end{pmatrix}. \tag{7.2–9}$$

Here is the initial matrix m.

```
In[1]:= m = {{1, 1}, {1, 0}}
Out[1]= {{1, 1}, {1, 0}}
```

`MatrixPower[]` computes powers of matrices. The elements of m^9 are $\begin{pmatrix} f_{10} & f_9 \\ f_9 & f_8 \end{pmatrix}$.

```
In[2]:= MatrixPower[m, 9] // MatrixForm
Out[2]//MatrixForm= 55    34
                    34    21
```

The reason for this property of m is that the characteristic polynomial of m is equal to the characteristic equation (7.2–5) of the Fibonacci numbers.

```
In[3]:= Det[ m - x IdentityMatrix[2] ]
                          2
Out[3]= -1 - x + x
```

```
fibf[n_] :=
    Module[{result = IdentityMatrix[2], nn = n-1, s = {{1, 1}, {1, 0}}},
        While[ nn > 1,
            If[OddQ[nn], result = result . s];
            s = s . s;
            nn = Floor[nn/2];
        ];
        result = result . s;
        result[[1, 1]] (* top left element *)
    ]
```

Listing 7.2–4   Fast matrix powers.

The program in Listing 7.2–4 is somewhat slower than is using `MatrixPower[]`, due to the overhead of the interpreted program.

The method is the same as `BinaryPower` (Listing 7.1–1). The variables `result` and `s` are now matrices. Therefore, we use the matrix product (written as `.`) instead of ordinary multiplication. The variable `result` is initialized to the identity matrix, which plays the role of 1.

This method is a bit slower than is `fibe`.   In[4]:= Timing[fibf[10^5];]

                                                    Out[4]= {2.24 Second, Null}

Computing the elements of the product of two 2×2 matrices takes eight integer multiplications. We need only one element of the result of the last multiplication outside the loop. This single element can be computed with just two integer multiplications. Therefore, we should not compute the whole matrix `result.s`, but only element $(1, 1)$. The elements v_{ik} of $r_{ij} \cdot s_{jk}$ are found with the usual formula for matrix products

$$v_{ik} = \sum_j r_{ij} s_{jk} . \tag{7.2–10}$$

This formula implies that v_{11} is $r_{11}s_{11} + r_{12}s_{21}$. If we insert this formula into our program, we arrive at the new program `fibg[]` (Listing 7.2–5), which runs about twice as fast as does `fibf[]`, but the asymptotic complexity remains the same.

```
fibg[n_] :=
    Module[{result = IdentityMatrix[2], nn = n-1, s = {{1, 1}, {1, 0}}},
        While[ nn > 1,
            If[OddQ[nn], result = result . s];
            s = s . s;
            nn = Floor[nn/2];
        ];
        result[[1,1]] s[[1,1]] + result[[1,2]] s[[2,1]]
    ]
```

Listing 7.2–5   Saving on the last multiplication.

This method is about twice as fast as `fibf`.   `In[5]:= Timing[fibg[10^5];]`

                                              `Out[5]= {1.03 Second, Null}`

7.2.6   Utilizing Symmetries

The matrices `result` and `s` are rather special. First, they are *symmetric* – that is, $m_{12} = m_{21}$. Therefore, we need to compute only three of their four elements. Second, their entries are successive Fibonacci numbers. Each one of them can be computed from the two others by a simple addition or subtraction. These two observations show that we need to compute only two of the four elements by expensive multiplications. To find the formulae for the elements, let us write the elements of `s` as s_{ij}, and the elements of `result` as r_{ij}. The square of s, $t = s.s$, can be found as follows (here, we use a new variable t for the result. In the programs we can assign the result back to the original variable `s` because the latter's old value is no longer needed.)

$$
\begin{aligned}
t_{11} &= s_{11}s_{11} + s_{12}s_{21} = s_{11}^2 + s_{12}^2, \\
t_{22} &= s_{21}s_{12} + s_{22}s_{22} = s_{12}^2 + s_{22}^2, \\
t_{12} &= t_{11} - t_{22}, \\
t_{21} &= t_{12}.
\end{aligned}
\tag{7.2–11}
$$

The result of $u = r.s$ is

$$
\begin{aligned}
u_{11} &= r_{11}s_{11} + r_{12}s_{21} - r_{11}s_{11} + r_{12}s_{12}, \\
u_{22} &= r_{21}s_{12} + r_{22}s_{22} = r_{12}s_{12} + r_{22}s_{22}, \\
u_{12} &= u_{11} - u_{22}, \\
u_{21} &= u_{12}.
\end{aligned}
\tag{7.2–12}
$$

In both cases, two of the four products involved are the same! We conclude that we can find these matrix products with three instead of eight scalar multiplications. Outside the loop, we need only two multiplications, as we saw earlier. To take advantage of this result, we shall no longer use variables for the whole matrices `s` and `result`, but work directly with their elements. We shall use variables `s11`, `s12`, and `s22`, and so on. We do not need `s21` because it is equal to `s12`. The resulting program, `fibh[]`, is shown in Listing 7.2–6.

This method is almost twice as fast as `fibg`.   `In[6]:= Timing[fibh[10^5];]`

                                              `Out[6]= {0.65 Second, Null}`

The number of iterations of the loop is $\lg n$ (the size of n in binary). The numbers that appear in the loop double at each iteration (the Fibonacci numbers are proportional to i). The whole computation takes, therefore, only a constant times the number of steps for single multiplication of numbers of length n. We can compute f_n in $M(n)$ steps! *Mathematica* uses an integer multiplication algorithm with $M(n) \approx n\log(n)$. It follows that we can compute large Fibonacci numbers asymptotically much faster than with the loop from Section 7.2.2.

```
fibh[n_] :=
    Module[{r11 = 1, r12 = 0, r22 = 1, s11 = 1, s12 = 1, s22 = 0, nn = n-1},
        While[ nn > 1,
            If[ OddQ[nn],
                {r11, r22} = r12 s12 + {r11 s11, r22 s22};
                r12 = r11 - r22
            ];
            {s11, s22} = s12^2 + {s11^2, s22^2};
            s12 = s11 - s22;
            nn = Quotient[nn, 2]
        ];
        r11 s11 + r12 s12
    ]
```

Listing 7.2–6 Utilizing symmetries.

7.2.7 Special Topic: An Even Faster Method

We can perform binary exponentiation also by traversing the exponent from bit n_{k-1} down to n_0; see Exercise 7.1. If done this way, additional identities between Fibonacci numbers can be used, for example

$$f_{n-1}f_{n+1} - f_n^2 = (-1)^n .\tag{7.2–13}$$

Such formulae allow us to compute Fibonacci numbers with *two* multiplications inside the loop, and a *single one* outside [43]; see Listing 7.2–7 for the fastest known program, fibj[]. This method is now also used by the built-in function Fibonacci[].

```
fibj[n_] :=
    Module[{r11 = 1, r12 = 0, r22 = 1, digits = IntegerDigits[n-1, 2], i, t},
        Do[ If[ digits[[i]] == 1, (* odd *)
                {r11, r22} = {r11(r11 + 2r12), r12(r11 + r22)};
                r12 = r11 - r22
            , (* else even *)
                t = r12(r11 + r22);
                {r11, r12} = {r11(r11 + 2r12) - t, t};
                r22 = r11 - r12
            ],
            {i, Length[digits]-1}
        ];
        If[ digits[[-1]] == 1,
            r11(r11 + 2r12),                    (* odd  *)
            r11(r11 + r22) - (-1)^((n-1)/2)  (* even *)
        ]
    ]
```

Listing 7.2–7 The fastest method known.

This method gives us another significant speed-up compared with `fibg`.

```
In[7]:= Timing[fibj[10^5];]
Out[7]= {0.12 Second, Null}
```

A variant of this method is built into *Mathematica*. The function is called `Fibonacci`.

```
In[8]:= Timing[Fibonacci[10^5];]
Out[8]= {0.14 Second, Null}
```

For example, we can compute the 10,000,000th Fibonacci number in about 19 seconds. The result is approximately

$$f_{10^7} \approx 1.12983\,43782\,25399\,76032 \cdot 10^{2\,089\,876} . \qquad (7.2\text{–}14)$$

It has 2,089,877 digits. Here are the first 1,997 of them:

```
  11 29834 37822 53997 60317 06363 77458 66372 94483 71904 89040 88151 35776 43245 53473 11679
33137 52421 97774 58247 74548 85033 29541 52973 79829 17618 97527 39285 43637 91302 93205 11080
39360 71609 47067 63227 61568 28424 89700 64197 36620 68255 55962 86851 20016 48785 24757 14279
90297 63435 33146 25437 48832 57472 80191 86803 44260 93376 13122 07871 80932 24952 47383 54896
45047 69641 15588 24438 10352 68921 04885 86302 82891 08325 78052 82510 91973 20550 13131 75430
39524 69745 20951 52991 52873 87889 12305 99963 21337 22895 61482 69938 55354 51421 38923 14918
16430 27404 15815 45933 03207 25972 48442 29945 90179 13355 42836 23442 60263 65272 46154 31201
28900 97417 31430 05927 26773 08812 15160 46861 80694 93942 72896 43128 03903 73271 84149 59744
80169 90022 35274 71956 09146 99473 75021 19772 50980 61063 48102 75868 45300 81480 44619 51748
27027 79357 34157 91787 70484 17134 44329 21027 34454 31566 67707 80853 58747 88855 76158 01979
11236 29805 11728 00438 66560 80547 84281 30090 93716 94862 21261 26722 04174 75093 59669 00205
85968 51837 15710 97533 70537 53104 17021 72377 50901 97191 26460 14841 94860 76150 31148 62814
48806 74336 82961 59389 40690 71537 46665 17020 19734 62650 50695 76052 88875 12885 85986 98715
41591 23306 40482 55866 33385 39959 34344 86481 73242 99707 28906 02522 43329 68148 31452 05324
34378 80699 34922 16228 25899 30595 61216 15723 38485 54057 29916 89169 14292 91942 57813 15246
48791 85431 96568 98393 94181 31716 36926 01546 64821 43144 35163 59574 57100 43018 24045 38253
33792 78975 38541 09280 30853 00212 72528 29224 22404 80298 13626 06558 85259 06745 67933 88589
40375 97341 01675 25755 53016 12822 58334 75708 19947 11991 30880 46978 54604 93179 12021 18241
23551 59596 46175 49536 47096 73339 66204 23680 17443 14372 37841 44707 28325 59840 45186 21030
71071 79856 62538 52983 33063 47356 19374 55610 74814 45416 60062 06636 98325 54254 26613 99152
47626 47328 19871 28825 46372 24608 02548 96453 24511 64839 34508 98390 23304 08830 90456 55981
27645 69943 79092 61067 88985 52277 58863 13325 76070 50615 49300 50850 37135 84630 45255 92491
15617 33946 39227 93051 39866 78790 93658 14542 23230 60592 15723 07483 68955 23891 12899 23625
87601 78719 80946 33679 50864 18634 26151 82841 05316 15376 43064 69492 90834 71924 84233 10087
86403 35046 59727 94929 54107 96696 22740 07367 36711 91419 35463 70034 08327 38470 09819 64960
```

7.2.8 Key Concepts

1. Recursive algorithms are inefficient if values are computed repeatedly.

2. Fibonacci numbers grow exponentially.

3. Computing the nth Fibonacci number has the same complexity as multiplying two n-digit numbers.

7.3   Special Topic: Dynamic Programming

Dynamic programming is a technique for avoiding the repeated computation of the same values in a recursive program. Each value computed is immediately stored. If the value is needed again, it is not computed but simply looked up in the table.

7.3.1   Recursion Can Be Expensive

In Section 7.2.1, we saw an example where the direct transformation of an inductive definition (of Fibonacci numbers) into a recursive set of rules gives an inefficient algorithm. Recall that Fibonacci numbers f_n are defined by this second order iteration (Equation 7.2–1):

$$
\begin{aligned}
f_1 &= 1, \\
f_2 &= 1, \\
f_n &= f_{n-1} + f_{n-2}.
\end{aligned}
$$

The resulting program `fiba[]`,

```
fiba[1] = fiba[2] = 1;
fiba[n_] := fiba[n-1] + fiba[n-2]
```

exhibits an exponential growth of computing time. The reason is the multiple computation of the same Fibonacci numbers f_i, for $2 < i < n$. See the illustration at the beginning of this chapter (on page 141).

A simple programming device, *dynamic programming*, lets us store each computed Fibonacci number as a new rule. If this number is needed again, it can be found immediately and needs not be recomputed. The program is given in Listing 7.3–1.

```
fibb[1] = fibb[2] = 1;
fibb[n_] := fibb[n] = fibb[n-1] + fibb[n-2]
```

Listing 7.3–1   Fibonacci numbers computed with dynamic programming.

How does it work? Definitions are *right associative;* therefore, the second definition is read as follows:

$$\texttt{fibb[n\_] := (fibb[n] = fibb[n-1] + fibb[n-2])}. \tag{7.3–1}$$

If we ask for the value of `fibb[10]`, for example, *Mathematica* evaluates the right side of this definition – that is,

$$\texttt{fibb[10] = fibb[9] + fibb[8]}. \tag{7.3–2}$$

Its right side, `fibb[9] + fibb[8]`, is now evaluated (giving 55). Now, the definition

$$fibb[10] = 55 \tag{7.3-3}$$

is carried out – that is, a *new* definition for `fibb` is added. This new definition is more specific than the existing one for `fibb[n_]` and is, therefore, put before the latter. If `fibb[10]` is needed again, the new definition returns the result immediately.

Initially, only these three definitions are given.	```In[1]:= ?fibb```
	```Global`fibb```
	```fibb[1] = 1```
	```fibb[2] = 1```
	```fibb[n_] := fibb[n] = fibb[n - 1] + fibb[n - 2]```

The computation of f_{10} needs all smaller values.	```In[2]:= fibb[10]``` ```Out[2]= 55```

These values have been defined during the previous computation.	```In[3]:= ?fibb```
	```Global`fibb```
	```fibb[1] = 1```
	```fibb[2] = 1```
	```fibb[3] = 2```
	```fibb[4] = 3```
	```fibb[5] = 5```
	```fibb[6] = 8```
	```fibb[7] = 13```
	```fibb[8] = 21```
	```fibb[9] = 34```
	```fibb[10] = 55```
	```fibb[n_] := fibb[n] = fibb[n - 1] + fibb[n - 2]```

The number of calls of `fibb` is reduced to n, but the additional definitions need much memory. Storing these definitions takes also some time, of order n^2. Because there are more efficient ways to compute Fibonacci numbers, this method is not used in practice. There are many problems, however, where no better algorithm is known. We shall look one of them – optimization – in the next section.

7.3.2 Example: The Knapsack Problem

Dynamic programming is used to solve many optimization problems. In an *optimization problem*, we try to maximize a certain function without violating given constraints.

The task in the *knapsack problem* is to fill a knapsack of given size optimally. There is a number of objects, each one having a given size and value. Which combination of objects maximizes the total value without violating the size limit?

Let there be n different kinds of objects. Let s_i be the size, and v_i be the value of the objects of type i. The knapsack has capacity s. The solution of the knapsack problem is described by n nonnegative integers m_i that give the number of objects of type i in the optimal knapsack. The knapsack problem can now be given formally as maximizing the value

$$\sum_{i=1}^{n} m_i v_i \qquad (7.3\text{--}4)$$

with the size constraint

$$\sum_{i=1}^{n} m_i s_i \leq s. \qquad (7.3\text{--}5)$$

Let us assume that the objects are ordered by size – that is, $s_1 \leq s_2 \leq \ldots \leq s_n$. It is easy to see that of two different objects of the same size only the more valuable one will be part of the optimal solution. Therefore, we can even assume $s_1 < s_2 < \ldots < s_n$. Also, we can assume that the values are increasing, too: $v_1 < v_2 < \ldots < v_n$.

The knapsack problem can be solved recursively. The function

```
Knapsack[{{s₁, v₁}, ..., {sₙ, vₙ}}, s]
```

finds the solution (and returns the optimal value) for given s_i, v_i, and s according to the following considerations.

1. If there are no objects – that is, $n = 0$ – the solution is 0:

```
Knapsack[{ }, s] = 0
```

2a. Otherwise, we can find recursively a solution that does not involve the last kind of object:

```
k₁ = Knapsack[{{s₁, v₁}, ..., {sₙ₋₁, vₙ₋₁}}, s]
```

2b. If $s \geq s_n$, we can tentatively put an object of type n into the knapsack and try to fill the remaining capacity $s - s_n$ optimally:

```
k₂ = Knapsack[{{s₁, v₁}, ..., {sₙ, vₙ}}, s - sₙ] + vₙ
```

Note that we must not exclude objects of type n in this recursive call because there might be more than one object of type n in the optimal solution.

3. The optimal solution is the larger one of k_1 and k_2.

Please convince yourself that the recursion always terminates. Correctness follows from the general principle that any part of the optimal solution is itself optimal. If the optimal solution contains one object of type i, the solution without this object is optimal for a knapsack of size $s - s_i$. Otherwise, there would be a better solution for the whole knapsack. We could simply add an object of type i back to the different optimal solution for size $s - s_i$.

In program Knapsack1.m (Listing 7.3–2), the function Knapsack[] does not return the optimal value but the *packing list*, that is, the list of objects in the optimal solution. The total value can be computed according to Equation 7.3–4. We perform this computation in the auxiliary function total[]. The objects are given as a list of size–value pairs.

```
size[object_] := object[[1]]
value[object_]  := object[[2]]

total[knapsack_, vs_]  := Plus @@  value /@ vs[[knapsack]] (* total value *)
contents[knapsack_, vs_] := Plus @@ size /@ vs[[knapsack]] (* total size *)

Knapsack[{}, s_Integer?NonNegative] := {}  (* Case 1 *)

Knapsack[vs_List, s_Integer?NonNegative] :=
    Module[{sn = size[Last[vs]],
            n = Length[vs], rest = Drop[vs, -1], k1, k2},
        k1 = Knapsack[rest, s];          (* 2a: without last object *)
        If[ s >= sn,
            k2 =  Knapsack[vs, s - sn]; (* 2b: with one last object *)
            k2 = Append[k2, n];
            If[ total[k1, vs] >= total[k2, vs], k1, k2 ] (* 3: the maximum *)
          ,
            k1
          ]
      ]
```

Listing 7.3–2 Knapsack1.m.

In this example, the sizes are $(3, 4, 7, 8, 9)$; the values are $(4, 5, 10, 11, 13)$.

```
In[1]:= objects =
            {{3, 4}, {4, 5}, {7, 10}, {8, 11}, {9, 13}};
```

The optimal solution consists of one object of type 1 and two objects of type 3.

```
In[2]:= Knapsack[ objects, 17 ]
Out[2]= {1, 3, 3}
```

Here is the optimal value achieved with this solution.

```
In[3]:= total[ %, objects ]
Out[3]= 24
```

The recursive computation can be illustrated graphically. For each recursive call of

$$\text{Knapsack}[\{\{s_1,\ v_1\},\ \ldots,\ \{s_n,\ v_n\}\},\ s],$$

we draw one node, labeled with the maximum reached. The two recursive calls that find k_1 and k_2 are connected by a line. The line corresponding the the larger value is drawn in bold.

This version of the package produces the illustrations.

```
In[4]:= << CSM`KnapsackG`
```

Here is the graphic for the previous example. The computation starts in the upper right corner with the largest values of n and s.

A vertical line from a node the the the node below it corresponds to a solution according to 2a, without the last kind of objects. A horizontal line to the left corresponds to a solution according to 2b, where the size of the knapsack has been reduced by the size of the last object; the length of this line equals the size of the corresponding object.

The vertical axis shows the number of different kinds of objects available, and the horizontal axis shows the size of the knapsack.

In[5]:= **KnapsackPlot[objects, 17];**

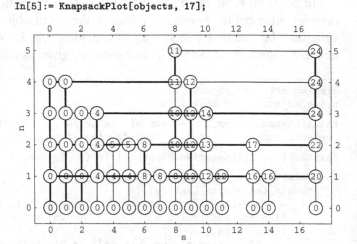

As in the program for Fibonacci numbers (see Section 7.3.1), certain values are computed several times. We can use the same idea of dynamic programming to store intermediate results to avoid this repeated computation. The final package Knapsack.m (Listing 7.3–3) shows dynamic programming for the knapsack problem.

We do the recursive computation locally inside the function Knapsack[]. The recursive function is a local variable named ks. The code for ks can determine the values and sizes

```
size[object_] := object[[1]]
value[object_]  := object[[2]]

total[knapsack_, vs_]  := Plus @@ value /@ vs[[knapsack]] (* total value *)
contents[knapsack_, vs_] := Plus @@ size /@ vs[[knapsack]] (* total size *)

Knapsack[vs_List, s_Integer?NonNegative] :=
    Module[{ks},
        ks[0, in_] = {};
        ks[n_, in_] := ks[n, in] =
            Module[{gn = size[vs[[n]]], k1, k2},
                k1 = ks[n-1, in];
                If[ in >= gn,
                    k2 =  ks[n, in - gn]; k2 = Append[k2, n];
                    If[ total[k1, vs] >= total[k2, vs], k1, k2 ]
                    ,
                    k1
                    ]
                ];
        ks[Length[vs], s]
    ]
```

Listing 7.3–3 Knapsack.m.

of the objects by consulting the parameter vs. Therefore, we do not need to pass the list of remaining objects as an argument of ks; it is sufficient to give the number of remaining types as argument. Any optimal solutions for smaller problems found during the recursion are stored as new definitions for ks, using ks[n_, in_] := ks[n, in] = ... There are at most s different sizes of smaller knapsacks and n different numbers of object types. The number of calls to ks[] is therefore certainly less than ns. Note that ns is the number of points in the rectangle shown in the previous picture. This method is quite efficient.

The following example shows us the values actually computed.

Here is a problem with only three kinds of objects.

```
In[1]:= Knapsack[{{3, 4}, {4, 5}, {7, 10}}, 8]
Out[1]= {2, 2}
```

This table shows the values stored. (Don't ask me how this works....)

```
In[2]:= Cases[
          DownValues[ks],
          (_[_[n_Integer, i_Integer]]:>r_) :>
             (knapsack[n, i]->r)
        ] // TableForm
Out[2]//TableForm= knapsack[1, 0] -> {}
                   knapsack[1, 1] -> {}
                   knapsack[1, 2] -> {}
                   knapsack[1, 4] -> {1}
                   knapsack[1, 5] -> {1}
                   knapsack[1, 8] -> {1, 1}
                   knapsack[2, 0] -> {}
                   knapsack[2, 1] -> {}
                   knapsack[2, 4] -> {2}
                   knapsack[2, 8] -> {2, 2}
                   knapsack[3, 1] -> {}
                   knapsack[3, 8] -> {2, 2}
```

7.3.3 Key Concepts

1. Dynamic programming allows the reuse of intermediate results.

2. Dynamic programming reduces the complexity of complicated recursive computations.

3. Many optimization problems can be solved by dynamic programming.

7.4 Long-Integer Arithmetic and Fast Multiplication

This section studies integer arithmetic. We shall look at the representation of big integers on computers and study typical algorithms. Computers have memory cells of a fixed size, which allow us to store only numbers of a certain maximum size. If we want to perform calculations with arbitrary-sized numbers (so-called long integers), we have to program their representation and the arithmetic ourselves. Long-integer arithmetic is already built into *Mathematica*; here, we see how it works.

7.4.1 Long Integers

The obvious representation of integers of arbitrary size is a generalization of the positional number system (binary, decimal) with a base $B > 1$. A number is represented as an array a_0, $a_1, \ldots, a_{n-1}$ of digits with

$$a = \sum_{i=0}^{n-1} a_i B^i, \qquad 0 \leq a_i < B.\tag{7.4–1}$$

The sign is stored separately and does not concern us here.

If we write our own program for long-integer arithmetic, we can choose the base B as we wish. If we set $B = 10$, we get our familiar decimal arithmetic. Because we are used to it, this choice makes it easier to understand the programs.

A long integer can simply be represented as the list of its digits a_i, for $i = 0, 1, \ldots, n - 1$. Because list elements are numbered starting with 1, the element $a[[i]]$ is the digit a_{i-1}. Addition or multiplication of digits can give intermediate values z that are larger than $B - 1$, the largest possible digit. If this happens, there is a *carry* into the next digit. This carry is equal to z div B, the quotient z/B rounded down. The function $\mathtt{carry}[z]$ returns this carry; $\mathtt{rem}[z]$ is the remainder of the digit without the carry. It is equal to $a \bmod B$, the remainder of the division of z by B. The data type for long integers contains these auxiliary functions, as well as constructors and selectors, as usual. The functions are in the package Bignum.m. Here is the specification and the simple implementation:

Function	Implementation	Description
digit[a, i]	a[[i+1]]	the ith digit of a
newNumber[n]	Table[0, {n}]	skeleton of a number of length n
length[a]	Length[a]	number of digits of a
carry[z]	Quotient[z, B]	carry into the next digit
rem[z]	Mod[z, B]	remainder after removing carry

The selector `digit[]` can be used also on the left side of an assignment, to change a digit in a number:

$$\text{digit}[sym, i] = new .$$

To redefine the assignment $ls = rs$, a definition of the form $sym/: (ls = rs) := expr$ can be given. Of course, the variable parts in ls and rs must be marked as pattern variables. sym is the head of ls. For `digit`, we used this definition:

$$\text{digit}/: (\text{digit}[a\_, i\_] = new\_) := (a[[i+1]] = new)$$

We set the base to 10.	`In[1]:= B = 10;`
The variable a is assigned a new long integer with length 2.	`In[2]:= a = newNumber[2]` `Out[2]= {0, 0}`
Now, we can define the digits. The unit digit is set to 1,	`In[3]:= digit[a, 0] = 1` `Out[3]= 1`
the tens digit is set to 2.	`In[4]:= digit[a, 1] = 2;`
The number a has digits $a_0 = 1$, $a_1 = 2$. Observe that the order of digits is the reverse of the usual notation.	`In[5]:= a` `Out[5]= {1, 2}`

The value of the number is computed according to Equation 7.4–1.	`In[6]:= Sum[ digit[a, i] B^i,`
	`          {i, 0, length[a]-1} ]`
	`Out[6]= 21`

7.4.2 Addition

For an example of an algorithm on long integers, let us look at addition. The method works in the way we learned it at school. The two numbers are added digit by digit, and the carry is added to the next digit. If the number a has n digits, and b has m digits, with $m \leq n$, the addition $c = a + b$ looks as follows:

$$
\begin{array}{ccccccccc}
 & a_{n-1} & \cdots & a_m & a_{m-1} & \cdots & a_1 & a_0 \\
+ & & & & b_{m-1} & \cdots & b_1 & b_0 \\
\hline
c_n & c_{n-1} & \cdots & c_m & c_{m-1} & \cdots & c_1 & c_0
\end{array}
\tag{7.4–2}
$$

We start with the digit at position zero. If we store the sum of a_i, b_i, and the carry in the auxiliary variables d_i, we get these formulae for the digits c_i:

$$
\begin{array}{llll}
d_0 &=& a_0 + b_0, & c_0 &=& d_0 \bmod B, \\
d_1 &=& a_1 + b_1 + d_0 \operatorname{div} B, & c_1 &=& d_1 \bmod B, \\
&\vdots& & &\vdots& \\
d_{m-1} &=& a_{m-1} + b_{m-1} + d_{m-2} \operatorname{div} B, & c_{m-1} &=& d_{m-1} \bmod B, \\
d_m &=& a_m + d_{m-1} \operatorname{div} B, & c_m &=& d_m \bmod B, \\
&\vdots& & &\vdots& \\
d_{n-1} &=& a_{n-1} + d_{n-2} \operatorname{div} B, & c_{n-1} &=& d_{n-1} \bmod B, \\
d_n &=& d_{n-1} \operatorname{div} B, & c_n &=& d_n.
\end{array}
\tag{7.4--3}
$$

We can write them in a more uniform way be defining $d_{-1} = 0$:

$$
\begin{array}{llllll}
d_i &=& a_i + b_i + d_{i-1} \operatorname{div} B, & c_i &=& d_i \bmod B, & i = 0, 1, \ldots, m-1, \\
d_i &=& a_i + d_{i-1} \operatorname{div} B, & c_i &=& d_i \bmod B, & i = m, \ldots, n-1, \\
& & & c_n &=& d_{n-1} \operatorname{div} B.
\end{array}
\tag{7.4--4}
$$

Observe that we no longer need the value of d_{i-1} after having computed d_i. Therefore, we need only *one* variable d, not a whole array. We can perform the calculations for each i in a loop. Listing 7.4–1 shows the resulting program.

```
plus[a_, b_] := plus[b, a] /; length[a] < length[b]

plus[a_, b_] :=
   Module[{c, n = length[a], m = length[b], i, d = 0},
       c = newNumber[n+1];
       Do[ d = digit[a, i] + digit[b, i] + carry[d];
           digit[c, i] = rem[d],
          {i, 0, m-1} ];
       Do[ d = digit[a, i] + carry[d];
           digit[c, i] = rem[d],
          {i, m, n-1} ];
       digit[c, n] = carry[d];
       If[ digit[c, n] == 0, c = Drop[c, -1] ]; (* normalize *)
       c
   ]
```

Listing 7.4–1   Addition of two long integers.

The first definition exchanges the two numbers if a is shorter than b. It may happen that the highest digit of the result c_n is equal to zero, if there was no carry into it. In this case, we remove digit c_n to keep the numbers normalized. In a normalized number, the highest digit is always nonzero.

Here are two numbers, $a = 9,899$ and $b = 101$.

```
In[7]:= a = {9, 9, 8, 9};\
        b = {1, 0, 1};
```

Their sum is 10,000.

```
In[8]:= plus[a, b]
Out[8]= {0, 0, 0, 0, 1}
```

In this example, there is no carry into the first digit; the sum has, therefore, a length of three instead of four.

```
In[9]:= plus[{9, 9, 8}, {1, 1}]
Out[9]= {0, 1, 9}
```

7.4.3 Multiplication: The Karatsuba Method

If we multiply two long integers with n digits in the naive way (the so-called schoolbook method), we need n^2 multiplications of digits. This number can be reduced drastically with the *Karatsuba method*. The Karatsuba method is not the asymptotically best possible, but it is efficient and easy to implement. It is also used in *Mathematica* for medium-sized numbers. An overview over the fastest methods for multiplication can be found in Knuth's book [35].

Let a and b be two long integers with n digits. We can view them as *two-digit* numbers with base B^m, where $m = \lceil n/2 \rceil$:

$$
\begin{aligned}
a &= a_0 + a_1 B^m, \\
b &= b_0 + b_1 B^m.
\end{aligned}
\tag{7.4--5}
$$

The product ab can be expressed as follows:

$$
\begin{aligned}
ab &= a_0 b_0 + (a_0 b_1 + a_1 b_0) B^m + a_1 b_1 B^{2m} \\
&= a_0 b_0 + ((a_0 + a_1)(b_0 + b_1) - a_0 b_0 - a_1 b_1) B^m + a_1 b_1 B^{2m}
\end{aligned}
\tag{7.4--6}
$$

We see that we need only *three* multiplications of half size (instead of the expected four). The three multiplications are $a_0 b_0$, $a_1 b_1$, and $(a_0 + a_1)(b_0 + b_1)$. This fact leads to an asymptotic improvement, if we use it recursively for the three multiplications. The number of multiplications, $T(n)$, is

$$
\begin{aligned}
T(n) &= 3T(n/2), \\
T(1) &= 1.
\end{aligned}
\tag{7.4--7}
$$

The solution of this recursive equation is

$$
T(n) = n^{\lg 3} \approx n^{1.58},
\tag{7.4--8}
$$

which is far better than n^2. The overhead for the extra additions and subtractions can be neglected because these operations are of order $O(n)$.

Mathematica uses a long integer base of 2^{16} on the computer on which this book was formatted.

```
In[1]:= l = 16; B = 2^l;
```

MultiplicationTime measures the time needed to multiply two numbers of length n. The numbers are chose such that most of their bits are one.

```
In[2]:= MultiplicationTime[n_] :=
            With[ {a = B^n - 1, b = B^n - 3},
                Timing[ a b ][[1]] /. Second -> 1
            ]
```

Here is a table of the times for $n = 1,000,$
$2,000, \ldots, 10,000.$

```
In[3]:= v40 = Table[ {n, MultiplicationTime[n]},
                    {n, 1000, 10000, 1000} ]
Out[3]= {{1000, 0.05}, {2000, 0.02}, {3000, 0.02},
         {4000, 0.03}, {5000, 0.06}, {6000, 0.06},
         {7000, 0.07}, {8000, 0.09}, {9000, 0.1},
         {10000, 0.11}}
```

This graphic shows a comparison with Versions 2.0 and 3.0 of *Mathematica* that used the naive algorithm and the Karatsuba algorithm, respectively. Version 4.0 uses even faster methods for such large numbers; see Section 7.2.

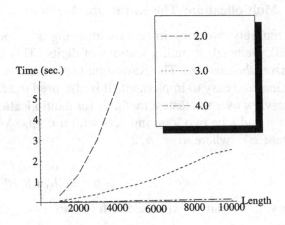

7.4.4 Key Concepts

1. Arbitrary-size numbers can be realized using a positional number system.

2. The schoolbook methods for arithmetic can easily be programmed for long integers.

3. Two numbers with n digits can be multiplied with fewer than n^2 digit multiplications.

7.5 Exercises

7.1 Repeated Squaring from Left to Right

Powers of numbers or matrices m^n can be computed by working on the exponent n from left to right (from the most significant to the least significant bit). This method has the advantage that each iteration of the loop requires only one multiplication with large numbers, whereas the second multiplication – if the bit is equal to one – is with the original m. For Fibonacci numbers, this matrix m consists only of zeroes and ones.

1. Program the left-to-right method in general form (for powers of numbers), similar to the definition of `BinaryPower[]` in Section 7.1.3.

2. Write a special version of the definition for the computation of the nth Fibonacci number and compare its run time with method `fibh[]` from Section 7.2.6.

7.2 Experimental Complexity

Make some experiments with the loop for computing the $n$the Fibonacci number (program `fibc[]` in Section 7.2.2) and estimate the time it would take to compute `fibc[10^7]`.

Hint: Use `Fit[]` to fit the measured times to the expected asymptotic expansion of the run time.

7.3 Long-Integer Arithmetic

In this exercise, we want to experiment with long-integer multiplication algorithms.

1. Write a program `times[a, b]` for the multiplication of two long integers similar to the program `plus[]` in Section 7.4.1. Use the naive schoolbook method for multiplication.

2. Implement the Karatsuba method.
   Hint: Numbers with a small number of digits should be multiplied with the naive method above.

3. For what size of numbers is the Karatsuba method faster than the simple algorithm?

Chapter 8
Operations on Vectors and Matrices

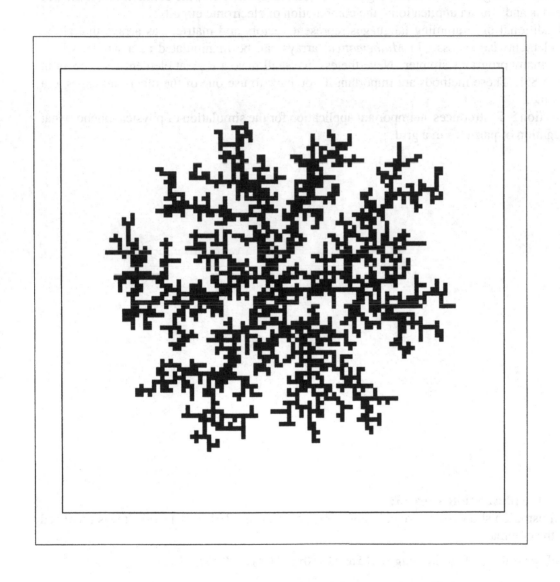

In this chapter, we look at arrays and a few of their uses. Vectors and matrices are important data structures for mathematical applications. They are simply represented as lists in *Mathematica*.

Section 8.1 studies one of the simplest operations on matrices: transposition. Its generalization leads to interesting applications. Inner and outer products (Section 8.2) are also important operations on matrices. They have many applications, especially when they are treated as generally as is possible in *Mathematica*.

From the large topic of linear algebra we treat, in Section 8.3, the solution of systems of equations and – as an application – the computation of electronic circuits.

Traditional programming languages represent vectors and matrices as arrays that allow only elementwise access. In *Mathematica*, arrays can be manipulated as a whole, which makes many programs simpler. Nevertheless, we shall have a look at elementwise access in Section 8.4. These methods are important if you have to use one of the other languages at a later time.

Section 8.5 introduces an important application for the simulation of physical phenomena: aggregation of particles in a grid.

About the illustration overleaf:
The illustration shows an aggregation of 2,001 particles in a 101 × 101 grid. It was produced with the command

```
Show[ gridGraphics[aggregate[initialGrid[50], 2000]] ].
```

The package Aggregate.m is developed in Section 8.5.

8.1   Vectors and Matrices

Mathematica represents vectors, matrices, and higher-order tensors as nested lists and provides many commands for manipulating them.

A vector (v_i) in an n-dimensional space $\mathbf{R}^n$ is represented as the list $\{v_1, v_2, \ldots, v_n\}$. An $m \times n$ matrix (a_{ij}) is represented as a list of m rows with n components each.

Here is a 3×3 matrix with symbolic elements. It is written as a list consisting of three sublists, each of length 3.	`In[1]:= mat = {{a11, a12, a13},`
	`            {a21, a22, a23},`
	`            {a31, a32, a33}};`

`MatrixForm[]` gives us the usual format of a matrix.	`In[2]:= MatrixForm[ mat ]`
	`Out[2]//MatrixForm= a11   a12   a13`
	`                    a21   a22   a23`
	`                    a31   a32   a33`

When you try this example in the *Mathematica* frontend, you will even see the customary parentheses:

$$\begin{pmatrix} a_{11} & a_{12} & a_{13} \\ a_{21} & a_{22} & a_{23} \\ a_{31} & a_{32} & a_{33} \end{pmatrix} .$$

A *tensor* is a higher-dimensional generalization of vectors and matrices. A tensor of *rank k* is described by elements with k indices, and represented by k-fold nested lists. Accordingly, a vector is a tensor of rank 1, and a matrix is a tensor of rank 2.

8.1.1   Transposition

A *transposition* (of a matrix) is a permutation of the indices or an interchange of rows and columns. The transpose a^t of an $m \times n$ matrix

$$a = \begin{pmatrix} a_{11} & a_{12} & \cdots & a_{1n} \\ a_{21} & a_{22} & \cdots & a_{2n} \\ \vdots & \vdots & & \vdots \\ a_{m1} & a_{m2} & \cdots & a_{mn} \end{pmatrix} \tag{8.1--1}$$

is the $n \times m$ matrix

$$a^t = \begin{pmatrix} a_{11} & a_{21} & \cdots & a_{m1} \\ a_{12} & a_{22} & \cdots & a_{m2} \\ \vdots & \vdots & & \vdots \\ a_{1n} & a_{2n} & \cdots & a_{mn} \end{pmatrix} . \tag{8.1--2}$$

The relation between a matrix and its transpose is best expressed in terms of matrix elements:

$$(a^t)_{ij} = a_{ji}. \tag{8.1-3}$$

The transposed matrix is obtained by inter-
changing rows and columns.

```
In[3]:= MatrixForm[ Transpose[mat] ]
Out[3]//MatrixForm= a11   a21   a31
                    a12   a22   a32
                    a13   a23   a33
```

The operation `Transpose[]` can perform more general index permutations than the simple transposition in Equation 8.1–3. The default levels permuted are {2, 1}, which means

$$(tr_{21}(m))_{i_1 i_2} = m_{i_2 i_1} , \tag{8.1-4}$$

that is, the usual transposition. You can use *repetition* of levels to select diagonal elements. A level specification of {1, 1} gives the vector of diagonal matrix elements:

$$(tr_{11}(m))_{i_1} = m_{i_1 i_1} . \tag{8.1-5}$$

Level specifications are given as an optional second argument of `Transpose[]`.

Here is the list (or vector) of all diagonal
elements.

```
In[4]:= Transpose[ mat, {1, 1} ]
Out[4]= {a11, a22, a33}
```

The *trace* of a matrix is defined as the sum of its diagonal elements. It can be programmed in this easy way.

`Plus @@` *list* replaces *list* by the sum of its
elements. (`@@` or `Apply` is explained in
Section 11.2.3.2.)

```
In[5]:= MatrixTrace[m_] := Plus @@ Transpose[m, {1, 1}]
```

In this way, we get the trace of `mat`.

```
In[6]:= MatrixTrace[ mat ]
Out[6]= a11 + a22 + a33
```

Transposition can be generalized to tensors.

To improve readability, we shall write tensors with subscripts.

```
In[7]:= Format[t_a] := Subscripted[t]
```

Here, we generate a $2 \times 2 \times 2 \times 2$ tensor,
that is, a tensor of rank four.

```
In[8]:= t = Table[ a[i, j, k, l], {i,2},
                   {j,2}, {k,2}, {l,2} ];
```

This command writes it in matrix form.	`In[9]:= MatrixForm[t]`
	`Out[9]//MatrixForm=`

$$
\begin{array}{cccc}
a_{1,1,1,1} & a_{1,1,1,2} & a_{1,2,1,1} & a_{1,2,1,2} \\
a_{1,1,2,1} & a_{1,1,2,2} & a_{1,2,2,1} & a_{1,2,2,2} \\
a_{2,1,1,1} & a_{2,1,1,2} & a_{2,2,1,1} & a_{2,2,1,2} \\
a_{2,1,2,1} & a_{2,1,2,2} & a_{2,2,2,1} & a_{2,2,2,2}
\end{array}
$$

Now we exchange levels two and three, that is,

$$(tr_{132}(t))_{i_1 i_2 i_3 i_4} = t_{i_1 i_3 i_2 i_4}.$$

`In[10]:= Transpose[ t, {1, 3, 2} ] // MatrixForm`

`Out[10]//MatrixForm=`

$$
\begin{array}{cccc}
a_{1,1,1,1} & a_{1,1,1,2} & a_{1,1,2,1} & a_{1,1,2,2} \\
a_{1,2,1,1} & a_{1,2,1,2} & a_{1,2,2,1} & a_{1,2,2,2} \\
a_{2,1,1,1} & a_{2,1,1,2} & a_{2,1,2,1} & a_{2,1,2,2} \\
a_{2,2,1,1} & a_{2,2,1,2} & a_{2,2,2,1} & a_{2,2,2,2}
\end{array}
$$

8.1.2 Exchange of Operations

A transposition requires the operations on the two levels that are exchanged to be the same. In the previous example, this operation was `List`, because a matrix is a list of lists. You can use `Thread[expr]` to exchange operations other than `List`.

The operations on the first level is `f`; the operation on the second level is `List`.	`In[1]:= f[{a, b}, {c, d}]`
	`Out[1]= f[{a, b}, {c, d}]`
`Thread[]` exchanges the two operations. We get a list of `f` objects.	`In[2]:= Thread[ % ]`
	`Out[2]= {f[a, c], f[b, d]}`
Elements that are not lists are duplicated as often as necessary.	`In[3]:= Thread[ f[{a, b, c}, x] ]`
	`Out[3]= {f[a, x], f[b, x], f[c, x]}`

This exchange is made automatically for most built-in mathematical functions. Whenever the arguments of these functions are lists, the function is applied to the elements of the lists, and the list of results is returned.

The square root is applied to the elements of the list. The result is a list of square roots.	`In[4]:= Sqrt[ {1, 2, 3, 4, 5} ]`
	`Out[4]= {1, Sqrt[2], Sqrt[3], 2, Sqrt[5]}`
Here is a sum of two lists. The elements are added pairwise.	`In[5]:= {1, 2} + {a, b}`
	`Out[5]= {1 + a, 2 + b}`
The second operand of `Power` is not a list and is duplicated. We get a list of second powers (squares).	`In[6]:= {a, b, c}^2`
	`Out[6]= {a^2, b^2, c^2}`

If you want to distribute ("thread") an operation other than list (h in this example), you must give the name of the operation as a second argument to `Thread[]`.

```
In[7]:= Thread[ h[a, b, c]^2, h ]
             2   2   2
Out[7]= h[a , b , c ]
```

8.1.3 Example: Manipulation of Equations

The operations performed to solve a simple equation by isolating the unknown variable are an example for the use of `Thread[]`.

Here is an equation that we want to solve for x.

```
In[1]:= a Log[x] + b == 0
Out[1]= b + a Log[x] == 0
```

First, we subtract b on both sides. The subtraction is not distributed onto the elements of the equation automatically.

```
In[2]:= % - b
Out[2]= -b + (b + a Log[x] == 0)
```

Only with `Thread[]`, do we get the desired result.

```
In[3]:= Thread[ %, Equal ]
Out[3]= a Log[x] == -b
```

Now, we can divide both sides by a.

```
In[4]:= Thread[ % / a, Equal ]
                      b
Out[4]= Log[x] == -(-)
                      a
```

Finally, we use exponentiation – the inverse of the logarithm – to isolate x.

```
In[5]:= Thread[ Exp[%], Equal ]
             -(b/a)
Out[5]= x == E
```

8.1.4 Key Concepts

1. Vectors, matrices, and tensors are represented in *Mathematica* as nested lists.

2. Transposition of matrices can be generalized to permutation of indices of tensors.

3. The trace of a matrix is the sum of its diagonal elements.

4. `Thread[]` exchanges operations with arguments that are lists.

8.2 Inner and Outer Products

Many operations on vectors can be viewed as generalized inner and outer products, where we use functions other than multiplication and addition.

8.2.1 Inner Products

The *dot product* of two vectors is a special case of the inner product of vectors, matrices, or – more generally – tensors.

The dot product is written as $v_1 . v_2$. The arguments v_1 and v_2 can be vectors or matrices. *Mathematica* does not distinguish between row and column vectors. A vector is simply a list of components and used as needed.

These two commands cause vectors a and b to be printed with indices.

```
In[1]:= Format[t_a] := Subscripted[t]; \
        Format[t_b] := Subscripted[t];
```

This command causes all results to be printed in matrix form.

```
In[2]:= $PrePrint = MatrixForm;
```

Here is a 3×3 matrix.

```
In[3]:= m = Table[ a[i, j], {i, 3}, {j, 3} ]

Out[3]= a      a      a
         1,1    1,2    1,3

        a      a      a
         2,1    2,2    2,3

        a      a      a
         3,1    3,2    3,3
```

We set v to a vector with three components.

```
In[4]:= v = Table[ b[i], {i, 3} ]

Out[4]= b
         1

        b
         2

        b
         3
```

The vector is considered a column vector (3×1). The result is again a column vector.

```
In[5]:= m . v

Out[5]= a      b  + a      b  + a      b
         1,1    1    1,2    2    1,3    3

        a      b  + a      b  + a      b
         2,1    1    2,2    2    2,3    3

        a      b  + a      b  + a      b
         3,1    1    3,2    2    3,3    3
```

Now it is treated as row vector (1×3). The result is again a row vector.

```
In[6]:= v . m
Out[6]= a    b  + a    b  + a    b
         1,1  1    2,1  2    3,1  3

         a    b  + a    b  + a    b
          1,2  1    2,2  2    3,2  3

         a    b  + a    b  + a    b
          1,3  1    2,3  2    3,3  3
```

Ordinary multiplication is done element by element. Therefore, the result is again a 3×3 matrix.

```
In[7]:= m  v
Out[7]= a    b    a    b    a    b
         1,1  1    1,2  1    1,3  1

         a    b    a    b    a    b
          2,1  2    2,2  2    2,3  2

         a    b    a    b    a    b
          3,1  3    3,2  3    3,3  3
```

The inner product of two tensors $(a_{i_1 i_2 \ldots i_m})$ and $(b_{k_1 k_2 \ldots k_n})$ is a tensor of rank $m + n - 2$ with these elements:

$$(a \cdot b)_{i_1 i_2 \ldots i_{m-1} k_2 \ldots k_n} = \sum_{j=1}^{d} a_{i_1 i_2 \ldots i_{m-1} j} b_{j k_2 \ldots k_n} , \qquad (8.2\text{--}1)$$

where the sum ranges over all indices of dimension m in a, and of dimension 1 in b (these two dimensions must agree). In the previous example, a was a 3×3 matrix (a_{ij}), and b was a 3 vector (b_k). The result is, therefore, a 3 vector (c_i) obtained by the ordinary formula for the multiplication of a matrix by a vector,

$$c_i = \sum_{j=1}^{3} a_{ij} b_j . \qquad (8.2\text{--}2)$$

The dot product of two vectors (u_i) and (v_k) is

$$u \cdot v = \sum_{j=1}^{d} u_j v_j , \qquad (8.2\text{--}3)$$

that is, a scalar.

The computation of an inner product requires two operations. A *multiplication* is used to combine corresponding elements, and an *addition* is used to sum the partial results. The operation `Inner[`*mult*, m_1, m_2, *add*`]` allows you to use arbitrary (binary) multiplication and addition operations instead of the default `Times` and `Plus`. The ordinary dot product $v_1 . v_2$, or `Dot[`v_1, v_2`]`, is the same as `Inner[Times, `v_1`, `v_2`, Plus]`.

The ordinary inner product is simply the dot product.

```
In[1]:= Inner[Times, {a, b, c}, {x, y, z}, Plus]
Out[1]= a x + b y + c z
```

If we use undefined operations (note the lowercase symbols `times` and `plus`), we can see how `Inner[]` works.

```
In[2]:= Inner[times, {a, b, c}, {x, y, z}, plus]
Out[2]= plus[times[a, x], times[b, y], times[c, z]]
```

8.2.2 Example: Connected Components

In an electronic circuit, certain points are connected by wires. If there are n points, we can represent the connections in a Boolean $n \times n$ matrix (a_{ij}), that is, a matrix whose elements are the Boolean values `True` or `False`. If there is a connection from point i to j, we set a_{ij} to `True`, otherwise to `False`. Observe that the matrix is symmetric because a connection from i to j is also a connection from j to i – that is, $a_{ij} = a_{ji}$.

Let us look at the Boolean inner product

$$a \cdot a = \texttt{Inner[And, } a, a, \texttt{ Or]} \,,$$

where the logical AND is used as multiplication and OR is used as addition. According to formula 8.2–1, this operation gives

$$(a \cdot a)_{ik} = \bigvee_{j=1}^{n} a_{ij} \wedge a_{jk} \,. \tag{8.2–4}$$

Element ik of $a \cdot a$ is true if and only if there is a connection from i to some j and from there to k; that is, if there is an *indirect* connection of length two. This computation can be iterated:

$$\begin{aligned} a^{(0)} &= E, \\ a^{(i)} &= a^{(i-1)} \cdot a, \qquad i = 1, 2, \dots, n. \end{aligned} \tag{8.2–5}$$

Matrix $a^{(i)}$ describes the connections of length i. E is the Boolean identity matrix having the values `True` in its diagonal (and `False` otherwise). It describes the trivial connections of length zero, because each point is connected to itself.

If we add up the matrices $a^{(i)}$ element by element with OR,

$$b = a^{(0)} \vee a^{(1)} \vee \dots \vee a^{(n)} \,, \tag{8.2–6}$$

we get a matrix b whose elements b_{ij} are equal to `True` if there is *some* connection between i and j. If all elements of b are `True`, our circuit is connected; otherwise it consists of several components that are completely independent of each other (indicating most likely an error in the wiring).

The Boolean sum can be taken inside the iteration. We get

$$\begin{aligned} a^{(0)} &= E \\ a^{(i)} &= a^{(i-1)} \vee a^{(i-1)} \cdot a, \qquad i = 1, 2, \dots, n. \end{aligned} \tag{8.2–7}$$

```
identity[n_] := Table[i===j, {i, n}, {j, n}]

inner[a_, b_] := Inner[And, a, b, Or]

or[a_, b_] := MapThread[Or, {a,b}, 2]

Components[a_] :=
    With[{n = Length[a]},
        Nest[ Function[{ai}, or[ai, inner[ai, a]]], identity[n], n ]
    ]
```

Listing 8.2–1   BooleMat.m.

Listing 8.2–1 shows the corresponding program. The operation `inner[`*a*`, `*b*`]` computes the Boolean inner product; `or[`*a*`, `*b*`]` is the Boolean sum. `Components[`*a*`]` finds the connected components.

In this example, we print all results in table form with labels for rows and columns. Here is how we can specify such formatting.

```
In[1]:= $PrePrint =
           TableForm[#, TableHeadings->Automatic]&;
```

Here is an example of a circuit with six points. There are wires between 1–2, 1–3, 2–3, 2–4, 3–4, 4–5, and 5–6.

```
In[2]:= circuit1
Out[2]=
```

	1	2	3	4	5	6
1	False	True	True	False	False	False
2	True	False	True	True	False	False
3	True	True	False	True	False	False
4	False	True	True	False	True	False
5	False	False	False	True	False	True
6	False	False	False	False	True	False

This matrix shows all connections of length two.

```
In[3]:= inner[%, %]
Out[3]=
```

	1	2	3	4	5	6
1	True	True	True	True	False	False
2	True	True	True	True	True	False
3	True	True	True	True	True	False
4	True	True	True	True	False	True
5	False	True	True	False	True	False
6	False	False	False	True	False	True

All points are connected, as this matrix consisting only of True shows.

```
In[4]:= Components[circuit1]
```

Out[4]=	1	2	3	4	5	6
1	True	True	True	True	True	True
2	True	True	True	True	True	True
3	True	True	True	True	True	True
4	True	True	True	True	True	True
5	True	True	True	True	True	True
6	True	True	True	True	True	True

In this circuit, the connection 4–5 is missing.

```
In[5]:= circuit2
Out[5]=
```

	1	2	3	4	5	6
1	False	True	True	False	False	False
2	True	False	True	True	False	False
3	True	True	False	True	False	False
4	False	True	True	False	False	False
5	False	False	False	False	False	True
6	False	False	False	False	True	False

As a consequence, the circuit consists of two components. Points 1 to 4 are connected, and so are points 5 and 6. There is no connection between these two sets of points.

```
In[6]:= Components[circuit2]
Out[6]=
```

	1	2	3	4	5	6
1	True	True	True	True	False	False
2	True	True	True	True	False	False
3	True	True	True	True	False	False
4	True	True	True	True	False	False
5	False	False	False	False	True	True
6	False	False	False	False	True	True

Boolean $n \times n$ matrices of the form used in this section are *adjacency matrices* of graphs. They specify which vertices in the graph are connected by an edge. The standard *Mathematica* package DiscreteMath`Combinatorica` contains many functions on graphs. Here, we solve the connection problem using the *Combinatorica* package [63].

We read the package.

```
In[7]:= Needs["DiscreteMath`Combinatorica`"]
```

Combinatorica needs graphs represented as lists of edges. The edges are the pairs of vertices whose corresponding entry in our adjacency matrix is True.

```
In[8]:= Position[circuit2, True]
Out[8]= {{1, 2}, {1, 3}, {2, 1}, {2, 3}, {2, 4},
         {3, 1}, {3, 2}, {3, 4}, {4, 2}, {4, 3}, {5, 6},
         {6, 5}}
```

This function converts the edge list into an internal representation of the graph.

```
In[9]:= gr2 = FromUnorderedPairs[%];
```

Here we find its components. As we have already seen, there are two components.

```
In[10]:= ConnectedComponents[gr2]
Out[10]= {{1, 2, 3, 4}, {5, 6}}
```

The package also contains commands to draw pictures of graphs.

```
In[11]:= ShowLabeledGraph[gr2];
```

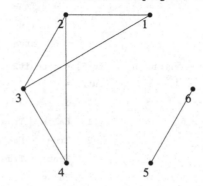

8.2.3   Outer Products

The *outer product* of two tensors $(a_{i_1 i_2 \ldots i_m})$ and $(b_{j_1 j_2 \ldots j_n})$ is a tensor of rank $m + n$ with elements

$$(a \otimes b)_{i_1 i_2 \ldots i_m j_1 j_2 \ldots j_n} = a_{i_1 i_2 \ldots i_m} b_{j_1 j_2 \ldots j_n} . \tag{8.2–8}$$

The outer product is computed by Outer[Times, a, b].

The outer product of two vectors is a matrix containing all possible products of elements of the two vectors.

```
In[1]:= Outer[Times, {a, b, c}, {x, y, z}] // MatrixForm
Out[1]//MatrixForm= a x    a y    a z
                    b x    b y    b z
                    c x    c y    c z
```

In a way similar to inner products, we can use another binary operation in place of multiplication. Outer[*mult*, a, b] uses the operation *mult* for combining the elements of a and b.

In this example, the elements of the two vectors are combined with g. Vectors are tensors of rank one; the result is, therefore, a tensor of rank two – that is, an ordinary matrix.

```
In[2]:= Outer[ g, {a, b, c}, {x, y, z} ] // MatrixForm
Out[2]//MatrixForm= g[a, x]    g[a, y]    g[a, z]
                    g[b, x]    g[b, y]    g[b, z]
                    g[c, x]    g[c, y]    g[c, z]
```

8.2.4 Special Topic: Vector Calculus

Many operations of vector calculus can be written as generalized inner and outer products. This formalism leads to compact programs.

8.2.4.1 Divergence

The *divergence* of an n-dimensional vector field $v = (e_1, e_2, \ldots, e_n)$, depending on n variables $(x_1, x_2, \ldots, x_n)$, is defined as

$$\text{div } v = \frac{\partial e_1}{\partial x_1} + \frac{\partial e_2}{\partial x_2} + \cdots + \frac{\partial e_n}{\partial x_n}. \tag{8.2–9}$$

This is an inner "product," with differentiation D[e, x] instead of multiplication.

```
Div[v_List, vars_List] := Inner[D, v, vars, Plus]
```

As an example, we compute the divergence of the ordinary gravitational or electric field in vacuum.

The radius or distance from the center is equal to the square root of the sum of the squares of the coordinates.

```
In[1]:= r = Sqrt[x^2 + y^2 + z^2]
                2    2    2
Out[1]= Sqrt[x  + y  + z ]
```

The magnitude of the field is $1/r^2$. The field points toward the origin. $-(x, y, z)/r$ is a unit vector pointing toward the origin.

```
In[2]:= e = -1/r^2 {x, y, z}/r
                  x                        y
Out[2]= {-(---------------), -(---------------),
            2    2    2 3/2      2    2    2 3/2
           (x  + y  + z )       (x  + y  + z )

          z
   -(---------------)}
      2    2    2 3/2
     (x  + y  + z )
```

Here is its divergence. We know that it should be zero. It is not trivial to see that this expression is indeed zero.

```
In[3]:= Div[ e, {x, y, z} ]
                  2                   2
              3 x                 3 y
Out[3]= --------------- + --------------- +
          2    2    2 5/2    2    2    2 5/2
         (x  + y  + z )     (x  + y  + z )

              2
          3 z                    3
   --------------- - ---------------
     2    2    2 5/2    2    2    2 3/2
    (x  + y  + z )     (x  + y  + z )
```

Simplifying it with Together returns the expected result.

```
In[4]:= Together[%]
Out[4]= 0
```

8.2.4.2 Gradient

The *gradient* is the vector of partial derivatives of a scalar field $s(x_1, x_2, \ldots, x_n)$ with respect to the coordinates:

$$\text{grad } s = (\frac{\partial s}{\partial x_1}, \frac{\partial s}{\partial x_2}, \ldots, \frac{\partial s}{\partial x_n}).$$

(8.2–10)

The scalar s must be differentiated with respect to each of the variables x_1, x_2, ..., x_n. We simply map the differentiation function over the list of variables.

```
Grad[s_, vars_List] := Map[ Function[{v}, D[s, v]], vars ]
```

The operation `Map[]` is explained in Section 11.2.3.1.

The vector field e from the previous section is the gradient of the potential $1/r$.

```
In[5]:= Grad[ 1/r, {x, y, z} ]

Out[5]= {-(———————————————), -(———————————————),
                   x                         y
            ——————————————            ——————————————
              2   2   2 3/2             2   2   2 3/2
            (x + y + z )              (x + y + z )

                      z
          -(———————————————)}
              2   2   2 3/2
            (x + y + z )
```

8.2.4.3 Jacobian

The *Jacobian* of a vector $(e_1, e_2, \ldots, e_m)$ with m components with respect to n variables $(x_1, x_2, \ldots, x_n)$ is the $m \times n$ matrix of partial derivatives

$$\begin{pmatrix} \frac{\partial e_1}{\partial x_1} & \frac{\partial e_1}{\partial x_2} & \cdots & \frac{\partial e_1}{\partial x_n} \\ \frac{\partial e_2}{\partial x_1} & \frac{\partial e_2}{\partial x_2} & \cdots & \frac{\partial e_2}{\partial x_n} \\ \vdots & \vdots & & \vdots \\ \frac{\partial e_m}{\partial x_1} & \frac{\partial e_m}{\partial x_2} & \cdots & \frac{\partial e_m}{\partial x_n} \end{pmatrix}.$$

(8.2–11)

This operation is an outer "product" with differentiation instead of multiplication.

```
Jacobian[f_List, vars_List] := Outer[D, f, vars]
```

Here is a symbolic Jacobian of three functions depending on two variables. The notation $f^{(i,j)}$ denotes a partial derivative: i times with respect to the first variable, j times with respect to the second variable.

```
In[6]:= Jacobian[{f[x, y], g[x, y], h[x, y]},
                 {x, y} ]  // MatrixForm

Out[6]//MatrixForm=   (1,0)            (0,1)
                    f     [x, y]     f     [x, y]

                      (1,0)            (0,1)
                    g     [x, y]     g     [x, y]

                      (1,0)            (0,1)
                    h     [x, y]     h     [x, y]
```

The internal form of the symbolic derivative $f^{(i,j)}$ is `Derivative[i, j][f]`.

```
In[7]:= InputForm[ D[f[x, y], {x, i}, {y, j}] ]
Out[7]//InputForm= Derivative[i, j][f][x, y]
```

8.2.4.4   Laplacian

The *Laplacian* ∇^2 of a scalar field s is defined as

$$\nabla^2 s = \text{div grad } s\,, \qquad\qquad (8.2\text{--}12)$$

which leads to this program:

```
Laplacian[s_, vars_List] := Div[ Grad[s, vars], vars ]
```

Here is the Laplacian of a general potential.

```
In[8]:= Laplacian[ s[x, y, z], {x, y, z} ]
           (0,0,2)            (0,2,0)
Out[8]= s        [x, y, z] + s        [x, y, z] +
           (2,0,0)
         s        [x, y, z]
```

Harmonic functions are functions whose
Laplacian is zero, for example the function $1/r$ from the previous sections.

```
In[9]:= Together[ Laplacian[ 1/r, {x, y, z} ] ]
Out[9]= 0
```

8.2.4.5   A Package for Vector Calculus

The package DivGrad.m (Listing 8.2–2) contains all functions defined in Section 8.2.4. Observe
how easy it was to program these functions. In particular, we did not use any explicit loops,
and the functions work with vectors of any number of components.

8.2.5   Key Concepts

1. The inner product is a generalization of the dot product.

2. Instead of addition and multiplication, other operations (e.g., Boolean operations) can be
   used in inner and outer products.

3. Outer products form all possible combinations of the elements of two tensors.

4. The operations of vector calculus can be described as generalized inner or outer products.

```
BeginPackage["CSM`DivGrad`"]

    (* simple vector calculus in Cartesian coordinates *)

Div::usage = "Div[v, varlist] computes the divergence of the vector field v
    w.r.t. the Cartesian coordinates varlist."

Laplacian::usage = "Laplacian[s, varlist] computes the Laplacian of the scalar
    field s w.r.t. the variables varlist."

Grad::usage = "Grad[s, varlist] computes the gradient of the scalar field s
    w.r.t. the variables varlist."

Jacobian::usage = "Jacobian[flist, varlist] computes the Jacobian of
    the functions flist w.r.t. the variables varlist."

Begin["`Private`"]

protected = Unprotect[{Jacobian}]

Div[v_List, vars_List]  := Inner[D, v, vars, Plus]

Grad[s_, vars_List] := Map[ Function[{v}, D[s, v]], vars ]

Laplacian[s_, vars_List] := Div[ Grad[s, vars], vars ]

Jacobian[f_List, vars_List] := Outer[D, f, vars]

Protect[Evaluate[protected]]

End[]

EndPackage[]
```

Listing 8.2–2   DivGrad.m.

8.3 Linear Algebra

Linear algebra is the foundation for many numerical problem-solving methods. We present a simple algorithm for the solution of linear equations and show an application: the analysis of electronic circuits.

8.3.1 Linear Equations

A system of linear equations with m equations and m unknowns $(x_1, x_2, \ldots, x_m)$ looks as follows:

$$
\begin{array}{ccccccc}
a_{11}x_1 & + & a_{12}x_2 & + & \cdots & + & a_{1m}x_m & = & b_1, \\
a_{21}x_1 & + & a_{22}x_2 & + & \cdots & + & a_{2m}x_m & = & b_2, \\
\vdots & & \vdots & & & & & & \\
a_{m1}x_1 & + & a_{m2}x_2 & + & \cdots & + & a_{mm}x_m & = & b_m.
\end{array}
\tag{8.3--1}
$$

Often, such a system is written in matrix notation. With $\mathbf{A} = (a_{ij})$, $\mathbf{x} = (x_j)$, and $\mathbf{b} = (b_i)$, we get,

$$
\mathbf{A} \cdot \mathbf{x} = \mathbf{b}, \tag{8.3--2}
$$

or, written out in full:

$$
\begin{pmatrix}
a_{11} & a_{12} & \cdots & a_{1m} \\
a_{21} & a_{22} & \cdots & a_{2m} \\
\vdots & \vdots & & \vdots \\
a_{m1} & a_{m2} & \cdots & a_{mm}
\end{pmatrix}
\cdot
\begin{pmatrix}
x_1 \\
x_2 \\
\vdots \\
x_m
\end{pmatrix}
=
\begin{pmatrix}
b_1 \\
b_2 \\
\vdots \\
b_m
\end{pmatrix}. \tag{8.3--3}
$$

Gaussian elimination is a simple method for the solution of such systems. It is based on the fact that the solution does not change if a multiple of one row of the matrix is added to another row. If we add c times row i to row j, we get

$$
a'_{jk} = a_{jk} + ca_{ik}, \qquad k = 1, \ldots, m, \tag{8.3--4}
$$

and, on the right side:

$$
b'_j = b_j + cb_i. \tag{8.3--5}
$$

Such a transformation is called a *row operation*. To make notation simpler, the matrix $\mathbf{A}$ and the right side $\mathbf{b}$ are combined to an $m \times (m + 1)$ matrix $\tilde{\mathbf{A}}$:

$$
\tilde{\mathbf{A}} =
\begin{pmatrix}
a_{11} & a_{12} & \cdots & a_{1m} & b_1 \\
a_{21} & a_{22} & \cdots & a_{2m} & b_2 \\
\vdots & \vdots & & \vdots & \vdots \\
a_{m1} & a_{m2} & \cdots & a_{mm} & b_m
\end{pmatrix}. \tag{8.3--6}
$$

In this notation, a row operation is expressed simply as

$$\tilde{a}'_{jk} = \tilde{a}_{jk} + c\tilde{a}_{ik}, \qquad k = 1, \ldots, m+1. \tag{8.3–7}$$

Our goal is to perform such row operations to put the matrix into triangular form. In triangular form, it looks like this:

$$\begin{pmatrix} a_{11} & a_{12} & a_{13} & \cdots & a_{1m} & b_1 \\ 0 & a'_{22} & a'_{23} & \cdots & a'_{2m} & b'_2 \\ 0 & 0 & a''_{33} & \cdots & a''_{3m} & b''_3 \\ \vdots & \vdots & \vdots & & \vdots & \vdots \\ 0 & 0 & 0 & \cdots & a''^{\ldots'}_{mm} & b''^{\ldots'}_m \end{pmatrix}. \tag{8.3–8}$$

This goal is achieved step by step. To set the the entries in the first column (in rows 2 to m) to zero, we can add $c = -a_{j1}/a_{11}$ times the first row to the jth row. According to Equation 8.3–7, the entries a_{j1} will become zero. If we do this operation for all rows, we get

$$\begin{pmatrix} a_{11} & a_{12} & a_{13} & \cdots & a_{1m} & b_1 \\ 0 & a'_{22} & a'_{23} & \cdots & a'_{2m} & b'_2 \\ 0 & a'_{32} & a'_{33} & \cdots & a'_{3m} & b'_3 \\ \vdots & \vdots & \vdots & & \vdots & \vdots \\ 0 & a'_{m2} & a'_{m3} & \cdots & a'_{mm} & b'_m \end{pmatrix}. \tag{8.3–9}$$

Next, we can eliminate the second column in rows 3 to m, and so on.

Mathematica makes it easy to program these elementary operations. A matrix is a list of rows, each row is a list (of elements). The ith row can simply be extracted as $mat[[i]]$. Arithmetic operations are automatically distributed on the elements of a list. Therefore, a row operation according to Equation 8.3–7 is simply $mat[[j]] = mat[[j]] + c\, mat[[i]]$; you need not program the loop over k. As usual, we can store the modified jth row in the original matrix because we no longer need the old values.

We ask for elements of the form a[i, j] to be written in the usual form with indices.

```
In[1]:= Format[t_a] = Subscripted[t];
```

Here is the original matrix with $m = 3$.

```
In[2]:= MatrixForm[
           mat = Table[ a[i, j], {i, 3}, {j, 4} ]
        ]
```

$$\text{Out[2]//MatrixForm=} \quad \begin{matrix} a_{1,1} & a_{1,2} & a_{1,3} & a_{1,4} \\ a_{2,1} & a_{2,2} & a_{2,3} & a_{2,4} \\ a_{3,1} & a_{3,2} & a_{3,3} & a_{3,4} \end{matrix}$$

Here is the row operation that adds c times the first row to the second row in symbolic form.

$$\text{In[3]:= mat[[2]] + c mat[[1]]}$$

$$\text{Out[3]= } \{c\, a_{1,1} + a_{2,1}, \ c\, a_{1,2} + a_{2,2}, \ c\, a_{1,3} + a_{2,3}, \ c\, a_{1,4} + a_{2,4}\}$$

The command `eliminateColumn[`*mat*`, `*i*`]` iterates the row operation over rows $i+1$ to m. It is used in `GaussianElimination[`*mat*`]` to put the matrix into triangular form, by performing it for $i = 1, 2, \ldots, m$ All these commands are in the package Linalg.m, reproduced in Listing 8.3–1.

```
nRows[mat_] := Dimensions[mat][[1]]

nColumns[mat_] := Dimensions[mat][[2]]

addColumn[mat_?MatrixQ, col_List] /; nRows[mat] == Length[col] :=
    Transpose[ Append[Transpose[mat], col] ]

eliminateColumn[ mat_?MatrixQ, i_Integer ] /; 1 <= i <= nColumns[mat] :=
    Module[{res = mat, m = nRows[mat], j, c},
        Do[ c = -res[[j, i]]/res[[i, i]];
            res[[j]] = res[[j]] + c res[[i]]
          , {j, i+1, m} ];
        res
    ]

GaussianElimination[ mat_?MatrixQ ] :=
    Module[{res = mat, m = Min[nRows[mat], nColumns[mat]], i},
        Do[ res = eliminateColumn[res, i], {i, 1, m-1} ];
        res
    ]

backSubstitution[mat_?MatrixQ] /; nColumns[mat] == 1 + nRows[mat] :=
    Module[{m = nRows[mat], i, k, x},
        x = Table[0, {m}];
        Do[ x[[i]] = (mat[[i, -1]] -
                    Sum[ x[[k]] mat[[i, k]], {k, i+1, m} ])/
                    mat[[i, i]];
          , {i, m, 1, -1} ];
        x
    ]

linearSystem[ a_?MatrixQ, b_?VectorQ ] /; nRows[a] === nColumns[a] === Length[b] :=
    backSubstitution[ GaussianElimination[ addColumn[a, b] ] ]
```

Listing 8.3–1 Linalg.m.

If the matrix is in triangular form, as shown in Equation 8.3–8, the solution $(x_1, x_2, \ldots, x_m)$ is easy to find. Multiplying the last row of the matrix by the vector **x** gives

$$a'_{mm} x_m = b'_m, \tag{8.3--10}$$

or

$$x_m = \frac{b'_m}{a'_{mm}} . \tag{8.3-11}$$

From the second-to-last row, we get

$$a'_{m-1,m-1}x_{m-1}a'_{m-1,m}x_m = b'_{m-1}, \tag{8.3-12}$$

or

$$x_{m-1} = \frac{(b'_{m-1} - a'_{m-1,m}x_m)}{a'_{m-1,m-1}} . \tag{8.3-13}$$

The general formula for row i is

$$x_i = \frac{a'_{i,m+1} - \sum_{k=i+1}^{m} a'_{ik}x_k)}{a'_{ii}} . \tag{8.3-14}$$

Note that b'_i is equal to $a'_{i,m+1}$. In *Mathematica*, this formula looks like this:

```
x[[i]] = (mat[[i,m+1]] - Sum[x[[k]] mat[[i, k]], {k,i+1,m}])/mat[[i,i]] .
```

As you can see in the command backSubstitution[*mat*], x is initialized to a list of length m. The values $x_m, x_{m-1}, \ldots, x_1$ are then computed in this order; therefore, the name *back substitution*.

Time for an example! First, we read the package.

```
In[1]:= << CSM`Linalg`;
```

This definition prints all outputs in matrix form.

```
In[2]:= $PrePrint = MatrixForm;
```

We generate a 3 × 3 matrix with random elements.

```
In[3]:= a = Table[ Random[Real, {-1, 1}], {3}, {3} ]
Out[3]= 0.507978     0.048887      0.519499

        0.979505     0.0374185    -0.0781593

       -0.882894     0.903669      0.0224132
```

Here is the right side of the equation.

```
In[4]:= b = Table[ Random[Real, {-1, 1}], {3} ]
Out[4]= -0.435791

        -0.753735

         0.352373
```

We add the right side as the last column of a.

```
In[5]:= addColumn[a, b]
Out[5]=
         0.507978     0.048887      0.519499     -0.435791

         0.979505     0.0374185    -0.0781593    -0.753735

        -0.882894     0.903669      0.0224132     0.352373
```

Elements of the first column are eliminated according to Equation 8.3–7.

```
In[6]:= eliminateColumn[ %, 1 ]
Out[6]=
      0.507978      0.048887      0.519499     -0.435791
      0.           -0.0568476    -1.07988       0.0865768
      0.            0.988637      0.925331     -0.405056
```

Next, the second column. The matrix is now in triangular form.

```
In[7]:= eliminateColumn[ %, 2 ]
Out[7]=
      0.507978      0.048887      0.519499     -0.435791
      0.           -0.0568476    -1.07988       0.0865768
      0.            0.           -17.8549       1.1006
```

The solution is obtained by back substitution.

```
In[8]:= x = backSubstitution[ % ]
Out[8]= -0.760977
        -0.352017
        -0.0616415
```

The verify the solution, we insert it into the equation.

```
In[9]:= a . x
Out[9]= -0.435791
        -0.753735
         0.352373
```

The result should be equal to *b*. We check it by subtraction. It is not completely accurate because of roundoff errors.

```
In[10]:= % - b
Out[10]=
         0.
                    -16
         1.11022 10

                    -17
        -5.55112 10
```

Chop[] can be used to remove small non-zero parts.

```
In[11]:= Chop[ % ]
Out[11]= 0
         0
         0
```

This function performs all solution steps and gives us the solution of $\mathbf{A} \cdot x = \mathbf{b}$ directly.

```
In[12]:= linearSystem[ a, b ]
Out[12]= -0.760977
         -0.352017
         -0.0616415
```

The method works also for symbolic systems! In this way, we can can find the formula for the solution of a general 2×2 system.

```
In[13]:= Simplify[ linearSystem[ {{a11,a12}, {a21,a22}},
                                 {b1,b2} ] ]
Out[13]=    a22 b1 - a12 b2
           ─────────────────
           -(a12 a21) + a11 a22

            a21 b1 - a11 b2
           ─────────────────
            a12 a21 - a11 a22
```

So far, we assumed that the elements a'_{ii} are always different from zero, because we have to divide by them. These elements are called *pivots*. A pivot may be zero even if the system of equations is *regular* – that is, has exactly one solution. If element a_{ii} is zero, we can find an element below it – that is, one of $a_{i,i+1}, \ldots, a_{im}$, that is different from zero. We exchange the two rows, and the algorithm can continue. We have to undo the exchanges at the end to put the solution into the right order. These manipulations are called *pivoting*. Pivoting is the topic of Exercise 8.6.

An algorithm for solutions of linear systems is already built into *Mathematica*. The function is called `LinearSolve[]`, and it can be used in the same way as our `linearSystem[]`.

8.3.2   Example: Passive Electronic Circuits

In electrical engineering, the imaginary unit is usually denoted by j instead of i, because current is denoted by i. In a *Mathematica* Notebook you can use the symbol $\mathfrak{j}$ on input, but the output will still be given in terms of $\mathfrak{i}$ or I. In this book, we want to use the symbol j on input and output; it is not difficult to teach *Mathematica* this convention.

This definition allows us to use the symbol j on *input*	`In[1]:= j = I;`

... and this format achieves the corresponding *output*.	`In[2]:= Unprotect[ Complex ];\`
	`Format[c_Complex] := Re[c] + HoldForm[j] Im[c];\`
	`Protect[ Complex ];`

We can work with complex numbers in j notation in the usual way.	`In[3]:= (1 + j)^2` `Out[3]= 2 j`

These two definitions are in the package Electronics.m. A definition that makes the frontend print I as $\mathfrak{j}$ is also in Electronics.m.

The analysis of passive circuits under a stationary alternating current leads to linear systems of equations. In equilibrium, all currents and voltages oscillate with a certain frequency ω and can be expressed as $u(t) = u_0 e^{j\omega t}$, and so on. The time dependency can be removed with the *impedance* formulation. For ordinary resistors, we have the equation $U = IR$ (Ohm's law). We can also apply this to the other two passive elements: capacitances and inductances. For a capacitor C, we have

$$U = \frac{I}{j\omega C}; \tag{8.3–15}$$

its impedance is $1/(j\omega C)$. For an inductance L, we get

$$U = I(j\omega L); \tag{8.3–16}$$

its impedance is $j\omega L$.

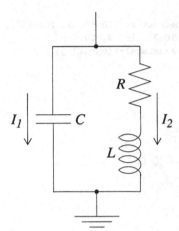

In the resonator shown at left, the total impedance is computed from the parallel impedances in the two branches. In the left branch, we get

$$z_1 = \frac{1}{j\omega C};$$ (8.3–17)

in the right branch, we have a sum of two impedances (because they are in series)

$$z_2 = R + j\omega L.$$ (8.3–18)

These two branches are in parallel, which gives

$$z = \frac{1}{1/z_1 + 1/z_2}.$$ (8.3–19)

Here are the two expressions in *Mathematica*.

```
In[4]:= z1 = 1/(j omega c);\
        z2 = r + j omega l;
```

Here is the formula for the impedance of the resonator.

```
In[5]:= z = Together[ 1/(1/z1 + 1/z2) ]

              -j (l omega - j r)
Out[5]=  ----------------------------
                            2
         -1 + c l omega  - j c omega r
```

Let us define it as a function. Note: if you use % in the body of a function, you must use an immediate definition (with =), instead of the usual delayed definition (with :=).

```
In[6]:= impedance[r_, l_, c_] = %;
```

In this way, we can plot the *frequency response* – that is, the impedance as a function of frequency – from 0 to 100 kHz. There is the characteristic maximum at the resonating frequency. Here it is for a resistor of 10 Ω and $C = 1\,\mu F$, $L = 1\,mH$.

```
In[7]:= Plot[
          Evaluate[Abs[impedance[10, 1.0 10^-3, 10^-6]]],
          {omega, 0, 100.0 10^3}
        ];
```

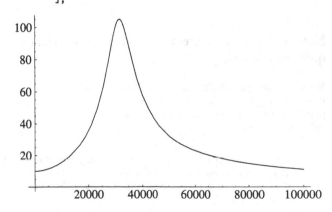

We can vary two parameters. Here we see
the quality Q of the resonator. It depends
on the damping resistor. With larger R, the
maximum becomes flatter and shifts toward
lower frequencies.

```
In[8]:= Plot3D[
          Evaluate[Abs[impedance[r, 1.0 10^-3, 10^-6]]],
          {omega, 0.0, 62 10^3}, {r, 9, 50.0},
          PlotRange->All, AxesLabel->{ω,r,Q} ];
```

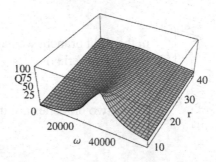

Instead of deriving the formula for the impedance step by step from the circuit, we can derive
the relationship between current and voltage in the various points of the circuit in a mechanical
way by using Kirchhoff's law. The resulting equations are linear and can be solved easily.

The first equation is Kirchhoff's law. The
next two are the equations for the relationship between current and voltage in the two
branches.

```
In[1]:= gl = { i == i1 + i2,
               u == i1/(j omega c),
               u == i2 r + i2 j omega l };
```

The equations are linear in i, i_1, and i_2 and
can be solved.

```
In[2]:= Solve[ gl, {i, i1, i2} ]
```

$$Out[2]= \left\{\left\{ i \to j\ c\ omega\ u - \frac{j\ u}{l\ omega - j\ r}, \right.\right.$$

$$\left.\left. i1 \to j\ c\ omega\ u,\ i2 \to \frac{-j\ u}{l\ omega - j\ r}\right\}\right\}$$

Now we know the current i as it depends on voltage u. The overall impedance is simply the
quotient $z = u/i$.

We substitute the solution in u/i and simplify the result. Please convince yourself
that the result is the same as in the previous
calculation on page 191.

```
In[3]:= Together[ u/i /. %[[1]] ]
```

$$Out[3]= \frac{-j\ (l\ omega - j\ r)}{-1 + c\ l\ omega^2 - j\ c\ omega\ r}$$

The interesting quantity z can be computed directly by adding an equation for it and
asking `Solve[]` to eliminate the auxiliary
variables u, i, i_1, and i_2.

```
In[4]:= Solve[Append[gl, z == u/i], {z}, {u, i, i1, i2}]
```

$$Out[4]= \left\{\left\{z \to \frac{-j\ (l\ omega - j\ r)}{-1 + c\ l\ omega^2 - j\ c\ omega\ r}\right\}\right\}$$

8.3.3   Key Concepts

1. Linear systems of equations can be solved by simple matrix operations.

2. Impedance formalism provides for an easy calculation of electronic circuits under stationary alternating currents.

8.4   Programs with Arrays

Programming with dynamic data structures in *Mathematica* and LISP is quite different from programming in traditional languages such as Pascal or C. We shall discuss the differences in the memory management underlying these two programming styles and then show how C-style programming with arrays looks like in *Mathematica*.

8.4.1   Memory Management

Working with dynamic data structures is quite simple in *Mathematica*. We saw examples in Section 6.3 (binary trees), and we shall see more in Section 9.2, where we work with lists. Such simple programs are possible only because *Mathematica* performs *memory management* itself. Every time we build a new expression with $e = h[e_1, \ldots, e_n]$ and assign it to a variable, a portion of our computer's memory must be reserved. A pointer to this part of the memory is then stored in the value field of the internal data structure for the symbol e. If we use the expression $h[e_1, \ldots, e_n]$ itself as an element of another expression, as in $f[e, \ldots]$, another pointer to the same piece of memory occupied by e is stored in this new expression. The expression is not duplicated. This method saves a lot of memory.

During a symbolic computation many expressions are created that are no longer in use at a later time. For example, if we assign a new value to the variable e, the old pointer to $h[e_1, \ldots, e_n]$ is overwritten. As soon as the last pointer to this expression has been overwritten, the expression can no longer be accessed; it has become *garbage*. This garbage accumulates in memory and would soon take up all available space.

One part of *Mathematica* serves to find and collect this garbage. Once reclaimed, we can use this memory to store new expressions. This action – called *garbage collection* – is automatic and invisible to the user.[1]

Traditional programming languages do not offer such garbage collection. It is left to us programmers to do it ourselves. To give you an idea of how it works, we can simulate such memory management techniques in *Mathematica*.

8.4.2   A Memory Model

The computer's memory is viewed as an array of cells. Each cell can store an integer. Cells are numbered sequentially, starting with 1. (In some programming languages, arrays start with index 0.) To represent n cells of memory, we use a list with n elements. The whole list is assigned to the variable a. The ith cell can be accessed using $a[[i]]$, and a new value can be

---

[1] This necessary task uses about 10% of the total computing time.

stored there with a[[i]] = *val*. In many programming languages, the notation a[i] is used instead; it means something different in *Mathematica*.

We create an array with 10 elements. The value Null marks the elements as uninitialized.

`In[1]:= a = Table[Null, {10}];`

We define two of the elements.

`In[2]:= a[[1]] = 5; a[[2]] = 7;`

Here, we retrieve element a_2.

`In[3]:= a[[2]]`

`Out[3]= 7`

8.4.3   Example: The Heap

A *heap* is a data structure similar to the binary tree. In this section, we shall store heaps in arrays and look at the most important algorithms in this representation. All functions described in this section are part of Heap.m.

Here is an array of 10 numbers.

`In[1]:= h = {21, 19, 19, 9, 17, 5, 8, 6, 4, 11};`

We can treat such an array as a binary tree. The root is at position 1, and the two successors of the node i are at positions $2i$ and $2i + 1$. The predecessor of node k is at position $\lfloor k/2 \rfloor$.

`In[2]:= HeapPlot[h, 10];`

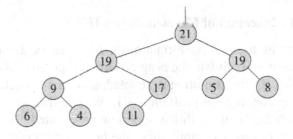

This picture shows the node numbers themselves. You can easily verify that the positions of successors and predecessors of nodes are as just described.

`In[3]:= HeapPlot[`
`           {1, 2, 3, 4, 5, 6, 7, 8, 9, 10}, 10];`

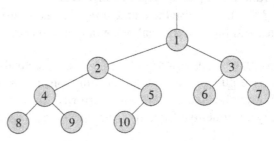

By storing the successors of a node at fixed positions, we need not store the structure of the tree explicitly. Compare this method with the data structure for binary trees in Section 6.3, where we needed the two fields `leftTree` and `rightTree` to store the successors. Note that a heap is always a *complete* binary tree – that is, the lowest level is filled in from the left, and it does not contain any holes.

A heap is *partially ordered*. The value at a node must be larger than the values in the two successors of the node (if it has any successors). In our example, the root (node 1) has two successors at positions 2 and 3; the nodes at positions 2–4 have also two successors each; the node at position 5 has one successor (at position 10), and the nodes at positions 6–10 have no successors. The partial order does not imply that the heap is completely ordered like a binary tree. All we can say is that the *largest* node is at the root.

In a heap of size n, the following conditions must be satisfied for all indices $i = 1, \ldots, n$:

$$\begin{aligned} h_i &\geq h_{2i}, &&\text{if } 2i \leq n, \\ h_i &\geq h_{2i+1}, &&\text{if } 2i + 1 \leq n, \end{aligned} \tag{8.4--1}$$

or, expressed differently:

$$h_k \leq h_{\lfloor k/2 \rfloor}, \quad k = 2, \ldots, n. \tag{8.4--2}$$

It turns out that it is easy to insert a new element into a heap so that these conditions are maintained.

8.4.3.1   Insertion of Elements into a Heap

If elements $h_1, \ldots, h_n$ form a heap, a new element can first be put at position $n + 1$. This placement may violate the heap condition Equation 8.4–2, but only at position $k = n + 1$. If $h_k > h_{\lfloor k/2 \rfloor}$, the condition is violated, and we can exchange elements k and $\lfloor k/2 \rfloor$ to satisfy the heap condition at position $n + 1$. We can then set $k = \lfloor k/2 \rfloor$, which is the next position at which the heap condition may now be violated. Again, we compare h_k with $h_{\lfloor k/2 \rfloor}$ and continue in this way, until either the heap condition is already satisfied (if $h_k \leq h_{\lfloor k/2 \rfloor}$), or until we reach $k = 1$.

The function `upHeap[h, k]` implements these steps for restoring the heap condition (Listing 8.4–1). Because the element $v = h_k$ takes part in all exchanges, we perform only half exchanges and put v at its final place only at the end. This idea saves half of all assignments.

We must give the function `upHeap[`h`, `k_0`]` the attribute `HoldFirst` to prevent evaluation of its first argument `h`. Inside the function, we want to modify the *value* of `h` (the list representing the heap). We can perform this modification only if `h` is not evaluated. Normally, arguments of functions are evaluated, however.

The first nine elements form a heap, the last   `In[4]:= h = {21, 19, 19, 9, 17, 5, 8, 6, 4, 20};`
one violates the heap condition.

```
p[k_Integer?Positive] := Floor[k/2]      (* Predecessor node *)

SetAttributes[ upHeap, HoldFirst ]

upHeap[h_Symbol, k0_] :=
    Module[{v = h[[k0]], k = k0},
        While[ p[k] > 0 && h[[ p[k] ]] < v,
            h[[ k ]] = h[[ p[k] ]];
            k = p[k]
        ];
        h[[k]] = v;
        h
    ]
```

Listing 8.4–1   Restoring the heap condition at the end of the heap.

This graphic shows it clearly. The predeces-   `In[5]:= HeapPlot[ h, 10 ];`
sor of 20 is 17. Its predecessor 19 is also too
small.

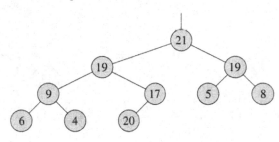

A sequence of exchanges puts the tenth ele-   `In[6]:= upHeap[ h, 10 ]`
ment at the right place.   `Out[6]= {21, 20, 19, 9, 19, 5, 8, 6, 4, 17}`

Now, the heap condition is satisfied every-   `In[7]:= HeapPlot[ h, 10 ];`
where.

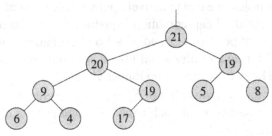

Insertion of elements into a heap is now a simple matter. We increase the size of the heap
by 1, put the new element at the end, and call upHeap[] (Listing 8.4–2). This function, too,
needs the attribute HoldAll to keep the second argument n unevaluated. The size of the heap
is stored in a variable whose value is modified inside insert to keep track of any changes
in size.

```
SetAttributes[ insert, HoldAll ]

insert[h_Symbol, n_Symbol, v_] := (h[[++n]] = v; upHeap[h, n]; h)
```

Listing 8.4–2   Inserting an element into a heap.

The variables h and n describe an empty heap with room for at most 10 elements.

```
In[8]:= h = newHeap[10]; n = 0;
```

This loop inserts eight random numbers into the heap.

```
In[9]:= Do[ insert[ h, n, Random[Integer, {0, 20}] ],
            {8}
        ]
```

Here is the resulting heap.

```
In[10]:= HeapPlot[ h, n ];
```

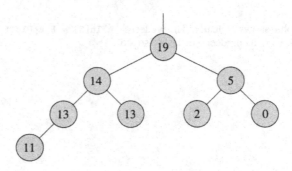

8.4.3.2   Deletion of the Largest Element

How can we remove the first (and largest) element from a heap? Because the heap must not have any holes, we can tentatively put the last element at the empty root $i = 1$. This placement may violate the heap condition Equation 8.4–1. To restore it, we find the larger of the two successors at positions $2i$ and $2i + 1$ and exchange it with position i. Then, we can set $i = 2i$ or $i = 2i + 1$, and continue until there are no more successors, which happens for $i > n/2$, or until the heap condition is no longer violated.

The function downHeap[h, n] implements these steps to restore the heap condition. Again, we perform only half exchanges and put the element $v = h_1$ at its final position at the end (Listing 8.4–3).

In the heap from the previous example, we exchange the first and last elements. Now, the heap condition is violated.

```
In[11]:= {h[[1]], h[[n]]} = {h[[n]], h[[1]]};\
         h

Out[11]= {11, 14, 5, 13, 13, 2, 0, 19, Null, Null}
```

A few exchanges restore it.

```
In[12]:= downHeap[ h, n ]

Out[12]= {14, 13, 5, 19, 13, 2, 0, 11, Null, Null}
```

```
SetAttributes[ downHeap, HoldFirst ]

downHeap[h_Symbol, n_] :=
   Module[{v = h[[1]], i = 1, j},
      While[ i <= n/2,
         j = 2i;
         (* find larger successor *)
         If[ j < n && h[[ j ]] < h[[ j+1 ]], j++ ];
         If[ v > h[[ j ]], Break[] ]; (* ok *)
         h[[ i ]] = h[[ j ]];
         i = j
      ];
      h[[ i ]] = v;
      h
   ]
```

Listing 8.4–3   Restoring the heap condition at the root of the heap.

Here is the result.   In[13]:= HeapPlot[h, n-1];

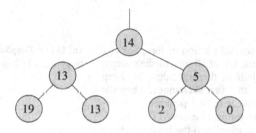

The deletion operation combines these steps into a function. It decrements to value of n by 1. For reasons soon to be seen, the function delete[] returns the element that was deleted (Listing 8.4–4).

```
SetAttributes[ delete, HoldAll ]

delete[h_Symbol, n_Symbol] :=
   Module[ {v = h[[1]]},
      h[[1]] = h[[n--]];
      downHeap[h, n];
      v
   ]
```

Listing 8.4–4   Deleting the largest element from a heap.

8.4.3.3 Heapsort

We can use the functions for inserting and deleting elements in a heap to implement an efficient sorting method. (See Section 6.2 for other sorting methods.) To sort a list, we insert all of its elements into a heap. The largest element is at the root of the heap. We can remove it with delete[]. Now the second largest element is at the root. We can remove it, and so on. We can, therefore, read out the elements in decreasing order.

We can put the removed elements at the end of the array used to store the heap. This part of the array is no longer used to hold the shrinking heap. In this way, the elements are put into the array with the largest one at the end; in other words, they are sorted in *ascending* order. The program is quite simple. It consists of two loops, first iterating from 1 to n, then from n down to 1.

```
HeapSort[a_List] :=
    Module[{n = 0, h = a, i},
        Do[ insert[ h, n, h[[i]] ], {i, 1, Length[a]} ];
        Do[ h[[i]] = delete[ h, n ], {i, Length[a], 1, -1} ];
        h
    ]
```

Listing 8.4–5   Sorting with a heap.

We wrote a special version of HeapSort[] that returns the list of all intermediate steps. In the first half of the algorithm, the heap is built up with a few exchanges. Then the largest element is in first position. It is exchanged with the last element. This last element is now sifted into the heap to restore the heap condition. Then, the (new) first element is exchanged with the second-to-last one, and so on.

```
In[14]:= HeapSortList[{1,5,2,4,3,7,6}] // TableForm
Out[14]//TableForm=
```

1	5	2	4	3	7	6
1	5	2	4	3	7	6
5	1	2	4	3	7	6
5	1	2	4	3	7	6
5	4	2	1	3	7	6
5	4	2	1	3	7	6
7	4	5	1	3	2	6
7	4	6	1	3	2	5
6	4	5	1	3	2	7
5	4	2	1	3	6	7
4	3	2	1	5	6	7
3	1	2	4	5	6	7
2	1	3	4	5	6	7
1	2	3	4	5	6	7
1	2	3	4	5	6	7

Heapsort has the same asymptotic complexity as Quicksort (i.e., $O(n \log n)$, see Section 6.2.3), but the inner loop is more complicated; so it runs only half as fast in practice.

8.4.3.4   A Look at Other Programming Languages

Listing 8.4–6 shows the fundamental heap operations in the language C. The programs are similar to the ones we developed for *Mathematica*. The syntax of the procedural part of *Mathematica* is (intentionally) similar to C. Note that we use pointers for the arguments that require the attributes HoldFirst or HoldAll.

8.4.4 Key Concepts

1. A heap is a partially ordered binary tree.

2. It is easy to insert an element or to delete the largest element in a heap.

3. We can use a heap for an efficient sorting method.

```c
void
upheap(int *h, int k)
{
    int         v = h[k];

    while (k/2 > 0 && h[k/2] < v) {
        h[k] = h[k/2];
        k = k/2;
    }
    h[k] = v;
}

void
insert(int *h, int *pn, int v)
{
    h[++*pn] = v;
    upheap(h, *pn);
}

void
downheap(int *h, int n)
{
    int         v = h[1], k = 1, j;

    while (k <= n/2) {
        j = 2 * k;
        if (j < n && h[j] < h[j + 1]) j++;
        if (v > h[j]) break;
        h[k] = h[j];
        k = j;
    }
    h[k] = v;
}

int
delete(int *h, int *pn)
{
    int         v = h[1];

    h[1] = h[(*pn)--];
    downheap(h, *pn);
    return v;
}
```

Listing 8.4–6   heap.c: Heap operations in C.

8.5   Application: Aggregation

This section presents a simple model for the aggregation of particles in a grid. A particle starts at a randomly chosen point and walks to one of the four neighboring points at each time step. If it comes next to an already aggregated particle, it stays where it is. The experiment is repeated many times, starting in a configuration with just one particle in the middle.

The grid positions are represented in a two-dimensional array. The value 0 denotes an empty position, 2 is used for an occupied site. The package Aggregate.m (Listing 8.5–1 on page 206) implements these functions:

initialGrid[*n*]	create initial configuration, grid size $2n + 1$
occupy[*grid*, {*x*, *y*}]	occupy grid position (x, y)
randomDirection	give a random direction (left, right, up, down)
walk[*grid*]	aggregate one particle
aggregate[*grid*, *n*]	aggregate n particles
gridGraphics[*grid*]	draw the grid

The functions from Aggregate.m.

initialGrid[*n*] creates a new grid with one particle in the center. The function walk[*grid*] chooses a random starting point in the grid and walks the particle until it comes next to an already occupied site or until it gets too far away. If the second case happens, it creates another particle until one has been successfully aggregated. To speed up the test whether the particle is next to another one, we mark the neighboring positions at the time a particle is aggregated (in the auxiliary function occupy[]). In this way, we can test whether a site is next to an occupied one by looking at this site only, not at all of its neighbors. This idea makes the program run faster because aggregation happens less frequently than moving around. Taking expensive calculations outside of inner loops is an important tool for improving the run time of programs.

Here is our initial configuration. Note the 2 in the center (marking it as occupied) and the neighborhood consisting of 1.

```
In[1]:= initialGrid[3] // MatrixForm
Out[1]//MatrixForm= 0   0   0   0   0   0   0
                    0   0   0   0   0   0   0
                    0   0   0   1   0   0   0
                    0   0   1   2   1   0   0
                    0   0   0   1   0   0   0
                    0   0   0   0   0   0   0
                    0   0   0   0   0   0   0
```

We aggregate one particle.

```
In[2]:= walk[%] // MatrixForm
Out[2]//MatrixForm= 0   0   0   0   0   0   0
                    0   0   0   0   0   0   0
                    0   0   0   1   0   0   0
                    0   0   1   2   1   0   0
                    0   0   1   2   1   0   0
                    0   0   0   1   0   0   0
                    0   0   0   0   0   0   0
```

This iteration aggregates 11 particles in a grid with radius five, and returns all intermediate grids.

```
In[3]:= NestList[walk, initialGrid[5], 11];
```

Now, we generate graphics of all intermediate grids in a 3 × 4 matrix.

```
In[4]:= Partition[ gridGraphics /@ %, 4 ];
```

Here are the pictures. They show how the aggregate grows one by one.

```
In[5]:= Show[ GraphicsArray[%] ];
```

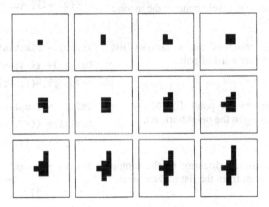

So far, we chose one of the four orthogonal directions. Another model allows also for diagonal movements, which gives a total of eight possible directions. The possible directions are stored in the list `neighborhood` and can easily be changed. Any change needs to be taken into account in the function `occupy[]` as well. This behavior is automatic because `occupy[]` uses the same list `neighborhood` to help mark the neighboring sites.

We generate a picture with 20 particles for the orthogonal neighborhood.

```
In[6]:= neighborhood = orthogonal;\
        gro =
          gridGraphics[aggregate[initialGrid[6], 20]];
```

Now, a picture with 20 particles, but for a diagonal neighborhood.

```
In[7]:= neighborhood = diagonal;\
        grd =
          gridGraphics[aggregate[initialGrid[6], 20]];
```

Here, both pictures are shown next to each other.

`In[8]:= Show[GraphicsArray[{gro, grd}]];`

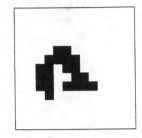 

Let us explain a few details of the programs in **Aggregate.m** (see Listing 8.5–1).

To generate the diagonal neighborhood, we first form an outer "product" (see Section 8.2.3) in which we combine all elements of the first list with all elements of the second list.

```
In[9]:= Outer[List, {-1, 0, 1}, {-1, 0, 1}]
Out[9]= {{{-1, -1}, {-1, 0}, {-1, 1}},
  {{0, -1}, {0, 0}, {0, 1}}, {{1, -1}, {1, 0}, {1, 1}}}
```

`Flatten[]` removes the outermost list brackets, leaving a list of pairs.

```
In[10]:= Flatten[ %, 1 ]
Out[10]= {{-1, -1}, {-1, 0}, {-1, 1}, {0, -1}, {0, 0},
  {0, 1}, {1, -1}, {1, 0}, {1, 1}}
```

We must remove the point {0, 0}, which does not belong to the neighborhood.

```
In[11]:= Complement[ %, {{0, 0}} ]
Out[11]= {{-1, -1}, {-1, 0}, {-1, 1}, {0, -1}, {0, 1},
  {1, -1}, {1, 0}, {1, 1}}
```

We obtain a random direction by choosing a random element from the list of directions.

```
In[12]:= neighborhood[[
         Random[Integer, {1, Length[neighborhood]}]
       ]]
Out[12]= {-1, 1}
```

To occupy a point $\{x, y\}$ with a particle, we must mark all neighboring points with the value `neighboring`, unless they are already occupied. We can avoid a conditional statement by taking the maximum of the old value and `neighboring`, provided that `occupied > neighboring`. Because we chose integer values 1 and 2 for `neighboring` and `occupied`, respectively, this condition is satisfied. We can obtain the coordinates of the neighboring points by adding to $\{x, y\}$ all elements of the array `neighborhood` in turn. The variable `f` contains the grid values in a two-dimensional array (a matrix). Therefore, we must perform the assignment

```
f[[x+dx, y+dy]] = Max[ f[[x+dx, y+dy]], neighboring ]
```

for all pairs $\{dx, dy\}$. We write the assignment as a pure function g with parameters dx and dy,

```
Function[{dx,dy}, f[[x+dx, y+dy]] = Max[f[[x+dx, y+dy]], neighboring]] ,
```

and apply it with

```
Apply[ g, neighborhood, {1} ]
```

to all pairs $\{dx, dy\}$ in the variable neighborhood.

We build the initial configuration by first creating an empty array with dimensions $(2n + 1) \times (2n + 1)$ (using Table[]), and then occupying the central cite. Because walk[] returns the new grid after aggregating a particle, we can apply it repeatedly to aggregate several particles. This iteration is best done with Nest[].

The graphics function Raster[] takes an array of graylevels as argument. 0 is black and 1 is white. Raster[] is used to make the grid graphics. Because the grid is already an array, we need only change the values 0, 1, and 2 into graylevels 0 and 1. The best way to do this is with a replacement rule.

```
In[13]:= Show[ Graphics[
            Raster[ {{0, 0.25, 0.5, 0.75, 1.0},
                     {1.0, 0.75, 0.5, 0.25, 0}} ],
            AspectRatio->Automatic, Frame->True,
            FrameTicks->None ] ];
```

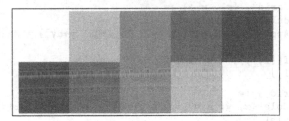

8.5.1 Key Concepts

1. Aggregation is a model of physical processes such as cloud formation, freezing, or sedimentation.

2. A simulation requires random numbers.

3. We can often take expensive calculations out of an inner loop to speed up the program.

```
BeginPackage["CSM`Aggregate`"]

initialGrid::usage = "initialGrid[n] gives the initial configuration
    with a radius n."
occupy::usage = "occupy[grid, {x, y}] occupies the grid position {x, y}."
walk::usage = "walk[grid] aggregates one particle."
gridGraphics::usage = "gridGraphics[g] generates a graphics of grid g."
aggregate::usage = "aggregate[grid, n] performs n experiments (with walk[])."
orthogonal::usage = "orthogonal is the orthogonal neighborhood."
diagonal::usage = "diagonal is the diagonal neighborhood."
neighborhood::usage = "neighborhood is the current neighborhood."

Begin["`Private`"]

orthogonal = {{1,0}, {0,1}, {-1,0}, {0,-1}}
diagonal = Complement[Flatten[Outer[List, {-1,0,1}, {-1,0,1}], 1], {{0, 0}}]
neighborhood = orthogonal (* default *)
randomDirection :=
    neighborhood[[ Random[Integer, {1, Length[neighborhood]}] ]]

occupied = 2; neighboring = 1; empty = 0;

occupy[grid_, {x_, y_}] :=
    Module[{f = grid},
        Apply[ Function[{dx,dy}, f[[x+dx, y+dy]] = Max[f[[x+dx, y+dy]], neighboring]],
                neighborhood, {1} ];
        f[[x, y]] = occupied;
        f ]

walk[grid_] :=
    Module[{x, y, n = Length[grid], c = (Length[grid]-1)/2},
        While[ True,
            {x, y} = Table[Random[Integer, {2, n-1}], {2}];
            If[ grid[[x, y]] == occupied, Continue[] ]; (* already occupied *)
            While[1 < x < n && 1 < y < n && grid[[x, y]] == empty,
                {x, y} = {x, y} + randomDirection ];
            If[ 1 < x < n && 1 < y < n,
                Return[occupy[grid, {x, y}]] ]           (* ok *)
    ]]

initialGrid[n_] := occupy[ Table[0, {2n+1}, {2n+1}], {n+1, n+1} ]
aggregate[grid_, m_] := Nest[ walk, grid, m ]

coloring = {occupied -> 0, neighboring -> 1, empty -> 1};
gridGraphics[ grid_, opts___ ] := Graphics[Raster[grid /. coloring],
    opts, AspectRatio->1, Frame->True, FrameTicks->None]

End[]

Protect[ initialGrid, occupy, walk, gridGraphics, aggregate ]
Protect[ orthogonal, diagonal ]

EndPackage[]
```

Listing 8.5–1   Aggregate.m.

8.6 Exercises

8.1 Simple Evaluations[2]

Give the result of evaluating the following expressions. If there are any nested functions, also give the most important intermediate steps. Assume that each example is evaluated in a fresh *Mathematica* session. Consecutive expressions in one example are evaluated one after another in the same session.

1. `p[x_, y_Integer] := x^(y-1)`
   `Thread[ p[1.1, {1, 2, 3.5}] ]`

2. `m = {{a11, a12, a13}, {a21, a22, a23}, {a31, a32, a33}};`
   `Rest[ Transpose[ Rest[ Transpose[m] ] ] ]`

3. `Inner[Power, {a, b, c}, {x, y, z}, Times]`

4. `Outer[D, {x - y, x y}, {x, y}]`

5. `Inner[ List, {a, b}, {x, y}, Dot ]`

8.2 Partitioning Lists[3]

Write a function `split[`*list*`, s]` that takes two lists as arguments. The first list, *list*, is any list, the second list, *s*, is a list of nonnegative integers. The result should be the partitioning of the first list into sublists whose lengths are given by the elements of *s* in turn.

The sublists have lengths 3, 0, 3, and 2, respectively.	`In[1]:= split[{a, b, c, d, e, f, g, h}, {3, 0, 3, 2}]` `Out[1]= {{a, b, c}, {}, {d, e, f}, {g, h}}`
If the inner list brackets are removed, the original list is restored.	`In[2]:= Flatten[ % ]` `Out[2]= {a, b, c, d, e, f, g, h}`

This partitioning is possible only if the sum of the elements of *s* is equal to the length of *list*. Formally, the result of

$$\text{split}[\{e_1, e_2, \ldots, e_n\}, \{s_1, s_2, \ldots, s_m\}]$$

is equal to

$$\{\{e_1, \ldots, e_{s_1}\}, \{e_{s_1+1}, \ldots, e_{s_1+s_2}\}, \ldots, \{e_{s_1+\ldots+s_{m-1}+1}, \ldots, e_{s_1+\ldots+s_m}\}\},$$

with $n = s_1 + \ldots + s_m$.

---

[2]Written examination, ETH Zürich, Department of Mathematics and Physics.

[3]Programming competition, *Mathematica* Conference 1992, Rotterdam.

8.3   Relative Maxima of a List[4]

Write a function `Maxima[`*list*`]` that finds all numbers in the list *list* that are larger than all preceding numbers in the list.

The result is a list of all those elements of the list that are larger than all preceding ones.	`In[3]:= Maxima[{4, 7, 5, 2, 7, 9, 1}]`
	
	`Out[3]= Maxima[{4, 7, 5, 2, 7, 9, 1}]`

8.4   Frequency Count

Write a function that counts how often each of the numbers $1 \ldots n$ occurs in a list of positive numbers. The result should be a list of frequencies $\{f_1, f_2, \ldots, f_n\}$, where f_i is the number of occurrences of i, and n is the largest number occurring in the list.

In this example, the number 1 occurs once, 2 does not occur at all, 3 occurs three times, and so on.	`In[4]:= Frequencies[{1, 3, 3, 4, 3, 5}]`
	
	`Out[4]= {1, 0, 3, 1, 1}`

8.5   Run-Length Coding[5]

The *run-length coding* of a list l is a list of pairs

$$r = \{\{e_1, k_1\}, \{e_2, k_2\}, \ldots, \{e_m, k_m\}\} \, .$$

The e_i are any expressions, the k_i are integers ≥ 1, and $m \geq 0$. The list r describes (encodes) the list

$$l = \{\underbrace{e_1, e_1, \ldots, e_1}_{k_1}, \underbrace{e_2, e_2, \ldots, e_2}_{k_2}, \ldots, \underbrace{e_m, e_m, \ldots, e_m}_{k_m}\} \, ,$$

where each element e_i occurs exactly k_i times in sequence. If the list l contains many repetitions of elements, the run-length coding is a short description of l.

Write a function `RunLength[`l`]` that finds the run-length coding of l.

In this list, the element `a` occurs once.	`In[1]:= RunLength[{a}]`
	
	`Out[1]= {{a, 1}}`

Here, we have one `a` and two `b`.	`In[2]:= RunLength[{a, b, b}]`
	
	`Out[2]= {{a, 1}, {b, 2}}`

The order of elements is important. The second `a` cannot be combined with the first one.	`In[3]:= RunLength[{a, b, a}]`
	
	`Out[3]= {{a, 1}, {b, 1}, {a, 1}}`

---

[4]Programming competition, *Mathematica* Conference 1992, Boston.

[5]Programming competition, *Mathematica* Conference 1991, San Francisco.

8.6   Pivoting Strategies

Modify the program for the solution of linear systems of equations Linalg.m such that pivots are searched in a column. Choose the element with the largest absolute value. See page 185.

8.7   Inverting Op Amp

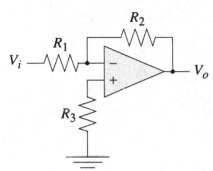

The circuit shown on the left is an inverting amplifier. Compute the *voltage gain* $A_v = V_o/V_i$ (see also Section 1.1.4).

The solution is valid also for arbitrary *impedances* instead of the resistors R_1 and R_2. Plot the frequency response for $R_1 = C = 2.0\,\mu F$ and $R_2 = 100\,\Omega$.

Chapter 9
List Processing and Recursion

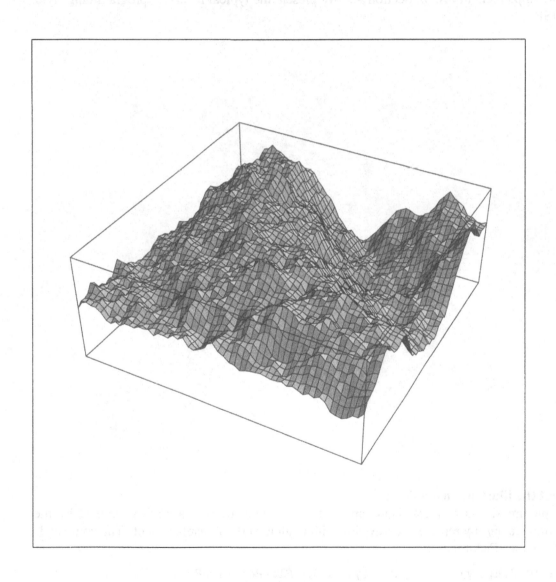

In this chapter, we study operations on nested data structures that are accessed exclusively by their selectors and constructors. This style of programming is typical for the language LISP. It is not particularly efficient in *Mathematica*, but it is simple to use. LISP is one of the oldest programming languages still used today. Its main application areas are artificial intelligence and symbolic computation. Many predecessors of *Mathematica* were written in LISP.

Section 9.1 defines the abstract data types for symbolic expressions and for lists and their simple implementations. In Section 9.2, we present the typical recursive programming style of LISP.

About the illustration overleaf:
The picture shows a fractal landscape. It was generated from a surface defined by the function $\sin(xy)$ by repeated subdivision with random vertical displacement. The commands used are (see Pictures.m):

```
Plot3D[ Sin[x y], {x, 0, 3}, {y, 0, 3}, PlotPoints->8];
Show[ Refine[%, 0.4, 0.9, 3], Axes->None ];
```

9.1 Symbolic Expressions and Lists

List processing has been the foundation of symbolic computation and artificial intelligence since the sixties. The programming language LISP uses list processing as fundamental operation. Lists are general data structures because they can be nested arbitrarily. In addition to list processing, recursion and functional programming are the most important features of LISP. *Mathematica* contains all operations available in LISP. It is, therefore, not difficult to program in the same way as one would in LISP. Lists are simply defined as an abstract data type.

9.1.1 Symbolic Expressions

LISP operates not only on lists, but on *symbolic expressions* (*S-expr*). LISP distinguishes between *atoms* and *composite expressions*. There is a similar distinction for expressions in *Mathematica*, see Section 2.4. Here is the abstract data type for symbolic expressions:

- Constants:

  all atoms: numbers, symbols, strings

- Constructors:

  $cons[e_1, e_2]$, a pair of expressions

- Selectors:

  $car[e]$, the first element of the pair e
  $cdr[e]$, the second element of the pair e

- Predicates:

  $pairQ[e]$, is e a pair?
  $atomQ[e]$, is e an atom?

- Equations:

$$
\begin{aligned}
car[cons[e_1, e_2]] &= e_1 \\
cdr[cons[e_1, e_2]] &= e_2 \\
atomQ[a] &= \text{True (for each atom a)} \qquad (9.1\text{--}1) \\
atomQ[cons[e_1, e_2]] &= \text{False} \\
pairQ[e] &= \,!atomQ[e]
\end{aligned}
$$

Observe, that the number of equations is infinite. There is one equation for $atomQ[a]$ for each atom a.

```
BeginPackage["CSM`Sexpr`"]

cons::usage = "cons[a, b] is the pair (a . b)."
car::usage  = "car[pair] is the first element of pair."
cdr::usage  = "cdr[pair] is the second element of pair."

pairQ::usage = "pairQ[e] is True if e is a pair."
atomQ::usage = "atomQ[e] is True if e is an atom."

Begin["`Private`"]

car[cons[e_, l_]] := e
cdr[cons[e_, l_]] := l

atomQ[_?AtomQ] = True     (* True for Mathematica atoms *)
atomQ[_cons] = False      (* pairs are not atoms *)
pairQ[e_] := !atomQ[e]    (* pairQ is the negation of atomQ *)

(* output formatting *)

Format[l_cons] := SequenceForm["(", Infix[l, " . "], ")"]

End[]

Protect[ car, cdr, cons, pairQ, atomQ ]

EndPackage[]
```

Listing 9.1–1   Sexpr.m: Symbolic expressions in *Mathematica*.

The implementation of this data type in *Mathematica* is simple (see Listing 9.1–1). We use
`cons[]` as constructor without any definitions for it. We can turn Equations 9.1–1 into rewrite
rules almost verbatim.

LISP Atoms are all atoms in *Mathematica* (`AtomQ[]` is a built in function). In LISP, pairs
`cons[`e_1`, `e_2`]` are normally written in the form `(`e_1` . `e_2`)`. It is easy to simulate this notation.

The symbol a is an atom.	`In[1]:= atomQ[a]`
	`Out[1]= True`
Here is a pair with the atoms a and b as elements.	`In[2]:= cons[a, b]`
	`Out[2]= (a . b)`
Its second element is b, of course.	`In[3]:= cdr[ % ]`
	`Out[3]= b`

9.1.2   Lists in LISP

Most LISP programs operate only on a subset of all symbolic expressions, the *lists*. Although
they are similar to lists in *Mathematica*, these LISP lists have different access functions. All
lists in this chapter are LISP lists, rather than *Mathematica* lists. A list is either equal to `nil`
(the empty list), or it is made up from a list l and an element e by `cons[e, l]`. The element e
is either an atom or another list. Some additional constants, constructors, and predicates are
defined for lists:

- Constants:

$$\texttt{nil}, \quad \text{the empty list}$$

- Constructors:

$$\texttt{list}[e_1, e_2, \ldots, e_n], \quad \text{for } n \geq 0$$

(There is one constructor for each $n \geq 0$)

- Predicates:

$$\texttt{nullQ}[e], \quad \text{is } e \text{ equal to } \texttt{nil}?$$

- Equations:

$$
\begin{aligned}
\texttt{nullQ[nil]} &= \texttt{True} \\
\texttt{nullQ[cons}[e_1, e_2]] &= \texttt{False} \\
\texttt{list[]} &= \texttt{nil} \\
\texttt{list}[e_1, e_2, \ldots, e_n] &= \texttt{cons}[e_1, \texttt{list}[e_2, \ldots, e_n]], \quad n > 0
\end{aligned}
$$

(9.1–2)

According to the equations, the list $\texttt{list}[e_1, e_2, \ldots, e_n]$ is represented by the symbolic expression $\texttt{cons}[e_1, \texttt{cons}[e_2, \ldots, \texttt{cons}[e_n, \texttt{nil}]\ldots]]$. The operation $\texttt{cons}[e, l]$ *prepends* a new element e to the list l. Again, we can derive the implementation directly from the equations. We use Sexpr.m, augmented by additional definitions, as shown in Listing 9.1–2.

```
list::usage = "list[e1, e2,..., en] is the Lisp list (e1 e2 ... en)."
nil::usage = "nil is the empty Lisp list."
nullQ::usage = "nullQ[l] is True if l is the empty list."

list[] = nil
list[e_, r___] := cons[e, list[r]]

nullQ[nil] = True
nullQ[_cons] = False
```

Listing 9.1–2 Part of Lisp.m: extensions for LISP lists.

The usual output format of a list $\texttt{list}[e_1, e_2, \ldots, e_n]$ is $(e_1 \ e_2 \ \ldots \ e_n)$, that is, with round parentheses and no comma between elements.

Here is the empty list.	`In[1]:= nil` `Out[1]= ()`
We prepend the atom `a` to it.	`In[2]:= cons[a, %]` `Out[2]= (a)`
An now the atom `b`.	`In[3]:= cons[b, %]` `Out[3]= (b a)`

Here is the list of the numbers $1, 2, \ldots, 5$.

```
In[4]:= l1 = list[1, 2, 3, 4, 5]
Out[4]= (1 2 3 4 5)
```

The selector `car[`*l*`]` gives the *first element* of a list.

```
In[5]:= car[l1]
Out[5]= 1
```

The selector `cdr[`*l*`]` gives the *rest* of a list, that is, the list without its first element.

```
In[6]:= cdr[l1]
Out[6]= (2 3 4 5)
```

The elements of a list can themselves be lists.

```
In[7]:= list[ nil, list[a, b], 2]
Out[7]= (() (a b) 2)
```

9.1.3   Key Concepts

1. Symbolic expressions are formed from atoms by a simple construction principle.

2. Lists in LISP are special symbolic expressions.

3. A nonempty list consists of a first element and a rest.

4. The empty list `nil` is both a list and an atom.

9.2 List Processing

In this section, we use the data type of LISP lists from Section 9.1.2 for the presentation of a few typical LISP programs. All programs are in the package Lists.m.

9.2.1 Recursion

Recursion is an important programming tool in LISP. Access to lists is rather special. We can access only the first element (with car[l]) and the rest of a list (with cdr[l]) directly. The rest of a nonempty list is also a list, which leads naturally to recursion. The parts of a list can be put together with cons[e, l].

The programming principle is as follows: An operation on a data structure is given by a number of rules. Among them are rules for special cases (empty structure, etc.) and – normally recursive – rules for the general case. These recursive rules take the data structure apart, perform the operation on the parts, and put the results back together with the recursively computed result of the rest of the structure.

Each recursive invocation must make some *progress* and call itself with a simpler problem. Only in this way can we guarantee that the recursion terminates always. This principle is analogous to induction proofs in mathematics.

Here is a simple example that illustrates these points. Let us develop a function squares[l] that squares the elements of a list of numbers. Because a list is either empty, or has been built by cons[e, l_1] from another list l_1, we must consider these cases:

- If l is empty, there is nothing to do. The result is again the empty list nil.

- Otherwise, l is of the form cons[e, l_1]. The first element is e. Its square becomes the first element of the desired result. The rest of the result is obtained by a recursive call of squares[] with argument *cdr*[l].

- The result of squaring the first element is combined with the result of the recursive call by cons[] to give the final result.

We obtain the following program:

```
squares[l_] :=
        If[ nullQ[l],
              nil,
              cons[ car[l]^2, squares[cdr[l]] ]
        ]
```

If we square the elements of the empty list, we get back the empty list.

```
In[1]:= squares[ nil ]
Out[1]= ()
```

The first element of the result is the square of the first element of the input. The rest of the result is equal to the squares of the rest of the input.

```
In[2]:= squares[ list[2, 3, 4, 5] ]
Out[2]= (4 9 16 25)
```

9.2.2   Applying Functions to Elements of Lists

The example in the preceding subsection can be generalized to a function map[f, l] that applies the function f to the elements of l and returns the list of the results.

```
map[f_, l_] :=
     If[ nullQ[l],
           nil,
           cons[ f[car[l]], map[f, cdr[l]] ]
     ]
```

The principle is simple: if the list l is not empty, we apply f to the first element and recursively to the rest of l. We combine the two results with cons[].

This call applies the factorial function to the numbers 1 to 6.

```
In[1]:= map[ Factorial, list[1, 2, 3, 4, 5, 6] ]
Out[1]= (1 2 6 24 120 720)
```

If we choose a symbolic (undefined) function f and symbolic arguments, we can easily see what happens.

```
In[2]:= map[ f, list[a, b, c] ]
Out[2]= (f[a] f[b] f[c])
```

9.2.3   Appending at the End of a List

The constructor cons[] prepends an element to a list. Appending an element is not that easy. Because we know how we can append an element to the empty list (how?), we can write a recursive program for append[l, e] that appends the element e at the end of the list l. We append e recursively at the end of the rest of l and combine the result with the unchanged first element of l.

```
append[l_, e_] :=
      If[ nullQ[l],
            list[e],
            cons[ car[l], append[cdr[l], e] ]
      ]
```

The new element x3 is put at the end of the list (x1 x2).

```
In[3]:= append[list[x1, x2], x3]
Out[3]= (x1 x2 x3)
```

9.2.4   Reversing Lists

To reverse the elements of a list, we append the first element at the end of the reversal of the rest of the list. (It's that simple!)

```
reverse[l_] :=
        If[ nullQ[l],
                nil,
                append[ reverse[cdr[l]], car[l] ]
        ]
```

This kind of reversal has quadratic complexity, which is not optimal. See Exercise 9.3 for a faster version of `reverse[]`.

```
In[4]:= reverse[ list[1, 2, 3, 4, 5] ]

Out[4]= (5 4 3 2 1)
```

9.2.5   Deleting Elements

To identify elements, we need a predicate that finds out whether two elements are the same. This predicate is SameQ[e_1, e_2], often written in the form e_1 === e_2. An element e can be removed from a list l in the following ways:

- If l is empty, there is nothing to do, because e does not occur in the list.

- If the first element of l is equal to e, the result is the rest of l.

- Otherwise, the first element of the result is the first element of l, and the rest of the result is the rest of l after having removed e from it.

This program requires a threefold branch, which we can program with

$$\texttt{Which}[test_1, \; val_1, \; test_2, \; val_2, \; \ldots, \; test_n, \; val_n] \; .$$

The tests are evaluated in sequence until one is found that returns True. The result is the corresponding val_i. The last test in the following Which[] statement is always True. There is nothing left to test in this case.

```
remove[l_, e_] :=
        Which[
                nullQ[l],   nil,
                car[l]===e, cdr[l],
                True,       cons[ car[l], remove[cdr[l], e] ]
        ]
```

This command removes the number 3 from the list (1 2 3 4 5).	`In[5]:= remove[ list[1, 2, 3, 4, 5], 3 ]` `Out[5]= (1 2 4 5)`
If the element to be removed does not occur, the list is returned unchanged.	`In[6]:= remove[ list[a, b, c], d ]` `Out[6]= (a b c)`
`remove[]` removes only the first occurrence!	`In[7]:= remove[ list[1, 2, 3, 2, 1], 2]` `Out[7]= (1 3 2 1)`

9.2.6   Inserting into Ordered Lists

The command insert[*l*, *e*] inserts a number *e* into an ordered list at the right place. If the new number is smaller than the first element of the list, it is put at the beginning; otherwise, it is inserted recursively.

```
insert[l_, e_] :=
      Which[
            nullQ[l],    list[e],
            e < car[l], cons[e, l],
            True,        cons[ car[l], insert[cdr[l], e] ]
      ]
```

In an empty list, the new element becomes the only element.	`In[8]:= insert[nil, 5]` `Out[8]= (5)`
Smaller elements are inserted at the beginning.	`In[9]:= insert[%, 3]` `Out[9]= (3 5)`
Larger elements are put at the end.	`In[10]:= insert[%, 7]` `Out[10]= (3 5 7)`

9.2.7   Nested Lists

All functions so far operated on *linear lists* – that is, we assumed that the elements of the lists are not lists themselves. If lists can be nested, we have to use recursion also along the first element, if it is a list. Because each element is either a list or an atom, we use atomQ[*e*] for this test. For example, let us replace all occurrences of the atom *a* by *b* in a nested list.

```
substAll[l_, a_, b_] :=
      Which[
        nullQ[l], nil,
        atomQ[l], If[ l === a, b, l ],
        True,     cons[ substAll[car[l], a, b],
                        substAll[cdr[l], a, b] ]
      ]
```

We need to substitute only if *l* is an atom. If it is equal to *a* it is replaced by *b*; otherwise, it remains unchanged. If *l* is not an atom, we recurse along car[*l*] and cdr[*l*].

Here is a nested list.	In[11]:= **list[a, nil, list[b, list[a], c], c]**
	Out[11]= (a () (b (a) c) c)
All occurrences of a are replaced by ap.	In[12]:= **substAll[%, a, ap]**
	Out[12]= (ap () (b (ap) c) c)

9.2.8 Predicates

All examples so far returned modified data structures as results. Predicates, however, test whether a condition is satisfied; they return only True or False. For example, consider a membership test: Is an element a member of a linear list?

```
memberQ[l_, e_] :=
     Which[
        nullQ[l],    False,
        e===car[l], True,
        True,        memberQ[cdr[l], e]
     ]
```

If the list *l* is empty, the element is not a member, and we return False. Otherwise, if the first element of *l* is equal to *e*, we can immediately return True; otherwise, we continue the search in the rest of *l*. Such programs are slowest when the condition is *not* satisfied. In a predicate, the recursion does not build up a new data structure; the given structure is only analyzed.

The membership test for nested lists needs to recur along car[*l*] and cdr[*l*]. The element occurs if it occurs in at least one of these parts. Therefore, the two results must be combined with OR. Note that we must test for *l* being an atom first because *l* is not always a list (in the first recursion), and nullQ is defined only for lists.

```
memberAllQ[l_, e_] :=
     Which[
        atomQ[l], l === e,
        nullQ[l], False,
        True,     memberAllQ[car[l], e] || memberAllQ[cdr[l], e]
     ]
```

Note the result *l* === *e* for the case where *l* is an atom. This is far more elegant than is If[*l* === *e*, True, False], an expression often written by beginners. The expression *l* === *e* is itself a predicate, returning True or False.

This list contains a nested sublist.

```
In[13]:= l = list[alpha, list[beta, gamma], delta]
Out[13]= (alpha (beta gamma) delta)
```

delta is an element of the linear list l.

```
In[14]:= memberQ[ l, delta ]
Out[14]= True
```

beta, however, is not an element of l.

```
In[15]:= memberQ[ l, beta ]
Out[15]= False
```

It occurs somewhere inside the nested list, however.

```
In[16]:= memberAllQ[ l, beta ]
Out[16]= True
```

9.2.9 Key Concepts

1. Recursion is the natural programming style in LISP.

2. Loops can be replaced by the application of functions to elements of lists.

3. Which[] is used for a multi-way branch.

9.3 Exercises

9.1 Operations on Lists[1]

Here is an abstract data type for lists:

- Constants:
  {}, the empty list

- Selectors:
  First[*list*], the *first element* of the list
  Rest[*list*], the *rest* of the list without its first element

- Constructors:
  Prepend[*list*, *elem*], gives a new list whose first element is *elem* and whose rest is *list*

- Predicates:
  ListQ[*list*], returns True, if *list* is a list

Define the following functions on lists, using rules (no loops or branches, but conditional rules if necessary). Lists may be accessed only with the given selectors and predicates.

1. join[l_1, l_2]: this function joins two lists

2. flatten[*list*]: this function turns a nested list into a linear list

3. count[l, e]: counts how often the element e occurs in the *linear* list l (Use === for testing equality)

Examples:

These two lists are simply spliced together.	In[1]:= join[{a, b, c}, {x, y}] Out[1]= {a, b, c, x, y}
Make sure to treat special cases correctly.	In[2]:= join[{}, {x, {y, z}}] Out[2]= {x, {y, z}}
All inner parentheses are removed.	In[3]:= flatten[{{a}, {b, c}, d}] Out[3]= {a, b, c, d}
An empty list is removed completely	In[4]:= flatten[{{}, {{1}, 2}}] Out[4]= {1, 2}
The element a occurs twice.	In[5]:= count[{a, b, a, x}, a] Out[5]= 2

---

[1]Written examination, ETH Zürich, Department of Mathematics and Physics.

In this list it occurs only once because the   `In[6]:= count[ {{a}, a, b}, a]`
list {a} is not the same as the symbol a.   `Out[6]= 1`

9.2   Program Analysis[1]

Consider these definitions. What does the function `f[]` do?

```
a[{}, e_] := {}
a[l_List, e_] := Prepend[ a[Rest[l], e], Prepend[First[l], e] ]
f[{}] := {{}}
f[l_List] := Join[ a[ f[Rest[l]], First[l] ], f[Rest[l]] ]
```

1. What is `f[{x}]`, `f[{x, y}]` and `f[{x, y, z}]`?

2. If `f` is called with a list of $n \geq 0$ elements (i.e., in the form `f[{`e_1, e_2, ..., e_n`}]`), what length does the result have?

3. Which well-known function is implemented by `f[{`e_1, e_2, ..., e_n`}]`? Assume that all e_i are pairwise distinct.

9.3   Operations on Linear Lists[1]

Consider the function `Mystery[`*list*`]` (*list* is a LISP list, see Section 9.1.2):

```
Mystery[l_] := mystery[l, nil]
mystery[nil, r_] := r
mystery[l_, r_] := mystery[ cdr[l], cons[car[l], r] ]
```

1. Describe what the function `Mystery[`*list*`]` does.

2. How many calls of `mystery[]` occur in the computation of `Mystery[`*l*`]`, if *l* is a list of length n?

3. Implement `Mystery[]` directly with a `While` loop (i.e., without the auxiliary function `mystery[]`). Use `Module` to declare local variables.

9.4   Sorting Lists

Choose one of the sorting methods from Section 6.2 that can be used for sorting LISP lists (Section 9.2) and implement it. The asymmetric access to lists (access is possible only to the first element and to the rest of a list) makes it necessary to adapt the algorithms for efficiency.

Chapter 10
Rule-Based Programming

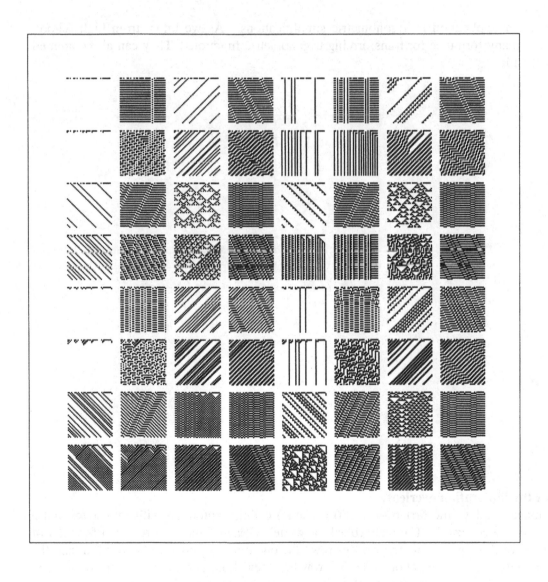

In this chapter, we discuss programming with rewrite rules. A rewrite rule is an equation that is used to rewrite an expression that matches the left side of the rule by the rule's right side. *Mathematica* offers a unique way to program formulae (from a handbook, say) directly as rewrite rules. In Section 10.1, we look at the foundation of rule-based programming: pattern matching. Section 10.2 shows how to use patterns in rewrite rules.

Then, in Section 10.3, we present the theory behind rule-based programming: normal forms and confluent rewrite systems. As an example, we treat normal forms of odd and even functions.

A larger application is trigonometric simplifications. As we know from high school, there are many formulae for transforming trigonometric functions. They can all be applied mechanically.

About the illustration overleaf:
The image displays the first 64 (of 256 possible) cellular automata with two states and a neighborhood of size 3. The state (black or white) of each point in a row is a function of the states of three points in the previous row: the one directly above the new point, and the former's left and right neighbors. The first row has been chosen at random and is the same in all pictures. The commands for this illustration are in the package Pictures.m.

10.1 Pattern Matching

Rule-based programming requires a mechanism for *pattern matching*. In *Mathematica*, pattern matching is a central part of the evaluator. How does it work? To understand it, we recall from Section 2.4 the structure of expressions. A composite expression (called a normal expression) has the form

$$h \, [\, e_1, \, e_2, \, \ldots, \, e_n \,],$$

where h and the e_i are themselves expressions; h is the *head* of the expression, and the e_i are the *elements*.

10.1.1 Patterns

A *pattern* is an expression in which certain parts are marked as *holes*. Such an expression describes a whole class of possible expressions: all expressions that we can obtain by filling in the holes. A hole is marked with the character _, which is called *blank*. Pattern matching consists of deciding whether a given expression matches the pattern. An expression *matches* a pattern if the holes in the pattern can be filled (with expressions) such that the filled-in pattern becomes equal to our expression.

For example, the expression f[5] matches the pattern f[_], because we can fill the hole in f[_] simply with the expression 5, to make it equal to f[5]. The expression f[5, 6] does not match the pattern. Whatever we fill in for the hole, we get an expression with *one* element, whereas f[5, 6] has *two* elements. The predicate MatchQ[*expr*, *pattern*] can be used to test whether an expression matches a pattern.

As we have seen, the expression f[5] matches the pattern f[_].

```
In[1]:= MatchQ[ f[5], f[_] ]
Out[1]= True
```

This expression does not match the pattern.

```
In[2]:= MatchQ[ f[5, 6], f[_] ]
Out[2]= False
```

The function Cases[{e_1, ..., e_n}, *pattern*] selects those e_i that match the pattern. It is well suited to conducting pattern-matching experiments because we can give it a list of candidate expressions and then see which ones match the pattern.

With Cases[], we can select from a list of expressions those that match the pattern.

```
In[3]:= Cases[ {f[5], f[5, 6], f[Sin[x]]}, f[_] ]
Out[3]= {f[5], f[Sin[x]]}
```

A pattern does not need to contain any holes. In this case, only expressions that are identical to the pattern match the pattern.

```
In[4]:= Cases[ {f[5], f[x], f[y], f[Sin[x]]}, f[x] ]
Out[4]= {f[x]}
```

A pattern can contain several holes. They can be filled in independently.

| This pattern describes all expressions with head f and exactly two (arbitrary) elements. | ```
In[5]:= Cases[
          {f[a], f[a, b], f[a, b, c], f[g[5], h[6]]},
          f[_, _]
        ]

Out[5]= {f[a, b], f[g[5], h[6]]}
``` |
| This pattern describes all expressions with head f and two elements. The first element must have the form g[_]. | ```
In[6]:= Cases[
          {f[a, b], f[g[a], b], f[g[5], z], f[x, g[y]]},
          f[g[_], _]
        ]

Out[6]= {f[g[a], b], f[g[5], z]}
``` |

The holes in a pattern can be named. A named blank is written *name_*. The name is a symbol. Pattern matching requires that two blanks having the same name must be filled in with the same expression. The object *name_* is also called a *pattern variable*. The blank alone, _, is called an *anonymous pattern variable*.

| This pattern describes exactly the expression with head f and two *identical* elements. Note that the numbers 2 and 2.0 are not considered identical. | ```
In[7]:= Cases[
          {f[5, 6], f[5, 5], f[g[y], g[y]], f[2, 2.0]},
          f[x_, x_]
        ]

Out[7]= {f[5, 5], f[g[y], g[y]]}
``` |
| Patterns can have holes in the head position. Here, we describe all expressions with head f that have two elements with identical heads and an arbitrary element. | ```
In[8]:= Cases[
          {f[g[y], g[y]], f[h[2], hh[2]], f[g[y], g[z]]},
          f[a_[_], a_[_]]
        ]

Out[8]= {f[g[y], g[y]], f[g[y], g[z]]}
``` |

10.1.2 Expressions of a Certain Type

Expressions to be filled in for a blank can be restricted to a certain type. The type of an expression is the latter's head. To allow only expressions with head *type*, we write *_type* for an anonymous pattern variable with the desired head, and *v_type* for a named pattern variable *v*. The type must be a symbol.

| This pattern selects all expressions with head h. Note that the last expression h itself does not match: Its head is Symbol. | ```
In[1]:= Cases[ {h[5], h[g[1]], hh[a], h[], h},
              _h ]

Out[1]= {h[5], h[g[1]], h[]}
``` |
| Here, we select all expressions with head f and an element of type Integer. | ```
In[2]:= Cases[ {f[1], f[1.0], f[Pi]},
                f[_Integer] ]

Out[2]= {f[1]}
``` |

10.1.3 Predicates

Expressions can be restricted to those satisfying a given predicate. A *predicate* is a function that returns either `True` or `False`. We write `_?`*pred* for an anonymous pattern variable with a predicate, and `v_?`*pred* for a named pattern variable *v* with a predicate. An expression *e* matches a pattern with a predicate only if the application of the predicate to the expression, that is, *pred*[*e*], gives `True`.

This pattern selects expressions of the form `a[n]`, where *n* must be a prime number.

```
In[3]:= Cases[
           {a[1], a[2], a[3], a[4], a[5], a[6], a[7]},
           a[ _?PrimeQ ]
        ]

Out[3]= {a[2], a[3], a[5], a[7]}
```

Here we ask for expressions having the form `f[n]`, where *n* is a nonnegative number.

```
In[4]:= Cases[
           {f[-1], f[0], f[1], f[2.5], f[z]},
           f[ _?NonNegative ]
        ]

Out[4]= {f[0], f[1], f[2.5]}
```

Note that the expression matches only if the predicate returns `True`. In the last example, `NonNegative[z]` returned neither `True` nor `False`, because `z` is not a number, and we, therefore, do not known whether it is negative. Examples of built-in predicates can be found in *The Mathematica Book* in Section 2.3.5. You can define your own predicates.

Here is a definition of a predicate that is true if the argument is larger than 5.

```
In[5]:= moreThan5[n_] := n > 5
```

Now we can select expressions whose element is larger than 5. The error message is generated by the evaluation `moreThan5[I]`, which *Mathematica* carries out to determine whether the predicate is satisfied. Complex numbers cannot be compared for size.

```
In[6]:= Cases[
           {f[-1], f[4], f[5], f[5.5], f[I]},
           f[ _?moreThan5 ]
        ]

Greater::nord: Invalid comparison with I attempted.

Out[6]= {f[5.5]}
```

10.1.4 Side Conditions

A mechanism more general than predicates is *side conditions*. To restrict a pattern, we write *pattern*/; *cond*. The side condition *cond* is any expression that may contain the pattern variables of *pattern*. If an expression matches the pattern in the first place, the condition is evaluated. If this evaluation returns `True`, the expression matches *pattern*/; *cond*. Therefore, an expression matches a conditional pattern only if it matches the pattern itself and if the condition is satisfied.

This pattern selects all expressions with two
elements, the first of which is smaller than
is the second. Note the use of the pattern
variables in the condition.

```
In[7]:= Cases[
            {f[2, 3], f[a, b], f[3, 3]},
            f[x_, y_]/; x < y
        ]

Out[7]= {f[2, 3]}
```

Side conditions are more general than predicates. That is, we could do without predicates
because each predicate can also be used in a side condition. Instead of f[_?p], we can use
f[x_/; p[x]]. These two forms are equivalent, but often, the form with the predicate is
easier to read.

This pattern describes the same expression
as does the pattern f[_?moreThan5] in
Section 10.1.3.

```
In[8]:= Cases[
            {f[-1], f[4], f[5], f[5.5], f[I]},
            f[ n_/; moreThan5[n] ]
        ]

Greater::nord: Invalid comparison with I attempted.

Out[8]= {f[5.5]}
```

One advantage of side conditions is that we
do not need to define a predicate first. We
can simply insert its definition right into the
pattern.

```
In[9]:= Cases[
            {f[-1], f[4], f[5], f[5.5], f[I]},
            f[ n_/; n>5 ]
        ]

Greater::nord: Invalid comparison with I attempted.

Out[9]= {f[5.5]}
```

The three ways to restrict pattern matching can be combined. For example, the pattern

$$f[n\_Integer?Positive/; IntegerQ[Sqrt[n]]]$$

describes expressions with positive integer arguments that are squares (whose square root is
an integer).

There are other kinds of patterns not treated here. A list of all pattern objects is given on
page 376.

10.1.5 Key Concepts

1. Patterns describe classes of expressions.

2. An expression matches a pattern if the latter's holes can be filled to make the filled pattern
    equal to the expression.

3. The class of expressions that match a pattern can be restricted by type or side conditions.

10.2   Rules and Term Rewriting

We have used patterns before we introduced them in this chapter. In a definition such as

$$gcd[a\_, b\_] := gcd[b, Mod[a, b]]$$

the left side is a pattern. The notation has been chosen to resemble ordinary function definitions in other programming languages. This chapter emphasizes the use of patterns for term rewriting.

10.2.1   Rewrite Rules

Term rewriting is done with *rewrite rules*. A rule has the form

$$pattern \to repl$$

or

$$pattern :> repl.$$

A rule specifies that we want to replace an expression matching the pattern by a new expression *repl*. Rules are applied to expressions with

$$expr \; /. \; rule \; .$$

Mathematica searches *expr* for parts that it can replace using the rule; it then performs the replacement. A few examples will clarify these notions.

The expression

    f[a, g[x], x^2, Sin[x], g[Pi]]

is searched for occurrences of the pattern x (which does not contain any variables), and each occurrence is replaced by 17. There are three such occurrences. The result is then evaluated further.

```
In[1]:= f[a, g[x], x^2, Sin[x], g[Pi]] /. x -> 17
Out[1]= f[a, g[17], 289, Sin[17], g[Pi]]
```

Here, each occurrence of the pattern g[_] is replaced by gg. There are two instances of g[_] in the expression.

```
In[2]:= f[a, g[x], x^2, Sin[x], g[Pi]] /. g[_] -> gg
                          2
Out[2]= f[a, gg, x , Sin[x], gg]
```

More interesting examples are those where the pattern contains variables. The names of the pattern variables can be used on the right side of the rule. They are replaced by the expression that matched the pattern variable.

On the right side, `t` is replaced by the expression filled in for the pattern variable `t_`. The pattern occurs twice in this example.

```
In[3]:= f[a, g[x], Sin[x], g[Pi]] /. g[t_] -> t^3
            3              3
Out[3]= f[a, x , Sin[x], Pi ]
```

Names of pattern variables are independent of symbols that may appear in the expression. The pattern variable `x_` has nothing to do with the symbol `x` occurring a few times in the expression.

```
In[4]:= f[a, g[x], Sin[x], g[Pi]] /. g[x_] -> x^3
            3              3
Out[4]= f[a, x , Sin[x], Pi ]
```

To verify this independence, we can rename the pattern variable (to `y`) and see that we get the same result as before.

```
In[5]:= f[a, g[x], Sin[x], g[Pi]] /. g[y_] -> y^3
            3              3
Out[5]= f[a, x , Sin[x], Pi ]
```

A mistake often made by beginners is to forget the underscore symbol. The pattern `g[x]` does not contain any variables; only literal occurrences are replaced (there is one). The expression `g[Pi]` does not match and is not replaced (compare it with the previous example).

```
In[6]:= f[a, g[x], Sin[x], g[Pi]] /. g[x] -> x^3
            3
Out[6]= f[a, x , Sin[x], g[Pi]]
```

Mathematica evaluates the left side of a replacement *expr* /. *rule* before the rule is applied. The mathematical formula

$$f'(x)\big|_{x=x_0} \tag{10.2–1}$$

for the calculation of the derivative of a function f at $x = x_0$ can therefore be written exactly as follows in *Mathematica*:

$$f'[x] /. x -> x0 .$$

As you know, it would be wrong first to replace the variable x and then to differentiate.

Here is the derivative of the sine function at zero.

```
In[7]:= Sin'[x] /. x -> 0
Out[7]= 1
```

The only difference between *pattern* -> *repl* and *pattern* :> *repl* is the time the right side *repl* is evaluated. In the first form, the right side is evaluated when the rule is encountered; in the second form, it is evaluated only after the rule has been applied. As a rule of thumb, we can say that :> should be used if the pattern contains variables that are used inside *repl* (for example, `f[x_] :> x^2`). If no pattern variables occur, the first form with -> can be used.

10.2.2   Several Rules

The replacement operator `/.` can take a list of rules as its right argument. The rules are tried in order until one is found that matches.

The expression `fk[3]` does not match the first rule. Therefore, the second rule is examined. It matches and is applied.

```
In[8]:= fk[3] /. {fk[1] -> 1, fk[n_] :> n fk[n-1]}
Out[8]= 3 fk[2]
```

Rules are applied only once to each part of an expression, even if the result of the first application would match the rule again. To evaluate the result further, we have to use the replacement operator again.

```
In[9]:= % /. {fk[1] -> 1, fk[n_] :> n fk[n-1]}
Out[9]= 6 fk[1]
```

Now the first rule matches and is applied. The result is then simplified in the usual way.

```
In[10]:= % /. {fk[1] -> 1, fk[n_] :> n fk[n-1]}
Out[10]= 6
```

The repeated replacement operator `//.` applies rules several times, until none of them matches anymore.

```
In[11]:= fk[3] //. {fk[1] -> 1, fk[n_] :> n fk[n-1]}
Out[11]= 6
```

The rules in this example are the rules for the computation of the factorial function $n! = n(n-1)\cdots 1$. Such rules can therefore be used to compute functions. So far, we defined functions in the form

$$fk[1] = 1 ,$$
$$fk[n\_] := n\ fk[n-1] .$$

These two possibilities are equivalent. If we perform the definitions with `=` and `:=`, they are applied automatically to all expressions evaluated later on. *Mathematica* uses essentially `//.` to apply the definitions. *Mathematica* treats definitions as rewrite rules. The theoretical connection between functions and term rewriting is explained in Section 11.1.

> If we give a definition of the form *pattern* `:=` *repl*, *Mathematica* will, from then on, perform the replacement *expr* `//.` *pattern* `:>` *repl* automatically with all expressions to be evaluated. A definition of the form x `=` *val* leads to the automatic replacement *expr* `//.` x `->` *val*.

10.2.3   Key Concepts

1. Rules have the form *pattern* `->` *repl* or *pattern* `:>` *repl*.

2. A replacement looks like this: *expr* `/.` *rule*.

3. In a replacement with several rules,

$$expr \;/.\; \{rule_1, \; rule_2, \; \ldots, \; rule_n\} \,,$$

the rules are tried in order.

4. No further rules are applied to the result of a rule application.

5. The operator `/.` traverses the rules once. The operator `//.` performs replacements until no more can be performed.

6. Definitions with `=` and `:=` are like rules with `->` and `:>` applied automatically to all expressions.

10.3   Simplification Rules and Normal Forms

Mathematica uses rewrite rules as the basis for its programming language. In this section, we look at rule-based programming proper. Rules allow you to perform simplifications mechanically. The result of a simplification is a normal form that can be used to decide whether two expressions are equivalent. The applications in this and next section are taken from mathematics, where transformations and simplifications play an important role.

10.3.1   The Normal Form of an Expression

An important concept for the simplification of expressions is the *normal form*. The number zero, for example, can be written in many different ways, such as 0, 1-1, i^2+1, or Cos[Pi/2]. All of them are *equivalent*, but we a have a clear notion of which of them is the simplest. Furthermore, we know how to convert the others into this simplest form. We write $0 \equiv 1-1$, to express *equivalence* of expressions. The expressions 0 and 1-1 are not *identical*, however. The distinction between expressions and their meaning (the number zero) is often blurred in mathematics. It is essential in symbolic computation, however.

A *simplifier* $S(e)$ is a function that transforms an expression e into another, equivalent expression, with the property that $S(S(e)) = S(e)$, or, in other words, that the result of a simplification cannot be simplified further. An expression e with $S(e) = e$ is called *irreducible* (it cannot be simplified). A simplifier is *canonical* if two equivalent expressions are simplified to the same expression; that is,

$$e_1 \equiv e_2 \rightarrow S(e_1) = S(e_2). \qquad (10.3\text{--}1)$$

If S is a canonical simplifier, the expression $S(e)$ is called a *normal form* of e. Every expression has exactly one normal form, and we have $e \equiv S(e)$.

If we can define a normal form for a class of expressions, two different but equivalent expressions can be simplified to the same normal form. Therefore, it becomes easy to decide whether two expressions are equivalent. To see whether $e_1 \equiv e_2$, we simply compute the normal forms $S(e_1)$ and $S(e_2)$ and see whether they are identical.

A normal form does not need to be the intuitively simplest form. For polynomials, for example, the fully expanded form is a normal form. We know how to expand polynomials, and two equal polynomials have the same expanded form. Expansion is a canonical simplifier. For some polynomials, the factored form is simpler, however.

To see whether these two polynomials are equivalent, we shall expand them.

```
In[1]:= {x^2-1, (x-1)(x+1)}

Out[1]= {-1 + x , (-1 + x) (1 + x)}
               2
```

The expanded forms are identical. The polynomials are, therefore, equivalent.

```
In[2]:= Expand[%]
          2      2
Out[2]= {-1 + x , -1 + x }
```

In this example, the normal form (the expanded form) is more complicated than is the factored form.

```
In[3]:= Expand[(x+1)^5]
                  2       3      4    5
Out[3]= 1 + 5 x + 10 x + 10 x + 5 x + x
```

In this example, the expanded form is simpler.

```
In[4]:= Expand[(-1 + x)(1 + x)(1 + x^2)(1 + x^4)]
              8
Out[4]= -1 + x
```

Mathematica performs certain simplifications automatically. For these examples, a canonical simplifier is applied without our intervention.

```
In[5]:= {0, 1-1, I^2+1, Cos[Pi/2]}
Out[5]= {0, 0, 0, 0}
```

Two expressions are *equivalent* if their meaning is the same.
Two expressions are *identical* if they look the same.

10.3.2 Term Rewriting as a Simplifier

An important class of simplifiers is obtained from rewrite rules. If r is a list of rules, the function S[*expr*], defined as

$$S[expr\_] := expr \; //. \; r \, ,$$

is a simplifier provided that two conditions are satisfied.

First, the application of rules must not lead to an infinite reduction. After finitely many rule applications, we must arrive at an irreducible expression. Rule sets with this property are called *Noetherian* (after the mathematician Emmy Nöther). An example of a rule that is not Noetherian is f[x_] :> f[g[x]].

The second condition is that the final result of the rule applications must not depend on the order in which the rules are applied. Such rule sets are called *confluent*.

These two rules are not confluent. Here is the result obtained if the first one is used first.

```
In[1]:= x //. {x -> a, x -> b}
Out[1]= a
```

We obtain a different result if the second rule is used first.

```
In[2]:= x //. {x -> b, x -> a}
Out[2]= b
```

These two rules are Noetherian and confluent.

```
In[3]:= f[g[2, 3], 4] //.
              {f[a_, b_] :> a b, g[x_, y_] :> x + y}
Out[3]= 20
```

A rule set is called *complete* if the corresponding simplifier S is canonical. If it is, we can determine the equivalence of two expressions simply by applying the rules to both expressions, and then seeing whether the results are identical.

This rule implements the distributive law $a(b_1 + b_2 + \ldots + b_n) = ab_1 + ab_2 + \ldots + ab_n$.	`In[4]:= dist = {a_*b_Plus :> Map[Function[e, a*e], b]};`
A symbolic example shows us how this rule works.	`In[5]:= a(b1 + b2 + b3 + b4) //. dist` `Out[5]= a b1 + a b2 + a b3 + a b4`

Application of the rules to the two expressions in the list shows us that the latter are equivalent.	`In[6]:= { a(c + d) + b c + b d,`
	`          c(a + b) + a d + b d } //. dist`
	`Out[6]= {a c + b c + a d + b d, a c + b c + a d + b d}`

Application of simplification rules is the main principle of *Mathematica*'s evaluator. If we give rules as definitions, they are used automatically to simplify expressions.

10.3.3 Example: Normal Forms of Even and Odd Functions

A function f is *even* if $f(-x) = f(x)$; it is *odd* if $f(-x) = -f(x)$. Examples of such functions are the trigonometric functions: They are all either even or odd.

An even function can be written in two ways, as $f(x)$ or as $f(-x)$. An odd function can be written as $f(x)$ or as $-f(-x)$. If we want to arrive at normal forms for such functions, we must decide on a single way of writing the functions. We demand that the argument not be negative in the normal form. The two rules given in Listing 10.3–1 perform this simplification.

```
oddEvenRules = {
    (f_Symbol?OddQ)[x_?Negative]  :> -f[-x],
    (f_Symbol?EvenQ)[x_?Negative] :>  f[-x]
}
```

Listing 10.3–1   OERules1.m: Simplification for negative arguments.

We use the standard predicates `EvenQ` and `OddQ`, which are defined for integers, to declare functions as even or odd. We do the declaration with a definition of the form

$$f /: \; \mathtt{OddQ}[f] = \mathtt{True} .$$

The restriction of the pattern `f_` to symbols is used for efficiency so that *Mathematica*'s evaluator will not have to consider too many expressions in pattern matching. These rules allow us to perform several simplifications.

We declare `e` as even and `o` as odd.	`In[1]:= e/: EvenQ[e] = True; \` `         o/: OddQ[o] = True;`

Application of the rules puts this expression into normal form. The usual rules of arithmetic lead to further simplifications.

```
In[2]:= o[-2] + o[2] + e[-1] + e[1] /.
            oddEvenRules
Out[2]= 2 e[1]
```

The simplification makes it clear that this sum is 0.

```
In[3]:= o[2] + o[-2] /. oddEvenRules
Out[3]= 0
```

Our rules are not yet complete. This expression is not simplified because -a does not satisfy the predicate `Negative[]`.

```
In[4]:= e[-a] /. oddEvenRules
Out[4]= e[-a]
```

10.3.3.1 Symbolic Arguments

We cannot say whether a symbolic argument is negative. Therefore, we want the normal form not to contain an *explicit* minus sign. Let us express this requirement using rules.

The obvious rule works in this simple case,

```
In[5]:= e[-a] /. e[-x_] :> e[x]
Out[5]= e[a]
```

but it is not sufficiently general.

```
In[6]:= e[-2a] /. e[-x_] :> e[x]
Out[6]= e[-2 a]
```

If we look at the internal forms of e[-2a] and of the pattern e[-x_], we can see why the expression does not match.

```
In[7]:= FullForm[{e[-2a], e[-x_]}]
Out[7]//FullForm=
 List[e[Times[-2, a]],
    e[Times[-1, Pattern[x, Blank[]]]]]
```

This pattern is more general. It allows an arbitrary negative number as a factor.

```
In[8]:= e[-2a] /. e[n_?Negative x_] :> e[-n x]
Out[8]= e[2 a]
```

We can declare x_ as optional. In this way, the rule also works for a purely numerical argument.

```
In[9]:= e[-2] /. e[n_?Negative x_.] :> e[-n x]
Out[9]= e[2]
```

Listing 10.3–2 shows the improved rules for numerical and symbolic arguments.

```
oddEvenRules = {
    (f_Symbol?OddQ)[n_?Negative x_.]  :> -f[-n x],
    (f_Symbol?EvenQ)[n_?Negative x_.] :>  f[-n x]
}
```

Listing 10.3–2   OERules2.m: Simplification of numerical and symbolic arguments.

10.3.3.2 Ordering of Expressions

If you enter b+a, it is turned into a+b. This form can hardly be called *simpler,* but the built-in ordering of expressions nevertheless defines a normal form for sums and products. Such an ordering is an important tool. Sorting a long sum makes it easy to combine like terms and to add all numbers occurring in the sum because numbers are ordered before symbolic expressions.

With the help of the ordering, we can define a normal form for even and odd functions having sums as arguments: The normal form shall not have a minus sign in the *first* term of the sum. Again, we try to find corresponding rules. This time it is not as easy because *Mathematica* will always examine all possible orderings of terms for pattern matching. In this case, we do not want it to do so.

This rule seems to work. It removes the minus sign in the first term.	```In[1]:= o[-a + b] /. o[n_?Negative x_ + y_] :> - o[-n x - y]```
	```Out[1]= -o[a - b]```
But it transforms the result back to the original expression, even though the first term does not have a minus sign.	```In[2]:= % /. o[n_?Negative x_ + y_] :> - o[-n x - y]```
	```Out[2]= o[-a + b]```
We can prevent this loop from happening by requiring that the negative term x be the first term.	```In[3]:= o[a - b] /. o[n_?Negative x_ + y_] :> - o[-n x - y] /; OrderedQ[{x, y}]```
	```Out[3]= o[a - b]```
This expression is simplified as it should be because the first term is a, rather than b.	```In[4]:= o[b - a] /. o[n_?Negative x_ + y_] :> - o[-n x - y] /; OrderedQ[{x, y}]```
	```Out[4]= -o[a - b]```
Again, we can declare x as optional to treat single numbers correctly.	```In[5]:= o[a - 1] /. o[n_?Negative x_. + y_] :> - o[-n x - y] /; OrderedQ[{x, y}]```
	```Out[5]= -o[1 - a]```

The rule just found cannot be used for sums of more than two terms. In such cases, the pattern y_ is matched with the sum of all remaining terms. Many single terms of the form n_?Negative x_. are ordered before sums, which allows the rule to be used in more than one way.

The single term -b is ordered before the sum a + c, and the rule is applied even though o[a - b + c] is in normal form.	```In[6]:= o[a - b + c] /. o[n_?Negative x_. + y_] :> - o[-n x - y] /; OrderedQ[{x, y}]```
	```Out[6]= -o[-a + b - c]```

The solution is a bit tricky. We must describe the whole sequence of summands with the pattern y__, and then test the ordering of the list of terms.

This rule is not applied here because the list {-b, a, c} is not ordered.	```In[7]:= o[a - b + c] /. o[n_?Negative x_. + y__] :> - o[-n x - Plus[y]] /; OrderedQ[{x, y}]```
	```Out[7]= o[a - b + c]```

In this case the rule is applied, as it should be.

```
In[8]:= o[-a + b - c] /. o[n_?Negative x_. + y__] :>
                    - o[-n x - Plus[y]] /; OrderedQ[{x, y}]

Out[8]= -o[a - b + c]
```

Listing 10.3–3 shows the complete rules for simplification of odd and even functions.

```
oddEvenRules = {
    (f_Symbol?OddQ)[n_?Negative x_.] :> -f[-n x],
    (f_Symbol?OddQ)[n_?Negative x_. + y__] :> -f[-n x - Plus[y]] /;
        OrderedQ[{n x, y}],
    (f_Symbol?EvenQ)[n_?Negative x_.] :> f[-n x],
    (f_Symbol?EvenQ)[n_?Negative x_. + y__] :> f[-n x - Plus[y]] /;
        OrderedQ[{n x, y}]
}
```

Listing 10.3–3   OERules.m: Normal forms for odd and even functions.

10.3.4   Key Concepts

1. Normal forms are unique forms of many equivalent, but different looking, expressions.

2. A simplifier is an idempotent function on expressions.

3. A canonical simplifier computes normal forms.

4. Noetherian and confluent reduction systems lead to canonical simplifiers.

10.4 Application: Trigonometric Simplifications

The simplifications discussed in Section 10.3.3 are performed automatically for trigonometric functions.

All these expressions have a minus sign in the first position. The cosine is even; the other functions are odd.

```
In[1]:= {Sin[-1], Cos[-x], Tan[b - a]}
Out[1]= {-Sin[1], Cos[x], -Tan[a - b]}
```

Trigonometric functions satisfy a number of further identities that we shall look at next. The presence of identities such as $\sin^2 x + \cos^2 x = 1$ means that there are many ways to write a trigonometric expressions. Let us try to find a normal form for them.

10.4.1 Normal Forms

Just as we did for ordinary polynomials (see Section 10.3.1), we can find a normal form for trigonometric expression by expanding them. Products and powers of trigonometric functions can be turned into sums using these three identities:

$$
\begin{aligned}
\sin x \sin y &= \frac{\cos(x-y)}{2} - \frac{\cos(x+y)}{2}, \\
\sin x \cos y &= \frac{\sin(x+y)}{2} + \frac{\sin(x-y)}{2}, \\
\cos x \cos y &= \frac{\cos(x+y)}{2} + \frac{\cos(x-y)}{2}.
\end{aligned}
\tag{10.4-1}
$$

An expression that does not contain any more products of trigonometric functions is a *linear* expression. Such an expression is a normal form. Listing 10.4–1 shows the three identities from Equation 10.4–1 as rewrite rules in *Mathematica*. As we shall see, they are not sufficient for transforming all trigonometric expressions into normal form.

```
trigLinearRules = {
    Sin[x_] Cos[y_] :> Sin[x+y]/2 + Sin[x-y]/2,
    Sin[x_] Sin[y_] :> Cos[x-y]/2 - Cos[x+y]/2,
    Cos[x_] Cos[y_] :> Cos[x+y]/2 + Cos[x-y]/2
}
```

Listing 10.4–1   TrigLinear1.m: Products of trigonometric functions as sums.

Here, all products are written as sums.

```
In[2]:= Sin[a] Cos[b] + Sin[a] Cos[a] +
        Cos[2a] Cos[3a] /. trigLinearRules
```

$$
Out[2]= \frac{Cos[a]}{2} + \frac{Cos[5\,a]}{2} + \frac{Sin[2\,a]}{2} + \frac{Sin[a - b]}{2} +
$$

$$
\frac{Sin[a + b]}{2}
$$

The operator `/.` applies the rules only once to each expression. As a consequence, some products remain.

```
In[3]:= Cos[a] Cos[2a] Cos[3a] Cos[4a] /.
          trigLinearRules
```

$$Out[3]= (\frac{Cos[a]}{2} + \frac{Cos[3\ a]}{2})\ Cos[3\ a]\ Cos[4\ a]$$

The operator `//.` applies the rules several times, until no more rules can be applied. Now, there are no more explicit products if sines and cosines.

```
In[4]:= Cos[a] Cos[2a] Cos[3a] Cos[4a] //.
          trigLinearRules
```

$$Out[4]= (\frac{Cos[a]}{2} + \frac{Cos[3\ a]}{2})\ (\frac{Cos[a]}{2} + \frac{Cos[7\ a]}{2})$$

The result is not in the desired form, however, because it still contains (implicit) products of trigonometric functions. Only after the distributive law is applied (with `Expand[]`) can the rules be applied again.

```
In[5]:= Expand[%] //. trigLinearRules
```

$$Out[5]= \frac{Cos[a]^2}{4} + \frac{\frac{Cos[2\ a]}{2} + \frac{Cos[4\ a]}{2}}{4} +$$

$$\frac{\frac{Cos[6\ a]}{2} + \frac{Cos[8\ a]}{2}}{4} + \frac{\frac{Cos[4\ a]}{2} + \frac{Cos[10\ a]}{2}}{4}$$

Expanding the result again shows that the rules cannot be applied again. Note that there are still powers of trigonometric functions left.

```
In[6]:= Expand[%]
```

$$Out[6]= \frac{Cos[a]^2}{4} + \frac{Cos[2\ a]}{8} + \frac{Cos[4\ a]}{4} + \frac{Cos[6\ a]}{8} +$$

$$\frac{Cos[8\ a]}{8} + \frac{Cos[10\ a]}{8}$$

Because we do not know beforehand how often we have to expand out products, it is best to use a fixed-point construction that applies the simplifier function as often as necessary. (`Function[]` is explained in Section 11.1.)

```
In[7]:= FixedPoint[
          Function[e, Expand[e //. trigLinearRules]],
          Cos[a] Cos[2a] Cos[3a] Cos[4a]
        ]
```

$$Out[7]= \frac{Cos[a]^2}{4} + \frac{Cos[2\ a]}{8} + \frac{Cos[4\ a]}{4} + \frac{Cos[6\ a]}{8} +$$

$$\frac{Cos[8\ a]}{8} + \frac{Cos[10\ a]}{8}$$

The preceding example shows that we need additional rules to simplify powers of trigonometric functions. Mathematically, `Cos[x]^2` is the same as `Cos[x] Cos[x]`. The square is stored differently (as `Power[Cos[x], 2]`), and, as a consequence, our rules do not match. The simplest way to derive the new rules is to view `Cos[x]^n` as `Cos[x] Cos[x] Cos[x]^(n-2)`, and then to use the previous rules to rewrite `Cos[x] Cos[x]`. We get:

```
Sin[x_]^n_Integer?Positive :> (1/2 - Cos[2x]/2) Sin[x]^(n-2)
Cos[x_]^n_Integer?Positive :> (1/2 + Cos[2x]/2) Cos[x]^(n-2)
```

The restriction of the exponent n to positive integers with n_Integer?Positive is necessary because rational or negative exponents lead to infinite application of the rules. (Can you explain why?)

As we have seen, it is necessary to multiply out intermediate results, and then to apply the rules again. We can write a function that performs these steps for us. We call it TrigLinear[*expr*]. Furthermore, we turn our small program into a package. It is shown in Listing 10.4–2.

```
BeginPackage["CSM`TrigLinear`"]

TrigLinear::usage = "TrigLinear[e] expands products and powers of
    trigonometric functions."

Begin["`Private`"]

trigLinearRules = {
    Sin[x_] Cos[y_] :> Sin[x+y]/2 + Sin[x-y]/2,
    Sin[x_] Sin[y_] :> Cos[x-y]/2 - Cos[x+y]/2,
    Cos[x_] Cos[y_] :> Cos[x+y]/2 + Cos[x-y]/2,
    Sin[x_]^n_Integer?Positive :> (1/2 - Cos[2x]/2) Sin[x]^(n-2),
    Cos[x_]^n_Integer?Positive :> (1/2 + Cos[2x]/2) Cos[x]^(n-2)
}

SetAttributes[TrigLinear, Listable]

TrigLinear[expr_] :=
    FixedPoint[ Function[e, Expand[e //. trigLinearRules]], expr ]

End[]

Protect[TrigLinear]

EndPackage[]
```

Listing 10.4–2   The first version TrigLinear.m.

The expression is simplified until all trigo-nometric functions occur only linearly.

In[1]:= **TrigLinear[Sin[x]^2 Cos[x]^3]**

$$Out[1]= \frac{Cos[x]}{8} - \frac{Cos[3\ x]}{16} - \frac{Cos[5\ x]}{16}$$

An important application of normal forms is to decide whether two different-looking expressions describe the same function. If we integrate a function and differentiate the result, we should get back the original function. Often, however, the result will look different. Because the linear form is a normal form for trigonometric functions, we can use TrigLinear[] to check the result.

First, we integrate $\sin^2 x \cos^2 x$.

In[2]:= **Integrate[Sin[x]^2 Cos[x]^2, x]**

$$Out[2]= \frac{x}{8} - \frac{Sin[4\ x]}{32}$$

Then, we differentiate the result. It looks different from the original expression.

```
In[3]:= D[ %, x ]
             1     Cos[4 x]
Out[3]=  -  -  -  --------
             8        8
```

We put the result into normal form. (It happens already to be in normal form.)

```
In[4]:= TrigLinear[ % ]
             1     Cos[4 x]
Out[4]=  -  -  -  --------
             8        8
```

Our original expression also is put into normal form. Now we can see immediately that the two expressions are the same.

```
In[5]:= TrigLinear[ Sin[x]^2 Cos[x]^2 ]
             1     Cos[4 x]
Out[5]=  -  -  -  --------
             8        8
```

We can check the equality of the expressions by putting both of them into normal form. This procedure is usually simpler than is trying to transform one expression into the other.

10.4.2 Simplifying Arguments

`TrigLinear[]` linearizes trigonometric functions and in doing so can introduce more complicated arguments of these functions.

The simple arguments x and y are turned into more complicated ones.

```
In[1]:= TrigLinear[ Cos[x] Cos[y] Sin[x] ]
             Sin[2 x - y]     Sin[2 x + y]
Out[1]=  ------------  +  ------------
                 4                4
```

We can try to find rules that will express functions with complicated arguments in terms of functions with simpler arguments. These two formulae allow the simplification of arguments involving sums of angles:

$$
\begin{aligned}
\sin(x + y) &= \sin x \cos y + \cos x \sin y, \\
\cos(x + y) &= \cos x \cos y - \sin x \sin y.
\end{aligned}
\qquad (10.4\text{--}2)
$$

It is not difficult to find rules that perform these simplifications.

Again, we have to think about special cases, multiples of an angle, in this case. The term $\sin(2x)$ is the same as $\sin(x + x)$, but it is stored differently; therefore, we need a special rule. More generally, we can write $\sin nx$, for positive integers n, as $\sin(x + (n - 1)x)$ and then use Equation 10.4–2. Note that we do not need any rules for negative multiples. Trigonometric functions are put into normal form by *Mathematica*, and these normal forms do not contain minus signs, as we saw at the beginning of Section 10.4. The rules and the function `TrigArgument[]`, which applies them, are in the package TrigArgument1.m, shown in Listing 10.4–3. `TrigArgument[]` uses `Together[]` to simplify the result (in the same way as `Expand[]` was used in `TrigLinear[]`).

```
BeginPackage["CSM`TrigArgument`"]

TrigArgument::usage = "TrigArgument[e] writes trigonometric functions
    of sums and products as products of simple trigonometric functions."

Begin["`Private`"]

trigArgumentRules = {
    Sin[x_ + y_] :> Sin[x] Cos[y] + Sin[y] Cos[x],
    Cos[x_ + y_] :> Cos[x] Cos[y] - Sin[x] Sin[y],
    Sin[n_Integer?Positive x_.] :> Sin[x] Cos[(n-1)x] + Sin[(n-1)x] Cos[x],
    Cos[n_Integer?Positive x_.] :> Cos[x] Cos[(n-1)x] - Sin[x] Sin[(n-1)x]
}

SetAttributes[TrigArgument, Listable]

TrigArgument[expr_] :=
    Together[ FixedPoint[ Function[e, e //. trigArgumentRules], expr ] ]

End[]

Protect[ TrigArgument ]

EndPackage[]
```

Listing 10.4–3   TrigArgument1.m: Simplification of arguments.

In this way, we can get back the input from line 1.

```
In[2]:= TrigArgument[%]

Out[2]= Cos[x] Cos[y] Sin[x]
```

Here is another example. First, we expand it out.

```
In[3]:= TrigLinear[Sin[x]^2]

Out[3]= 1   Cos[2 x]
        - - -------
        2      2
```

Now, we try to get back the original expression. The result looks different, however.

```
In[4]:= TrigArgument[%]

              2         2
        1 - Cos[x]  + Sin[x]
Out[4]= --------------------
                 2
```

To prove that it is right, we put it into normal form.

```
In[5]:= TrigLinear[%]

Out[5]= 1   Cos[2 x]
        - - -------
        2      2
```

The preceding example shows that `TrigArgument[]` does not give normal forms. There are several possible ways to write a trigonometric expression, if we allow products of trigonometric functions. This fact is a consequence of identities such as $\sin^2 x + \cos^2 x = 1$.

10.4.3 Advanced Topic: The Complexity of Rule Application

In our rules for `TrigArgument[]`, we replaced `Sin[n x]` by an expression involving `Sin[(n-1) x]`. The advantage of this method is that the rule is easy to derive. Repeated application of rules performs the iteration automatically. The disadvantage is the slow speed of such rules for large values of n, as run-time measurements show.

This command generates a table of the time needed for the application of our rules for $\sin(nx)$, for $n = 5, 6, \ldots, 15$. The times double for each successive expression.

```
In[1]:= Table[ Timing[ TrigArgument[Sin[n x]] ][[1]],
                {n, 4, 14} ] /. Second -> 1
Out[1]= {0.02, 0.02, 0.04, 0.08, 0.17, 0.32, 0.64, 1.3,
         2.62, 5.3, 10.6}
```

We can find much faster rules if we use a formula that expresses $\sin(nx)$ and $\cos(nx)$ directly in terms of $\sin x$ and $\cos x$. Such formulae can be found in mathematics handbooks.

$$\begin{aligned}
\sin(nx) &= n\cos^{n-1} x \sin x - \binom{n}{3} \cos^{n-3} x \sin^3 x + \cdots, \\
\cos(nx) &= \cos^n x - \binom{n}{2} \cos^{n-2} x \sin^2 x + \cdots.
\end{aligned} \qquad (10.4\text{–}3)$$

An important aspect of *Mathematica* is that it is very easy to program such formulae directly as rules. The result is shown in Listing 10.4–4.

```
Sin[n_Integer?Positive x_.] :>
    Sum[ (-1)^((i-1)/2) Binomial[n, i] Cos[x]^(n-i) Sin[x]^i, {i, 1, n, 2} ],

Cos[n_Integer?Positive x_.] :>
    Sum[ (-1)^(i/2) Binomial[n, i] Cos[x]^(n-i) Sin[x]^i, {i, 0, n, 2} ]
```

Listing 10.4–4   TrigArgument2.m: A formula for multiple angles.

The new rules are much faster and show only a linear growth of run time that is almost unnoticeable here.

```
In[1]:= Table[ Timing[ TrigArgument[Sin[n x]] ][[1]],
                {n, 20, 35} ] /. Second -> 1
Out[1]= {0.02, 0.01, 0.02, 0.01, 0.02, 0.02, 0.02,
         0.02, 0.03, 0.02, 0.02, 0.02, 0.03, 0.02, 0.03, 0.02}
```

If there was no formula for expressing powers and multiples directly in terms of single functions, we could still improve efficiency by expressing $\sin(nx)$ as $\sin(\frac{n}{2}x + \frac{n}{2}x)$ for even n, and as $\sin(\frac{n+1}{2}x + \frac{n-1}{2}x)$ for odd n. This method is often called *divide and conquer*. Here are the corresponding rules. They are part of TrigArgument3.m, shown in Listing 10.4–5.

Run times turn out to be irregular. They depend on the representation of n in binary. Asymptotically, they are of the order $O(n \log n)$. This complexity is between those of the previous two versions.

```
In[1]:= Table[ Timing[ TrigArgument[Sin[n x]] ][[1]],
                {n, 20, 35} ] /. Second -> 1
Out[1]= {0.08, 0.18, 0.11, 0.17, 0.05, 0.2, 0.12, 0.23,
         0.09, 0.23, 0.13, 0.2, 0.06, 0.29, 0.22, 0.39}
```

These improvements can also be applied to `TrigLinear[]` from Section 10.4.1 to express $\sin^n x$ directly in terms of $\sin x$ and $\cos x$.

Functions for transforming trigonometric expressions in many ways are now built into *Mathematica*. Our `TrigLinear[]` is called `TrigReduce[]`, and `TrigArgument[]` is `TrigExpand[]`.

```
Sin[n_Integer?EvenQ x_.] :>
    Sin[n/2 x] Cos[n/2 x] + Sin[n/2 x] Cos[n/2 x]

Sin[n_Integer?OddQ x_.] :>
    Sin[(n+1)/2 x] Cos[(n-1)/2 x] + Sin[(n-1)/2 x] Cos[(n+1)/2 x]

Cos[n_Integer?EvenQ x_.] :>
    Cos[n/2 x] Cos[n/2 x] - Sin[n/2 x] Sin[n/2 x]

Cos[n_Integer?OddQ x_.] :>
    Cos[(n+1)/2 x] Cos[(n-1)/2 x] - Sin[(n+1)/2 x] Sin[(n-1)/2 x]
```

Listing 10.4–5   TrigArgument3.m: Divide and conquer.

10.4.4   Key Concepts

1. The fully linearized form of trigonometric expressions is a normal form.

2. Even though integer powers are products, they need to be treated specially in pattern matching.

10.5   Exercises

10.1   Simple Evaluations[1]

Give the result of evaluating the following expressions. If there are any nested functions, also give the most important intermediate steps. Assume that each example is evaluated in a fresh *Mathematica* session. Consecutive expressions in one example are evaluated one after another in the same session.

1. `0 <= x < y <= 7 /. { x -> 5, y -> 7 }`

2. `abs[x_] := x /; x > 0`
    `abs[x_] := -x /; x < 0`
    `Map[ abs, {-1, 1/3, 0, I} ]`

3. `sign[x_] := If[x < 0, -1, 1]`
    `{sign[-2.33], sign[c], sign[sign[-1]]}`

10.2   Pattern Matching[2]

Describe the terms that match this pattern:

$$g[\ x\_ \ + \ n\_Integer \ y\_. \ ] \ .$$

Which parts (if any) of the following expressions can be filled in for the pattern variables `x_`, `y_`, and `n_`?

1. `g[ u + 3 x + 2 ]`

2. `g[ 2 u∧2 + v ]`

3. `g[ 6 ]`

4. `g[ a u + 6 ]`

5. `g[ u∧3 - v ]`

6. `g[ u∧3 / 2 ]`

---

[1]Written examination, ETH Zürich, Department of Mathematics and Physics.
[2]Béatrice Amrhein, ETH Zürich.

10.3 Differentiation of Expressions[3]

Write a package that defines a function diff[*expr, var*] to differentiate expressions symbolically.

The derivative of an arithmetic expression U with respect to x, $\left(\frac{dU}{dx}\right)$, is defined recursively by differentiation rules that are applied to U. From a handbook, we take the following rules (U and V are arbitrary arithmetic expressions, and c is a constant):

$$\frac{dc}{dx} \longrightarrow 0$$

$$\frac{dx}{dx} \longrightarrow 1$$

$$\frac{d-U}{dx} \longrightarrow -\frac{dU}{dx}$$

$$\frac{dU+V}{dx} \longrightarrow \frac{dU}{dx} + \frac{dV}{dx}$$

$$\frac{dUV}{dx} \longrightarrow \frac{dU}{dx}V + U\frac{dV}{dx}$$

$$\frac{dU^c}{dx} \longrightarrow cU^{c-1}\frac{dU}{dx}$$

$$\frac{d\exp(U)}{dx} \longrightarrow \exp(U)\frac{dU}{dx}$$

$$\frac{d\ln(U)}{dx} \longrightarrow \frac{1}{U}\frac{dU}{dx}$$

$$\frac{dU^V}{dx} \longrightarrow U^V\frac{dV\ln(U)}{dx}$$

1. Write these rules as definitions for diff[]. Not all of these rules are strictly necessary. Which ones are sufficient to differentiate all the functions given?

2. These definitions can be augmented by rules for special functions, such as sine, cosine, and so on. The function diff[] becomes more powerful in this way. Implement a few of these rules.

10.4 L-Systems

An *L-System* consists of a word over some alphabet and a set of rewrite rules for replacing symbols or subwords by other words.

Words are associative, so we should define these attributes for our data type for words.

```
In[1]:= SetAttributes[word, {Flat, OneIdentity}]
```

Here is a word over the alphabet consisting of the three symbols m, l, and r.

```
In[2]:= gen = word[m, r, r, m, r, r, m]
Out[2]= word[m, r, r, m, r, r, m]
```

Our set of rules consists of a single rule for replacing the symbol m by the given word.

```
In[3]:= rules = {m -> word[m, l, m, r, r, m, l, m]}
Out[3]= {m -> word[m, l, m, r, r, m, l, m]}
```

---

[3]Dominik Gruntz, ETH Zürich.

One application of the rules replaces every occurrence of m by a word; the result is flattened out, due to the attribute `Flat`.

```
In[4]:= gen1 = gen /. rules
Out[4]= word[m, l, m, r, r, m, l, m, r, r, m, l, m, r,
        r, m, l, m, r, r, m, l, m, r, r, m, l, m]
```

We can visualize the resulting words using an idea from *Turtle graphics*, a simple graphic model used in the language Logo. The turtle sits originally at the origin and faces right. Each letter in our word is interpreted as a command for the turtle to change either its location by moving a certain distance in the current direction, or by turning a certain amount. As the turtle moves, it leaves a visible trail behind.

By interpreting m as a move, and l and r as turns by 60° to the left and right, respectively, the generator gen describes a triangle, and the first iteration gen1 corresponds to the figure on the left.

If we apply the rules four times to the generator, using

```
Nest[# /. rules &, gen, 4]
```

we arrive at a word whose interpretation is shown on the right. This example generates the *Koch curve* or *snowflake* fractal curve.

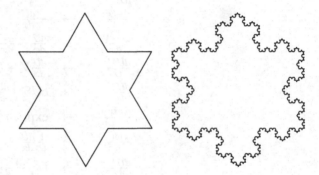

1. Define a suitable data type for representing the possible states of the turtle.

2. Design a way to specify an *interpretation* of a word by giving the effect each letter of the alphabet has on the state of the turtle.

3. Program a function for converting a word to a list of points, given an interpretation and the start state of the turtle.

4. Plot the line connecting the points to obtain pictures similar to the ones given here.

5. Optionally remove duplicate points from the line before plotting it. The words will often consist of long sequences of turns between the moves, leading to many occurrences of the same point in lines. For better rendering, only one of a sequence of identical points should be drawn.

Experiment with various generators, rule sets, and interpretations, such as the *flowsnake*. The alphabet consists of {m1, m2, r, l}, the rules are

```
m1 -> word[l, m2, r, m1, m1, r, r, m1, r, m2, l, l, m2, l, m1]
m2 -> word[m2, r, m1, r, r, m1, l, m2, l, l, m2, m2, l, m1, r]
```

Both, m1 and m2 are interpreted as moves, and r and l as 60° turns as before.

Here is the fourth iteration of the flowsnake.
The generator is simply a straight line, that
is, word[m1].

Chapter 11
Functions

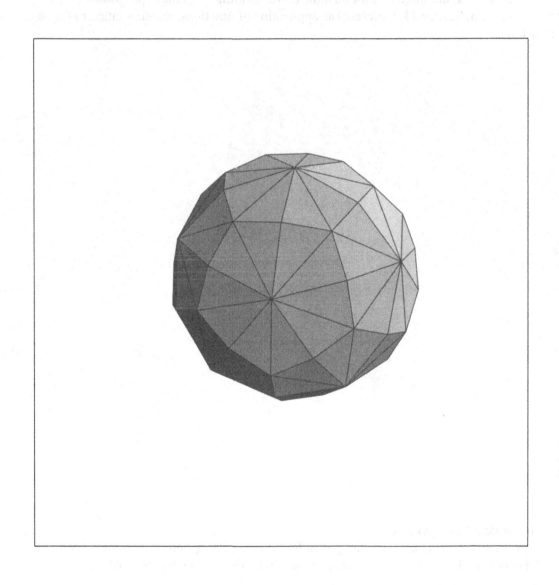

In this chapter, we study functions. Functions are of central importance in mathematics, but they play a peripheral role in computer science because many programming languages have only rudimentary means of working with them. The functional languages, including *Mathematica*, are an important exception.

The ideas used in functional languages go back to λ calculus, which we explain in Section 11.1. Then, we show how we can program with functions as values. This possibility often leads to programs that are more elegant than the corresponding procedural programs.

The last section, Section 11.3, presents an application of functions: the simulation of linear shift registers.

About the illustration overleaf:
The picture shows a *Picagon*. The picagon is formed by putting certain pyramids onto the faces of a dodecahedron. The graphic was produced with this command (see Pictures.m):

```
Show[ Polyhedron[Picagon], Boxed->False ].
```

11.1   A Notation for Functions (λ Calculus)

Functions are the most important concept in mathematics. Interestingly, there is no universally adopted notation for functions. To define the function that squares its argument, for example, we may write

$$f(x) = x^2,$$ (11.1–1)

and then use the expression $f(x)$ sometimes for the function itself, sometimes for the function value at x. We would like to make a definition of the form

$$f = ?$$ (11.1–2)

instead. Sometimes one writes

$$f: x \mapsto x^2.$$ (11.1–3)

11.1.1   λ Notation

As a notation for functions, the λ *notation* was proposed in the thirties by A. Church. In this notation, we write

$$f = \lambda x.x^2.$$ (11.1–4)

for the function that squares its argument. The function $\lambda x.x^2$ can be applied to an argument a. The result (the value of the function at a) is obtained by substituting the argument for the λ variable x.

$$(\lambda x.x^2)(a) \longrightarrow a^2.$$ (11.1–5)

In general, we can turn an expression e involving the variable x into a function of x. This function is denoted by $\lambda x.e$. *Mathematica* offers this possibility as well. Instead of λ, we use the symbol `Function`, and we write `Function[x, e]`. The new mechanism allows us to use a function without defining it beforehand or even giving it a name. Without it, we would always have to define a function by name using

$$\texttt{f[x\_] := e}.$$ (11.1–6)

Both, `f` and `Function[x, e]`, are a notation for the function and the two are interchangeable. To apply the function to an argument a, we write either `f[a]` or `Function[x, e][a]`. The latter form looks probably strange at first. The expression `Function[x, e]` is called a *pure function*.

This command defines `f` as the function with   `In[1]:= f[x_] := 1 + x^2`
$f(x) = 1 + x^2$.

The variable g is assigned a pure function that is the same as f.

```
In[2]:= g = Function[x, 1 + x^2]

Out[2]= Function[x, 1 + x ]
                           2
```

Both can be used in the same way.

```
In[3]:= {f[3], g[3]}

Out[3]= {10, 10}
```

In this way, the function can be used without a prior definition and without a name for it.

```
In[4]:= Function[x, 1 + x^2][3]

Out[4]= 10
```

11.1.2 Advanced Topic: Properties of Pure Functions

λ *calculus* is the mathematical study of formal systems of functions. Three properties of pure functions are of particular interest for us. They are called β reduction, α conversion, and η conversion. In the pure function $\lambda x.e$, the variable x is called the *formal parameter*, and e is the *body* of the function.

The first property (β reduction) describes how pure functions are applied to their arguments. We write $(\lambda x.e)(a)$ for the application of the function $\lambda x.e$ to argument a. We do the application by *substituting* the argument for every occurrence of the formal parameter in the body of the function. The substitution of the variable x by the expression a in e is written

$$[x \rightarrow a]e. \tag{11.1–7}$$

Therefore, $(\lambda x.e)(a)$ is equal to $[x \rightarrow a]e$. For example,

$$(\lambda x.x^2)(2) = [x \rightarrow 2]x^2 = 2^2 = 4. \tag{11.1–8}$$

In *Mathematica*, the application of a pure function looks as follows:

$$\text{Function}[x, e][a].$$

A substitution mechanism is part of the language (see Section 10.2). We can, therefore, express the rule for β reduction $[x \rightarrow a]e$ in *Mathematica* as

$$e \; / . \; x \; \text{->} \; a \; .$$

The result of function application is 4, as expected.

```
In[1]:= Function[x, x^2][2]

Out[1]= 4
```

This expression is equivalent to the previous function application. It shows how pure functions are applied to arguments.

```
In[2]:= x^2 /. x -> 2

Out[2]= 4
```

There is one subtlety. In the expression e /. x -> a the terms e and x are evaluated before substitution takes place. However, in a function application `Function[x, e][a]`, the body e is evaluated only *after* replacing the formal parameter x by its value a. We can preserve this behavior by using the more complicated form

`ReleaseHold[ Hold[e] /. HoldPattern[x] -> a]`

for the substitution. This expression is essentially the same as e /. x -> a, except that e and x are not evaluated before the substitution takes place.

To show why `Hold[]` and `HoldPattern[]` are necessary, we give the global variable x a value.	`In[3]:= x = 17` `Out[3]= 17`
Even with the global value for x, this expression is still evaluated correctly.	`In[4]:= ReleaseHold[ Hold[x^2] /. HoldPattern[x] -> 2 ]` `Out[4]= 4`
The simplified form of the replacement, however, gives an incorrect result.	`In[5]:= x^2 /. x -> 2` `Out[5]= 289`

The second property (α conversion) says that the name of the formal parameter does not matter. If we replace the variable x in `Function[x, e]` by y, wherever it occurs, we get the same function. The function $(\lambda x.e)$ is therefore the same as $(\lambda y.[x \rightarrow y]e)$.

Here is an example of a pure function.	`In[1]:= Function[x, Sqrt[x] + Sin[x] + E^(2x)]` `Out[1]= Function[x, Sqrt[x] + Sin[x] + E`$^{2 x}$`]`
This expression describes the exact same function.	`In[2]:= % /. x -> y` `Out[2]= Function[y, Sqrt[y] + Sin[y] + E`$^{2 y}$`]`

As we have seen, the expression `Function[x, e][a]` is evaluated by replacing each occurrence of x in e by the argument a. It is intuitively clear that the name of the variable does not matter. This is true, however, only if the new name y did not already occur in e. *Mathematica* treats names of formal parameter as local variables and renames them if necessary to avoid naming conflicts with other variables. A detailed explanation of how this is done can be found in [54]. This kind of substitution (that respects names of formal parameters) must be performed using `With[{x = y}, e]`. Ordinary substitution, e /. x -> y, does not care about naming conflicts.

Ordinary substitution violates the semantics of λ calculus. The resulting function *doubles* its argument, instead of adding the global symbol x to the argument.	`In[3]:= Function[x, x + y] /. y -> x` `Out[3]= Function[x, x + x]`

With[] gives the correct result, that is, a   In[4]:= With[{y = x}, Function[x, x + y]]
function that adds x to its argument. The
variable x outside Function[] is different   Out[4]= Function[x$, x$ + x]
from the formal parameter sharing its name.
Mathematica renamed the formal parameter
to x$.

The third property (η conversion) says that a pure function of the form $\lambda x.f(x)$ is the same
as f. In *Mathematica*, Function[x, $f[x]$] is simply f itself.

This pure function is merely a complicated   In[5]:= Function[x, Sin[x]]
way to write the sine function.
                                             Out[5]= Function[x, Sin[x]]

Its application to an argument returns the   In[6]:= { Function[x, Sin[x]][a], Sin[a] }
same result as the application of Sin itself.
                                             Out[6]= {Sin[a], Sin[a]}

11.1.3   Short Forms of Pure Functions

Because the name of the formal parameter in a pure function is unimportant, *Mathematica* can
provide special symbols for the use as formal parameters. The expressions #1, #2, and so on
are used for the first, second, and so on formal parameters of a pure function. Their internal
form is Slot[i]. If you use these formal parameters, you do not have to declare them, and you
can leave out the first argument of Function[]. Instead of Function[{#1, #2}, e], you
can write Function[e]. Another (small) abbreviation allows you to use # for #1. The short
form Function[e] can be written using the special postfix operator &. You can therefore
write e& for Function[e]. The operator & has low priority, just above assignment (see
Section B.4).

The whole expression the the left of & is part   In[1]:= 1 + # + #^2 & [5]
of the body of the pure function. $1 + 5 + 5^2$ Out[1]= 31
gives 31.

In this context, you must write the paren-   In[2]:= f[a] /. f -> (1+# &)
theses *around* the pure function to avoid the
whole substitution to be treated as the func-   Out[2]= 1 + a
tion's body.

11.1.4   Constant Pure Functions

The formal parameter need not necessarily occur in the body. If it does not occur, the function
value does not depend on the argument, the function is *constant*. The expression 1&, or
Function[1], for example, describes a constant function that gives – independent of its
argument – always the value 1.

Independent of its argument (5, here) we   `In[3]:= 1&[5]`
always get the value 1.   `Out[3]= 1`

11.1.5   Key Concepts

1. Functions themselves are values that can be used in our programs.

2. A concise notation for functions is λ calculus.

3. The application of a function to its argument happens by substitution for the formal parameter.

4. Names of formal parameters are unimportant as long as no naming conflicts occur.

11.2   Functions as Values

Traditional programming languages make it hard to work with functions. Functions have to be defined and then compiled. Little can be done with such static objects. As we have just seen, *Mathematica* makes it easy to define and use functions. Functions are, therefore, values that you can pass around as parameters, return as values of functions, and so on. This section explores some of the possibilities of the functional programming style.

11.2.1   Functions Returning Functions

Because we now have a way to describe new functions without having to make a definition for a symbol, we can return such functions as values of other functions.

Here is the definition of `constant[val]`,
a function whose *result* is a constant pure
function that always returns *val*.

```
In[1]:= constant[x_] := x&
```

k7 is now a constant pure function.

```
In[2]:= k7 = constant[7]

Out[2]= 7 &
```

It always returns the value 7.

```
In[3]:= k7[666]

Out[3]= 7
```

11.2.2   Application: Infinite Data Structures

In Section 12.3, we need to model a potentially infinite memory. *Potentially infinite* means that we will never, of course, store an infinite number of data elements at the same time, but that we do not know beforehand how many there will be. If we knew that there were never more than n elements, we could simply store them in a list of length n. `l = Table[0, {n}]` could be used to initialize the list with zeroes, and `ReplacePart[l, new, i]` could be used to change the value at position i. The value at position i could be looked at with `l[[i]]`.

In this example we set $n = 10$.

```
In[1]:= l = Table[0, {10}]

Out[1]= {0, 0, 0, 0, 0, 0, 0, 0, 0, 0}
```

The number 77 is stored at position 2.

```
In[2]:= l1 = ReplacePart[l, 77, 2];
```

Here are the elements no. 2 and 3 of `l1`.

```
In[3]:= {l1[[2]], l1[[3]]}

Out[3]= {77, 0}
```

Observe that we did not modify the original
list `l`. This property will be important in
our application.

```
In[4]:= l[[2]]

Out[4]= 0
```

If we were allowed to destructively modify the list, the solution to our problem would be simple. We could store the values as rules for the "function" l.

This definition establishes the default value.	`In[1]:= l[_] := 0`
The "list" l behaves like an infinite list that contains the value 0 everywhere.	`In[2]:= l[10000000]` `Out[2]= 0`
To store the value 77 at position 2, we simply make this definition.	`In[3]:= l[2] = 77;`
Here are the elements no. 2 and 3 of l.	`In[4]:= {l[2], l[3]}` `Out[4]= {77, 0}`

How can we combine both properties, potentially infinite and nondestructive? Mathematically, an infinite list l is a function from $\mathbf{Z}$ to the set of expressions. The function value at i, $l(i)$, is the value stored at position i. If we want to store the value e at position i, we get a new function l' with the definition

$$l'(j) = \begin{cases} e, & \text{if } i = j \text{ ;} \\ l(j) & \text{otherwise ,} \end{cases} \tag{11.2–1}$$

because the new function differs only at position i from the old one; it is the same everywhere else. We need an implementation of this abstract data type:

Constants	`empty`	an empty list
Constructors	`update[`l`, `e`, `i`]`	a new list with e at position i
Selectors	l`[`i`]`	the value at position i

One possible implementation uses functions. Translated into *Mathematica*, Equation 11.2–1 means that l' is

$$\text{Function[j, If[j===i, e, l[j]]] .}$$

The constructor `update[`l`, `e`, `i`]` can be implemented as

$$\text{update[l\_, e\_, i\_] := Function[j, If[j===i, e, l[j]]] ,}$$

and the empty list is simply a constant pure function:

$$\text{empty = Function[i, 0] .}$$

Initially, the list is a constant pure function that always returns zero.	`In[1]:= l = Function[i, 0];`
l behaves like an infinite list.	`In[2]:= l[10000000]` `Out[2]= 0`

We use `update[]` to store the number 77 at position 2.

```
In[3]:= l1 = update[1, 77, 2];
```

Here are the elements no. 2 and 3 of `l1`.

```
In[4]:= {l1[2], l1[3]}

Out[4]= {77, 0}
```

The original list has not been modified.

```
In[5]:= l[2]

Out[5]= 0
```

11.2.3 Functions as Arguments

We have seen that it is easy to define functions. There are two ways to define them: *definitions* and *pure functions*.

We can make a definition to define the function `f1`.

```
In[1]:= f1[x_] := x^2
```

Instead, we can also use a pure function.

```
In[2]:= f2 = Function[x, x^2]

Out[2]= Function[x, x ]
```

The two possibilities are equivalent and they give the same result.

```
In[3]:= {f1[5], f2[5]}

Out[3]= {25, 25}
```

Pure functions can be used to give functions as arguments to other functions. Let us describe the most important of these functional operations.

11.2.3.1 Applying Functions to Elements (`Map`)

Functional thinking can lead to simple programs. Let us look at an example: we want to square the elements of a list `l`. Many languages leave us no other option than to write a loop in which we assign the squares of the elements of `l` to the elements of a new list `r`.

```
q1[l_List] :=
    Module[{r, n = Length[l]},
        r = Table[0, {n}];        (* Result array    *)
        Do[ r[[i]] = l[[i]]^2,    (* assign elements *)
            {i, 1, n}
        ];
        r
    ]
```

Mathematica makes it unnecessary to create the list of results explicitly. We can simply use `Table[`*elem*`, `*iterator*`]` to generate the elements. They are collected in a list automatically.

```
q2[l_List] :=
    Module[{n = Length[l], i},
        Table[ l[[i]]^2,          (* generate elements *)
            {i, 1, n}
        ]
    ]
```

The body of `Table` is of the form $f[\ l[[i]]\ ]$, that is, the *same* function is applied to all elements of `l`. The operation that applies functions to elements of a list is built into *Mathematica*. It is `Map[`*function*, *list*`]`. Using it, we arrive at a much simpler program.

```
q3[l_List] := Map[ Function[x, x^2], l ]
```

The operation `Map[]` takes a *function* as its first argument. This is a good place to use pure functions.

The way such operations work is easy to see if we use purely symbolic arguments.	`In[4]:= Map[ f, {e1, e2, e3, e4, e5} ]` `Out[4]= {f[e1], f[e2], f[e3], f[e4], f[e5]}`
To square the elements, we use a pure function that squares its argument.	`In[5]:= Map[ Function[x, x^2], {e1, e2, e3, e4, e5} ]` `Out[5]= {e1^2, e2^2, e3^2, e4^2, e5^2}`
In this easy way, we get the squares of numbers in a list.	`In[6]:= Map[ Function[x, x^2], {1, 2, 3, -1, I} ]` `Out[6]= {1, 4, 9, 1, -1}`
The infix operator `/@` can be used in place of `Map[]`.	`In[7]:= f /@ {e1, e2, e3, e4, e5}` `Out[7]= {f[e1], f[e2], f[e3], f[e4], f[e5]}`

We do not want to fail to mention that this particular example can be computed in an even simpler way. *Mathematica* applies arithmetic and mathematical functions automatically to elements of lists.

There cannot be a simpler way!	`In[8]:= {1, 2, 3, -1, I} ^ 2` `Out[8]= {1, 4, 9, 1, -1}`

11.2.3.2 Applying Functions to Expressions (`Apply`)

The operation `Apply[`f, *expr*`]` performs a simple operation: It replaces the head of *expr* by f. This operation has surprisingly diverse uses.

The expression `{a, b, c}` has head `List`. If we replace the head by `f`, we get this result.	`In[1]:= Apply[ f, {a, b, c} ]` `Out[1]= f[a, b, c]`

The new head is now Plus: we get the *sum* of the elements of the list!

```
In[2]:= Apply[ Plus, {a, b, c} ]
Out[2]= a + b + c
```

This simple definition is all it takes to compute the average of the elements of a list.

```
In[3]:= average[l_List] :=
            Apply[Plus, l] / Length[l]
```

Again, symbolic arguments make it easy to see what is going on. Here is the formula for the average of two numbers.

```
In[4]:= average[{a, b}]
        a + b
Out[4]= -----
          2
```

We can compute the expected value when throwing an ordinary die.

```
In[5]:= average[{1, 2, 3, 4, 5, 6}]
        7
Out[5]= -
        2
```

This definition is for the calculation of the absolute value of vectors. First, we square the elements; then, we sum them; and finally, we extract the square root.

```
In[6]:= abs[v_List] := Sqrt[ Apply[ Plus, v^2 ] ]
```

Here is the formula for

$$\left| \begin{pmatrix} x \\ y \\ z \end{pmatrix} \right|$$

```
In[7]:= abs[{x, y, z}]
                2   2   2
Out[7]= Sqrt[x + y + z ]
```

Note that the definition works for vectors of arbitrary dimension.

The infix operator @@ can be used in place of Apply[].

```
In[8]:= f @@ g[x, y]
Out[8]= f[x, y]
```

11.2.3.3 Iterating Function Application (Nest)

Iterated function application consists in applying a function again and again to the result of the previous application, that is, we build the sequence x, $f(x)$, $f(f(x))$, ... The operation Nest[f, x, n] applies the function f n times to the initial value x.

Here is the tenfold nesting with purely symbolic values.

```
In[9]:= Nest[ f, x, 10 ]
Out[9]= f[f[f[f[f[f[f[f[f[f[x]]]]]]]]]]
```

The function $\lambda x. 1 + \frac{1}{x}$ is applied 10 times to the value 1.0. The result is an approximation of the Golden Ratio φ.

```
In[10]:= Nest[ Function[x, 1 + 1/x], 1.0, 10 ]
Out[10]= 1.61798
```

NestList[], instead of Nest[], shows all intermediate values.

```
In[11]:= NestList[ Function[x, 1 + 1/x], 1.0, 10 ]
Out[11]= {1., 2., 1.5, 1.66667, 1.6, 1.625, 1.61538,
          1.61905, 1.61765, 1.61818, 1.61798}
```

If we choose an exact number as starting point, we get a rational approximation of φ.

```
In[12]:= Nest[ Function[x, 1 + 1/x], 1, 10 ]

Out[12]= 144
         ───
          89
```

A symbolic starting point gives a continued fraction.

```
In[13]:= Nest[ Function[x, 1 + 1/x], a, 5 ]

Out[13]= 1 + ──────────────────────
                            1
             1 + ──────────────────
                              1
                 1 + ──────────────
                                1
                     1 + ──────────
                                  1
                         1 + ──────
                                  1
                             1 + ─
                                 a
```

A finite approximation of a continued fraction is an ordinary rational expression. Together[] puts it over a common denominator.

```
In[14]:= Together[ % ]

         5 + 8 a
Out[14]= ───────
         3 + 5 a
```

Interestingly, the coefficients of the rational approximation of the Golden Ratio are successive Fibonacci numbers. See also Section 7.2.

```
In[15]:= NestList[Function[x, Together[1 + 1/x]], a, 5]

              1 + a  1 + 2 a  2 + 3 a  3 + 5 a  5 + 8 a
Out[15]= {a, ─────, ───────, ───────, ───────, ───────}
                a     1 + a    1 + 2 a  2 + 3 a  3 + 5 a
```

We used such function iteration mostly for numerical computations, for example in Section 1.1.1 and in Section 3.4.4.

11.2.4 Key Concepts

1. Potentially infinite data structures are finite but have no fixed limit on size.

2. Iteration of functions is an important tool for efficient programs and for finding approximate numerical solutions.

3. If an iteration converges, the limit is a fixed point of the iterated function.

11.3   Example: Simulation of Shift Registers

An application of Nest[] and NestList[] is the simulation of systems that evolve in discrete time steps. At each time step, the system is in a certain state. The new state in the next time step is a function of the old state. If we program the state transition as a function, we can perform the simulation with Nest[]. NestList[] returns the evolution history of the system.

A *linear shift register with feedback* of length k consists of k cells that hold the values 0 or 1. At each time step, the contents of the cells are shifted to the right and the new content of the first cell is the sum (modulo 2) of certain other cells (the so-called *taps*).

We can treat a shift register as a function that computes the new cell contents from the old ones. The contents of the cells are described as a list of zeroes and ones. The constructor shiftRegister[*taps*] creates this function for a shift register whose taps are given by the list of positions *taps*. The program is shown in Listing 11.3–1. (Think about how the definition of shiftRegister works.)

Here is a shift register with taps at the given positions.	`In[1]:= s = shiftRegister[{5, 7, 10, 15}];`
We choose a random initial configuration of 15 bits.	`In[2]:= z0 = Table[Random[Integer], {15}]` `Out[2]= {1, 1, 0, 1, 0, 1, 1, 0, 0, 0, 1, 1, 0, 1, 0}`
Here are the contents after one time step. All bits moved to the right, and the new first bit is a function of the bits at the tap positions.	`In[3]:= s[z0]` `Out[3]= {1, 1, 1, 0, 1, 0, 1, 1, 0, 0, 0, 1, 1, 0, 1}`

We can let the register run for 25 steps.	`In[4]:= NestList[ s, z0, 25 ] // Short`
	`Out[4]//Short=`
	`  {{1, 1, 0, 1, 0, 1, 1, 0, 0, 0, 1, 1, 0, 1, 0}, <<25>>}`

It is best to draw a picture of the states of the register. The contents of the cells at one time step are shown vertically (from bottom to top). Successive steps are shown next to each other. Ones are shown in white, and zeroes are in black.	`In[5]:= Show[ Graphics[Raster[Transpose[%]]],`
	`            AspectRatio->Automatic ];`

For many of these shift registers, the sequence derived from the contents of the first cell is a good pseudorandom sequence.

```
In[6]:= First /@ %%
Out[6]= {1, 1, 1, 0, 0, 1, 0, 1, 1, 1, 1, 1, 0, 1, 1,
         0, 1, 1, 1, 0, 1, 1, 0, 0, 1, 1}
```

```
shiftRegister[taps_List] :=
    Function[cells,
        Prepend[ Drop[cells, -1],
            Mod[ Plus @@ cells[[taps]], 2]
        ]
    ]
```

Listing 11.3–1   LSR.m: Shift registers.

11.4   Exercises

11.1   Simple Evaluations[1]

Give the result of evaluating the following expressions. If there are any nested functions, also give the most important intermediate steps. Assume that each example is evaluated in a fresh *Mathematica* session. Consecutive expressions in one example are evaluated one after another in the same session.

1. ```
   g[x_] := 1 + 1/x
   Nest[g, a, 2]
   ```

2. ```
   i[i_] := i^I
   Nest[i, I, 2]
   ```

11.2   Unbounded Data Structures

Realize some other implementation for the potentially infinite lists from Section 11.2.2. Some Ideas:

1. Binary trees (see Section 6.3). Note that old information has to be overwritten if an already existing key is inserted again.

2. A list of rules of the form $\{i_1 \text{->} e_1, \ldots, i_n \text{->} e_n\}$. To store a new value at position i, you can simply prepend a new rule. For efficiency reasons it may be necessary to remove other rules for the same i to prevent the rule list from growing too much.

3. *Your own idea.*

Compare efficiency (run time and memory needed) of various implementations.

11.3   Shift Registers

Use the package LSR.m to implement a random number generator, as indicated in Section 11.3.

11.4   Bell Polynomials

The nth *Bell polynomial* $B_n(x; g(t))$ is the coefficient of t^n in the Taylor series of $e^{xg(t)}$ at $t = 0$. We assume $g(0) = 0$. The formula for the Taylor series gives:

$$e^{xg(t)} = \sum_{k=0}^{\infty} B_n(x) \frac{t^n}{n!} \tag{11.4–1}$$

---

[1]Written examination, ETH Zürich, Department of Mathematics and Physics.

- Example 1: $g(t) = t$:

$$\begin{aligned} e^{xt} &= \sum_{k=0}^{\infty} x^n \frac{t^n}{n!} \\ B_n(x;t) &= x^n \end{aligned}$$ (11.4–2)

- Example 2: $g(t) = \log(1+t)$:

$$\begin{aligned} e^{x\log(1+t)} &= \sum_{k=0}^{\infty} x^{\underline{n}} \frac{t^n}{n!} \\ B_n(x;\log(1+t)) &= x^{\underline{n}} \end{aligned}$$ (11.4–3)

The *falling factorial* $x^{\underline{n}}$ is defined as

$$x^{\underline{n}} = \prod_{i=0}^{n-1} (x-i) = x(x-1)\ldots(x-n+1).$$ (11.4–4)

Write a package that implements the function BellP[n, x, g] to compute the Bell polynomial $B_n(x;g)$.

The identity is a good way to test our function (Example 1).

```
In[1]:= BellP[10, x, Identity]
            10
Out[1]= x
```

Here are the falling factorials up to degree four. (Example 2).

```
In[2]:= Table[ BellP[i, x, Log[1+#]&], {i, 0, 4} ]
                       2          2     3
Out[2]= {1, x, -x + x , 2 x - 3 x  + x ,

              2       3     4
   -6 x + 11 x  - 6 x  + x }
```

Their construction becomes apparent in factored form.

```
In[3]:= Factor[%]
Out[3]= {1, x, (-1 + x) x, (-2 + x) (-1 + x) x,

    (-3 + x) (-2 + x) (-1 + x) x}
```

Chapter 12
Theory of Computation

1	91	188	290	386
2	93	210	320	387
3	94	211	321	411
2	96	212	322	412
4	97	211	323	412
5	99	213	324	413
6	100	214	324	414
8	102	215	325	415
9	103	214	326	416
10	105	216	327	417
12	106	217	328	418
13	108	219	329	420
14	109	220	330	421
13	111	222	332	423
15	112	223	333	424
16	114	225	335	425
17	115	226	336	424
18	117	262	337	426
19	118	263	336	427
20	130	264	338	428
21	131	265	339	429
22	133	266	341	430
23	134	267	342	431
24	136	268	366	432
25	137	269	367	433
26	139	269	367	434
27	140	270	368	435
28	142	271	369	436
29	143	272	370	438
30	171	273	371	439
32	172	274	372	441
33	174	275	373	442
35	175	277	375	444
36	177	278	376	427
38	178	280	378	445
39	180	281	379	446
41	181	282	380	447
42	182	281	379	448
44	183	283	381	449
45	182	284	382	451
67	184	286	384	452
68	185	287	16	454
90	187	289	385	0

In this chapter, we present one foundation of theoretical computer science. Theory of computation studies the fundamental limits of algorithmic computation – independent of practical considerations of run time and memory size. We shall characterize the class of computable functions and show that there are functions that cannot be computed by any machine.

Section 12.3 presents Turing machines, one of the abstract machine models used as a tool for proving theorems about computability. Despite its abstract nature, we will be able to develop real programs for it and run them on a simulator. This material is adapted from [50, 53]. Finally, in Section 12.4 we show exactly how the partial recursive functions can be computed on Turing machines.

About the illustration overleaf:
This picture shows the computation of the predecessor function on a Turing machine. See Section 12.4.

12.1 Computable Functions

A program (a definition in *Mathematica*) computes a function transforming its input into an output. Theory of computation investigates the question of which functions are computable in principle without regard to limits of memory size and run time. That is, we assume that we have all the memory needed and that the computer is fast enough, whatever the computation performed. The large number of different data types and program constructs offered in real programming languages make such fundamental questions difficult to answer. It is easy to see, however, that we can restrict ourselves to programs working with natural numbers. All other data types, such as strings, can be represented easily as numbers. In the end, every computation takes place on a computer whose memory cells can be viewed as numbers.

We can restrict ourselves to functions on natural numbers, having some number k of arguments, that is, functions

$$f : \mathbf{N}^k \to \mathbf{N}, \qquad k \geq 0. \tag{12.1–1}$$

The case $k = 0$ describes functions of no arguments, that is, *constants*. Zero is considered a natural number: $\mathbf{N} = \{0, 1, 2, \ldots\}$.

In this section, we shall define a class of mathematical functions, the partial recursive functions, and show that we can compute all of them on a computer.

12.1.1 The Natural Numbers

As a data type, the natural numbers are defined by the constant 0, and the successor function $s\colon n \mapsto n + 1$ (see Section 5.1.1). A set of natural numbers containing 0, and, with each n also the number $s(n)$, contains all natural numbers. This property is the foundation of proofs by induction, see Section 5.1.1. We can define addition and multiplication inductively as follows:

$$\begin{aligned}
m + 0 &= m, \\
m + s(k) &= s(m + k), \\
m \cdot 0 &= 0, \\
m \cdot s(k) &= m \cdot k + m.
\end{aligned} \tag{12.1–2}$$

It is not difficult to write a *Mathematica* program for such definitions. Obviously, these functions can be computed.

12.1.2 The Primitive Recursive Functions

We want to formalize the informal principle of recursion to obtain a rigorously defined class of functions. An inductive definition of a class of objects defines certain fundamental objects and provides construction methods for obtaining new objects from already constructed ones. This principle is similar to the definition of a data type from constants (the fundamental objects) and constructors (see Chapter 5). The most important of these construction methods is the schema of primitive recursion, which we used in Equation 12.1–2. We want to generalize and formalize it. The result is the class of *primitive recursive functions*. The class of primitive recursive functions is defined inductively as follows:

1. The constant 0 is a (nullary) primitive recursive function.

2. The *successor function* s is a (unary) primitive recursive function.

3. For each $n \geq 1$ and $k \leq n$, the *projection function* p_k^n, with

$$p_k^n(m_1, m_2, \ldots, m_n) = m_k, \tag{12.1–3}$$

   is a primitive recursive function.

4. The *composition* of primitive recursive functions is primitive recursive:
   Let $f, g_1, \ldots, g_p$ be primitive recursive, $n \geq 0$, then h, with

$$h(m_1, \ldots, m_n) = f(g_1(m_1, \ldots, m_n), \ldots, g_p(m_1, \ldots, m_n)), \tag{12.1–4}$$

   is a primitive recursive function.

5. Let f and g be primitive recursive, $n \geq 0$, and

$$\begin{aligned} h(0, m_1, \ldots, m_n) &= f(m_1, \ldots, m_n), \\ h(s(k), m_1, \ldots, m_n) &= g(k, h(k, m_1, \ldots, m_n), m_1, \ldots, m_n), \end{aligned} \tag{12.1–5}$$

   Then, h is a primitive recursive function (schema of recursion).

It is rather cumbersome to adhere strictly to this formalism. To see that the addition $+(m_1, m_2)$ is primitive recursive, for example, we need to write Equation 12.1–2 in this way:

$$\begin{aligned} +(0, m) &= p_1^1(m), \\ +(s(k), m) &= g(k, +(k, m), m), \\ g(k, l, m) &= s(p_2^3(k, l, m)). \end{aligned} \tag{12.1–6}$$

In particular, the projection functions are mostly notational inconvenience. We shall, therefore, simply insert the corresponding arguments. For example, we can define g as $g(k, l, m) = s(l)$. It should be obvious which projections to use, if we wanted to be strict.

    We still have to prove that the schema of recursion 12.1–5 does indeed define a proper function h. The method of proof is, of course, induction (see Exercise 12.1).

12.1.3 Which Functions Are Primitive Recursive?

All basic arithmetic functions are primitive recursive. We looked already at addition and multiplication. The *predecessor function* $p(n)$, with

$$
\begin{aligned}
p(0) &= 0, \\
p(n) &= n - 1, \quad n > 0,
\end{aligned}
\tag{12.1--7}
$$

is also primitive recursive:

$$
\begin{aligned}
p(0) &= 0, \\
p(s(k)) &= k.
\end{aligned}
\tag{12.1--8}
$$

Note that $p(0) = 0$ because we deal only with *nonnegative* integers.

The *arithmetic difference* $m \mathbin{\dot-} n$ is used in place of ordinary subtraction because there are no negative numbers.

$$
m \mathbin{\dot-} n = \begin{cases} m - n, & \text{if } m \geq n; \\ 0 & \text{otherwise.} \end{cases}
\tag{12.1--9}
$$

It is easy to show that the arithmetic difference is primitive recursive:

$$
\begin{aligned}
m \mathbin{\dot-} 0 &= m, \\
m \mathbin{\dot-} s(n) &= p(m \mathbin{\dot-} n).
\end{aligned}
\tag{12.1--10}
$$

For the last operation, division, see Exercise 12.3.

12.1.4 Programming Constructs

Programs are our main source of functions. If we assume that we work only with natural numbers, every program (or subprogram) is a function of natural numbers.

Let us now look at programming constructs and find out which ones lead to primitive recursive functions. The simplest programming constructs are predicates, branches, and loops. We can view predicates as functions returning a natural number. We use the value 0 for True, and any value greater than 0 means False.

The conditional statement or branch If[*pred, then, else*] is also primitive recursive because we can define it strictly as a primitive recursive function if(k, m_1, m_2) that returns m_1 for $k = 0$, and m_2 for $k > 0$:

$$
\begin{aligned}
\text{if}(0, m_1, m_2) &= p_1^2(m_1, m_2) & = m_1, \\
\text{if}(s(k), m_1, m_2) &= p_4^4(k, \text{if}(k, m_1, m_2), m_1, m_2) & = m_2.
\end{aligned}
\tag{12.1--11}
$$

Functions defined with *bounded iteration* are primitive recursive. A bounded iteration is a loop whose number of iterations is known already at the beginning – that is, the number of iterations does not depend on values computed during the iteration. The Do loop in *Mathematica* is such a bounded iteration; the While loop is not, in general. Here is an example of a function computed with a Do loop. We want to show that it corresponds to a primitive recursive function.

```
x2 = 1;
Do[ x2 = x2 * x3, {x3, 1, x1} ]
```

This program uses the variables x_1, x_2, and x_3. The value of x_2 after program termination is, therefore, a function of x_1, x_2, and x_3, $\varphi(x_1, x_2, x_3)$. Which well-known function is it? The iteration is over x_1. If $x_1 = 0$, the loop is never executed, and we get

$$\varphi(0, x_2, x_3) = 1. \tag{12.1--12}$$

Now, the induction step. For $x_1 + 1$ instead of x_1, the loop is iterated one more time, and in the last traversal x_3 is equal to $x_1 + 1$. After the next-to-last traversal, x_2 is equal to $\varphi(x_1, x_2, x_3)$ (by induction), and we get

$$\varphi(x_1 + 1, x_2, x_3) = \varphi(x_1, x_2, x_3) \cdot (x_1 + 1). \tag{12.1--13}$$

Equations 12.1–12 and 12.1–13 together are an example of the schema of primitive recursion. The function computed by them is the factorial function of x_1

$$\varphi(x_1, x_2, x_3) = x_1!. \tag{12.1--14}$$

12.1.5   The Partial Recursive Functions

The class of primitive recursive functions is too small for the notion of computability. While loops, for example, often lead to functions that are not primitive recursive. There are also programs that do not halt for every input value. Such behavior leads to *partial functions*. A function is partial if its domain is not necessarily the whole of $\mathbf{N}^k$. A simple example of a partial function is the square root. It is defined only for natural numbers that are perfect squares, that is, for $n = 0, 1, 4, 9, \ldots$.

We can describe partial functions by a single new construction in addition to the primitive recursive functions, the μ schema. The functions defined in this way are called the *partial recursive functions*.

6. (μ schema). Let f and g be primitive recursive; then h, with

$$h(m_1, \ldots, m_n) = f(\mu k[g(m_1, \ldots, m_n, k)]) \tag{12.1--15}$$

is a partial recursive function. $\mu k[g(m_1, \ldots, m_n, k)]$ is the least k with $g(m_1, \ldots, m_n, k) = 0$, if one exists, undefined otherwise.

As an example, consider the square root function just mentioned. Let

$$\delta(n_1, n_2) = (n_1 \dot{-} n_2) + (n_2 \dot{-} n_1). \tag{12.1--16}$$

$\delta(n_1, n_2)$ is zero if and only if $n_1 = n_2$. Now, we can define the square root $w(m)$:

$$w(m) = \mu k[\delta(m, k \cdot k)].$$ (12.1–17)

If m is a square, then $w(m) = \sqrt{m}$; otherwise, $w(m)$ is undefined.

The μ schema formalizes the While loop. The square root function can be programmed as follows:

```
k = 0;
While[ Not[ m == k^2 ], k++ ];
k
```

If you run this program with an input m that is not a square, the loop will never terminate! "Undefined" usually means for functions given by programs that the program does not terminate.

12.1.6 The Ackermann Function

All primitive recursive functions are total. Partial recursive function may be – but need not be – total, as we have seen. The class of *recursive functions* is the class of all partial recursive functions that are total. The question arises whether this class is larger than is the class of primitive recursive functions: Are there functions that are total, but not primitive recursive?

An example of a total function that is not primitive recursive is the *Ackermann function*. It is a binary function defined as

$$\begin{array}{rcl} A(0, y) & = & y + 1, \\ A(x, 0) & = & A(x - 1, 1), \\ A(x, y) & = & A(x - 1, A(x, y - 1)). \end{array}$$ (12.1–18)

It can be shown that primitive recursive functions cannot grow too fast. A primitive recursive function $\varphi(y)$, obtained by n-fold application of the schema of primitive recursion 12.1–5, cannot grow faster than $A(n, y)$. If $A(x, y)$ were primitive recursive, then $f(n) = A(n, n)$ would also be primitive recursive. This is impossible because $A(n_1, y)$ grows faster than $A(n_2, y)$ for $n_1 > n_2$. There should be a n_0, such that $f(n) < A(n_0, n)$.

The Ackermann function can easily be defined in *Mathematica*.

```
In[1]:= Ackermann[ 0, y_ ] := y + 1; \
        Ackermann[ x_, 0 ] := Ackermann[ x - 1, 1 ]; \
        Ackermann[ x_, y_ ] :=
            Ackermann[ x - 1, Ackermann[x, y-1] ];
```

$A(1, i)$ is equal to $i + 2$.

```
In[2]:= Table[Ackermann[1, i], {i, 0, 10}]
Out[2]= {2, 3, 4, 5, 6, 7, 8, 9, 10, 11, 12}
```

$A(2, i)$ is equal to $2i + 1$.

```
In[3]:= Table[Ackermann[2, i], {i, 0, 10}]
Out[3]= {3, 5, 7, 9, 11, 13, 15, 17, 19, 21, 23}
```

Because of the deep recursion involved, the recursion limit has to be increased.

```
In[4]:= $RecursionLimit = Infinity
Out[4]= Infinity
```

$A(3, i)$ is equal to $2^{i+3} - 3$.

```
In[5]:= Table[Ackermann[3, i], {i, 0, 4}]
Out[5]= {5, 13, 29, 61, 125}
```

The value $A(4, 1) = A(3, A(4, 0)) = A(3, A(3, 1)) = A(3, 13) = 2^{16} - 3 = 65533$ cannot be computed with this method in reasonable time.

Our knowledge of $A(3, y)$ allows us to speed up the calculations.

```
In[6]:= Ackermann[3, y_] := 2^(y + 3) - 3
```

Now we can even compute $A(4, 2)$ quickly, but we cannot print out the result.

```
In[7]:= Timing[ a42 = Ackermann[4, 2];]
Out[7]= {0. Second, Null}
```

The result has 19,729 digits.

```
In[8]:= N[a42]
                             19728
Out[8]= 2.003529930406846 10
```

The next number, $A(4, 3)$, already has $6.03 \cdot 10^{19727}$ digits! The whole universe is not big enough to print this number.

```
In[9]:= Log[10.0, 2] %
                            19727
Out[9]= 6.03122606263029 10
```

12.1.7   Recursive Functions Are Computable

It is not difficult to see that all partial recursive functions can be computed (in principle) on a computer. We have to convince ourselves that the schema of primitive recursion (Equation 12.1–5), and the μ schema (Equation 12.1–15) can be programmed. As an example, let us look at the definition of addition according to Equations 12.1–2 and 12.1–6. They can be programmed like this in *Mathematica*:

```
plus[0, m_] := m
plus[s[k_], m_] := s[plus[k, m]]
```

Here is the computation of $2 + 1 = 3$.

```
In[1]:= plus[ s[s[0]], s[0] ]
Out[1]= s[s[s[0]]]
```

Primitive recursion corresponds to the definition of the data type for natural numbers (see also Section 5.1.1). Induction for k can be used to show that the computation of h is finite for any k. The μ schema leads to a While loop.

12.1.8   Key Concepts

1. Arbitrary data processing on computers can be reduced to the computation of functions of natural numbers.

2. Computability is a theoretical concept, independent of any restrictions on memory size and run time.

3. Partial functions can also be regarded as computable.

4. Undefined places of a function correspond to programs that do not halt.

12.2   Models of Computation

After we saw that recursive functions are computable, we are interested in the reverse question: Which functions can be computed at all? It is obvious that there are functions that cannot be computed: The number of possible programs is countable, but the number of functions $N \rightarrow N$ is uncountable.

12.2.1   Machine Models

To see which functions can be computed in principle, we have to think about what kinds of computers we can reasonably imagine. To answer this question, we study abstract machine models. Such models are free of restrictions concerning memory size and computing time. The most important of these models is the *Turing machine*, named after the computer pioneer Alan Turing. This model is very simple, but it is obvious that none of the sophisticated features of today's computers extend the class of functions computable on them. Every computation on one of today's computers could be done in principle on a Turing machine.

The simplicity of the Turing machine allows us to prove that every function computable on it is partial recursive. (We cannot give this proof here; it is too complicated.) Both theorems taken together show that the computable functions are *exactly* the partial recursive functions.

12.2.2   Equivalence of Machine Models

Over time, many different machine models have been proposed. In each case, it turned out that the functions computable on the new models are exactly the partial recursive functions. An important tool for proving two models equivalent is *simulation*. A program is developed that runs on one machine and that interprets programs written for the other machine. That is, one machine is simulated on another machine. We can think of *Mathematica*'s programming language as a machine model. The *program Mathematica* is nothing but an interpreter of *Mathematica*'s programming language on a certain computer. An interpreter for Turing machines in *Mathematica* is developed in Section 12.3.

A. Church summed up these insights in what is now called *Church's thesis*:

> *The computable functions are exactly the partial recursive functions.*

This statement cannot be proved. We cannot exclude the possibility that some day a physical process will be discovered that can be used to compute nonrecursive functions.

12.2.3   The Halting Problem

An important noncomputable function is the *halting problem*. Computer programs can be encoded as numbers. This encoding allows us to think about functions operating on programs.

Because computable functions can themselves be represented as programs, we can see that programs can receive other programs as input. This statement is not as strange as it may seem at first. A compiler, for example, is a program that takes another program as input and produces a program as output (normally written in machine language). An interpreter is also such a program. It takes another program P and its input E as inputs, and produces the same output that the program P would have produced with input E. If the program P with input E got into an infinite loop, the interpreter would also fail to halt.

An interesting question is: Is there a program H that can find out whether another program P with input E will halt in finite time (without taking an infinite amount of time to find out). That is, we ask for a total function $H(P, E)$ that returns 0 (for `True`) if P halts with input E, and 1 (for `False`) otherwise. The predicate

$$H(P, E) : \text{ Program } P \text{ halts with input } E \text{ in finite time}$$

cannot be computable. The assumption that it is computable, that there is a *program* computing H, leads to a contradiction. Define

$$G(z) = \text{if}(H(z, z) = 0, loop, halt).$$

(*loop* means to go into an infinite loop, for example, $\mu k[1]$.)

If H were computable, G would be, too. Look at $G(G)$: The execution of program G with input G terminates if and only if $H(G, G) > 0$, that is, if program G with input G does *not* halt! Therefore, the halting problem is *undecidable*, that is, there is no program that can decide whether any program halts on any given input.

The undecidability of the halting problem does not mean that we can never decide whether a particular program halts. But there is no single program that can answer this question for *all* programs.

A related intriguing concept is the halting probability, explained in Chaitin's book [11].

12.3   Turing Machines

The *Turing machine* was devised by Alan Turing as a theoretical model of a computer. On one hand, the machine is simple enough that the class of functions computable on it can be described exactly (the partial recursive functions); on the other hand, the model is universal – that is, all functions computable on any other model can also be computed on the Turing machine. This property is shown by simulating the other models on the Turing machine.

In this section we want to develop a simulator for Turing machines themselves. In the next section, we shall show that the partial recursive functions are Turing computable.

12.3.1   The Machine Model

The Turing machine consists of an infinite memory (of which we will always use only a finite portion). The memory can be thought of as a linear arrangement of cells. We call the memory the *tape* of the Turing machine. Each cell contains one symbol taken from a finite alphabet. We shall develop only machines whose alphabet consists of two symbols, *empty* (_) and *mark* (*). All but finitely many cells contain the empty symbol.

The Turing machine can access only one cell at a time. We can think of this cell as the position of a read/write head. The machine is in one of finitely many *states*, which we can label with positive integers. The program of a Turing machine consists of finitely many instructions. An instruction reads the symbol under the head and performs three actions:

- It writes a symbol into the cell under the head, overwriting the symbol present. The new symbol may be the same as the old one, in which case the contents of the cell are not changed.

- It moves the head one cell to the right or left, or it stays where it is. We denote this action by l, r, and s.

- The machine enters a new state.

The cycle is then repeated: The machine reads the symbol under the head, and so on.

The behavior of the Turing machine is given completely by the list of instructions (the Turing table) and the original contents of the tape. Instructions are quintuplets of the form

```
instruction[state, symbol, newsymbol, move, newstate] .
```

The machine halts if the new state is equal to 0. We assume that the machine starts in state 1. It is taken to be an error if there is no instruction for the current state and symbol read. We shall not (knowingly) develop machines that fall into an errror state for a correct input.

We can use a simulator for Turing machines to assemble instruction sequences in *Mathematica* and then look at the actions of the corresponding Turing machine step by step. Here is an example. This is the list of instructions:

state	symbol	newsymbol	move	newstate
1	_	_	r	2
2	*	*	r	2
2	_	*	l	3
3	*	*	l	3
3	_	_	s	0

The course of a computation is best visualized with a picture.

Each line depicts the configuration before the execution of an instruction. On the left is the current state, followed by a portion of the tape. The position of the head is marked by a gray square.

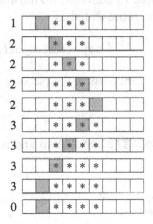

The machine starts in state 1 with a blank under the head. According to the first instruction it writes a blank, moves to the right, and goes into state 2. Now it finds a mark, writes another mark, moves to the right, and stays in state 2. After three more steps it finds a blank, writes a mark, moves to the left, and continues in state 3. In state 3 it *skips* all further marks going left and, finally, comes to a halt on the cell it started from.

Overall, this machine increments the number of consecutive marks by 1. It implements the successor function, if we represent natural numbers as sequences of marks.

12.3.2 The Tape of the Turing Machine

The first thing we need is a data type for the tape of the Turing machine. We developed a suitable data type for infinite lists in Section 11.2.2. Because the head of a Turing machine moves only a little, writing over an old part of the tape happens much more frequently than does venturing into new parts of the tape. The implementation given in Section 11.2.2 is not particularly efficient for this kind of usage. We can keep the abstract data type, however, with a few additional functions:

Constants	emptyTape[b]	an empty tape
Constructors	update[t, s, i]	same tape as t, but with s in cell i
	newTape[$list$, b, p_0]	a new tape from a list
Selectors	$t[i]$	the symbol in cell i
	low[t]	the smallest nonempty cell
	high[t]	the largest nonempty cell

Observe that the constructor emptyTape[b] takes an argument that specifies the chosen empty symbol. Our implementation in the package Tape.m, shown in Listing 12.3–1, uses an ordinary list that is enlarged as needed. In addition, we must store the true index of the first element of the list. Tapes are, therefore, represented as

$$\text{tape}[list,\ offset,\ b]\ .$$

Please try to understand the functions in the package. As output format we choose

$$<\ t_1\ t_2\ \ldots\ t_6\ \ldots>\ ,$$

showing a portion of the tape. The variables b and m contain the symbols used for empty and mark.

newTape[] makes it easy to set up the initial tape contents for a Turing machine.

```
In[3]:= t = newTape[{b, m, m, m}, b]
Out[3]= < _ * * * _ _ ...>
```

Here is how we give a new value for the tape position 6.

```
In[4]:= t1 = update[ t, m, 6 ]
Out[4]= < _ * * * _ * ...>
```

12.3.3   Instructions and Configurations

We saw already how we can specify instructions. Internally, however, we want to store them as rules

$$\{state,\ symbol\}\ \text{->}\ \{newsymbol,\ move,\ newstate\}\ ,$$

to allow us to use the built-in mechanism of rule application for finding the instruction for a given state and symbol. The data type for instructions defines the five selectors state[], symbol[], newstate[], newsymbol[], and move[] for extracting the respective components of instructions. The Turing table is stored as a list (of instructions). Listing 12.3–2 shows the simple implementation of the data type.

The *configuration* of a Turing machine is given by the current state, the contents of the tape, and the position of the head. We use the data type

$$config[state, \ tape, \ head]$$

with the expected selectors state[], tape[] and head[], as well as symbol[*config*] as an

```
BeginPackage["CSM`Tape`"]

emptyTape::usage = "emptyTape[b] is an empty tape with blank b."
update::usage = "update[tape, sym, i] is a tape differing from tape at position i
    where its value is sym."
newTape::usage = "newTape[list, b, p0:1] is a tape taken from a list.
    The first element is at position p0."
low::usage = "low[tape] is the least index of a nonempty cell."
high::usage = "high[tape] is the largest index of a nonempty cell."

Begin["`Private`"]  g

(* list[[j]] is the position i = offset + j *)

emptyTape[b_] := tape[{}, 0, b]

tape[list_, offset_, b_][i_Integer]/; 0 < i-offset <= Length[list] :=
        list[[i-offset]]
tape[list_, offset_, b_][i_Integer] := b

tape/: update[ tape[list_, offset_, b_], new_, i_Integer ] :=
    Which[ i-offset <= 0,
                tape[ Join[ {new}, Table[b, {offset-i}], list ], i-1, b ],
            i-offset > Length[list],
                tape[ Join[ list, Table[b, {i-offset-Length[list]-1}], {new} ],
                    offset, b ],
            True,
                tape[ ReplacePart[list, new, i-offset], offset, b ] ]

newTape[l_List, b_, p0_:1] := tape[ l, p0-1, b]

tape/: low[tape[list_, offset_, b_]] :=
    Module[{j = 1},
        While[ j <= Length[list] && list[[j]] === b, j++ ];
        If[ j <= Length[list], offset + j, Infinity ] ]

tape/: high[tape[list_, offset_, b_]] :=
    Module[{j = Length[list]},
        While[ j >= 1 && list[[j]] === b, j-- ];
        If[ j >= 1, offset + j, -Infinity ] ]

Format[t_tape] := SequenceForm[ "< ", Infix[Array[t, 6, 1], " "], " ...>" ]
Protect[ tape ]

End[]
Protect[ emptyTape, update, newTape, low, high ]
EndPackage[]
```

Listing 12.3–1 Tape.m.

abbreviation for `tape[`*config*`][head[`*config*`]]`, to make it easier to look at the symbol under the head.

```
instruction[state_, symbol_, newsym_, move_, newst_] :=
        {state, symbol} -> {newsym, move, newst}

state[instruction[state_, symbol_, newsym_, move_, newst_]] := state

symbol[instruction[state_, symbol_, newsym_, move_, newst_]] := symbol

newsymbol[instruction[state_, symbol_, newsym_, move_, newst_]] := newsym

move[instruction[state_, symbol_, newsym_, move_, newst_]] := move

newstate[instruction[state_, symbol_, newsym_, move_, newst_]] := newst
```

Listing 12.3–2   Part of Turing.m: Instructions.

12.3.4 Simulation

The execution of an instruction leads from the old configuration to a new configuration that reflects the effects of the instruction. The pair (*state, symbol under head*) determines which instruction is executed. Because we store instructions as rules, we can simply apply the list of instructions to this pair to get the new state, new symbol, and the movement of the head. These three pieces of information allow us to change the configuration accordingly. The function `nextConfiguration[` *config, instructions*`]` performs these steps, see Listing 12.3–3.

```
nextConfiguration[c_config/; state[c]==0, instructions_] := c

nextConfiguration[c_config, instr_List] :=
    Module[{newst, newsym, move},
        {newsym, move, newst} = {state[c], symbol[c]} /. instr;
        If[ Head[newst] === Symbol,
            Message[ nextConfiguration::noinstr, state[c], symbol[c]];
            Return[c] ];
        config[ newst,
                update[tape[c], newsym, head[c]],
                head[c] + move /. moverules
              ]
    ]

moverules = {r -> 1, l -> -1, s -> 0}

nextConfiguration::noinstr = "No instruction with state `1` and symbol `2` found."
```

Listing 12.3–3   Part of Turing.m: Configurations.

The first definition makes sure that no more changes take place after entering the halt state (state 0). The error message is generated if no instruction is applicable to the current state and symbol. This condition means an error in either the instructions or the contents of the tape. In general, the new state is taken from the instruction, the tape is updated by writing the new symbol at the current head position, and the head position is changed according to the move. The symbolic moves r, l, and s are first translated into corresponding offsets in the positions (−1, 1, or 0).

An auxiliary function initialConfiguration[*list*] creates an initial configuration by creating an initial tape from the given list of symbols, setting the state to 1 and the putting the head over the first symbol in the list.

To simulate a computation, we need to set up the initial configuration, and then repeatedly apply the function nextConfiguration[]. It is best to use Nest[] for this iteration. To simulate *n* computation steps, we use

Nest[nextConfiguration[#, *instructions*]&, *config*, *n*] .

If we want to see the intermediate steps, we use NestList[] instead.

These are the instructions of the machine we showed in action on page 283.

```
In[5]:= addOne // TableForm
Out[5]//TableForm= {1, _} -> {_, r, 2}
                   {2, *} -> {*, r, 2}
                   {2, _} -> {*, l, 3}
                   {3, *} -> {*, l, 3}
                   {3, _} -> {_, s, 0}
```

Here is an initial configuration with three marks on the tape. The head is on the blank before the marks.

```
In[6]:= m0 = initialConfiguration[{b, m, m, m}]
Out[6]= config[1, < _ * * * _ _ ...>, 1]
```

We execute nine steps. The machine is now in state 0, that is, it has halted.

```
In[7]:= NestList[ nextConfiguration[#, addOne]&,
             m0, 9 ] // TableForm
Out[7]//TableForm= config[1, < _ * * * _ _ ...>, 1]
                   config[2, < _ * * * _ _ ...>, 2]
                   config[2, < _ * * * _ _ ...>, 3]
                   config[2, < _ * * * _ _ ...>, 4]
                   config[2, < _ * * * _ _ ...>, 5]
                   config[3, < _ * * * * _ ...>, 4]
                   config[3, < _ * * * * _ ...>, 3]
                   config[3, < _ * * * * _ ...>, 2]
                   config[3, < _ * * * * _ ...>, 1]
                   config[0, < _ * * * * _ ...>, 1]
```

Most of the time we want to let the machine run until it halts. We made sure that the function nextConfiguration[] does not modify the halt state. A configuration with state 0 is, therefore, a *fixed point* of nextConfiguration[]. The operation FixedPoint[] works like Nest[], but it continues applying the function until a fixed point is reached.

The machine runs until it comes to a halt. The result is the final configuration.

```
In[8]:= FixedPoint[ nextConfiguration[#, addOne]&, m0 ]
Out[8]= config[0, < _ * * * * _ ...>, 1]
```

`FixedPointList[]`, instead of `FixedPoint[]`, returns the list of intermediate configuration (like `NestList[]`).

The command `run[`*config*, *instructions*`]`, shown in Listing 12.3–4, uses `FixedPoint[]` in the way just shown. An optional third argument specifies the maximal number of steps to perform. It is meant as an "emergency exit" for machines that may not halt. `runList[]` returns all intermediate configurations. In addition to an initial configuration, both commands can take also a list describing the initial contents of the tape as an argument.

```
run[c_config, instr_List, n_:Infinity] :=
      FixedPoint[ nextConfiguration[#, instr]&, c, n ]

run[init_List, instructions_, n_:Infinity] :=
      run[initialConfiguration[init], instructions, n]

runList[c_config, instr_List, n_:Infinity] :=
   Module[{configs},
      configs = FixedPointList[ nextConfiguration[#, instr]&, c, n ];
      If[ Length[configs] < n + 1, Drop[configs, -1], configs ]
   ]

runList[init_List, instructions_, n_:Infinity] :=
      runList[initialConfiguration[init], instructions, n]
```

Listing 12.3–4   Part of Turing.m: Running the simulator.

A programming detail: If a fixed point is reached, that is, if the machine halts in fewer than n steps, the output of `FixedPointList[]` contains the last configuration twice, and we remove the last one. If we stop because of the limit on the number of steps instead, the result is a list of length $n + 1$, and we leave it alone.

This machine removes the last one of a sequence of marks. It implements the predecessor function.

```
In[9]:= sub1 = {
            instruction[ 1, b, b, r, 2],
            instruction[ 2, m, m, r, 2],
            instruction[ 2, b, b, l, 3],
            instruction[ 3, m, b, l, 4],
            instruction[ 3, b, b, s, 0],
            instruction[ 4, m, m, l, 4],
            instruction[ 4, b, b, s, 0]
         };
```

We let it run to completion.

```
In[10]:= runList[ {b, m, m}, sub1 ] // TableForm
Out[10]//TableForm= config[1, < _ * * _ _ _ ...>, 1]
                    config[2, < _ * * _ _ _ ...>, 2]
                    config[2, < _ * * _ _ _ ...>, 3]
                    config[2, < _ * * _ _ _ ...>, 4]
                    config[3, < _ * * _ _ _ ...>, 3]
                    config[4, < _ * _ _ _ _ ...>, 2]
                    config[4, < _ * _ _ _ _ ...>, 1]
                    config[0, < _ * _ _ _ _ ...>, 1]
```

A picture makes it easier to see how it works.   `In[11]:= PlotTuring[ % ];`

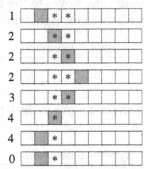

This machine with three states is called a *busy beaver*. If it is started on an empty tape, it runs for 21 steps before halting. No other machine with three states runs for more steps before halting.

```
In[12]:= beaver3a = {
             instruction[ 1, b, m, r, 2],
             instruction[ 1, m, m, r, 0],
             instruction[ 2, b, m, l, 2],
             instruction[ 2, m, b, r, 3],
             instruction[ 3, b, m, l, 3],
             instruction[ 3, m, m, l, 1]
         };
```

Here, we see the busy beaver in action. It writes five marks on the tape. There are five different machines with three states that write a total of six marks before halting (but taking less than 21 steps to do so). Can you find one of them?

The option `Columns->n` causes the configurations to be shown in n columns instead of in only one.

`In[13]:= PlotTuring[runList[{}, beaver3a], Columns->2];`

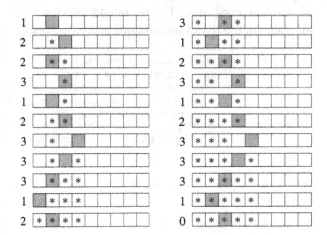

12.3.5   Assembly Programming

Programming Turing machines is rather cumbersome. It resembles programming today's computers in machine language. The first tool to simplify this task is an assembler (see also Section 1.3). Assemblers provide for the definition of macros. *Macros* are instruction sequences for often-used subprograms that can be inserted (expanded) inside other programs.

The simplest of these macros are moves to the right and left. The instruction sequence `right` moves the head one position to the right without changing the contents of the tape:

state	symbol	newsymbol	move	newstate
1	_	_	r	0
1	*	*	r	0

A similar sequence can be given for a move to the left. The following sequence, called `noop`, does nothing at all:

state	symbol	newsymbol	move	newstate
1	_	_	s	0
1	*	*	s	0

It is often needed as a filler in more complicated constructions.

Our most important tool for developing programs is the composition of instruction sequences in a way that the second sequence is executed after the first one. For this composition to work, we first have to relabel to states in the second sequence so that they do not collide with the states of the first sequence. Then we replace each halt state (new state 0) in the first sequence by the first state of the second sequence. In this way we "jump" to the second sequence after the first one has completed. The term *relocation* is used for such manipulations of machine programs. The command `relocate[`*instructions*`, `*offset*`, `*return*`]` adds *offset* to all states in the list of instructions and replaces each halt state by the return state.

```
relocate[instr_List, offset_, return_] :=
    instr /. {instruction[st_, sy_, nsy_, mv_, 0]  :>
                instruction[st+offset, sy, nsy, mv, return],
            instruction[st_, sy_, nsy_, mv_, nst_] :>
                instruction[st+offset, sy, nsy, mv, nst+offset]}
```

Listing 12.3–5   Part of TuringMacros.m: Relocating instructions.

Here is the instruction sequence for the move to the right.

```
In[1]:= right
Out[1]= {{1, _} -> {_, r, 0}, {1, *} -> {*, r, 0}}
```

We relocate it by adding one to all states.

```
In[2]:= r2 = relocate[ right, 1, 0]
Out[2]= {{2, _} -> {_, r, 0}, {2, *} -> {*, r, 0}}
```

Here, we change each halt state by a jump to state 2.

```
In[3]:= r1 = relocate[ right, 0, 2]
Out[3]= {{1, _} -> {_, r, 2}, {1, *} -> {*, r, 2}}
```

The combined sequence causes a move by two cells to the right.

```
In[4]:= Join[ r1, r2 ]
Out[4]= {{1, _} -> {_, r, 2}, {1, *} -> {*, r, 2},
        {2, _} -> {_, r, 0}, {2, *} -> {*, r, 0}}
```

To compose two instruction sequences, we find the highest state in the first one and then relocate the second sequence by this amount, and, finally, change each halt state in the first sequence as indicated. Composition is *associative,* that is, we can compose an arbitrary number of sequences. To take advantage of associativity, we need only give the symbol compose the attributes Flat and OneIdentity.

```
maxState[{}] = 0
maxState[instr_List] := Max[ state /@ instr ]

SetAttributes[ compose, {Flat, OneIdentity} ]

compose[instr1_, instr2_] :=
    With[{offset = maxState[instr1]},
        Join[ relocate[instr1, 0, offset+1],
              relocate[instr2, offset, 0] ]
    ]

compose[instr1_] := instr1
```

Listing 12.3–6   Part of TuringMacros.m: Composing instructions.

Here is a composed sequence for a move by three places to the right.

```
In[5]:= compose[ right, right, right ]
Out[5]= {{1, _} -> {_, r, 2}, {1, *} -> {*, r, 2},
         {2, _} -> {_, r, 3}, {2, *} -> {*, r, 3},
         {3, _} -> {_, r, 0}, {3, *} -> {*, r, 0}}
```

A conditional loop is another useful tool. As long as the symbol under the head is a mark, we execute an instruction sequence once, then we test the symbol again, and so on. The implementation is simple:

```
while[ instr_ ] :=
    Join[ { instruction[1, b, b, s, 0],
            instruction[1, m, m, s, 2] },
          relocate[ instr, 1, 1 ]
    ]
```

Listing 12.3–7   Part of TuringMacros.m: The while loop.

The while loop allows us to assemble a program that jumps over a sequence of marks. First, we move to the right (because we always start on the cell before the marks); then we move right *while* the current symbol is still a mark.

```
In[6]:= compose[
            right,
            while[ right ]
        ]
Out[6]= {{1, _} -> {_, r, 2}, {1, *} -> {*, r, 2},
         {2, _} -> {_, s, 0}, {2, *} -> {*, s, 3},
         {3, _} -> {_, r, 2}, {3, *} -> {*, r, 2}}
```

We test the program on a tape having three marks.

`In[7]:= runList[ {b, m, m, m}, % ];`

The graphic shows you how it works. You can also see that programs assembled with macros are often not as efficient as possible. Can you find a more efficient version?

`In[8]:= PlotTuring[ % ];`

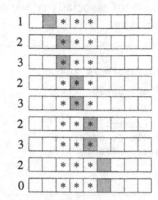

In the next section, we shall need a few more macros. They are also defined in the package TuringMacros.m. These macros work on tapes on which a number of *arguments* are encoded. An argument is a sequence of marks. Arguments are separated from each other by exactly one blank.

`skip[n]`	skip n arguments to the right
`skip[-n]`	skip n arguments to the left
`shiftleft[n]`	shift n arguments one cell to the left
`eat1[n]`	delete the first of n arguments
`copy[n, m]`	copy n arguments over m others

Additional macros defined in TuringMacros.m.

12.3.6   Key Concepts

1. The Turing machine is an idealization of a computer.

2. A simulator is a program that performs Turing machine calculations in some other computation model (e.g., in *Mathematica*).

12.4 Recursive Functions Are Turing Computable

We presented the partial recursive functions in Section 12.1. Now, we want to show that these functions can be computed on Turing machines. We have to show how we can program the six construction principles for partial recursive functions (pages 274 and 276). Because we frequently combine small programs to form larger ones, we have to make sure that the programs fit together well. We have the following requirements:

- The natural number n is represented by n consecutive marks.

- Arguments of a function are separated by exactly one blank.

- The tape to the right of the arguments is empty.

- The computation starts in state 1 with the head on the blank immediately before the first argument.

- The machine does not use the tape to the left of the initial cell.

- At the end of a computation, the head is again on the initial cell with the result following on the right.

Such conventions are called a *calling convention*. A calling convention defines the interface between the calling program and the called subprogram. It plays an important role in the compilation of higher-level languages.

All functions presented here are in the package TuringRecursive.m.

12.4.1 The Basic Functions

The first two constructions, zero and the successor, are simple.

Zero is a a function of no arguments that must write zero marks on the tape, that is, it does nothing at all.

```
In[1]:= zero = noop

Out[1]= {{1, _} -> {_, s, 0}, {1, *} -> {*, s, 0}}
```

The successor skips its argument, adds a mark, and skips back.

```
In[2]:= plus1 =
        compose[
          skip[1],
          {instruction[1, b, m, r, 0]}, (* write 1 *)
          skip[-1]
        ];
```

In this picture, we see how it works. We compute $s(2) = 3$.

```
In[3]:= PlotTuring[ runList[{b, m, m}, plus1],
                    Columns->2 ];
```

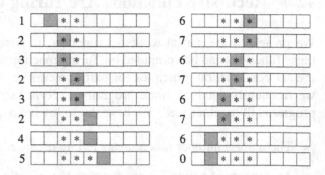

It is a good idea to check that such definitions also work for special inputs, such as the number 0.

```
In[4]:= PlotTuring[ runList[{b}, plus1],
                    Columns->2 ];
```

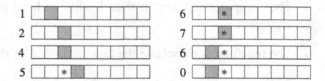

12.4.2 Projections

The projection $p_k^n(m_1, \ldots, m_n)$ returns argument m_k. Therefore, we must delete the first $k - 1$ arguments, shifting the remaining ones to the left; then, we skip the result and delete any remaining arguments m_{k+1} to m_n.

The conditional If[] in this macro is used only for efficiency: If we project onto the last argument, there are no remaining ones to delete.

```
p[k_, n_] :=
    compose[
      compose @@ Table[eat1[j], {j, n, n-k+2, -1}],
      If[ k < n,
      compose[
          skip[1],
          compose @@ Table[eat1[j], {j, n-k, 1, -1}],
          skip[-1] ],
      noop
      ]
    ]
```

Listing 12.4–1   Part of TuringRecursive.m: Projections.

Here is the computation of $p_2^3(1, 2, 1) = 2$. It is rather long.

```
In[5]:= runList[{b, m, b, m, m, b, m}, p[2, 3]] // Short
Out[5]//Short=
    {config[1, < _ * _ * * _ ...>, 1], <<77>>,
        config[0, < _ * * _ _ _ ...>, 1]}
```

12.4.3 Composition

The macro comp[n, f, {g_1, ..., g_p}] generates the program for a function h, with

> h[m1_, m2_, ..., mn_] :=
> f[g_1[m1, m2, ..., mn], g_2[...], ..., g_p[m1, m2, ..., mn]],

provided that f, g_1, ..., g_p are programs for the corresponding functions. First, we must evaluate the functions g_1, ..., g_p with arguments m_1, ..., m_n, and then apply the function f to the p results. Because we need the original arguments several times, we copy them to the end of the tape and run the program for g_i on this copy.

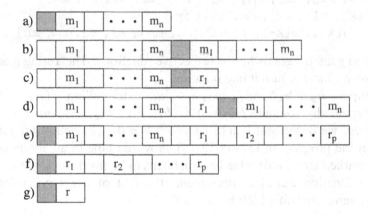

Figure 12.4–1 Composition of functions on a Turing machine.

Figure 12.4–1 shows the idea. Line a shows the initial configuration with n arguments on the tape. We copy them to the end (line b). Now, we can run the program for g_1; it leaves a result r_1, as shown in line c. According to our calling convention, the program does not use the tape to the left of the initial position, a property that is important here. Now, we copy the arguments again, ready to run g_2 (line d). Line e shows the tape after all programs g_1 through g_p were run. We can now delete the original arguments and run f, as shown in line f. The last line shows the final result. Listing 12.4–2 shows the code that implements these steps.

```
comp[ n_, f_, gs_List ] :=
  With[{p = Length[gs]},
    compose[
      compose @@ Table[
        compose[
            copy[n, n+i-1], (* copy arguments *)
            gs[[i]],        (* execute g_i *)
            skip[-(n+i-1)]  (* back to the beginning *)
        ], {i, 1, p} ],
      compose @@ Table[eat1[i+p], {i, n, 1, -1}],
      f
    ]
  ]
```

Listing 12.4–2   Part of TuringRecursive.m: Composition.

12.4.4   Primitive Recursion

The macro pr[n, f, g] generates the program for a function h, with

$$h[0, m1\_, m2\_, \ldots, mn\_] := f[m1, m2, \ldots, mn],$$
$$h[k\_, m1\_, m2\_, \ldots, mn\_] :=$$
$$g[k-1, h[k-1, m1, m2, \ldots, mn], m1, m2, \ldots, mn],$$

provided that f and g are programs for the respective functions. The Turing machine does not offer recursion, so we have to turn it into iteration.

First, we compute $h_0 = h[0, m_1, m_2, \ldots, m_n]$, by calling $f[m_1, m_2, \ldots, m_n]$. In the loop, we repeatedly compute $h_{i+1} = g[i, h_i, m_1, m_2, \ldots, m_n]$ for $i = 0, 1, \ldots$. After each iteration, we decrement k until we reach $k = 0$. The details are rather awkward. The comments in the program in Listing 12.4–3 show the tape in an abbreviated way. The head position is marked by : , unless the head happens to be inside an argument.

The auxiliary function sub1[n] decrements the first of $n + 1$ arguments by 1. The remaining n arguments are shifted left by one cell.

As an example of a primitive recursive function, we look at the predecessor function shown to be primitive recursive in Section 12.1.3. Written strictly, its definition is

$$\begin{aligned} p(0) &= 0, \\ p(s(k)) &= p_1^2(k, p(k)), \end{aligned} \qquad (12.4\text{–}1)$$

that is, $f = 0$ and $g = p_1^2$.

First, we generate the programs for the aux-   In[6]:= **f = zero;**
iliary functions f and g.

                                                In[7]:= **g = p[1, 2];**

Here is the program for the predecessor. It consists of 722 instructions.

```
In[8]:= (predecessor = pr[ 0, f, g ]) // Short
Out[8]//Short=
    {{1, _} -> {_, r, 2}, {1, *} -> {*, r, 2}, <<719>>,
     {454, *} -> {*, s, 0}}
```

The computation of the predecessor of 1 takes already 215 steps. The result is 0, of course. The graphic on the title page of this chapter (page 271) shows the computation.

```
In[9]:= runList[ {b, m}, predecessor ] // Short
Out[9]//Short=
    {config[1, < _ * _ _ _ _ ...>, 1], <<213>>,
     config[0, < _ _ _ _ _ _ ...>, 1]}
```

The μ schema is left as Exercise 12.5.

```
pr[n_, f_, g_] :=
compose[              (*:k m1...mn                    *)
  skip[n+1],          (* k m1...mn:                    *)
  zero,               (* k m1...mn:0                   *)
  skip[-n],           (* k:m1...mn 0                   *)
  copy[n, n+1],       (* k m1...mn 0:m1...mn           *)
  f,                  (* k m1...mn 0:h0                *)
  skip[-(n+2)],       (*:k m1...mn 0 h0                *)
  right,              (* k m1...mn 0 h0                *)
  while[ (* k > 0 *)
    compose[
      left,           (*:k' m1...mn:i hi               *)
      sub1[n+2],      (*:k m1...mn i hi                *)
      skip[n+1],      (* k m1...mn:i hi                *)
      copy[2, 2],     (* k m1...mn i hi:i hi           *)
      skip[-(n+2)],   (* k:m1...mn i hi i hi           *)
      copy[n, n+4],   (* k m1...mn i hi i hi:m1...mn   *)
      skip[-2],       (* k m1...mn i hi:i hi m1...mn   *)
      g,              (* k m1...mn i hi:hi'            *)
      skip[-2],       (* k m1...mn:i hi hi'            *)
      copy[1, 3],     (* k m1...mn i hi hi':i          *)
      plus1,          (* k m1...mn i hi hi':i'         *)
      skip[-1],       (* k m1...mn i hi:hi' i'         *)
      copy[1, 2],     (* k m1...mn i hi hi' i':hi'     *)
      skip[-4],       (* k m1...mn:i hi hi' i' hi'     *)
      eat1[5],        (* k m1...mn:hi hi' i' hi'       *)
      eat1[4],        (* k m1...mn:hi' i' hi'          *)
      eat1[3],        (* k m1...mn:i' hi'              *)
      skip[-(n+1)],   (*:k m1...mn i' hi'              *)
      right           (* k m1...mn i' hi'              *)
    ]
  ],
  left,               (*:0 m1...mn k hk                *)
  p[n+3, n+3]         (*:hk                            *)
]
```

Listing 12.4–3 Part of TuringRecursive.m: Primitive recursion.

We showed that the partial recursive functions are Turing computable. The converse could be shown as well: all Turing computable functions are partial recursive. The tool for this proof is the *universal Turing machine*. The details are too involved to be presented here.

12.4.5 Key Concepts

1. On Turing machines, all functions can be computed that are also computable on any other computer.

2. The Turing machine computes exactly the partial recursive functions.

12.5 Exercises

12.1 Recursion Schema and Induction Proofs

Give the proof mentioned at the end of Section 12.1.2 that the recursion 12.1–5 defines a total function.

12.2 Programming Recursive Functions

We saw that recursive functions are programmable. Give a practical proof by showing how they can be programmed in *Mathematica*.

1. Show in detail how each function defined strictly by primitive recursion (Section 12.1.2) can be programmed in *Mathematica*. Show that the computation terminates for each value of the arguments.

2. Show how the μ schema can be programmed in *Mathematica*.

12.3 Integer Division

Show that integer division, a div b, and remainder, a mod b, are primitive recursive. For two integers a and b, with $b > 0$, the so-called *div-mod identity* holds:

$$a = (a \text{ div } b) b + (a \text{ mod } b).$$ (12.5–1)

Furthermore, we have

$$0 \leq (a \text{ mod } b) < b.$$ (12.5–2)

(In *Mathematica* these two functions are Quotient[a, b] and Mod[a, b].)

12.4 Addition on a Turing Machine

This exercise will show you that programs constructed strictly according to the schema of primitive recursion are usually very inefficient.

1. Generate the instructions for addition according to the schema of primitive recursion (see Sections 12.4 and 12.1.2.) How many instructions do you get? How many steps does the program take to add 1 and 1?

2. Find a much simpler and faster program for adding two numbers.

12.5   The μ Schema on Turing Machines

Write a macro mu[n, f, g], that generates the Turing program for the μ schema

$$h(m_1, \ldots, m_n) = f(\mu k[g(m_1, \ldots, m_n, k)]).$$

See Section 12.4.

Chapter 13
Databases

In this chapter, we give an introduction to databases. As an example, we discuss a database of classical music recordings. Databases are the most important commercial application of computers. Large collections of data are valuable resources of companies. The administration of such collections of data requires reliable and powerful database management programs. A precise mathematical modeling of databases provides a tool for their simple maintenance. The most often used model is the relational database model.

Section 13.1 discusses the design of databases. We show how redundancy in the data is removed by splitting the tables into several connected parts. In Section 13.2, we discuss the fundamental operations of relational algebra.

Data entry and queries are the topic of Section 13.3. We show how we can enter data into a database, and how we can formulate queries to extract the information in a readable form. Finally, in Section 13.4, we mention some aspects of larger, commercial database applications.

About the illustration overleaf:
The illustration shows a fractal curve by B. Mandelbrot, described in [56]. The picture is from [44, 51]. The commands for this illustration are in the package Pictures.m.

13.1 Database Design

Databases model aspects of the real world. Objects from the real world are called *entities*. Entities are related through certain *relationships*. An entity is described by *attributes*, that is, the properties we are interested in for our application.

A database models only part of reality. In a diary, for example, the entities are *persons*. As attributes we may use name, first name, address, phone number, date of birth, that is, only a few of the properties of these persons. There may also be legal restrictions on what kind of personal data can be stored.

13.1.1 A Database of Music Recordings

Here is a simple example of a database. We want to maintain data about our record collection. This example shows well the hierarchical organization of many collections of data. On a record (nowadays more likely on a CD), we find recordings of several works. The record has a *number*, a *label* (the publishing company), and a *title*. Each work has a *title* and a *composer*. Our first attempt simply lists the attributes, one line per recording. Table 13.1–1 shows such a list.

		Music		
record title	*label*	*record number*	*work title*	*composer*
Das Konzert November 1989	Sony	45830	Conc. for Piano and Orch. No. 1	Beethoven, L. v.
Das Konzert November 1989	Sony	45830	Symphony No. 7	Beethoven, L. v.
Horovitz at Carnegie Hall	RCA	7992-2	Conc. for Piano and Orch. No. 5	Beethoven, L. v.
Horovitz at Carnegie Hall	RCA	7992-2	Conc. No. 1 for Piano and Orch.	Tchaikovsky, P. I.
Beethoven's Symphonies	London	430400-2	Symphony No. 6	Beethoven, L. v.
Beethoven's Symphonies	London	430400-2	Symphony No. 7	Beethoven, L. v.
Beethoven: The Piano Conc.	Angel	63360	Conc. for Piano and Orch. No. 1	Beethoven, L. v.
Beethoven: The Piano Conc.	Angel	63360	Conc. for Piano and Orch. No. 4	Beethoven, L. v.
Beethoven: The Piano Conc.	Angel	63360	Conc. for Piano and Orch. No. 5	Beethoven, L. v.

Table 13.1–1 A simple list of music recordings.

Many database programs for personal computers work in this simple way. It has an important drawback: There is *redundancy* in the database. The record title and the label, for example, are uniquely determined by the record number. We can see that the values of these two attributes arc the same in all lines with the same record number. Such redundancy wastes storage space. Worse, it may lead to inconsistent updates of the database. If we wanted to translate the record title into a foreign language, for example, we have to perform the same change in many different lines. During such work, errors can creep in easily.

13.1.2 Splitting the Lists

We can solve the redundancy problems by splitting the list. We define two entities with the following attributes:

- The entity *records* has attributes *record title, label*, and *record number.*
- The entity *recordings* has attributes *work title* and *composer.*

The connection between the two lists is given by the relationship between the two entities. The relationship between records and recordings,

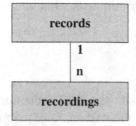

Record x contains recording y,

is a 1–n (one-to-many) relationship, because each record may contain several recordings, but each recording is contained on exactly one record. The figure on the left describes this relationship. Note how the line between the two entities is labeled to express the 1–n relationship. The relationship is established by including the attribute *record number* in the list *recordings*. This attribute is a key in the list *records*. A *key* is an attribute whose values are unique in a list. Table 13.1–2 shows the two new lists corresponding to the entities *records* and *recordings*.

Records		
record title	*label*	*record number*
Das Konzert November 1989	Sony Classical	45830
Horovitz at Carnegie Hall	RCA	7992-2
Beethoven's Symphonies	London	430400-2
Beethoven: The Piano Conc.	Angel	63360

Recordings		
record number	*work title*	*composer*
45830	Conc. for Piano and Orch. No. 1	Beethoven, L. v.
45830	Symphony No. 7	Beethoven, L. v.
7992-2	Conc. for Piano and Orch. No. 5	Beethoven, L. v.
7992-2	Conc. No. 1 for Piano and Orch.	Tchaikovsky, P. I.
430400-2	Symphony No. 6	Beethoven, L. v.
430400-2	Symphony No. 7	Beethoven, L. v.
63360	Conc. for Piano and Orch. No. 1	Beethoven, L. v.
63360	Conc. for Piano and Orch. No. 4	Beethoven, L. v.
63360	Conc. for Piano and Orch. No. 5	Beethoven, L. v.

Table 13.1–2   Splitting into lists for records and recordings.

A one-to-many relationship in a list is resolved by splitting the list into two lists. The relationship is then established by including a key for the first list in the second list.

Another source of redundancy lies in the attribute pairs *work title* and *composer name*. Each

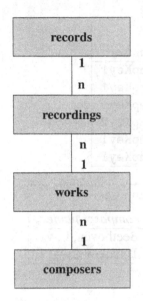

such pair describes a work of classical music uniquely and can occur several times if we own several recordings of the same work. (In our example, Beethoven's seventh symphony occurs twice). Furthermore, there is usually more than one work by a given composer. To remove these redundancies, we define the new entity *works*, with attributes *workKey*, *work title*, and *compKey*, and the entity *composers*, with attributes *compKey* and *composer name*. In both cases, there is no attribute that could naturally be used as key. To remedy this situation, we create the artificial attributes *compKey* and *workKey*. The values of these attributes do not matter; we can use symbols. Often, numbers are used for this purpose as well. We need only ensure that each value occurs at most once.

The relationship between *works* and *recordings* is $1-n$. A work can occur in several recordings, and each recording consists of exactly one work. Therefore, we replace the columns *work title* and *composer name* in the list *recordings* by *workKey*. The relationship between *composers* and *works* is also $1-n$. The figure on the left shows the new relationships and Table 13.1–3 shows the new lists.

Another attribute, *recKey*, serves as key in the list *recordings*. We shall need it soon.

Splitting the lists to remove redundancy puts the database into *normal form*.

13.1.3 Many-to-Many Relationships

We would like also to store some information about the musicians performing in a recording. The relationship between artists and recordings,

Artist x performs in recording y ,

is an $n-m$ or *many-to-many* relationship because each artist may perform in several works, and each work may have several artists performing it. The only possibility we have to establish such a relationship without redundancy, is to define another list *performers* for it. The new information about performers gives rise to these two new entities:

- *artists,* with attributes *artist name, instrument,* and the key *artistKey*

- *performers,* with attributes *recKey,* and *artistKey*

Note that the list performers contains only pairs of keys from other lists. It is used only to implement a relationship and does not correspond to a natural entity in the real world. Table 13.1–4 shows a few sample entries in the two new lists. Observe that the orchestra is treated as the instrument of the conductor. Figure 13.1–1 shows the final layout of our music database.

Works		
workKey	*work title*	*compKey*
work1	Conc. for Piano and Orch. No. 1	compKey1
work2	Symphony No. 7	compKey1
work3	Conc. for Piano and Orch. No. 5	compKey1
work4	Conc. No. 1 for Piano and Orch.	compKey2
work5	Symphony No. 6	compKey1
work9	Conc. for Piano and Orch. No. 4	compKey1

Recordings		
recKey	*workKey*	*record number*
rec1	work1	45830
rec2	work2	45830
rec3	work3	7992-2
rec4	work4	7992-2
rec5	work5	430400-2
rec6	work2	430400-2
rec7	work1	63360
rec10	work9	63360
rec11	work3	63360

Composers	
compKey	*composer name*
compKey1	Beethoven, L. v.
compKey2	Tchaikovsky, P. I.

Table 13.1–3 Second split of the music database.

Artists		
artistKey	*artist name*	*instrument*
art1	Barenboim, Daniel	Berliner Philharmoniker
art2	Barenboim, Daniel	Piano
art3	Horovitz, Vladimir	Piano
art4	Reiner, Fritz	RCA Victor Symphony
art5	Solti, Sir Georg	Chicago Symphony Orch.
art6	Klemperer, Otto	New Philharmonia Orch.

Performers	
recKey	*artistKey*
rec1	art1
rec1	art2
rec2	art1
. . .	. . .
rec11	art6

Table 13.1–4 Information about interpreters of works.

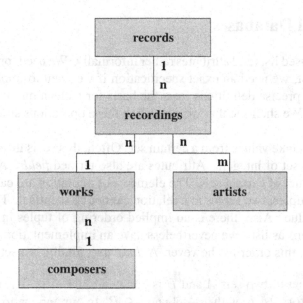

Figure 13.1–1   Layout of the music database.

13.1.4 Key Concepts

1. Data about aspects of the real world are represented by entities, attributes, and relationships.

2. Redundancy in a list is removed by splitting the list into several lists.

3. Relationships are of kind 1–1, 1–n, or n–m.

4. The layout of a database shows entities and their relationships.

13.2 Relational Databases

So far, we have discussed lists and attributes rather informally. We need formalize these notions for two reasons. First, we need an exact specification if we want to implement databases on a computer. Second, precise definitions form the basis for a clean mathematical treatment of database operations. We shall see that we can define these operations simply as operations on sets.

Each attribute can take values from a certain set. Often, this set is the set of all strings over some alphabet or the set of integers. Attributes are also termed *fields*. A *relation* is a subset of the Cartesian product of certain sets. The elements of a relation are called *tuples*. Because relations are *sets* of tuples, two tuples in a relation cannot be identical. They must differ in at least one attribute value. Also, there is no implied ordering of tuples in a relation. Because we implement relations as lists, we nevertheless have an implementation-dependent ordering; We will never rely on this ordering, however. A *database*, finally, is a set of relations.

The Cartesian product of two sets A and B is denoted by $A \times B$. The elements of $A \times B$ are all tuples of the form (a, b) with $a \in A$ and $b \in B$. In our application, the sets A and B will be the sets of all possible values of attributes.

The lists in Section 13.1 are such relations. The list *artists* from Table 13.1–4, for example, contains the attributes *artistKey* , *artist name*, and *instrument*. The values of *artistKey* are symbols; the values of *artist name* and *instrument* are strings. The relation contains six tuples; here is one of them:

> ```
> {art1, "Barenboim, Daniel", "Berliner Philharmoniker"}.
> ```

A tuple is, therefore, a *row* in the list. Table 13.2–1 describes all relations and attributes of the music database. The field "type" describes the type of values of the attributes. Keys are denoted by an asterisk.

13.2.1 An Implementation of Relations

We can implement a relation as a data type with this representation:

> ```
> relation[{attributes...}, {tuples...}] .
> ```

The two components can be extracted with the selectors `Fields[rel]` and `Tuples[rel]`. `Fields[]` gives the list of fields or attributes. The constructor

> ```
> newRelation[{attributes...}, {tuples...}]
> ```

creates a new relation with the given attributes and tuples. The output format for relations is

$$\texttt{R[\{}attributes...\texttt{\}, Short[\{}tuples...\texttt{\}]]} \; ,$$

which prints the tuples in abbreviated form. Later we will show how information from a database is presented in human-readable form. All of these functions are part of the package DB.m.

The variable `artists` contains the relation artists from our example.	`In[1]:= artists` `Out[1]= R[{artistKey, artistName, instrument}, {<<12>>}]`
Here are its attributes.	`In[2]:= Fields[artists]` `Out[2]= {artistKey, artistName, instrument}`

Here is a shortened list of its tuples.	`In[3]:= Short[ Tuples[artists] ]`
	`Out[3]//Short=`
	`{{artistKey$108, Klemperer, Otto,`
	`    New Philharmonia Orch.}, <<11>>}`

To explain the database operations, we shall often use relations with symbolic attributes and values.	`In[4]:= r1 = newRelation[{A, B}, {{a1, b1}, {a2, b2}}]` `Out[4]= R[{A, B}, {{a1, b1}, {a2, b2}}]`

Music		
Relation	*Attributes*	*Type*
records	record title	string
	label	string
	record number*	string
recordings	recKey*	symbol
	workKey	symbol
	record number	string
works	workKey*	symbol
	compKey	symbol
	work title	string
composers	compKey*	symbol
	composer name	string
artists	artistKey*	symbol
	artist name	string
	instrument	string
performers	recKey	symbol
	artistKey	symbol

Table 13.2–1   Relations and attributes of the music database.

13.2.2 Relational Algebra

This section presents the operations of *relational algebra*. Certain operations are defined on relations, much like arithmetic operations are defined on numbers. These operations are used to formulate database queries (in Section 13.3). To visualize these operations, we shall use – in addition to the relations of our music database – small relations with symbolic entries. Here is a list of these relations:

Name	Attributes	Tuples
r1	A, B	(a_1, b_1), (a_2, b_2)
r2	n, m, o	$(x, 2, 1.44)$, $(y, 3, 2.50)$, $(z, 4, 1.20)$
r3	A1, A2, A3	(a, b, c), (a, b, d), (a, f, c)
r4	A, B	(a, α), (b, α), (c, δ), (c, γ)
r5	B, C	$(\alpha, 5)$, $(\gamma, 6)$, $(\gamma, 8)$, $(\kappa, 7)$
r6	A1, A2, A3	(a, b, c), (e, b, d)

Relations are *sets*. We can, therefore, apply the ordinary set operations *union* $r \cup s$, *intersection* $r \cap s$, and *difference* $r - s$ to relations, provided that the relations involved have the same attributes. In *Mathematica*, these operations are called `Union[]`, `Intersection[]`, and `Complement[]`, respectively.

The union contains all tuples occurring in at least one of the relations.

```
In[5]:= Union[ r3, r6 ]
Out[5]= R[{A1, A2, A3},

        {{a, b, c}, {a, b, d}, <<1>>, {e, b, d}}]
```

The intersection contains only those tuples that occur in both relations.

```
In[6]:= Intersection[ r3, r6 ]
Out[6]= R[{A1, A2, A3}, {{a, b, c}}]
```

The difference (or complement) contains those tuples occurring in the first but not in the second relation.

```
In[7]:= Complement[ r3, r6 ]
Out[7]= R[{A1, A2, A3}, {{a, b, d}, {a, f, c}}]
```

13.2.3 Selection

An important operation is the selection of a subset of the tuples according to some criteria. The function `Select[relation, cond]` is provided for this purpose. The condition is written as a Boolean expression involving the names of the attributes. The result of selection is another relation with the same attributes as the input relation.

Only one tuple in r2 satisfies this condition, so the result is a relation with only one tuple.

```
In[8]:= Select[ r2, m < 4 && o > 2.0 ]
Out[8]= R[{n, m, o}, {{y, 3, 2.5}}]
```

Here, we select from the relation `records` all tuples in which the attribute label has the value *Sony Classical*.

```
In[9]:= Select[ records, label == "Sony Classical"]
Out[9]= R[{recordTitle, label, recordNumber},
          {{Das Konzert November 1989, <<1>>, 45830}}]
```

13.2.4 Projection

The *projection* of a relation onto a subset of its attributes is a new relation containing only the projected attributes. Remaining ones are removed. In the tuples, the values corresponding to the removed attributes are also removed. This operation corresponds to deletion of *columns* in a list. It may happen that formerly different tuples become equal after projection. Only one of each set of equal tuples is retained.

Consider the following example. The relation r_3 has attributes A_1, A_2, and A_3. Its tuples are $\{(a, b, c), (a, b, d), (a, f, c)\}$. The projection onto attributes A_1 and A_2, denoted by $\pi_{A_1, A_2}(r_3)$, would contain the tuples $\{(a, b), (a, b), (a, f)\}$ because we have to remove the third element of each tuple. The first two of these tuples are now equal, and only $\{(a, b), (a, f)\}$ remain.

Here is the example we just explained in detail.

```
In[10]:= Projection[ r3, {A1, A2} ]
Out[10]= R[{A1, A2}, {{a, b}, {a, f}}]
```

This projection removes the attributes *artist-Key* and *Instrument*. Only the name remains.

```
In[11]:= Projection[ artists, {artistName} ]
Out[11]= R[{artistName},
           {{Barenboim, Daniel}, <<9>>, {Wand, Guenter}}]
```

Here are the names of all artists in the database.

```
In[12]:= Tuples[ % ]
Out[12]= {{Barenboim, Daniel}, {Horovitz, Vladimir},
          {Klemperer, Otto}, {Norman, Jessye}, {Reiner, Fritz},
          {Runkel, Reinhild}, {Schunk, Robert},
          {Solti, Sir Georg}, {Sotin, Hans},
          {Toscanini, Arturo}, {Wand, Guenter}}
```

13.2.5 The Join

In Section 13.1, we removed redundancy in a database by splitting the lists. We established the relationships by an attribute occurring in both lists. To work with a database, there must be a possibility to reverse this process, that is, to join two relations into one. This operation is the *natural join*. It combines tuples from two relations into tuples of a new relation. The selection of tuples to combine is done through the common attribute.

A simple example shows how the join works. Let the relation r have attributes A and B, and the relation s have the attributes B and C. The join $r \bowtie s$ has attributes A, B, and C. It consists of all tuples (a, b, c) for which $(a, b) \in r$ and $(b, c) \in s$ hold.

Here is relation r4 with four tuples.

```
In[13]:= r4 = newRelation[{A, B}, {
                {a, alpha}, {b, alpha},
                {c, delta}, {c, gamma}} ];
```

Here is relation r5.

```
In[14]:= r5 = newRelation[{B, C}, {
                {alpha, 5}, {gamma, 6},
                {gamma, 8}, {kappa, 7}} ];
```

The join $r_4 \bowtie r_5$ has attributes A, B, and C.

```
In[15]:= Join[ r4, r5 ]
Out[15]= R[{A, B, C}, {{a, alpha, 5}, <<2>>,
            {c, gamma, 8}}]
```

Here are its tuples. Please convince yourself that this output is correct.

```
In[16]:= Tuples[ % ]
Out[16]= {{a, alpha, 5}, {b, alpha, 5}, {c, gamma, 6},
            {c, gamma, 8}}
```

Often, the common attribute is a key. In this case, the join undoes the split of the list into two relations.

Earlier, we split the list of works to avoid redundancy. The join reverses this step.

```
In[17]:= Join[ works, composers ]
Out[17]= R[{workKey, compKey, workTitle, composerName},
            {<<18>>}]
```

The keys are no longer needed and can be projected away.

```
In[18]:= Projection[ %, {workTitle, composerName} ]
Out[18]= R[{workTitle, composerName}, {<<18>>}]
```

These operations give a human-readable list of the works and their composers.

```
In[19]:= Tuples[ % ] // TableForm
Out[19]//TableForm=
    Conc. for Piano and Orch. No. 1    Beethoven, L. v.
    Conc. for Piano and Orch. No. 2    Beethoven, L. v.
    Conc. for Piano and Orch. No. 3    Beethoven, L. v.
    Conc. for Piano and Orch. No. 4    Beethoven, L. v.
    Conc. for Piano and Orch. No. 5    Beethoven, L. v.
    Conc. No. 1 for Piano and Orch.    Tchaikovsky, P. I.
    Pictures at an Exhibition          Mussorgsky, M.
    Symphony No. 1                     Beethoven, L. v.
    Symphony No. 1                     Schubert, Franz
    Symphony No. 2                     Beethoven, L. v.
    Symphony No. 2                     Schubert, Franz
    Symphony No. 3                     Beethoven, L. v.
    Symphony No. 4                     Beethoven, L. v.
    Symphony No. 5                     Beethoven, L. v.
    Symphony No. 6                     Beethoven, L. v.
    Symphony No. 7                     Beethoven, L. v.
    Symphony No. 8                     Beethoven, L. v.
    Symphony No. 9                     Beethoven, L. v.
```

The join is also defined in other cases, where relations have more than one, or no attributes in common. If there are several common attributes, the values of all of them must agree. If two relations have no common attributes, there is no restriction on the combination of tuples. Each tuple in the first relation is combined with each tuple in the second relation. The result is the *Cartesian product* of the two relations.

Relations `r1` and `r2` have no common attributes. The join consists of all attributes of `r1` and `r2`.

```
In[20]:= Join[ r1, r2 ]
Out[20]= R[{A, B, n, m, o},
    {{a1, b1, x, 2, 1.44}, <<5>>}]
```

Its tuples are all possible combinations of tuples from `r1` and `r2`. Their number is, therefore, equal to the product of the number of tuples of `r1` and `r2`, that is, $2 \times 3 = 6$.

```
In[21]:= Tuples[ % ] // TableForm
Out[21]//TableForm= a1    b1    x    2    1.44
                    a1    b1    y    3    2.5
                    a1    b1    z    4    1.2
                    a2    b2    x    2    1.44
                    a2    b2    y    3    2.5
                    a2    b2    z    4    1.2
```

13.2.6   Renaming Attributes

Renaming is an auxiliary function that changes the name of the attributes without affecting the tuples.

Here we rename the attribute A of `r4` to As. Renamings are simply given as replacement rules.

```
In[22]:= r4a = Rename[ r4, A -> As ]
Out[22]= R[{As, B}, {{a, alpha}, {b, alpha}, <<1>>,
    {c, gamma}}]
```

Renaming becomes necessary if we want to form the join of a relation with itself.

```
In[23]:= s4 = Join[ r4, r4a ]
Out[23]= R[{A, B, As},
    {{a, alpha, a}, <<4>>, {c, gamma, c}}]
```

Here are the tuples of this join.

```
In[24]:= Tuples[ % ] // TableForm
Out[24]//TableForm= a    alpha    a
                    a    alpha    b
                    b    alpha    a
                    b    alpha    b
                    c    delta    c
                    c    gamma    c
```

13.2.7   Key Concepts

1. Relations are subsets of a Cartesian product.

2. The operations of relational algebra are the set operations, selection, projection, and the natural join.

3. The join undoes a split of a list.

13.3   Data Entry and Queries

Data entry studies the methods used to put information into a database. This operation is not as simple as it may seem, however, because we must be careful to maintain consistency of the database.

Queries return the stored information in a readable form. The main problem is to combine and select data in a way that gives us exactly the information we are interested in. A query does not modify the database.

13.3.1   Database Queries

The relational algebra from Section 13.2.2 is the main tool for formulating *queries*. It allows us to select data according to various criteria. Here are two examples of queries.

First, we are interested in the contents of the CD *Das Konzert November 1989*, given in Berlin after the opening of the Berlin Wall.

We begin by choosing from the recordings those that are present on the CD, whose number is 45830.

```
In[1]:= Select[ recordings, recordNumber == "45830" ]
Out[1]= R[{recKey, workKey, recordNumber},
    {{recKey$16, workKey$14, 45830}, <<1>>}]
```

Now, we join the result with the relations needed to get all information.

```
In[2]:= Join[ %, works, composers,
                    performers, artists ];
```

Finally, we project onto the interesting attributes, removing in particular all keys.

```
In[3]:= Projection[ %, {composerName, workTitle,
                        artistName, instrument} ];
```

We have the information, but it is not yet in a readable form.

```
In[4]:= Tuples[ % ]
Out[4]= {{Beethoven, L. v.,
    Conc. for Piano and Orch. No. 1, Barenboim, Daniel,
    Berliner Philharmoniker},
   {Beethoven, L. v., Conc. for Piano and Orch. No. 1,
    Barenboim, Daniel, Piano},
   {Beethoven, L. v., Symphony No. 7, Barenboim, Daniel,
    Berliner Philharmoniker}}
```

There is a standard way to present such hierarchical data in a readable way, the *report*. The operation

$$\texttt{Report}[\textit{relation}, \, n_1, \, \ldots, \, n_k]$$

prints the tuples of a relation in an easy-to-read way. It shows subordinate information using indentation. Each line contains n_i attributes. Information that is the same as in the previous tuple is not repeated.   Our example shows immediately how this command works.   The attributes composer name and work title are subordinate and are printed on different lines. Attributes artist name and instrument are at the same level, and are, therefore, printed on the same line.

As we explained, this report consists of three levels.   The lowest level contains two attributes, the other two levels contain one each. We can see at a glance that two works by Ludwig van Beethoven were performed at this concert.

```
In[5]:= Report[ %%, 1, 1, 2 ];

Beethoven, L. v.
     Conc. for Piano and Orch. No. 1
          Barenboim, Daniel, Berliner Philharmoniker
          Barenboim, Daniel, Piano
     Symphony No. 7
          Barenboim, Daniel, Berliner Philharmoniker
```

The second example presents a more complicated query: Find all records that do not contain any works by Beethoven. Negation can be implemented by finding first all tuples violating the condition (that do contain at least one work by Beethoven), and then computing a complement.

This relation contains all records and the composers of all works present on them.

```
In[6]:= Join[ records, recordings, works, composers ];
```

We need only the record number and the names of the composers.

```
In[7]:= Projection[ %, {recordNumber, composerName} ];
```

We select all tuples with the composer Beethoven.

```
In[8]:= Select[ %, composerName == "Beethoven, L. v." ];
```

Here is a list of all records containing works by Beethoven.

```
In[9]:= b = Projection[ %, {recordNumber} ]
Out[9]= R[{recordNumber},

    {{430400-2}, {45830}, {63360}, {7992-2}}]
```

Here is a list of *all* records.

```
In[10]:= a = Projection[ records, {recordNumber} ]
Out[10]= R[{recordNumber},

    {{430400-2}, {45830}, <<3>>, {GD 60 449 QH}}]
```

The difference a - b is the desired list of all records without any Beethoven.   There are two such records.

```
In[11]:= Complement[ a, b ]
Out[11]= R[{recordNumber},

    {{CDC 7 47874 2}, {GD 60 449 QH}}]
```

If we want more information about these records, we have to add it back with a join, and then project onto the interesting attributes.

```
In[12]:= Join[ %,
               records,
               recordings,
               works,
               composers ];
```

```
In[13]:= Projection[ %, {label, recordNumber,
                 recordTitle, workTitle, composerName} ];
```

Here are the titles of these records and the works contained on them.

```
In[14]:= Report[ %, 3, 2 ];

EMI, CDC 7 47874 2, Schubert, Symphonies Nos. 1&2, Wand
        Symphony No. 1, Schubert, Franz
        Symphony No. 2, Schubert, Franz
RCA, GD 60 449 QH, Mussorgsky/Tchaikovsky
        Conc. No. 1 for Piano and Orch., Tchaikovsky, P. I.
        Pictures at an Exhibition, Mussorgsky, M.
```

13.3.2 Data Entry

Before we can work with a database, we have to enter the data somehow. Entering new information into a database has to be done in such a way that it does not violate the *consistency* of the database. If we enter new tuples into the relation works, for example, we also have to enter the corresponding composers into the relation composers, if they are not there already. If we do it wrong, there will either be dangling references – that is, values of *compKey* that do not have an entry in composers – or we may enter the same composer with two different keys.

To ensure consistency, we will not manipulate the relations directly, but instead will write a data entry program that guarantees these dependencies. Only this program will modify the relations. These operations can be used in such a program:

- addTupleTo[*relation*, *tuple*] adds a new tuple to a relation.

- addWithKeyTo[*relation*, *tuple*, *key*] generates a new value for the key attribute *key* and then inserts a tuple with this key value. This operation is used to generate unique key values.

- InputField[*attribute*, *type*, *prompt*] asks for the value of the given attribute. This function performs the actual input from the user.

- FindOrAdd[*relation*, *attributes*, *defaults*, *key*] implements the entry of dependent information. The information is first searched in the database. It is requested from the user only if it is not there.

The hierarchical division of the database into records, recordings, and artists leads to a data entry program with three nested loops. The outermost loop asks for the data for a whole record; within it, there is a loop over the recordings on this record; innermost is the loop over the performers of a work. The function DataEntry is part of the package Music.m, and it is shown in Listing 13.3–1.

Here is a sample data entry session. We enter a CD with two violin concertos by Mozart. The program continues to ask for more information until we tell it with ∧D that no more data are to follow. Under the Notebook frontend, the dialogues appear in their own window. Data entry can by terminated by . in this window. The lines

Found: {*tuple*}

are printed if dependent information is already in the database. In our example, this happens when the second work on the record is entered because we just entered the composer a few lines before.

```
In[15]:= DataEntry
recordNumber: 410 020-2
label:  Deutsche Grammophon
recordTitle:  Mozart Violin Concertos Nos. 3&5
  next work on record 410 020-2
  composerName:  Mozart, W. A.
  workTitle:  Violin Conc. No. 3
    next performer of Violin Conc. No. 3
    artistName:  Perlman, Itzhak
    instrument:  Violine
    next performer of Violin Conc. No. 3
    artistName:  Levine, James
    instrument:  Wiener Philharmoniker
    next performer of Violin Conc. No. 3
    artistName:  ^D
  next work on record 410 020-2
  composerName:  Mozart, W. A.
  Found: {compKey$16, Mozart, W. A.}
  workTitle:  Violin Conc. No. 5
    next performer of Violin Conc. No. 5
    artistName:  Perlman, Itzhak
    instrument:  Violine
    Found: {artistKey$29, Perlman, Itzhak, Violine}
    next performer of Violin Conc. No. 5
    artistName:  Levine, James
    instrument:  Wiener Philharmoniker
    Found: {artistKey$35, Levine, James, Wiener Philharmoniker}
    next performer of Violin Conc. No. 5
    artistName:  ^D
  next work on record 410 020-2
  composerName:  ^D
recordNumber:  ^D
```

13.3.3 Key Concepts

1. The two main operations on databases are queries and data entry.

2. A report is a list of hierarchical information.

3. Negations in a query lead to expressions involving the difference of relations.

4. Data entry consists of several operations that belong together to keep the database consistent.

```
DataEntry :=
    Module[{record, recno, work, workt, workk,
            perfk, artist, ak},
    While[ True, (* loop over records *)
        record = FindOrAdd[ records, {recordNumber} ];
        If[ record === EndOfFile, Break[] ];
        recno = recordNumber /. rules[ records, record ];
        While[ True, (* loop over works/recordings *)
            Print["next work on record ", recno];
            composer = FindOrAdd[ composers, {composerName},
                                    {}, compKey ];
            If[ composer === EndOfFile, Break[] ];
            compk = compKey /. rules[ composers, composer ];
            work = FindOrAdd[ works, {workTitle},
                            {compKey->compk}, workKey ];
            If[ work === EndOfFile, Break[] ];
            workk = workKey /. rules[ works, work ];
            workt = workTitle /. rules[ works, work ];
            perfk = addWithKeyTo[ recordings, {workk, recno},
                            recKey ];
            While[ True, (* loop over artists *)
                Print["next performer of ", workt];
                artist = FindOrAdd[ artists, {artistName, instrument},
                                    {}, artistKey ];
                If[ artist === EndOfFile, Break[] ];
                ak = artistKey /. rules[ artists, artist ];
                addTupleTo[ performers, {perfk, ak} ]
            ]
        ];
        Print[""];
    ]
    ]
```

Listing 13.3–1   DataEntry from Music.m.

13.4   Commercial Databases

There is much more to say about databases than we could fit in this chapter. In conclusion, we mention some topics important for real-world databases.

13.4.1   Database Management Programs

Consistency of databases is so important that our naive solution with special data entry programs is insufficient for larger applications. The problem is made worse by the fact that in a large organization many users (humans and programs) access a database concurrently. Think about a bank where many transactions take place simultaneously in various branch offices. A database system is therefore separated into two components:

- The *server* maintains the data and allows only well-defined access through an interface. It also enforces consistency conditions. Another task of the server is to maintain data integrity in case of computer malfunction or a loss of power.

- The *access programs* use the interface to the server for queries and data entry. Using the interface guarantees that no inconsistent modifications can take place. *On-line programs* allow real-time access to the database, for example, at a cashier's register in a bank. *Batch programs* run overnight or on weekends and print account statements, for example.

13.4.2   Query Languages

One of the most often used interfaces or query languages is named SQL. In SQL, our example from page 314 would look like this:

```
select   composerName, workTitle, artistName, instrument
    from   recordings, works, composers, performers, artists
    where recordings.recordNumber = "45830" and
          recordings.workKey = works.workKey and
          works.compKey = composers.compKey and
          recordings.recKey = performers.recKey and
          performers.artistKey = artists.artistKey
go
```

Projection, selection, and join can be combined in one command. This language is an example of *relational calculus*, an alternative to our relational algebra. The operations of relational algebra are easier to implement, but relational calculus is easier to use.

13.4.3   Data Storage

Larger databases no longer fit into the main memory of a computer. Data are stored on secondary storage devices, such as disks and tapes. Only a small part of the data are brought into main memory to perform the relational operations. Because access to secondary storage is comparatively slow, the efficient organization of such accesses is an important part of implementing the operations. One tool for speeding up access is an index. An *index* is a small table that lists for each occurring key value the address of the tuples having this key value. Because keys are often used in natural joins, indices make this operation much faster.

13.4.4   Transactions

A *transaction* is a sequence of related elementary updates. In our example, entering the data for a whole CD is a transaction. If a transaction is interrupted because of a hardware of software failure, the database might be left in an inconsistent state. Database servers therefore guarantee that a transaction either completes successfully or is completely undone. This mechanism guarantees consistency of the database under all circumstances.

13.5 Exercises

13.1 An Exercise Database[1]

The database of classical music recordings used in this chapter is available for your own exercises.

The package Music.m contains the auxiliary functions for working with the database.

```
In[1]:= << CSM'Music'
```

The command load loads the example data from the file music.db.

```
In[2]:= load;
```

Here, for example, is a report listing all records and the works contained on these records.

```
In[3]:= report[allrecords];
```

```
Beethoven's Symphonies, London, 430400-2
        Beethoven, L. v.
            Symphony No. 1
            Symphony No. 2
            Symphony No. 3
            Symphony No. 4
            Symphony No. 5
            Symphony No. 6
            Symphony No. 7
            Symphony No. 8
            Symphony No. 9
Beethoven: The Piano Concertos, Angel, 63360
        Beethoven, L. v.
            Conc. for Piano and Orch. No. 1
            Conc. for Piano and Orch. No. 2
            Conc. for Piano and Orch. No. 3
            Conc. for Piano and Orch. No. 4
            Conc. for Piano and Orch. No. 5
Das Konzert November 1989, Sony Classical, 45830
        Beethoven, L. v.
            Conc. for Piano and Orch. No. 1
            Symphony No. 7
Horovitz at Carnegie Hall, RCA, 7992-2
        Beethoven, L. v.
            Conc. for Piano and Orch. No. 5
        Tchaikovsky, P. I.
            Conc. No. 1 for Piano and Orch.
Mussorgsky/Tchaikovsky, RCA, GD 60 449 QH
        Mussorgsky, M.
            Pictures at an Exhibition
        Tchaikovsky, P. I.
            Conc. No. 1 for Piano and Orch.
Schubert, Symphonies Nos. 1&2, Wand, EMI, CDC 7 47874 2
        Schubert, Franz
            Symphony No. 1
            Symphony No. 2
```

---

[1]From "Databases" [47], reprinted in [51].

Some standard queries of the form report[*name*] are predefined. Here, for example, is the code that produced the report:

```
report[ allrecords ] :=
    Module[{rel},
        rel = records;
        rel = Join[ rel, recordings ];
        rel = Join[ rel, works ];
        rel = Join[ rel, composers ];
        rel = Projection[ rel,
            {recordTitle, label, recordNumber,
             composerName, workTitle} ];
        Report[rel, 3, 1]
    ]
```

The data entry command DataEntry is defined also in Music.m. After entering new data, you can write the modified database to the file music.db using save. A backup copy of the old file is first put into music.db.bak.

13.2   An Address Database

Find entities, attributes, and relationships for a simple address database. Develop the corresponding layout of relations. Which attributes can be used as keys? Provide for the entry of optional information, such as phone and fax number(s), occupation, and so on. Test your design by solving the following problems with it:

1. Print a list of all persons having the same address.

2. Make entries for father and son having the same first and last names and living at the same address.

3. Change of name at marriage.

4. Addresses in various countries, for example:

MathConsult Dr. R. Mäder
Samstagernstraße 58a
8832 Wollerau
Switzerland

Tel: +41 1 687 4051, Fax: +41 1 687 4054

Chapter 14
Object-Oriented Programming

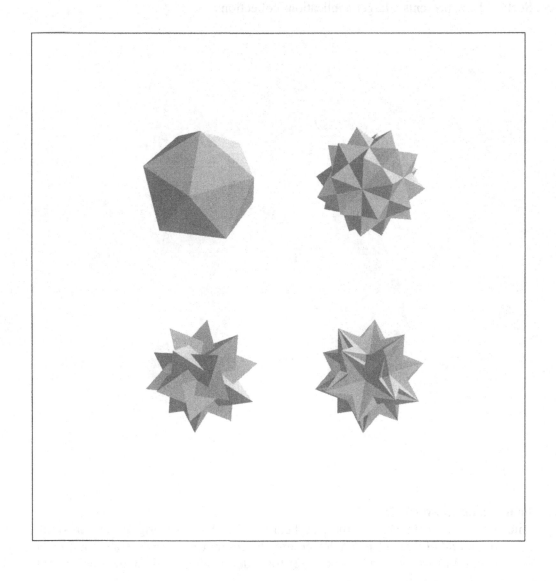

In this chapter, we introduce object-oriented programming, a programming style that is rapidly gaining in importance.

Section 14.1 introduces the concepts of object-oriented programming: objects, methods, and classes. In Section 14.2, we shall look at a simple example of an object-oriented program: maintenance of bank accounts. The section shows how classes can be used to share code between closely related data types.

A list of principles of object-oriented programming is given in Section 14.3. The last section, Section 14.4, presents a larger application: collections.

About the illustration overleaf:
The graphic shows four stellations of the icosahedron. Top left: the original icosahedron; top right the compound of five octahedra; lower left: the compound of five tetrahedra; Lower right: the compound of tne tetrahedra. See [52] for a description of all stellations and for *Mathematica* code to generate them.

14.1   Introduction

We always emphasized two principles of good programming: abstract data types and modularization (packages). So far, we have not implemented the idea that data and functions belong together on the lowest level of individual data elements. The components of abstract data types are themselves data elements; there is no room for functions. So far, we could combine data and functions only at the level of a package.

14.1.1   Objects and Methods

The combination of data and operations at the level of single *objects* is the first important idea behind object-oriented programming. An object is, therefore, a collection of data elements together with the functions operating on them. These functions are called *methods*. Methods are always applied to an object, which is called the *receiver* of the method invocation. We shall represent method invocation as an ordinary function call, that is, as

$$method[object, \ arguments\ldots] \ .$$

The first argument is the receiver, any remaining arguments are additional parameters of the method.

14.1.2   Classes

Methods are normally not defined for each object separately, but only for *classes* of objects. A class is characterized by the fact that all objects belonging to this class know the same methods, that is, they show the same behavior.

   In addition to the methods, objects contain also data elements. The data elements of an object are called *instance variables*. Such an instance variable is like a component in a composite data type (see Section 5.1). All objects in a class have the same set of variables, but each object has its own private *values* for these variables. An object is also called an *instance* of its class.

14.1.3   Inheritance

The second important concept in object-oriented programming is *inheritance*. Often, related data types have common characteristics. We can take advantage of these common aspects and program some of the methods in a way that does not depend on which of the similar classes an object belongs to. The program works in the same way for objects from any of the related classes. The common characteristics can, therefore, be extracted and can be put

into a new class. The other classes are then made *subclasses* of the new class. They inherit
instance variables and methods from their *superclass*, and need to define only those variables
and methods that are special to them. This code sharing in a superclass makes programs easier
to maintain because there is no duplication of almost identical pieces of code scattered over
several data types. A modification needs to be programmed only once and is made available
to all subclasses automatically.

14.1.4   Object-Oriented Programming in *Mathematica*

Object-oriented programming is not built into *Mathematica*. It has been implemented in
the package Classes.m. This package needs to be read in for all examples in this chapter
(using Needs["CSM`Classes`"]). We shall not show the command for reading it in, but
always assume that it has been read. How the package Classes.m works is unimportant for
our applications of object-oriented programming. Readers interested in this question should
consult [51], where the package Classes.m is explained.

14.2   Example: Bank Accounts

A simple version of account management software is well suited to explain the ideas of object-oriented programming. The instance variables of an account object describe its internal state. The balance is such a variable. In addition, we store the name of the owner of the account as an additional instance variable. Which methods are needed? First, we need a way to create new accounts. Then, there are methods for depositing and withdrawing money from the account, and for balance enquiry. These instance variables and methods define the class Account. The following syntax is used to declare classes:

$$\text{Class}[class, \; superclass, \; \{ivars...\}, \; \{methods...\}] \, .$$

The *ivars* are the instance variables; a method is a pair

$$\{name, \; implementation\} \, .$$

Listing 14.2–1 shows the declaration of the class Account.

```
Class[ Account, Object,
    {balance, owner},
    {{new,      Function[{bal,own}, new[super]; balance=bal; owner=own]},
     {Balance,  Function[{}, balance]},
     {Deposit,  Function[{amt}, balance += amt]},
     {Withdraw, Function[{amt}, balance -= amt]},
     {Owner,    Function[{}, owner]}
    }
]
```

Listing 14.2–1   Accounts.m: The class Account.

The superclass of Account is Object, the superclass of all classes. This class is used if there is no other class that we can use as a superclass. The two instance variables are balance and owner.

Now we consider the methods. Methods are implemented as *pure functions*. Please make sure that you understand Section 11.1, where pure functions are explained. The method new is used to create instances of Account. The arguments bal and own in the method are used to initialize the instance variables, the initial balance and the name of the owner of the new account. The body of the method new is

$$\text{new[super]; balance=bal; owner=own} \, .$$

The first action, new[super], invokes the method new in the superclass of the new object. In this way, the superclass can perform its own initializations. Afterward, the two instance variables are initialized from the values of the two parameters.

When we read in the file Accounts.m, the class `Accounts` is defined.

```
In[1]:= << CSM`Accounts`
```

Now we can create new account objects by sending the message `new` to the *class*. The result is an object whose internal structure is invisible.

```
In[2]:= a1 = new[ Account, 1000, "Roman E. Maeder" ]

Out[2]= -Account-
```

The method `new` is special (it is called a *class method*) because its receiver is not an object, but a class. Because it is used to create objects in the first place, there is no object on which we could invoke this method.

    The method `Balance` should return the current balance. It does not need any parameters, and we can, therefore, write it as a constant pure function that returns the value of the instance variable `balance` – that is, simply as `Function[balance]`, or `Function[{}, balance]` to make it clear that it does not take any arguments. The same is true for the method `Owner` that returns the owner's name, which is the value of the instance variable `owner`.

Objects behave like ordinary data elements to which we can apply functions.

```
In[3]:= Balance[a1]

Out[3]= 1000
```

If we deposit an amount `amt` in the account, the balance is increased accordingly. The amount deposited is the argument of the method `Deposit`. Its implementation simply increments the balance – that is, we can use `Function[{amt}, balance += amt]`. Similar remarks apply to withdrawal.

The new balance is returned as value.

```
In[4]:= Deposit[ a1, 200 ]

Out[4]= 1200
```

A withdrawal decreases the balance.

```
In[5]:= Withdraw[ a1, 500 ]

Out[5]= 700
```

In addition to the user-defined methods, each class inherits certain standard methods from the class `Object`.

The method `Class` returns the class to which an object belongs.

```
In[6]:= Class[ a1 ]

Out[6]= Account
```

`Methods` gives a list of all known methods.

```
In[7]:= Methods[ a1 ]

Out[7]= {Balance, Class, delete, Deposit,
    InstanceVariables, isa, Methods, new, NIM, Owner,
    SuperClass, Withdraw}
```

The method `InstanceVariables` returns the names of all instance variables.

```
In[8]:= InstanceVariables[ a1 ]

Out[8]= {balance, owner}
```

Note that objects have many properties of abstract data types. The instance variables can be accessed only using the defined methods. The methods `Balance` and `Owner` correspond to *selectors*, `new` is a *constructor*. In a moment, we shall see the advantages of object-oriented programming over ordinary data types. We want to define a *subclass* of `Account`.

A *savings account* is an account whose balance must always be positive (you do not get credit on a savings account). All other properties can be inherited from the class `Account` – that is, we can make savings accounts a subclass of `Account`. Only the method for withdrawals needs to be redefined to check the balance before allowing a withdrawal. Everything else is inherited from the superclass. The definition of class `SavingsAccount` is in Listing 14.2–2.

```
Class[ SavingsAccount, Account,
      { },
      {{Withdraw, Function[{amt}, If[ Balance[self] < amt,
                                Message[Account::nomoney, Balance[self], amt],
                                Withdraw[super, amt] ]
              ]}
      }
]

Account::nomoney = "Balance `1` insufficient for withdrawal of `2`."
```

Listing 14.2–2 Accounts.m: The class `SavingsAccount`.

No new instance variables are needed; therefore, the empty list is given as second argument in the declaration. The method `Withdraw` first checks whether the balance is sufficient by comparing the balance with the amount to be withdrawn. The balance is obtained with the method `Balance` sent to the receiver, denoted by the variable `self`, whose value is always the receiver of the currently executing method. If the balance is insufficient, an error message is generated. Otherwise, the withdrawal can take place. We perform it by invoking the *same* method `Withdraw` of the superclass of the receiver! Similar to `self`, the variable `super` stands for the receiver of the current method, but viewed as a member of its superclass. This mechanism causes the code from the superclass to be invoked, performing the withdrawal.

The method `new` is inherited from the class `Account`.	`In[9]:= sa1 = new[ SavingsAccount, 100, "Janet Smith" ]` `Out[9]= -SavingsAccount-`

If we try to withdraw too much money, an error message is generated.	`In[10]:= Withdraw[ sa1, 110 ]`
	`Account::nomoney:`
	`    Balance 100 insufficient for withdrawal of 110.`

Smaller amounts can be withdrawn as usual.	`In[11]:= Withdraw[ sa1, 90 ]` `Out[11]= 10`

14.3   Principles of Object-Oriented Programming

Here are a few guidelines for object-oriented programming. Examples of programs can be found in the previous and following sections.

1. A class combines data (instance variables) and functions (methods).

2. An object is an instance of a class. Each object has its own values of the instance variables and reacts to all methods defined in its class.

3. A class inherits all variables and methods from its superclass.

4. An object is created with the class method new[*class*, ...]. The first action in the body of the method new should be an invocation of new[super].

5. Method invocation has the form *message*[*object*, *arguments*...]. The first parameter is the receiver of the method.

6. Methods are pure functions that take the arguments of a method invocation as parameters.

7. Inside the body of a method, the names of the instance variables stand for the variables of the receiver of the method.

8. Other methods of the receiver can be called by using the object self as the receiver.

9. A method having the same name as a method in the superclass *specializes* this method. In this way, the behavior of objects of the subclass is modified.

10. To call a method of the superclass that has been specialized, use super as the receiver.

11. An abstract class is a class of which there will never be any objects. It serves to define the common characteristics of a number of subclasses.

12. The class Object is the abstract superclass of all other classes.

Table 14.3–1 lists the methods that are predefined for all classes in our implementation of object-oriented programming.

Method	Description
new[*class*, ...]	create a new object
Methods[*obj*]	give all known methods of *obj*
InstanceVariables[*obj*]	give the names of all instance variables of *obj*
Class[*obj*]	give the class of *obj*
SuperClass[*obj*]	give the superclass of the class of *obj*
isa[*obj*, *class*]	return True, if *obj* belongs to *class* or one of its subclasses
delete[*obj*]	delete the object (normally not needed)

Table 14.3–1   Standard methods for all classes.

14.4   Application: Collections

A *collection* is a container for data. We have seen examples of collections in other parts of this book: binary trees in Section 6.3, lists in Section 9.2, and heaps in Section 8.4.3. The object-oriented language Smalltalk provides a well-designed set of collections that we want to implement in *Mathematica*. The package Collect.m contains the code for all classes described here.

The abstract base class is collection. There will be no objects of this class; it serves only to describe the common characteristics of all kinds of collections. An important subclass is the class of indexed collections, whose elements are accessed using a key. The complete hierarchy of classes is shown in Figure 14.4–1.

Table 14.4–1 shows all methods to be implemented for collections. Remarkably, all methods from the first group can be implemented in the abstract class collection in terms of the method do, as shown in Listing 14.4–1. Only the iterator do needs to be defined in the subclasses. This kind of code sharing is typical of well-written object-oriented programs. It also means that it is easy to add new collections: All we need is figure out a way to apply a function to all of its elements in turn.

The operation of *folding* fold[*coll*, v_0, *g*] applies the binary function *g* to all elements of the collection *coll* and the result of the last application, respectively. It corresponds to the operation Fold[*g*, v_0, *list*] (see Section 2.3.9). fold is implemented by initializing a local variable v with the initial value v_0 and then iterating Function[v = g[v, #]] over the

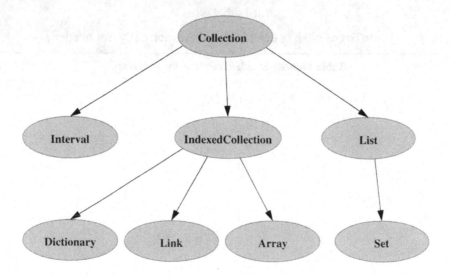

Figure 14.4–1   The class hierarchy of collections.

collection (using do). The final value of v is the result.

The number of elements in a collection can be found by folding the function #1+1&. It simply counts the elements. The collection is empty if the number of elements is zero.

To find out whether a certain element *elem* is a member of the collection, we iterate over the collection and compare *elem* with all elements present. If we find one that is equal, we can immediately return True. We can perform such an exit from a running loop with Throw[*result*]. It terminates any computation going on inside Catch[]. If we do not find the element, the loop runs to completion, and we return False.

The method select[*coll, predicate*] generates a list (one of the collections treated in Section 14.4.1) containing all elements of *coll* satisfying the given predicate. It is implemented by folding

$$\texttt{Function[If[}predicate\texttt{[\#2], add[\#1, \#2]]; \#1]}$$

The second argument of the folded function is one of the elements of the collection. The

Methods defined for all collections	
do[*coll, f*]	apply the function *f* to all elements of *coll*
fold[*coll*, v_0, *g*]	iterate the binary operation *g* over *coll*, initialized with v_0
size[*coll*]	the number elements in *coll*
isEmpty[*coll*]	True, if *coll* is empty
includes[*coll, elem*]	True, if *elem* is an element of *coll*
select[*coll, predicate*]	give the list of elements satisfying *predicate*

Additional methods for lists and sets	
add[*list, elem*]	insert *elem* into the list or set *list*

Additional methods for indexed collections	
binaryDo[*icoll, f*]	apply the function *f* to all (key, value) pairs
includesKey[*icoll, key*]	True, if *key* occurs as key in *icoll*
at[*icoll, key*]	returns the value stored under the key *key*
atPut[*icoll, key, val*]	insert a value under the given *key*

Table 14.4–1 Methods for collections.

element is tested with the given predicate. If we get True we add the element to the list, which is the first argument of the folded function. If the predicate is not satisfied, we return the old list to allow the folding to continue correctly. Initially, the list is set to a new empty list with new[list].

```
Class[ collection, Object,
    {},
    {{fold,      Function[{v0, g},
                     Module[{v = v0}, do[self, (v = g[v, #])&]; v] ]},
     {size,      Function[{}, fold[self, 0, #1+1&] ]},
     {isEmpty,   Function[{}, size[self] == 0 ]},
     {includes,  Function[{elem},
                     Catch[ do[self, If[#===elem, Throw[True]]&]; False ] ]},
     {select,    Function[{pred},
                     fold[self, new[list], (If[pred[#2], add[#1, #2]]; #1)&] ]}
    }
]
```

Listing 14.4–1   The abstract class collection.

14.4.1 Ordinary Collections

So far, we programmed only the abstract base class collection. Now we turn to the subclasses, the collections we can use to store data. Each collection needs only an implementation of the method do and the constructor new.

14.4.1.1 Interval

The simplest collection is the *interval*. An interval is created with

$$new[\ interval,\ l,\ u,\ s\ ]\ .$$

Its elements are the numbers l, $l + s$, $l + 2s$, ..., u. In *Mathematica*, we would use Range[l, u, s] to generate these elements in a list. The declaration of interval is shown in Listing 14.4–2.

```
Class[ interval, collection,
    {lower, upper, step},
    {{do,  Function[{f}, Do[ f[i], {i, lower, upper, step}]]},
     {new, Function[{l, u, s}, new[super]; {lower, upper, step}={l, u, s}]]}
    }
]
```

Listing 14.4–2   The collection interval.

Note that we do not need to generate and store the elements of the interval explicitly. We need only to remember the bounds and the increment (these three instance variables are initialized when the interval is created). We can perform the iteration do using the command Do[].

We generate the interval 1, 2, 3, 4, 5.	```In[1]:= i1 = new[interval, 1, 5, 1]```
	```Out[1]= -interval-```
To look at its elements, we can simply apply the function Print to its elements.	```In[2]:= do[i1, Print]```
	```1```
	```2```
	```3```
	```4```
	```5```
Folding with Plus gives us the sum of the elements.	```In[3]:= fold[i1, 0, Plus]```
	```Out[3]= 15```
The number of elements is five.	```In[4]:= size[i1]```
	```Out[4]= 5```
The number 3 is a member of the interval.	```In[5]:= includes[i1, 3]```
	```Out[5]= True```
The number 7 is not included.	```In[6]:= includes[i1, 7]```
	```Out[6]= False```
The language Smalltalk uses intervals for iteration. Here is a loop in typical Smalltalk fashion. It prints the squares of 1, 3, 5, 7, and 9.	```In[7]:= do[new[interval, 1, 9, 2], Print[#^2]&]```
	```1```
	```9```
	```25```
	```49```
	```81```

14.4.1.2 List

Lists are implemented with an auxiliary data type, the link. A link consists of three parts: a key field, a value field, and a field for the next link. Links are used to implement linked lists, another important dynamic data structure (other than binary trees and heaps, see Section 9.2). Links are indexed collections (see Section 14.4.2) whose implementation is not treated here. (The class definition is in the package Collect.m.) A link is created with new[link, *key, val, next*]. The class list needs one instance variable for the head of the linked list of its elements. A new list is created with

new[list] .

We implement the iteration do by passing it on to the first link. We add an element with add[*list, elem*]. To add an element, we create a new link with the element as its value field and the old list head as the next link. The key field is not used, because lists are not indexed collections. See Listing 14.4–3.

```
Class[ list, collection,
    {head},
    {{do,    Function[{f}, do[head, f]]},
     {add,   Function[{elem}, head = new[link, 0, elem, head]; self]},
     {new,   Function[{}, new[super]; head=nullLink]}
    }
]
```

Listing 14.4–3 The collection `list`.

We create a new empty list and assign it to `11`.

```
In[8]:= 11 = new[list]
Out[8]= -list-
```

We add two elements to it.

```
In[9]:= 11 = add[11, a];\
        11 = add[11, b];
```

To look at the list, we iterate the `Print` function over it.

```
In[10]:= do[ 11, Print ]
b
a
```

The result of a selection is a list. In this example, we select all prime numbers from the interval 1 . . . 25.

```
In[11]:= select[ new[interval, 1, 25, 1], PrimeQ ]
Out[11]= -list-
```

Instead of printing the elements, we can alternatively put them into an ordinary list to see them.

```
In[12]:= res={}; do[ %, PrependTo[res,#]& ]; res
Out[12]= {2, 3, 5, 7, 11, 13, 17, 19, 23}
```

14.4.1.3 Set

Sets can be implemented in terms of lists. Therefore, we declare the class `set` as a subclass of `list`; see Listing 14.4–4. The only difference between a set and a list is that an element cannot be a member of a set more than once. Therefore, we specialize the method `add` to test the new element before adding it to the list. We used this idea already for our savings accounts in Listing 14.2–2.

```
Class[ set, list,
    {},
    {{add,   Function[{elem}, If[!includes[self, elem], add[super, elem]]; self ]}
    }
]
```

Listing 14.4–4 The collection `set`.

14.4.2 Indexed Collections

The abstract base class `indexedCollection` (Listing 14.4–5) implements many of the additional methods of indexed collections. They need three basic methods that have to be implemented in all subclasses. The iterator binaryDo[*icoll*, *f*] applies the binary function *f* to all keys and values. The method atPut[*icoll*, *key*, *val*] adds a value under the key *key*, and atIfAbsent[*icoll*, *key*, *proc*] returns the value stored under *key*, if such a key exists; otherwise, it calls the parameterless procedure *proc*. The other methods do, includesKey, and at can be implemented in terms of the three basic methods.

```
Class[ indexedCollection, collection,
    {},
    {{do,          Function[{f}, binaryDo[self, f[#2]&]]},
     {includesKey, Function[{key},
                       Catch[atIfAbsent[self, key, Throw[False]&]; True] ]},
     {at,          Function[{key},
                       atIfAbsent[self, key,
                          Message[indexedCollection::nsk, key, self]&]
                   ]}
    }
]
indexedCollection::nsk = "Key `1` is not in `2`."
```

Listing 14.4–5 Indexed collections.

The method do uses binaryDo to apply the function *f* to the values only. The method includesKey[*icoll*, *key*] tries to find the value under the given key. If it succeeds, we know that the key is in fact present, and we can return True; otherwise, the exception procedure in atIfAbsent is called, and it returns with False. Finally, at is implemented in terms of atIfAbsent as well. If the key does not exist, an error message is generated.

14.4.2.1 Array

The simplest indexed collection is the *array* (Listing 14.4–6). The keys are the integers from 1 to the size of the array. An array is created with

$$\text{new}[\text{ array}, \textit{size}, v_0 \text{ }] \text{ .}$$

Its elements are initialized with the default value v_0. Because the keys are successive integers, we need not store them. We need to store only the values (in a *Mathematica* list). For the iteration binaryDo, we generate the keys as an interval and then iterate over the interval. atIfAbsent simply tests whether the key is in the range $1 \ldots n$, where n is the size of the array. The auxiliary method boundCheck performs this test.

Arrays have a special version of the method size that is much faster than is the default method in the base class collection. We are always free to specialize methods for efficiency reasons, even it is not strictly required to do so.

Here, we create an array with 10 elements, initialized to 0.

```
In[13]:= a1 = new[ array, 10, 0 ]
Out[13]= -array-
```

This loop stores the value i^2 in the element   In[14]:= binaryDo[a1,
with index i.   Function[{i, val}, atPut[a1, i, i^2]]]

Here is the element with index 8.   In[15]:= at[a1, 8]

                                                        Out[15]= 64

```
Class[ array, indexedCollection,
    {ar},
    {{binaryDo,    Function[{f},
                     do[ new[interval, 1, size[self], 1], f[#, at[self, #]]& ] ]},
     {atIfAbsent,  Function[{key, proc},
                     If[ boundCheck[self, key], ar[[key]], proc[] ] ]},
     {atPut,       Function[{key, val},
                     If[ boundCheck[self, key],
                         ar[[key]] = val,
                         Message[array::nsk, key, size[self]] ];
                     self ]},
     {size,        Function[{}, Length[ar] ]},
     {boundCheck,  Function[{i}, TrueQ[1 <= i <= size[self]] ]},
     {new,         Function[{size, v0}, new[super]; ar = Table[v0, {size}] ]}
    }
]

array::nsk = "Array index `1` is not in the range (1...`2`)."
```

Listing 14.4–6   The collection `array`.

14.4.2.2   Dictionary

Our last example is the *dictionary*. A dictionary is an indexed collection where keys and values can be arbitrary expressions. The simplest implementation is a linked list (using the link, as in the collection `list`). Such an implementation is rather inefficient, because keys can be found only by linear search.

A useful technique for improving access times is *hashing*. A hashing function computes an integer value from any expression. It may happen that two expressions will be hashed to the same integer, but a good hashing function will distribute the possible values evenly over the range of expressions. Other possible implementations for dictionaries are binary trees and ordered lists (see Exercise 14.2).

A hashing function is built into *Mathemati-*   In[16]:= Hash /@ {1, 1.5, I, a, f[x]}
ca.

                                                        Out[16]= {659992243, 676422052, 389582518, 13947657,

                                                          544912441}

In our dictionary, the expressions are classified into a number of *bins* (see Listing 14.4–7). The hashing function `Mod[Hash[`*expr*`], `n`]` gives n different values (from 0 to $n - 1$). It can

```
Class[ dictionary, indexedCollection,
    {linktable},
    {{binaryDo,    Function[{f}, do[linktable, binaryDo[#, f]&] ]},
     {atIfAbsent,  Function[{key, proc},
                       atIfAbsent[ at[linktable, bin[self, key]], key, proc ] ]},
     {atPut,       Function[{key, val}, With[{slot = bin[self, key]},
                       atPut[ linktable, slot, atPut[at[linktable, slot], key, val] ];
                       self ]]},
     {new,         Function[{n}, new[super]; linktable = new[array, n, nullLink] ]},
     {bin,         Function[ {key}, Mod[Hash[key], size[linktable]] + 1 ]}
    }
]
```

Listing 14.4–7 The collection `dictionary`.

be used to find the bin for an expression. All keys ending up in the same bin are then stored in a linked list. If we choose the number of bins larger than the expected number of entries of the dictionary, these lists will be short and can be searched quickly.

A dictionary is, therefore, an array of links. The size of the array (the number of bins) is set when the dictionary is created with

$$\text{new[dictionary, } n \text{] .}$$

The only instance variable of `dictionary` is the array `linktable`. At initialization, it is set to an array of empty links (the constant `nullLink` is an empty link). The auxiliary method `bin[`*dict, key*`]` returns the number of the bin to use for the given key. The method `binaryDo` iterates over the array (using `do`) and calls `binaryDo` again for the elements of the array (these elements are links, which are an indexed collection). The methods `atIfAbsent` and `atPut` first determine the bin to use and then call the same method for the corresponding link.

The implementation of `dictionary` makes heavy use of other collections. As a consequence, this rather complicated collection has a very short implementation.

We generate a dictionary with 10 bins.

```
In[17]:= cup = new[dictionary, 10]
Out[17]= -dictionary-
```

We enter data of offices of Cambridge University Press in various countries. The countries are the keys, the phone numbers are the values. These data were also used in Section 6.1.3.

```
In[18]:= atPut[cup, "USA",       "+1 212 924 3900"];\
         atPut[cup, "Australia", "+61 3 9568 0322 9"];\
         atPut[cup, "Spain",     "+34 1 360 45 65"];\
         atPut[cup, "Argentina", "+541 322-5040"];\
         atPut[cup, "Brazil",    "+55 11 259 2122"];\
         atPut[cup, "Egypt",     "+202 3935157"];\
         atPut[cup, "France",    "+331 39 14 46 91"];\
         atPut[cup, "Greece",    "+30 1 9213020"];\
         atPut[cup, "India",     "+91 11 3274196"];\
         atPut[cup, "Poland",    "+48 2 654 18 09"];\
         atPut[cup, "Thailand",  "+66 2 255 4620"];\
         atPut[cup, "Turkey",    "+216 346 3046"];\
         atPut[cup, "Japan",     "+81 813 32914541"];
```

Now, we can easily find the phone numbers.

```
In[19]:= at[ cup, "Thailand" ]
Out[19]= +66 2 255 4620
```

On the other hand, we have to search the whole dictionary to find the country, given the number +202 3935157.

```
In[20]:= binaryDo[ cup, Function[{key, val},
                If[val === "+202 3935157", Print[key]]] ]
Egypt
```

This example shows how we can exploit common characteristics of related data types in object-oriented programming. This kind of programming is typical for the language Smalltalk.

14.5 Exercises

14.1 Binary Trees as Collections

Implement binary trees (Section 6.3) as an indexed collection (Section 14.4). The nodes should have a key and value field each.

14.2 Different Implementations of Dictionaries

Implement the class `dictionary` in another way than was done in Listing 14.4–7. Here are a few possibilities:

1. Using binary trees (see Section 6.3)

2. As an ordered list (see Section 6.1.3)

3. *Your own idea*

Appendix A

Further Reading

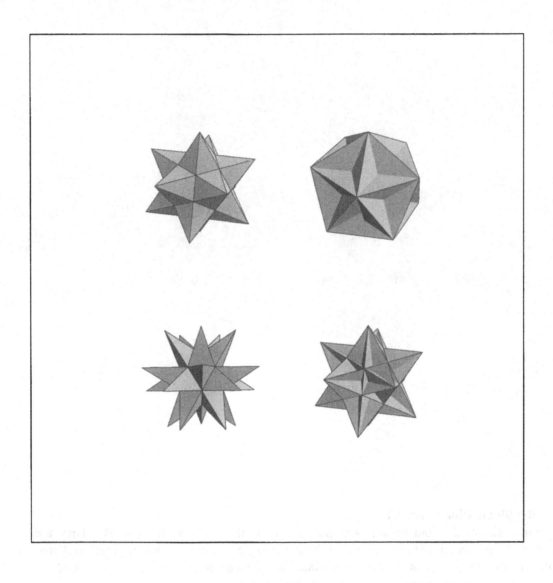

This appendix contains an annotated bibliography for the topics programming styles, teaching with *Mathematica*, literature on *Mathematica*, and computer science. Section A.1.5 provides the references for the topics treated in this book. Section A.1.5 gives the concise bibliographical data.

About the illustration overleaf:
The picture shows the four regular star polyhedra (Kepler–Poinsot polyhedra). They are regular by definition but not convex. From the left to right and top to bottom: small stellated dodecahedron, great dodecahedron, great stellated dodecahedron, great icosahedron. The code for this picture is taken from [51] and shown in Pictures.m.

A.1   A Guide to the Literature

A.1.1   Programming

Functional programming originated with the language LISP in 1960 [55]. A clean implementation is the dialect Scheme, developed at MIT [1, 64]. A delightful introduction to LISP is *The Little LISPer* [20]. This booklet starts with the basics and leads right into the center of the programming style so typical of LISP. *Pure functions* (see Section 11.1) are of central importance in LISP, where they are called *Lambda expressions*. The theoretical background of functional programming is λ calculus. A comprehensive presentation can be found in Barendregt's book [4]. We look at functional programming in Chapter 9 and in Section 11.2.

Object-oriented programming got its start with the language Simula [5]. Today, the languages Smalltalk [25] and C++ [66] are widely used, with Java [3] quickly catching up. A particularly recommended book on object-oriented programming is [10]. It discusses the concepts using four object-oriented languages: Smalltalk, C++, Object Pascal and Objective C. Other recommended books are [6, 14, 57]. In this book, Chapter 14 is about object-oriented programming.

The important concept of *modularization,* with its two central ideas of encapsulation and interface definition, is realized in many procedural languages such as Ada and Modula-2. The theoretical background was described by Parnas in 1972 [58]. We treat these concepts in Chapter 4.

An overview over the various programming styles in the way they present themselves in *Mathematica* can be found in [45] and [51].

Readers interested in the development of programming languages can find a collection of the most important works on the origin of all major languages in Horowitz's book [29].

A.1.2   Teaching with *Mathematica*

Mathematica is used more and more in teaching. A complete introductory course in calculus has been developed by H. Porta und J. Uhl at the University of Illinois [17]. Its authors described the underlying ideas in an excellent article in the *Mathematica Journal* [9]. Other examples of classroom material using *Mathematica* are in [7, 16, 19, 24, 30, 31]. There is also a journal devoted to *Mathematica* in education, aptly named *Mathematica in Education and Research*.

A.1.3   Literature on *Mathematica*

The official *Mathematica* manual is Wolfram's book [74]. The *Mathematica Journal* contains articles on all aspects of *Mathematica*. Further material on programming in *Mathematica* can be found in our books [54, 51, 53]. Various *Mathematica* topics are treated in the books by Wickham-Jones [73] and Wagon [72]. Applications of *Mathematica* in various sciences are in [15, 22, 26, 70, 71], among many others.

A.1.4   Other Topics in Computer Science

Everything about discrete mathematics (recursion equations, closed form solution of sums, combinatorics, and so on) can be found in [37]. A good reference for algorithmics is Sedgewick [61], and, of course, there are the volumes of Knuth's *The Art of Computer Programming* [34, 35, 36].

Gersting's text [23] contains elements of discrete mathematics and some chapters on the theory of computation and finite automata. An impressive collection of survey articles on the occasion of the 50th anniversary of Turing's important work on computability [67] was edited by Herken [27]. A new approach, algorithmic information theory, was pioneered by Chaitin [11], who uses *Mathematica* for some of his programs.

A newer book on numerical mathematics of special interest to *Mathematica* users is [62]. A recommended book on databases is [68].

A.1.5   Various References

The Collatz or $3x+1$ problem from Section 3.2 is discussed further in an article by Lagarias [39]. A description of fast searching methods for the $3x + 1$ problem can be found in [42]. The diode equation from Section 1.1.6 is taken from [15]. The proof that there are three fourth powers whose sum is again a forth power (Section 2.1.1) is by Elkies [18]. The various computation methods for Fibonacci numbers in Section 7.2 are taken from [43]. The Karatsuba multiplication method from Section 7.4.3 originated in [32] (English translation in [33]).

λ calculus was introduced by Church [12] (Section 11.1). The collections in Section 14.4 are from Budd's book [10]. Their implementation in *Mathematica* was first given in [49].

Turing's work for the British defense is described in his interesting biography [28] (Section 1.2). The Turing machine is from his work in 1936 [67]. Church's thesis was also postulated in 1936 [13].

The Ackermann function was given in [2] as an example of a total but not primitive recursive function. The busy beaver problem is by Rado [60]. An overview of the current research in this area can be found in [8].

The oscillator in Section 3.4.5 is named after van der Pol who described it in 1926 [69]. The examples with op amps in Section 1.1.4 and in Exercise 8.7 are taken from the book [65]. The Koch curve is from [38] the flowsnake is due to W. Gosper [21] (Exercise 10.4).

A.2 References

[1] H. Abelson and G. J. Sussman. *Structure and Interpretation of Computer Programs*. The MIT Press, Cambridge, MA, 1985.

[2] W. Ackermann. Zum Hilbertschen Aufbau der reellen Zahlen. *Math. Ann.*, 99:118–33, 1928.

[3] Ken Arnold and James Gosling. *The Java Programming Language*, 2nd edition. Addison Wesley Longman, Reading, MA, 1998.

[4] H. P. Barendregt. *The Lambda Calculus*, revised edition. Studies in Logic 103. North Holland, Amsterdam, 1984.

[5] G. M. Birtwistle, O.-J. Dahl, B. Myhrhaug, and K. Nygaard. *SIMULA Begin*. Studentlitteratur Sweden, Lund, 1979.

[6] Grady Booch. *Object Oriented Design with Applications*. The Benjamin/Cummings Publishing Company, Redwood City, CA, 1991.

[7] Bart Braden. *Discovering Calculus with Mathematica*. John Wiley & Sons, New York, 1992.

[8] Allen H. Brady. The busy beaver game and the meaning of life. In Rolf Herken, *The Universal Turing Machine: A Half Century Survey*. Kammerer & Unverzagt, Hamburg–Berlin, 1988.

[9] Don Brown, Horacio Porta, and Jerry Uhl. Calculus&Mathematica: Courseware for the nineties. *The Mathematica Journal*, 1(1), 1990.

[10] Timothy Budd. *An Introduction to Object-Oriented Programming*. Addison-Wesley, Reading, MA, 1991.

[11] Gregory J. Chaitin. *The Limits of Mathematics*. Springer-Verlag, New York, 1998.

[12] A. Church. A set of postulates for the foundation of logic. *Annals of Math.*, 33-34, 1932–33.

[13] A. Church. An unsolvable problem in elementary number theory. *Amer. J. Math.*, 58:345–63, 1936.

[14] Brad J. Cox and Andrew J. Novobilski. *Object-Oriented Programming*, second edition. Addison-Wesley, Reading, MA, 1991.

[15] Richard Crandall. *Mathematica for the Sciences*. Addison-Wesley, Reading, MA, 1991.

[16] Philip Crooke and John Ratcliffe. *A Guidebook to Calculus with Mathematica*. Wadsworth Publishing Company, 1991.

[17] Bill Davis, Horacio Porta, and Jerry Uhl. *Calculus&Mathematica*. Addison-Wesley, Reading, MA, 1994.

[18] Noam D. Elkies. On $A^4 + B^4 + C^4 = D^4$. *Math. of Computation*, 51:825–35, October 1982.

[19] James K. Finch and Millanne Lehmann. *Exploring Calculus with Mathematica*. Addison-Wesley, Reading, MA, 1992.

[20] Daniel P. Friedman and Matthias Felleisen. *The little LISPer*. The MIT Press, Cambridge, MA, 1987.

[21] M. Gardner. Mathematical games. *Scientific American*, December 1976.

[22] Richard J. Gaylord and Paul R. Wellin. *Computer Simulations with Mathematica*. TELOS/Springer-Verlag, Santa Clara, CA, 1994.

[23] Judith L. Gersting. *Mathematical Structures for Computer Science*, second edition. W. H. Freeman, San Francisco, CA, 1987.

[24] Oliver Gloor, Beatrice Amrhein, and Roman E. Maeder. *Illustrated Mathematics*. TELOS/Springer-Verlag, Santa Clara, CA, 1995. CD-ROM with booklet.

[25]   Adele Goldberg and David Robson. *Smalltalk-80: The Language*. Addison-Wesley, Reading, MA, 1989.

[26]   Theodore Gray and Jerry Glynn. *Exploring Mathematics with Mathematica*. Addison-Wesley, Reading, MA, 1991.

[27]   Rolf Herken, editor. *The Universal Turing Machine: A Half Century Survey*. Kammerer & Unverzagt, Hamburg–Berlin, 1988.

[28]   Andrew Hodges. *Alan Turing: the Enigma*. Burnett Books, London, 1983.

[29]   E. Horowitz, editor. *Programming Languages: A Grand Tour*, second edition. Computer Science Press, New York, 1985.

[30]   Cliff J. Huang and Philip S. Crooke. *Mathematics and Mathematica for Economists*. Blackwell Publishers, Malden, MA, 1997.

[31]   E. Johnson. *Linear Algebra with Mathematica*. Brooks/Cole, Pacific Grove, CA, 1995.

[32]   A. Karatsuba and Yu. Ofman. Multiplication of many-digital numbers by automatic computers. *Doklady Akademii nauk SSSR*, 145(2):293–94, 1962. (in Russian).

[33]   A. Karatsuba and Yu. Ofman. Multiplication of multidigit numbers on automata. *Soviet physics doklady*, 7(7):595–96, 1963.

[34]   D. E. Knuth. *Fundamental Algorithms, The Art of Computer Programming*, Vol. 1, 3rd edition. Addison-Wesley, Reading, MA, 1997.

[35]   D. E. Knuth. *Seminumerical Algorithms, The Art of Computer Programming*, Vol. 2, 3rd edition. Addison-Wesley, Reading, MA, 1997.

[36]   D. E. Knuth. *Sorting and Searching, The Art of Computer Programming*, Vol. 3, 3rd edition. Addison-Wesley, Reading, MA, 1997.

[37]   Donald E. Knuth, Ronald L. Graham, and Oren Patashnik. *Concrete Mathematics*. Addison-Wesley, Reading, MA, 1989.

[38]   H. von Koch. Sur une courbe continue sans tangente, obtenue par une construction géométrique élémentaire. *Arkiv för Matematik, Astronomi och Fysik*, 1:681–704, 1904.

[39]   Jeffrey C. Lagarias. The 3x+1 problem and its generalizations. *The American Mathematical Monthly*, 92(1):3–23, Jan. 1985.

[40]   Leslie Lamport. LATEX: *A Document Preparation System*. Addison-Wesley, Reading, MA, 1986.

[41]   Leslie Lamport. *MakeIndex: An Index Processor for* LATEX, Software Manual, February 17, 1987.

[42]   Gary T. Leavens and Mike Vermeulen. $3x + 1$ search programs. *Computers and Mathematics with Applications*, 24(11):79–99, December 1992.

[43]   Roman E. Maeder. Fibonacci on the fast track. *The Mathematica Journal*, 1(3):42–46, 1991.

[44]   Roman E. Maeder. Fractal curves. *The Mathematica Journal*, 1(4):28–33, 1991.

[45]   Roman E. Maeder. *Mathematica* as a programming language. *Dr. Dobbs Journal*, February 1992.

[46]   Roman E. Maeder. Minimal surfaces. *The Mathematica Journal*, 2(2):25–30, 1992.

[47]   Roman E. Maeder. Databases. *The Mathematica Journal*, 3(2):40–47, 1993.

[48]   Roman E. Maeder. *Informatik für Mathematiker und Naturwissenschaftler — Eine Einführung mit Mathematica*. Addison-Wesley (Germany), Bonn, 1993.

[49]   Roman E. Maeder. Object-oriented programming. *The Mathematica Journal*, 3(1):23–31, 1993.

[50]   Roman E. Maeder. Turing machines and code-optimization. *The Mathematica Journal*, 3(3):36–45, 1993.

[51] Roman E. Maeder. *The Mathematica Programmer*. AP Professional, San Diego, CA, 1994.

[52] Roman E. Maeder. The stellated icosahedra. *Mathematica in Education*, 3(1), 1994.

[53] Roman E. Maeder. *The Mathematica Programmer II*. Academic Press, New York, 1996.

[54] Roman E. Maeder. *Programming in Mathematica*, third edition. Addison-Wesley, Reading, MA, 1996.

[55] John McCarthy. Recursive functions of symbolic expressions and their computation by machine I. *J. ACM*, 3:184–95, 1960.

[56] Michael McGuire. *An Eye for Fractals*. Addison-Wesley, Reading, MA, 1991.

[57] Bertrand Meyer. *Object-Oriented Software Construction*. Prentice Hall, Englewood Cliffs, NJ, 1988.

[58] D. L. Parnas. A technique for software module specification with examples. *Comm. ACM*, 15(5), May 1972.

[59] Oren Patashnik. *BIBTEXing*, February 8, 1988.

[60] T. Rado. On non-computable functions. *Bell Sys. Tech. J.*, 877–84, May 1962.

[61] Robert Sedgewick. *Algorithms in C*. Addison-Wesley, Reading, MA, 1990.

[62] R. Skeel and Jerry Keiper. *Elementary Numerical Computing with Mathematica*. McGraw-Hill, New York, 1993.

[63] Steven S. Skiena. *Implementing Discrete Mathematics: Combinatorics and Graph Theory with Mathematica*. Addison-Wesley, Reading, MA, 1990.

[64] George Springer and Daniel P. Friedman. *Scheme and the Art of Programming*. McGraw-Hill, New York, 1989.

[65] David F. Stout and Milton Kaufman. *Handbook of Microcircuit Design and Application*. McGraw-Hill, New York, 1980.

[66] Bjarne Stroustrup. *The C++ Programming Language*, second edition. Addison-Wesley, Reading, MA, 1991.

[67] Alan M. Turing. On computable numbers with an application to the entscheidungsproblem. *P. Lond. Math. Soc. (2)*, 42:230–65, 1936-37.

[68] Jeffrey D. Ullman. *Principles of Database and Knowledge-base Systems*, volume 14 of *Principles of Computer Science Series*. Computer Science Press, Rockville, Maryland, 1988.

[69] B. van der Pol. On relaxation oscillations. *Phil. Mag.*, 2:978–92, 1926.

[70] H. Varian, editor. *Economic and Financial Modeling with Mathematica*. Springer Verlag, 1992.

[71] H. Varian, editor. *Computational Economics and Finance*. TELOS/Springer Verlag, New York, 1996.

[72] Stan Wagon. *Mathematica in Action*. W. H. Freeman, San Francisco, 1990.

[73] Tom Wickham-Jones. *Mathematica Graphics: Techniques and Applications*. TELOS/Springer-Verlag, Santa Clara, CA, 1994.

[74] Stephen Wolfram. *The Mathematica Book*, 4th edition. Wolfram Media/Cambridge University Press, New York, 1999.

[75] Konrad Zuse. Computerarchitektur aus damaliger und heutiger Sicht. Technical Report 180, Informatik ETH, Zurich, 1992.

Appendix B
More Information About *Mathematica*

Section B.1 gives an overview of *Mathematica*'s capabilities; is best used for a computer demonstration. The emphasis in this book has been on programming and not on the many functions built into *Mathematica*. Nevertheless, it is useful to know more about the things you can do. Graphics, especially, have been used in many places to illustrate algorithms. Section B.2 contains the programs for the graphics on the title pages of all chapters.

Sections B.3 and B.4 are a concise reference for *Mathematica*'s programming language. It does not replace the manual but is sufficient for those parts of *Mathematica* used in this book.

About the illustration overleaf:
A butterfly-shaped parametric curve. The picture was produced with this command (see Pictures.m):

```
ParametricPlot[
    (Exp[Cos[phi]] - 2Cos[4phi] + Sin[phi/12]^5)*{Cos[phi], Sin[phi]},
    {phi, 0, 12Pi}, PlotPoints -> 100, Axes -> None ];
```

B.1   Computations You Can Do with *Mathematica*

This section gives some examples from mathematics, the sciences, and engineering, which can be computed with *Mathematica*. It provides an overview of the built-in functions and the use of numerical, symbolic, and graphical methods. Further examples can be found in *The Mathematica Book*.

B.1.1   Calculations with Arbitrary-Size Numbers

Complex numbers with integer real and imaginary parts are called *Gaussian integers*. Here, $2 + 3i$ is raised to the power 77.

```
In[1]:= (2 + 3I)^77
Out[1]= 74123044320760466908976013782472536242678 82 +
        21065280862059058362439170750811346943822 03 I
```

Here is the sum of the first 120 terms of the harmonic series as an exact rational number.

```
In[2]:= Sum[ 1/i, {i, 1, 120} ]
Out[2]=
    18661952910524692834612799443020757786224277983797
    ──────────────────────────────────────────────────
    34759565539135580345945855936592012865331873 98464
```

Here is a 40-digit approximation of it.

```
In[3]:= N[%, 40]
Out[3]= 5.368868287353394912822154939438701013894
```

Mathematical constants, such as π, can be computed to arbitrary precision.

```
In[4]:= N[ Pi, 200 ]
Out[4]= 3.1415926535897932384626433832795028841971 69399\
        37510582097494459230781640628620899862803 482534211706\
        79821480865132823066470938446095505822317 253594081284\
        81117450284102701938521105559644622948954 9303820
```

Mathematica keeps track of the precision of all numbers it works with. Every computation introduces a certain amount of roundoff error, so that the precision of intermediate results usually decreases gradually.

We start with the number 100 exact to 60 decimal digits of precision.

```
In[5]:= N[100, 60]
Out[5]= 100.000000000000000000000000000000000000000 00000000\
        00000000000000
```

The exponential e^{100} does not decrease the precision noticeably, but the number of digits to the right of the decimal points decreases.

```
In[6]:= Exp[ % ]
Out[6]= 2.6881171418161354484126255158001358736111 1877\
        374192241519 10^43
```

The precision of the sine function $\sin e^{100}$ depends essentially on the number of available digits after the decimal point. As a consequence, this result has much less than 100 digits precision.

```
In[7]:= Sin[ % ]
Out[7]= 0.14219812365824
```

If possible, *Mathematica* computes ahead and may be able to figure out the required input precision to achieve a result of a desired precision. This adaptive precision control is a major new feature of Version 3.0.

If we ask for 60 digits of $\sin e^{100}$ directly, we get the desired precision. The computation we just performed step by step is done at a higher precision automatically.

```
In[8]:= N[ Sin[Exp[100]], 60 ]
Out[8]= 0.1421981236582386377245030647868525633473760 9\
    563878023658927
```

The same method can also be used to decide exact computations by performing a suitable numerical computation to a high-enough precision. Even though the computations involve numerical approximations, the results is guaranteed to be correct, due to careful control of precision.

Is e^π less than π^e? We can decide if we know both values to sufficient precision.

```
In[9]:= E^Pi < Pi^E
Out[9]= False
```

The two values are close enough that a simple calculation in our head would not easily find the correct answer.

```
In[10]:= N[ {E^Pi, Pi^E} ]
Out[10]= {23.1407, 22.4592}
```

B.1.2 Numerical Methods

Numerical integration can find approximations to integrals that cannot be computed in closed form, such as this example, $\int_0^\pi \sin \sin x \, dx$.

```
In[1]:= NIntegrate[ Sin[Sin[x]], {x, 0, Pi} ]
Out[1]= 1.78649
```

Integrals with infinite domain of integration can also be computed numerically.

```
In[2]:= NIntegrate[ Exp[-x^2], {x, 0, Infinity} ]
Out[2]= 0.886227
```

NSum[] finds numerical approximations for infinite sums. Here is the sum $\sum_{i=1}^\infty 1/i^2$.

```
In[3]:= NSum[ 1/i^2, {i, 1, Infinity} ]
Out[3]= 1.64493
```

The exact value for this sum is known ($\pi^2/6$), which allows us to confirm the accuracy of the numerical approximation.

```
In[4]:= N[ Pi^2/6 ]
Out[4]= 1.64493
```

B.1.3   Graphs of Functions

This command plots the graph of sin x in the range $(0, 2\pi)$. The output line `-Graphics-` represents the internal symbolic form of the graphic object.

```
In[5]:= Plot[Sin[x], {x, 0, 2Pi}]
```

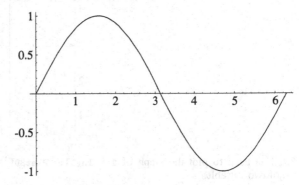

```
Out[5]= -Graphics-
```

Certain aspects of previous graphics can be changed in a new rendering. Here, we add a plot label. Normally, we terminate graphics commands with the semicolon to suppress to output of `-Graphics-`.

```
In[6]:= Show[%, PlotLabel -> "The Sine Function"];
```

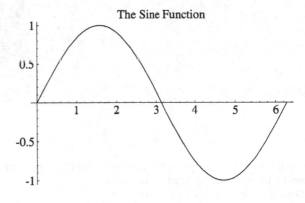

If a function has singularities, *Mathematica* limits the plot range and does not try to plot all function values.

```
In[7]:= Plot[Tan[x], {x, 0, 2Pi}];
```

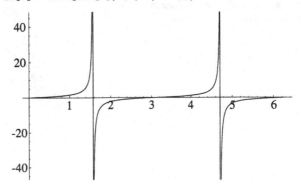

Nevertheless, it is often useful to give the plot range explicitly.

```
In[8]:= Show[ %, PlotRange -> {-5, 5} ];
```

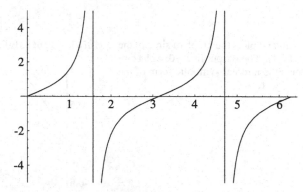

Plot3D[] is used to plot the graph of a function of two variables.

```
In[9]:= Plot3D[ Sin[x y], {x, -3, 3}, {y, -3, 3} ];
```

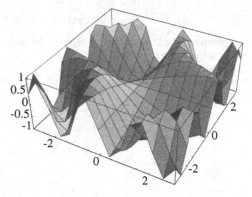

The option PlotPoints gives the number of places to evaluate the function in each dimension. A higher value gives a nicer picture but increases the computing time considerably. Axes->None suppresses the axes and tick marks.

```
In[10]:= Plot3D[ Sin[x y], {x, -3, 3}, {y, -3, 3},
              PlotPoints -> 40, Axes -> None ];
```

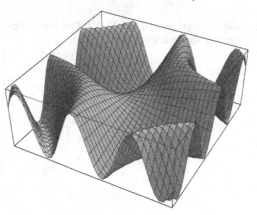

B.1.4   Parametric Curves and Surfaces

A parametric curve is given by the x and y coordinates as a function of a parameter t. Here is an example of a *Lissajous curve*.

```
In[1]:= ParametricPlot[{Sin[2t], Sin[3t]}, {t, 0, 2Pi}];
```

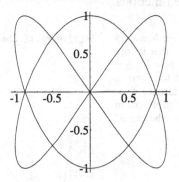

Here is a spiral, a parametric curve in three dimensions.

```
In[2]:= ParametricPlot3D[ {Sin[t], Cos[t], t/6},
                          {t, -2Pi, 2Pi} ];
```

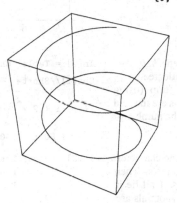

If the x, y, and z coordinates depend on two parameters, we get a parametric surface. Here is a catenoid.

```
In[3]:= ParametricPlot3D[
          {Cosh[z] Cos[phi], Cosh[z] Sin[phi], z},
          {phi, 0, 2Pi}, {z, -1, 1} ];
```

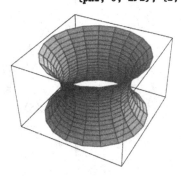

B.1.5   Special Functions

All built-in functions can be evaluated in the complex plane to arbitrary precision. We can, therefore, plot all of these functions.

Here is the absolute value of the Riemann ζ function on the *critical line,* that is, the numbers of the form $1/2 + yi$, here for $y = 0\ldots31$. We can see the first four zeroes of the ζ function on the critical line. One of the most important unsolved problems in mathematics is the question of whether all zeroes lie exactly on this line.

```
In[1]:= Plot[ Abs[Zeta[0.5 + y I]], {y, 0, 31} ];
```

We generate a table of the first ten *Chebyshev polynomials* $T_i(x)$. $T_i(x)$ is of degree i.

In the shortened output form (using `Short[]`) any suppressed terms are marked by `<<n>>`, where n indicates the number of terms left out.

```
In[2]:= Table[ ChebyshevT[i, x], {i, 1, 10} ] // Short
Out[2]//Short=

{x, -1 + 2 x , -3 x + <<1>>, <<6>>,

                2        4         6         8         10
     -1 + 50 x  - 400 x  + 1120 x  - 1280 x  + 512 x  }
```

A picture shows immediately the characteristic properties of these polynomials. Their values in the range $-1 \le x \le 1$ all lie in the interval $[-1, 1]$. These polynomials are, therefore, often used for interpolation.

```
In[3]:= Plot[ Evaluate[%], {x, -1.1, 1.1},
              PlotRange->{-2, 2},
              PlotStyle->Thickness[0.001]
        ];
```

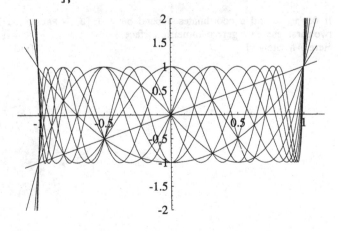

B.1.6 Calculus and Algebra

Differentiation is a purely mechanical operation (because of the chain rule), which is best left to a machine.

```
In[1]:= D[ Log[Log[Log[Log[x]]]], x ]
```

$$Out[1]= \frac{1}{x \, Log[x] \, Log[Log[x]] \, Log[Log[Log[x]]]}$$

Mathematica employs methods to find inner derivatives, making it easy to perform this integration back to the expression we started with.

```
In[2]:= Integrate[ %, x ]
Out[2]= Log[Log[Log[Log[x]]]]
```

Integrals of rational functions can be found by partial fraction expansion.

```
In[3]:= Integrate[ (1+2x)/(x^2-1), x ]
```

$$Out[3]= \frac{3 \, Log[-1 + x]}{2} + \frac{Log[1 + x]}{2}$$

This integral cannot be expressed in terms of elementary functions. *Mathematica* knows most nonelementary functions, such as the *error function* erf(x).

```
In[4]:= Integrate[ E^-x^2, x ]
```

$$Out[4]= \frac{Sqrt[Pi] \, Erf[x]}{2}$$

The definite integral

$$\int_0^1 \frac{x^2}{\sqrt{1-x^4}(1+x^4)}\,dx$$

can be found only with advanced methods.

```
In[5]:= Integrate[x^2/(Sqrt[1-x^4](1+x^4)), {x, 0, 1}]
```

$$Out[5]= \frac{Pi}{8}$$

These methods can also deal with unbounded integration domains.

```
In[6]:= Integrate[ Log[x] (1 + x^2)^(-2),
                    {x, 1,Infinity} ]
```

$$Out[6]= \frac{4 \, Catalan - Pi}{8}$$

The limit $\lim_{x \to 0} \frac{\sin x}{x}$ can easily be found with *de l'Hôpital's rule*.

```
In[7]:= Limit[ Sin[x]/x, x -> 0 ]
Out[7]= 1
```

Mathematica can find (generalized) *Taylor series*. This example has the remarkable property that the coefficient of x^{n-1} in the series expansion of

$$\frac{x^n}{(1 - e^{-x})^n}$$

is always one. Here is $n = 9$.

```
In[8]:= Series[ x^9/(1 - E^-x)^9, {x, 0, 9} ]
```

$$Out[8]= 1 + \frac{9 \, x}{2} + \frac{39 \, x^2}{4} + \frac{27 \, x^3}{2} + \frac{1069 \, x^4}{80} + \frac{801 \, x^5}{80} +$$

$$\frac{29531 \, x^6}{5040} + \frac{761 \, x^7}{280} + x^8 + \frac{25713 \, x^9}{89600} + O[x]^{10}$$

There are also methods for finding infinite sums exactly.

```
In[9]:= Sum[1/i^2, {i, 1, Infinity}]
```

$$Out[9]= \frac{Pi^2}{6}$$

B.1.7 Differential Equations

Some simple differential equations can be solved exactly. Here is the *harmonic oscillator*. C[1] and C[2] are the two constants of integration.

```
In[1]:= DSolve[ {x''[t] + x[t] == 0}, x[t], t ]
Out[1]= {{x[t] -> C[2] Cos[t] - C[1] Sin[t]}}
```

If initial conditions are given, the constants of integration are determined fully.

```
In[2]:= DSolve[ {x''[t] + x[t] == 0,
                 x[0] == 0, x'[0] == 1},
                x[t], t ]
Out[2]= {{x[t] -> Sin[t]}}
```

This command asks for the numerical solution of the system of differential equations

$$x_1' = x_2,$$
$$x_2' = -x_1 - \alpha x_2 + \beta \cos(\omega t),$$

for $t = 0 \dots 12\pi$, with $\alpha = 0.01$, $\beta = 0.1$, and $\omega = 1.1$. The two solutions are returned as interpolating functions.

```
In[3]:= NDSolve[{x1'[t] == x2[t], x2'[t] ==
                 -x1[t] - .01 x2[t] + .1 Cos[1.1t],
                 x1[0] == 2, x2[0] == 0},
                {x1, x2}, {t, 0, 12Pi}, MaxSteps->1000]
Out[3]= {{x1 ->
    InterpolatingFunction[{{0., 37.6991}}, <>],
    x2 -> InterpolatingFunction[{{0., 37.6991}}, <>]}}
```

The solutions are assigned to the variables x1 and x2.

```
In[4]:= {x1, x2} = {x1, x2} /. %[[1]];
```

Interpolating functions can be evaluated for arbitrary values of t and can also be plotted. Here is a *phase space* representation of the solution.

```
In[5]:= ParametricPlot[{x1[t], x2[t]}, {t, 0, 12Pi},
                       AspectRatio->1];
```

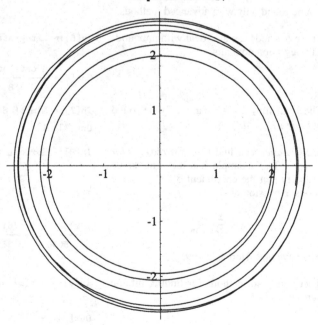

B.1.8   Systems of Equations

Here, we compute the intersection of a circle and a hyperbola, that is, the common solutions of the equations for the circle $x^2 + y^2 = 4$ and the hyperbola $xy = 1$. The four solutions are given in exact form.

```
In[1]:= Solve[ {x^2 + y^2 == 4, x y == 1}, {x, y} ]//
        Simplify

Out[1]= {{x -> -(Sqrt[2 - Sqrt[3]] (2 + Sqrt[3])),
         y -> -Sqrt[2 - Sqrt[3]]},

        {x -> Sqrt[2 - Sqrt[3]] (2 + Sqrt[3]),
         y -> Sqrt[2 - Sqrt[3]]},

        {x -> -((-2 + Sqrt[3]) Sqrt[2 + Sqrt[3]]),
         y -> Sqrt[2 + Sqrt[3]]},

        {x -> (-2 + Sqrt[3]) Sqrt[2 + Sqrt[3]],
         y -> -Sqrt[2 + Sqrt[3]]}}
```

The nested roots can be simplified further.

```
In[2]:= ToRadicals[RootReduce[%]]

Out[2]= {{x -> -Sqrt[2 + Sqrt[3]],
         y -> -Sqrt[2 - Sqrt[3]]},

        {x -> Sqrt[2 + Sqrt[3]], y -> Sqrt[2 - Sqrt[3]]},

        {x -> Sqrt[2 - Sqrt[3]], y -> Sqrt[2 + Sqrt[3]]},

        {x -> -Sqrt[2 - Sqrt[3]], y -> -Sqrt[2 + Sqrt[3]]}}
```

As usual, N[] gives us a numerical approximation.

```
In[3]:= N[ % ]

Out[3]= {{x -> -1.93185, y -> -0.517638},

        {x -> 1.93185, y -> 0.517638},

        {x -> 0.517638, y -> 1.93185},

        {x -> -0.517638, y -> -1.93185}}
```

This equation of fifth degree cannot be solved in closed form. *Mathematica* returns the solutions in a symbolic form (as algebraic numbers) that can be used for further manipulations or numerical approximation.

```
In[4]:= Solve[ x^5 + 2x + 1 == 0 ]

Out[4]= {{x -> Root[1 + 2 #1 + #1^5 & , 1]},

        {x -> Root[1 + 2 #1 + #1^5 & , 2]},

        {x -> Root[1 + 2 #1 + #1^5 & , 3]},

        {x -> Root[1 + 2 #1 + #1^5 & , 4]},

        {x -> Root[1 + 2 #1 + #1^5 & , 5]}}
```

Here is a 10-digit approximation of the five solutions. One of them is real valued, the other four are complex.

```
In[5]:= N[ %, 10 ]

Out[5]= {{x -> -0.486389},

        {x -> -0.701874 - 0.879697 I},

        {x -> -0.701874 + 0.879697 I},

        {x -> 0.945068 - 0.854518 I},

        {x -> 0.945068 + 0.854518 I}}
```

Mathematica can perform a complete case analysis. If $a \neq 0$, there are two solutions according to the well-known formula for quadratic equations. If $a = 0$ and $b \neq 0$, the equation is linear. Otherwise, a, b, and c must all be zero, and any x is a solution.

```
In[6]:= Reduce[ a x^2 + b x + c == 0, x ]

                   -b - Sqrt[b  - 4 a c]
Out[6]= x == ------------------------- && a != 0 ||
                       2 a

                   2
             -b + Sqrt[b  - 4 a c]
        x == ------------------------- && a != 0 ||
                   2 a

        a == 0 && b == 0 && c == 0 ||

                        c
        a == 0 && x == -(-) && b != 0
                        b
```

Using purely symbolic coefficients, we can find the general solution (x_1, x_2) of the linear system

$$\begin{pmatrix} m_{11} & m_{12} \\ m_{21} & m_{22} \end{pmatrix} \cdot \begin{pmatrix} x_1 \\ x_2 \end{pmatrix} = \begin{pmatrix} b_1 \\ b_2 \end{pmatrix}.$$

```
In[7]:= Together[
            LinearSolve[ {{m11, m12}, {m21, m22}},
                         {b1, b2} ]
        ]

         b2 m12 - b1 m22      b2 m11 - b1 m21
Out[7]= {---------------, ---------------------}
         m12 m21 - m11 m22  -(m12 m21) + m11 m22
```

B.1.9   Animated Graphics

Unfortunately, we cannot show animated graphics in a book, but we can at least show the individual frames of an animation sequence. The package `Graphics`Animation`` contains the animation commands, and FlipBookAnimation.m causes the static rendering of the frames.

Figure B.1–1 shows eight frames of the transition from the catenoid to the helicoid. The command `CartesianSurface[]` is taken from the package `MathProg`MinimalSurfaces`` described in [46] and [51].

```
Needs["Graphics`Animation`"]

<< FlipBookAnimation.m

Needs["MathProg`MinimalSurfaces`"]

Animate[ CartesianSurface[Exp[I arg] E^-z, E^z, z, {-2, 2, 4/20}, {-Pi, Pi, Pi/14},
                 PlotRange->{{-7.5,7.5}, {-7.5,7.5}, {-7.5,7.5}},
                 Boxed->False, Axes->None ],
         {arg, 0, Pi/2}, Frames->8, Closed->False
];
```

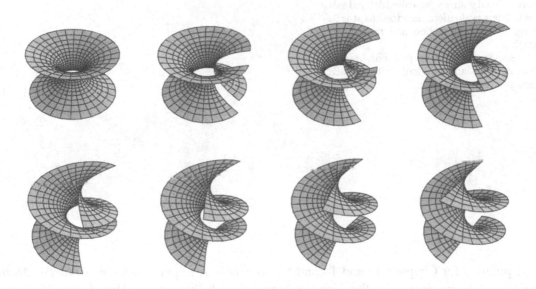

Figure B.1–1   The transition from the catenoid to the helicoid.

B.2   The Code for the Illustrations in this Book

Here is the package Pictures.m used to produce the graphics on the title pages of the chapters. The graphics for Chapter n is obtained by evaluation of the symbol chapter$n$. The symbol appendix$n$ gives the picture for Appendix n.

Reading the package sets up the definitions, but does not produce any graphic output.

```
In[1]:= << CSM`Pictures`
```

The symbols chapter$n$ and appendix$n$ were defined with := (so-called delayed values). Their evaluation, here for chapter6, triggers the computation and renders the graphic.

   Some pictures, such as this one, use random numbers and will look different each time you reevaluate them.

```
In[2]:= chapter6;
```

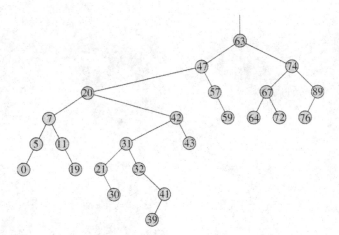

The pictures for Chapters 13 and 14 and for Appendix A require packages from *The Mathematica Programmer* [53]; they are not included with this book. The picture for Chapter 10 requires a package for cellular automata that is no longer part of the standard *Mathematica* packages. It is available from *MathSource*, however (item No. 0200-282, see http://www.mathsource.com/Content22/Applications/Complexity/0200-282).

   Please note that some graphics may take a long time to compute. You can look at them first at a lower quality by changing parameters and options, such as PlotPoints.

```
(* packages from Computer Science with Mathematica *)

Needs["CSM`BinaryTree`"]
Needs["CSM`ComplexParametricPlot`"]
Needs["CSM`Aggregate`"]
Needs["CSM`Iterate`"]
Needs["CSM`TuringRecursive`"]
Get["CSM`Collatz2`"]
```

```
(* standard packages *)

Needs["Graphics`Animation`"]
Get["FlipBookAnimation`"]

(* not part of this book's packages: *)

Get["CellularAutomata`"]                  (* from Mathematica 2.2 or from MathSource *)
Needs["MathProg`FractalExamples`"]   (* The Mathematica Programmer *)
Needs["MathProg`Icosahedra`"]         (* The Mathematica Programmer *)
Needs["MathProg`UniformPolyhedra`"]  (* The Mathematica Programmer *)

(* more standard packages *)

Needs["Geometry`Polytopes`"]
Needs["Graphics`Polyhedra`"]

chapter1 :=
    Animate[ FunctionIteration[ 4#(1-#)&, {0.099, 0.1, 0.101}, 0, n, {0, 1},
                                Frame->True, FrameTicks->None ],
            {n, 1, 9, 1} ];

grid := grid = Table[If[PrimeQ[x + I y], 0, 1], {x, 0, 255}, {y, 0, 255}]

chapter2 := Show[Graphics[Raster[grid]], AspectRatio -> Automatic]

chapter3 := ListPlot[Table[CollatzLength[i],{i,1,1000}]]

randCoeff := 2Random[Integer, {0, 1}] - 1
RandHorner[n_Integer, x_] := Nest[Function[p, p x + randCoeff], 1, n]

chapter4 := ComplexParametricPlot[ RandHorner[20,Exp[I t]]/Sqrt[21],
            {t, 0, 2Pi}, PlotStyle->Thickness[0.002],
            PlotPoints->100, AspectRatio->Automatic ]

Cuboids[n_, m_] := Graphics3D[ Cuboid /@ Table[Random[Integer, {0, m-1}], {n}, {3}] ]

chapter5 := Show[ Cuboids[500, 20] ]

RandomTree[n_] := Tree[ Table[Random[Integer, {0, 3n}], {n}], Identity ]
CSM`BinaryTree`Private`diskr = 0.5 (* make nodes larger   *)
CSM`BinaryTree`Private`ys = 2      (* more vertical space *)

chapter6 := plotTree[ RandomTree[30], DefaultFont->{"Times-Roman", 8},
                    Prolog->Thickness[0.001] ]

`fibx
fib[1] := {Point[{fibx++, 1}]}
fib[2] := {Point[{fibx++, 2}]}
fib[n_] :=
    Module[{n1 = n-1, n2 = n-2, xo = fibx++, a, b, c, d},
        a = Line[{ {xo, n}, {fibx, n1} }]; b = fib[n1];
        c = Line[{ {xo, n}, {fibx, n2} }]; d = fib[n2];
        {Point[{xo, n}], a, b, c, d} ]
FibonacciPlot[n_] :=
    Module[{lines},
        fibx = 0;
```

```
        lines = fib[n];
        lines = {PointSize[1.0/fibx], lines};
        Show[ Graphics[Flatten[lines]], Frame->True,
              PlotRange -> {All, {0.5, n + 0.5}} ] ]

chapter7 := FibonacciPlot[9]

chapter8 := Show[gridGraphics[aggregate[initialGrid[50], 2000]]]

InsertMiddle[l_List] :=
    Flatten[Apply[{#1, (#1+#2)/2}&, Partition[l, 2, 1], {1}], 1] ~Join~ {l[[-1]]}
DoOrDie[ e_, d_, {i_, j_}/;OddQ[i+j] ] := e + Random[Real, {-d, d}]
DoOrDie[ e_, d_, {_, _} ] := e

Refine[ SurfaceGraphics[gr_, opts___], d_ ] :=
    Module[{net},
        net = Map[ InsertMiddle, gr, {0, 1} ];
        net = MapIndexed[ DoOrDie[#1, d, #2]&, net, {2} ];
        SurfaceGraphics[net, opts] ]
Refine[ s_SurfaceGraphics, d_, r_, 0 ] := s
Refine[ s_SurfaceGraphics, d_, r_, n_Integer?Positive ] :=
    Refine[ Refine[s, d], r d/2, r, n-1 ]

graph := graph = Plot3D[ Sin[x y], {x, 0, 3}, {y, 0, 3},
        PlotPoints->8, DisplayFunction->Identity ]

chapter9 := Show[ Refine[graph, 0.4, 0.9, 3], Axes->None,
                  DisplayFunction->$DisplayFunction ]

automata[n_] :=
    Module[{init, pics},
        init = Table[ Random[Integer, {0, 1}], {n}];
        Block[{$DisplayFunction=Identity},
            pics = Table[ ShowCA[EvolveCA[init, NumberedRule[i], n-1]], {i, 0, 63} ]
        ];
        pics = GraphicsArray[ Partition[pics, 8] ];
        Show[pics, DisplayFunction->$DisplayFunction, AspectRatio->1] ]

chapter10 := automata[40]

SuperStellateFace[face_] :=
    Module[{apex, i, i1, r = Norm[face[[1]]], l = Length[face], nf},
        apex = r Unitize[Plus @@ face / l];
        nf = Table[ i1 = Mod[i, l] + 1;
                    nv = r Unitize[ face[[i]] + face[[i1]] ];
                    {Polygon[{face[[i]], apex, nv} ],
                      Polygon[{nv, apex, face[[i1]]}]},
                   {i, l}];
        Flatten[nf, 1] ]
Norm[v_] := Sqrt[Plus @@ (v^2)]
Unitize[v_] := v/Norm[v]

SuperStellate[thing_] := thing /. Polygon[vl_] :> SuperStellateFace[vl]

chapter11 := Show[ SuperStellate[Polyhedron[Dodecahedron]], Boxed->False ]
```

```
chapter12 := PlotTuring[ runList[ {b, m}, pr[0, zero, p[1, 2]] ],
                         Columns->5, DefaultFont->{"Times-Roman", 6.0} ]

chapter13 := Show[ Mandelbrot[4] ]

icosa = {{1, 3}, {36, 18}};

chapter14 := Show[GraphicsArray[Map[Icosahedra[#, Boxed->False]&, icosa, {2}]],
                  GraphicsSpacing -> 0]

polyopts = Sequence @@ {PlotRange->All, Boxed->False}
p1 := p1 = Graphics3D[MakeUniform[ w1[5, 2, 5/2] ], polyopts];
p2 := p2 = Graphics3D[MakeUniform[ w1[5/2, 2, 5] ], polyopts];
p3 := p3 = Graphics3D[MakeUniform[ w1[3, 2, 5/2] ], polyopts];
p4 := p4 = Graphics3D[MakeUniform[ w1[5/2, 2, 3] ], polyopts];

appendixA := Show[ GraphicsArray[{{p1, p2}, {p3, p4}}, GraphicsSpacing->0] ]

appendixB := ParametricPlot[
      (Exp[Cos[phi]] - 2Cos[4phi] + Sin[phi/12]^5)*{Cos[phi], Sin[phi]},
      {phi, 0, 12Pi}, PlotPoints->100, AspectRatio->Automatic, Axes->None ]

index := Show[ Graphics3D[MakeUniform[ w1[2, 5/2, 3] ]] ]
```

B.3   *Mathematica*'s Evaluation Method

Mathematica performs a computation in three phases:

- Read the input and convert it into internal form as an expression.

- Evaluate the expression.

- Format the result for output.

After outputting the result, *Mathematica* is once more ready for new input. This cycle repeats until *Mathematica* itself is terminated.

Under the Notebook frontend, the input consists of the contents of the cell that is sent to the kernel with the Evaluate Selection menu command or the ENTER key. In the direct dialog with the kernel, lines are read until a syntactically complete expression has been input.

B.3.1   Conversion into Internal Form

Expressions in internal form are either atoms (numbers, symbols, or strings), or they are composite expression of the form

$$h \,[\, e_1, \, e_2, \, \ldots, \, e_n \,]\,,$$

where h and the e_i are themselves expressions. We looked at this building principle for expressions in Section 2.4.

Expressions can be entered in this form, if desired. Much easier for us humans is, however, the use of *operators*. There are prefix operators, such as $-x$, postfix operators, such as f', and infix operators, such as $a + b + c$, as well as some special cases, such as $\{a, b, c\}$ and $l[[i]]$. *Mathematica*'s *parser*, which reads your input, converts expressions involving operators into internal form. The most important operators and their internal forms are listed in the tables in Section B.4. To guarantee a unique way of conversion, each operator is equipped with a *priority*. Such priorities are familiar from mathematics: multiplication, for example, has a higher priority than addition.

B.3.2   Evaluation of Expressions

Mathematica evaluates an expression by applying various transformation rules to it. Many such rules are built into *Mathematica*; others can be defined by the user. For example, if we evaluate the definition f[x_] := x^2, a new rule is established that from now on is applied to all matching expressions (see also Section 10.2).

B.3.2.1   The Different Kinds of Rules

To restrict the number of rules that have to be tried on each expression, each rule is associated with a symbol. There are several cases (h, f, and s denote symbols):

- A definition of the form

$$h := body$$

  belongs to the symbol h. Such a rule is called an *ownvalue*.

- A definition of the form

$$h[\ \ldots\ ] := body$$

  belongs to the symbol h. Such a rule is called a *downvalue*.

- A definition of the form

$$f/:\ h[\ \ldots,\ f[\ldots],\ \ldots\ ] := body$$

  or

$$f/:\ h[\ \ldots,\ f,\ \ldots\ ] := body$$

  belongs to the symbol f. Such a rule is called an *upvalue*. Upvalues are associated with symbols occurring as *arguments* of the left side.

- A definition of the form

$$s[\ f[\ldots],\ \ldots\ ] := body\ ,$$

  where s is one the special symbols N, Default, Attributes, or Format, belongs to f. The declaration $f/:$ is not needed in these cases.

- A definition of the form

$$h[\ldots][\ \ldots\ ] := body$$

  belongs to the symbol h. Such a rule is called a *subvalue*. Because the head of the left side is not a symbol, no rule can be associated to it.

Together with the built-in rules of the same types, these user-defined rules form the set of rules according to which every expression is evaluated.

B.3.2.2   The Evaluator

The evaluator works in a loop and continues until no more rules can be applied to an expression. Whenever the application of a rule changed an expression, it starts again from the beginning.

Atoms are easy to evaluate. *Numbers* and *strings* evaluate to themselves, that is, no change takes place. *Symbols* having a value (defined with *symbol* = *val* or *symbol* := *val*) evaluate to this value. Symbols without a value evaluate to themselves.

The evaluation of *composite expressions* is more complicated. First, the head and the elements are evaluated recursively. The evaluation of certain elements can be prevented by the attributes `HoldFirst` and `HoldRest`.

$s[\ e_1,\ e_2,\ \ldots,\ e_n\ ]$	
Attribute of s	Meaning
`HoldFirst`	e_1 is not evaluated
`HoldRest`	e_2 through e_n are not evaluated
`HoldAll`	no element is evaluated

Other nonstandard evaluation of elements takes place for many programming constructs, such as definitions, loops, conditional statements, and logical operations. See Section A.4.2 of *The Mathematica Book*.

After the evaluation of head and elements, the attributes `Flat` and `Orderless` are taken into account. If the head has the attribute `Orderless`, the elements are sorted into standard order. The attribute `Flat` causes nested occurrences of the head to be flattened out.

Attributes are set in this way.

```
In[1]:= SetAttributes[f, Flat];\
        SetAttributes[g, Orderless];
```

All nested occurrences of f are flattened.

```
In[2]:= f[x, f[a, b], y, f[c]]
Out[2]= f[x, a, b, y, c]
```

Elements of g are sorted.

```
In[3]:= g[a, 2, -3.5, z]
Out[3]= g[-3.5, 2, a, z]
```

Addition is associative and commutative, that is, it has both of these attributes (among others).

```
In[4]:= Attributes[Plus]
Out[4]= {Flat, Listable, NumericFunction, OneIdentity,
        Orderless, Protected}
```

The next step in evaluation is governed by the attribute `Listable`. If the head h has this attribute and if there are any lists among the elements, these lists are exchanged with h (using `Thread[]`, as explained in Section 8.1.2).

Most mathematical functions have the attribute `Listable`.

```
In[5]:= Sin[{a, 1, Pi}]
Out[5]= {Sin[a], Sin[1], 0}
```

Finally, *rules* are applied. Applicable rules are those that are associated with the head of the expression or with the heads of elements. Rules are examined in the following order:

- User-defined rules with a left side

$$h[\ldots, f[\ldots], \ldots]$$

or
$$h[\dots,\ f,\ \dots]\ ,$$

associated with f (upvalues).

- Built-in upvalues.
- User-defined rules with a left side
$$h[\ \dots\ ]$$

or
$$h[\dots][\ \dots\ ]\ ,$$

associated with h (downvalues and subvalues).

- Built-in downvalues and subvalues.

In each case, *pattern matching* (see Section 10.1) is used to find out whether a rule is applicable. If a rule is applicable, the expression is replaced by the right side of the rule, and evaluation starts over. An example of a user-defined upvalue can be found on page 163. There, we modified assignment for digit[].

B.3.2.3   Control of Run-Away Evaluations

The evaluator has safeguards against infinite recursion (when evaluating the head or the elements) and against infinite iteration (when applying rules).

Variable	Meaning
$RecursionLimit	limit for the recursion
$IterationLimit	limit for the iteration

For these examples, we set the limits to small values.

```
In[1]:= $RecursionLimit = 20;\
        $IterationLimit = 100;
```

Such a definition leads to infinite recursion.

```
In[2]:= f[x_] := h[f[x]]
```

After reaching the recursion limit, further evaluation is prevented by Hold.

```
In[3]:= f[1]
$RecursionLimit::reclim: Recursion depth of 20 exceeded.
Out[3]= h[h[h[h[h[h[h[h[h[h[h[h[h[h[h[h[h[h[h[
                Hold[f[1]]]]]]]]]]]]]]]]]]]]]
```

Such a definition leads to infinite iteration.

```
In[4]:= g[x_] := g[2x]
```

After reaching the iteration limit, further evaluation is prevented by Hold.

```
In[5]:= g[1]
$IterationLimit::itlim: Iteration limit of 100 exceeded.
Out[5]= Hold[g[2 6338253001141147007483516602688]]
```

B.3.3   Output Formatting

The internal form of the result is converted into print form by application of format rules. *Mathematica* supports several formats. The most important formats are `OutputForm` (a two-dimensional representation), `InputForm` (a form that can be read back into *Mathematica*), `FullForm` (the unchanged internal form), as well as `TeXForm`, `CForm`, and so on for special applications.

The frontend offers print-quality mathematical typesetting through the new format types `StandardForm` and `TraditionalForm`.

The default format is *output form,* a two-dimensional representation.

```
In[1]:= expr = Exp[x^2]/3
           2
          x
         E
Out[1]= ───
          3
```

Input form can be read back into *Mathematica*.

```
In[2]:= InputForm[expr]
Out[2]//InputForm= E^x^2/3
```

Here is the *internal form* of the expression.

```
In[3]:= FullForm[expr]
Out[3]//FullForm=
     Times[Rational[1, 3], Power[E, Power[x, 2]]]
```

This form is suitable for input into TeX. Formatted, it looks like this:

```
In[4]:= TeXForm[expr]
Out[4]//TeXForm= \frac{e^{x^2}}{3}
```

$$\frac{e^{x^2}}{3}.$$

This form can be inserted into C programs.

```
In[5]:= CForm[expr]
Out[5]//CForm= Power(E,Power(x,2))/3.
```

For formatting, the expression `Format[`*result, format*`]` is evaluated (in the standard way, as explained in Section B.3.2). The default for *format* is `OutputForm`. Many formatting rules are built in. You can also define your own formatting rules. We have done so in some places in this book, for example in Section 5.2.3. Please consult *The Mathematica Book* (Section 2.8) for more information on formatting.

B.3.4   The Main Loop

In addition to the three main actions *input, evaluation,* and *output,* a number of other things take place during a computation. Here is the complete description of an evaluation.

- Print the input prompt `In[n]:=` (not under the frontend).

- Read input (as a string).

- Apply the function `$PreRead`, if it is defined, to the input string.

- Print syntax errors, if necessary.

- Assign `InString[n]`.

- Convert input string into internal form.

- Apply the function `$Pre`, if it is defined, to the input expression.

- Assign `In[n]`.

- Evaluate expression.

- Apply the function `$Post`, if it is defined, to the result.

- Assign `Out[n]`.

- Apply the function `$PrePrint`, if it is defined, to the result.

- Print expression if it is not `Null`.

- Increment `$Line`.

The variables `$Pre`, `$Post`, and `$PrePrint` allow us to change the behavior of *Mathematica* at will. If we work frequently with vectors and matrices, for example, we can use `$PrePrint = MatrixForm` to force all results in matrix form (we did so in Section 8.2).

B.4 Syntax of Operators

In the following table, operators are ordered by decreasing priority. Operators in the same group have equal priorities. The Grouping column explains how several consecutive binary operators are grouped. If no parentheses are given, the operator can take an arbitrary number of arguments (it is associative). If there is no entry, the operator cannot be used without explicit parentheses. (For example, $expr_1?expr_2?expr_3$ is not possible.) The column is also empty for unary operators.

Input Form	*Internal Form*	*Grouping*
digits . digits	(floating-point number)	
expr::*string*	`MessageName[`*expr*`, "`*string*`"]`	
expr::*string₁*::*string₂*	`MessageName[`*expr*`, "`*string₁*`", "`*string₂*`"]`	
expressions with `#`	(see below)	
expressions with `%`	(see below)	
expressions with `_`	(see below)	
`<<` *filename*	`Get["`*filename*`"]`	
expr₁?*expr₂*	`PatternTest[`*expr₁*`, `*expr₂*`]`	
expr₁[*expr₂*, ...]	*expr₁*[*expr₂*, ...]	(e[e])[e]
expr₁[[*expr₂*, ...]]	`Part[`*expr₁*`, `*expr₂*`, ...]`	(e[[e]])[[e]]
expr++	`Increment[`*expr*`]`	
expr--	`Decrement[`*expr*`]`	
++*expr*	`PreIncrement[`*expr*`]`	
--*expr*	`PreDecrement[`*expr*`]`	
expr₁ @ *expr₂*	*expr₁*[*expr₂*]	e @ (e @ e)
expr₁ /@ *expr₂*	`Map[`*expr₁*`, `*expr₂*`]`	e /@ (e /@ e)
expr₁ //@ *expr₂*	`MapAll[`*expr₁*`, `*expr₂*`]`	e //@ (e //@ e)
expr₁ @@ *expr₂*	`Apply[`*expr₁*`, `*expr₂*`]`	e @@ (e @@ e)
expr!	`Factorial[`*expr*`]`	
expr!!	`Factorial2[`*expr*`]`	
expr'	`Derivative[1][`*expr*`]`	
expr₁ <> *expr₂*	`StringJoin[`*expr₁*`, `*expr₂*`]`	e <> e <> e
expr₁^*expr₂*	`Power[`*expr₁*`, `*expr₂*`]`	e^(e^e)
expr₁ . *expr₂* . *expr₃*	`Dot[`*expr₁*`, `*expr₂*`, `*expr₃*`]`	e . e . e
-*expr*	`Times[-1, `*expr*`]`	
+*expr*	*expr*	

Syntax, Part 1.

Input Form	Internal Form	Grouping
$expr_1$/$expr_2$	`Times[`$expr_1$`, Power[`$expr_2$`, -1]]`	(e / e) / e
$expr_1$ $expr_2$ $expr_3$	`Times[`$expr_1$`, `$expr_2$`, `$expr_3$`]`	e e e
$expr_1$ * $expr_2$ * $expr_3$	`Times[`$expr_1$`, `$expr_2$`, `$expr_3$`]`	e * e * e
$expr_1$ + $expr_2$ + $expr_3$	`Plus[`$expr_1$`, `$expr_2$`, `$expr_3$`]`	e + e + e
$expr_1$ - $expr_2$	`Plus[`$expr_1$`, Times[-1, `$expr_2$`]]`	(e - e) - e
$expr_1$ == $expr_2$	`Equal[`$expr_1$`, `$expr_2$`]`	e == e == e
$expr_1$!= $expr_2$	`Unequal[`$expr_1$`, `$expr_2$`]`	e != e != e
$expr_1$ > $expr_2$	`Greater[`$expr_1$`, `$expr_2$`]`	e > e > e
$expr_1$ >= $expr_2$	`GreaterEqual[`$expr_1$`, `$expr_2$`]`	e >= e >= e
$expr_1$ < $expr_2$	`Less[`$expr_1$`, `$expr_2$`]`	e < e < e
$expr_1$ <= $expr_2$	`LessEqual[`$expr_1$`, `$expr_2$`]`	e <= e <= e
$expr_1$ === $expr_2$	`SameQ[`$expr_1$`, `$expr_2$`]`	e === e === e
$expr_1$ =!= $expr_2$	`UnsameQ[`$expr_1$`, `$expr_2$`]`	e =!= e =!= e
!$expr$	`Not[`$expr$`]`	!(!e)
$expr_1$ && $expr_2$	`And[`$expr_1$`, `$expr_2$`]`	e && e && e
$expr_1$ || $expr_2$	`Or[`$expr_1$`, `$expr_2$`]`	e || e || e
$expr_1$ | $expr_2$	`Alternatives[`$expr_1$`, `$expr_2$`]`	e | e | e
$symb$:$expr$	`Pattern[`$symb$`, `$expr$`]`	
$expr_1$ /; $expr_2$	`Condition[`$expr_1$`, `$expr_2$`]`	(e/;e)/;e
$expr_1$ -> $expr_2$	`Rule[`$expr_1$`, `$expr_2$`]`	e->(e->e)
$expr_1$:> $expr_2$	`RuleDelayed[`$expr_1$`, `$expr_2$`]`	e->(e->e)
$expr_1$ /. $expr_2$	`ReplaceAll[`$expr_1$`, `$expr_2$`]`	(e/.e)/.e
$expr_1$ //. $expr_2$	`ReplaceRepeated[`$expr_1$`, `$expr_2$`]`	(e//.e)//.e
$expr_1$ += $expr_2$	`AddTo[`$expr_1$`, `$expr_2$`]`	
$expr_1$ -= $expr_2$	`SubtractFrom[`$expr_1$`, `$expr_2$`]`	
$expr_1$ *= $expr_2$	`TimesBy[`$expr_1$`, `$expr_2$`]`	
$expr_1$ /= $expr_2$	`DivideBy[`$expr_1$`, `$expr_2$`]`	
$expr$ &	`Function[`$expr$`]`	
$expr_1$ // $expr_2$	$expr_2$`[`$expr_1$`]`	(e // e) // e
$expr_1$ = $expr_2$	`Set[`$expr_1$`, `$expr_2$`]`	e = (e = e)
$expr_1$:= $expr_2$	`SetDelayed[`$expr_1$`, `$expr_2$`]`	
$expr_1$ ^= $expr_2$	`UpSet[`$expr_1$`, `$expr_2$`]`	e = (e = e)
$expr_1$ ^:= $expr_2$	`UpSetDelayed[`$expr_1$`, `$expr_2$`]`	
$symb$/: $expr_1$ = $expr_2$	`TagSet[`$symb$`, `$expr_1$`, `$expr_2$`]`	
$symb$/: $expr_1$:= $expr_2$	`TagSetDelayed[`$symb$`, `$expr_1$`, `$expr_2$`]`	
$expr_1$; $expr_2$	`CompoundExpression[`$expr_1$`, `$expr_2$`]`	e ; e ; e
$expr_1$;	`CompoundExpression[`$expr_1$`, Null]`	e ; e ; e ;

Syntax, Part 2.

Input Form	Internal Form
#	Slot[1]
#*n*	Slot[*n*]
%	Out[ ]
%%	Out[-2]
%%...%	Out[-*n*]
%*n*	Out[*n*]
_	Blank[ ]
_*h*	Blank[*h*]
__	BlankSequence[ ]
__*h*	BlankSequence[*h*]
___	BlankNullSequence[ ]
___*h*	BlankNullSequence[*h*]
_.	Optional[Blank[ ]]
*symb*_	Pattern[*symb*, Blank[ ]]
*symb*_*h*	Pattern[*symb*, Blank[*h*]]
*symb*__	Pattern[*symb*, BlankSequence[ ]]
*symb*__*h*	Pattern[*symb*, BlankSequence[*h*]]
*symb*___	Pattern[*symb*, BlankNullSequence[ ]]
*symb*___*h*	Pattern[*symb*, BlankNullSequence[*h*]]
*symb*_.	Optional[Pattern[*symb*, Blank[ ]]]

Special Input Forms.

expr and *expr*$_i$	any expression
symb, *h*	a symbol
string and *string*$_i$	a string
filename	a file name
n	an integer (in decimal)
digits	a sequence of digits

Meaning of variables in the tables.

Complete tables of all special input forms are given in Appendix A.2.7 of *The Mathematica Book*. These tables are also available on-line in the *Help Browser*.

Index

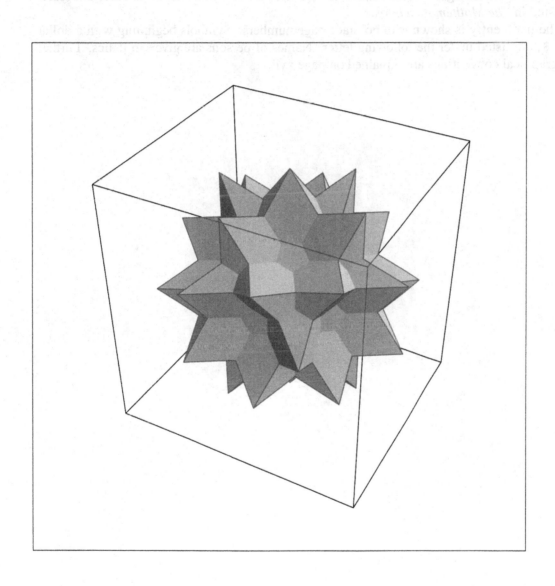

A complete index for *Mathematica* is in *The Mathematica Book*. *Mathematica* commands are listed here only if they are used in this book. You will find here all the commands developed in our example packages. These commands are not part of *Mathematica* and are, therefore, not listed in *The Mathematica Book*.

The main entry is shown with boldface page numbers. Symbols beginning with a dollar sign, $, are listed under the following letter. Names of persons are given in italics. Further typographical conventions are explained on page xvii.

About the illustration overleaf:
The *great icosidodecahedron*. It consists of triangles and pentagrams arranged alternatingly.